BARRON'S

HOW TO PREPARE FOR THE

ExCET

EXAMINATION FOR THE CERTIFICATION OF EDUCATORS IN TEXAS

PROFESSIONAL DEVELOPMENT TESTS

Sandra Luna McCune, Ph.D.
Department of Elementary Education
College of Education
Stephen F. Austin State University

Donnya E. Stephens, Ed.D.
Department of Secondary Education and
Educational Leadership
College of Education
Stephen F. Austin State University

Mary Ella Lowe, Ed.D.
Department of Elementary Education, Retired
College of Education
Stephen F. Austin State University

2ND EDITION

BARRON'S

All inquiries should be addressed to:

Barron's Educational Series, Inc.
250 Wireless Boulevard
Hauppauge, New York 11788
http://www.barronseduc.com

Library of Congress Catalog Card No.: 99-42038

International Standard Book No. 0-7641-0771-2

Library of Congress Cataloging-in-Publication Data

McCune, Sandra K.
    How to prepare for the ExCET : Examination for the
Certification of Educators in Texas : professional development
tests / Sandra Luna McCune, Donnya E. Stephens, Mary Ella Lowe. —
2nd ed.
        p.   cm.
    At head of title: Barron's.
Includes bibliographical references.
ISBN 0-7641-0771-2
1. Teaching—Texas--Examinations—Study guides. 2.
Teachers—Certification—Texas. I. Stephens, Donnya E. (Donnya
Elle) II. Lowe, Mary Ella. III. Title. IV. Title: Barron's how to
prepare for the ExCET
    LB1763.T4M33 1999
    379.1'57'09764—dc21

                                                                99-42038
                                                                CIP

PRINTED IN THE UNITED STATES OF AMERICA
9 8 7 6

CONTENTS

PREFACE

How to Prepare for the ExCET was written because we believe preservice teachers in Texas needed a thorough, comprehensive, and cohesive review book for the elementary and secondary Professional Development ExCET tests. This book is specifically designed around the state-mandated professional development competencies, and it contains current information on theory and practice for teachers. To help you prepare adequately, there are a full-length diagnostic test and a full-length practice test of 90 questions each for both the elementary and secondary levels. To facilitate understanding and retention, the answers are keyed to the competencies, with explanations supported by educational theory of effective practice. Upon completion of this book, not only will you be better prepared to take the professional development ExCET, but you will be better prepared to be a Texas public school teacher. Good luck!

Sandra Luna McCune
Donnya E. Stephens
Mary Ella Lowe

PART ONE

Get Ready for the Professional Development ExCET Test

CHAPTER 1

WHAT IS THE ExCET?

General Information

ExCET stands for the Examination for the Certification of Educators in Texas. The ExCET is not just one test—there are actually over sixty ExCET tests that educators in Texas may take. The tests and the testing program that goes with them are the result of legislation passed by the Texas legislature in 1981. If you want to teach in a Texas public elementary or secondary school, you will have to take and pass at least two ExCET tests. First of all, you will have to demonstrate general knowledge about learning, teaching, and professional conduct by passing a professional development ExCET—which is what this book is designed to help you do. In addition, if you want to be an elementary teacher, you will have to pass the Elementary Comprehensive ExCET; if you want to be a secondary teacher, you will have to pass comprehensive ExCET tests in your field or fields of specialization. Each test is based on a set of competencies written to correspond with state guidelines and current research on teaching practices. Anyone who wants to teach in Texas must pass ExCET tests, so this is an obstacle between you and your goal of being a Texas teacher. It is the law, so you have no choice but to take the tests.

In 1995 the legislature created the State Board for Educator Certification (SBEC) to govern the standards for public school educators. The 15-member appointed board is responsible for managing the development and administration of the ExCETs. Passing standards for the tests are reviewed periodically, and recommendations from these reviews are presented to SBEC. The board sets the minimum score required to pass each ExCET based on the recommendations.

Commonly Asked Questions About the ExCET

Who is eligible to take the ExCET?

According to the *ExCET Registration Bulletin*, to be eligible to take an ExCET test, you must meet one of the following requirements:

1. You have completed the program requirements of an approved certification program in a Texas college or university and you have obtained an official authorization-to-test bar code label from your certification officer.

2. You are enrolled in your last semester of a certification program in a Texas college or university at the time of administration of the test

registered for and you have obtained an official authorization-to-test bar code label from your certification officer.

3. You are in the spring semester prior to summer completion of program requirements in a Texas college or university at the time of administration of the test registered for and you have obtained an official authorization-to-test bar code label from your certification officer.

4. You are in the second semester of the one-year internship of an alternative certification program approved by SBEC and you have obtained an official authorization-to-test bar code label from your certification officer.

5. You are fully certified by a state other than Texas and are seeking a Texas teacher certificate in the same certification area. In addition, you have applied for and received a review of your credentials by SBEC.

6. You hold a current one-year certificate issued by the Texas Education Agency and you have obtained an official authorization-to-test bar code label from your certification officer.

7. You have completed a bachelor's degree and hold a valid Texas classroom certificate, but are seeking an additional certification or endorsement and you have obtained an official authorization-to-test bar code label from your certification officer.

Must I obtain an authorization-to-test bar code label?

You must obtain an official authorization-to-test bar code label from the certification officer at your institution if you are seeking certification by one of the following certification routes:

- University-Based Initial Educator Preparation Certification
- University-Based Additional Educator Preparation Certification
- Alternative Certification Educator Preparation

This step may take additional time, so plan ahead to avoid a late registration or emergency registration fee. You must affix an official authorization-to-test bar code label to the registration form every time you register for an ExCET—even if you have registered and tested previously. Registration forms without the official authorization-to-test bar code label will not be processed and will be returned.

When should I take the ExCET?

You should take the ExCET at the point in your preparation program at which you become eligible to take the test. You should delay taking the ExCET until you have had an opportunity to apply what you have learned in your program to actual teaching situations. You will need to demonstrate this kind of thinking on the ExCET. This is why you shouldn't take the test too early. Once you are certain when you should take the ExCET, sign up as soon as possible. Application deadlines for the tests are very strict, and you will have to pay monetary penalties for being late to register. The best thing for you to do is obtain an *ExCET Registration Bulletin* the semester *before* you become eligible to take the tests, so that you do not miss the deadline for regular registration. You can pick up a registration bulletin at the teacher certificate office at your institution or at your regional educational service center, or you may request one by calling the SBEC Information and Support Center toll-free at (888) 863-5880 or by sending an e-mail request (along with your mailing address) to sbec@esc20.net.

When are the tests given?

The ExCET tests are given three times a year (usually in February, April, and October) at locations throughout the state, with two additional special testings in June and December at limited sites. You can find information on test dates, site locations, fees, registration procedures, and policies in the current *ExCET Registration Bulletin* or at the SBEC Web page (address: www.sbec.state.tx.us).

Registration deadlines are strictly enforced. Registration forms generally must be postmarked about one month before the test date. Late registration, until about three weeks before the test, requires an additional late fee ($30 in 1999). If you really get in a bind and miss the regular registration deadline *and* the late registration deadline, you can call (413) 256-2888 and "emergency register" (for a limited site). You will have to pay an additional fee ($70 in 1999) if you find yourself in this situation.

How many tests should I take in one day?

You should not take more than two tests in one day, so that you will have adequate time in which to take the tests. Each testing day has two five-hour test sessions: morning from 8 AM to 1 PM and afternoon from 2 PM to 7 PM. When you register, if you plan to take two tests, you should request to take one in the morning session and one in the afternoon session. You will be expected to complete all tests listed on the ticket stub for a particular session within the allotted five hours.

Are the tests timed?

The individual tests in a session are not timed, so you may allot the five hours for the session to the test(s) as you choose. If you have scheduled two tests in a session, you should plan to spend about two and a half hours on each test. If you are scheduled to take one test in a session, even if it is a short test, you may spend the entire five hours on the test. If you complete the test(s) before the end of the test session, you may leave after giving your test materials to the test administrators.

Are special testing arrangements available?

If you have a disabling condition (visual, physical, hearing, or so on), special testing arrangements and test materials can be made available for you. You have to fill out an Alternative Testing Arrangements Request Form and send it in, along with all necessary documentation, by the *regular registration deadline*. You can find the form in the *Registration Bulletin*. You can also use this form to request a Friday administration of the test if you are unable to take the test on Saturdays because of your religious convictions. A letter from your clergy on the clergy's letterhead, verifying the religious basis for your request, must be included with your form. You should write your name, social security number, and phone number on all correspondence to ensure proper handling of your documentation. Don't forget to make copies of everything before you mail it in.

What are the fees for the test?

The current fees (in 1999) for regular registration are $72 for one test, $144 for two tests, $216 for three tests, and $288 for four tests. The fee for late registration is an additional $30 charge. If you fail to meet either the regular registration deadline or the late registration deadline, you can register by telephone up until four days before the test is given and pay an emergency registration fee of $70 in addition to the regular fees. All fees must be paid by check or money order to NES. Do not send cash to the testing service.

May I change my registration if I need to?

Yes. You must complete a Change of Registration Request Form, available in the *ExCET Registration Bulletin*. If the completed form is postmarked no later than the regular registration deadline for the test administration date for which you originally registered, the change of registration fee is $15 (as of 1999).

What should I bring to the test site?

After you mail in your registration form, you should receive an admission ticket by one week before the test date. If you have not received your admission ticket by this time or if you have lost your admission ticket, call NES immediately at (413) 256-2888. You can still get into the test site with proper identification if you notify NES in time. Your admission ticket will list your name, address, test date, site address, information about your site assignment, educator preparation program, your route to certification, and a reminder of what to bring to the test site. Check the information on your admission ticket to make sure it is correct. You will not be allowed to make changes at the test site. The day of the test, you should bring your admission ticket and two forms of identification, including one that is government-issued with a recent photograph, to the test site. In addition, you should bring several sharpened No. 2 pencils, a simple twist-type pencil sharpener (so that you need not waste time walking back and forth to a pencil sharpener if your point breaks), a good eraser, an accurate watch (so that you can pace yourself during the test), and, if desired, some mints (for a quick energy boost if you get hungry or tired). You are *not* allowed to bring calculators or calculator watches, watches that beep, photographic or recording devices, audiotapes, highlighters, dictionaries, spell checkers, slide rules, briefcases, backpacks, packages, cellular phones, beepers, notebooks, textbooks, scratch paper, or any written material inside the testing room. Also, you are *not* allowed to eat, drink, or smoke inside the testing room.

What time do I need to be at the test site?

You should be at the test site by 7:30 AM for the morning session and 1:30 PM for the afternoon session. The testing will begin one-half hour after these reporting times. If you arrive up to thirty minutes after testing starts, the Test Administration Manager will have to decide if you will be admitted to the test session. These decisions are made on a case-by-case basis, so you should not count on being admitted if you arrive after the testing has begun. If you are admitted TDD late, you will not be given additional time to make up for what you missed by being late, and you will have to sign a statement agreeing to that condition.

When will I receive my test(s) results?

Your score reports will be mailed approximately four weeks after you take the test. You will receive a score report, mailed separately, for each test you take. To protect the confidentiality of your score(s), no results are given over the telephone or by fax machine.

May I cancel my score(s)?

You may cancel your test score(s) for one or more tests in a given test administration by sending a request *in writing* to National Evaluation Systems, Inc., P.O. Box 4721, Amherst, MA 01004-4721. A Score Cancellation Form will be available at the test site on the day of the test. Don't forget to ask for one if you think you may want to cancel your score(s). If you have not received verification of cancellation of your score(s) within twenty-one days of your letter, call National Evaluation Systems at (413) 256-2888 right away. You are not entitled to a refund if you cancel your scores.

How many times may I retake a test?

You may retake a test as many times as is necessary to pass; however, you must submit a new registration form and pay the full fees every time you retake a test.

Is there a number I may call if I have questions about the ExCET program?

If you have questions about how to complete any of the forms in the registration bulletin, your payment, test administration, or your score report, call National Evaluation Systems at (413) 256-2888. Individuals with hearing impairments using a TDD may call (413) 256-8032. For questions relating to certification, contact the SBEC Information and Support Center toll-free at (888) 863-5880 or e-mail the center at sbec@esc20.net.

CHAPTER 2

WHAT ARE THE PROFESSIONAL DEVELOPMENT TESTS?

General Information

To be certified to teach in Texas, you must pass one of the two state-mandated professional development ExCET tests: the Elementary Professional Development ExCET or the Secondary Professional Development ExCET. If you are seeking All-Level certification, you may take either the elementary or the secondary test. You decide which level test to take based on the level at which you are planning to teach. This book will help you prepare for either of the professional development tests. Both tests are based on the same set of broad competencies that are meant to ensure that entry-level teachers have the necessary professional knowledge to teach effectively in Texas public schools.

The Professional Development ExCET Competencies

The professional development ExCET tests are designed to measure proficiency in three domains: Understanding Learners (approximately 33 percent of test), Enhancing Student Achievement (approximately 40 percent of test), and Understanding the Teaching Environment (approximately 27 percent of test). Each domain is defined by a list of specific professional competencies. These competencies are listed below. A fuller description of the competencies is provided in Chapter 4 and the review chapters for each domain.

Domain I—Understanding Learners

Competency 001: The teacher uses an understanding of human developmental processes to nurture student growth through developmentally appropriate instruction.

Competency 002: The teacher considers environmental factors that may affect learning in designing a supportive and responsive classroom community that promotes all students' learning and self-esteem.

Competency 003: The teacher appreciates human diversity, recognizing how diversity in the classroom and the community may affect learning and creating a classroom environment in which both the diversity of groups and the uniqueness of individuals are recognized and celebrated.

Competency 004: The teacher understands how learning occurs and can apply this understanding to design and implement effective instruction.

Competency 005: The teacher understands how motivation affects group and individual behavior and learning and can apply this understanding to promote student learning.

Domain II—Enhancing Student Achievement

Competency 006: The teacher uses planning processes to design outcome-oriented learning experiences that foster understanding and encourage self-directed thinking and learning in both individual and collaborative settings.

Competency 007: The teacher uses effective verbal, nonverbal, and media communication techniques to shape the classroom into a community of learners engaged in active inquiry, collaborative exploration, and supportive interactions.

Competency 008: The teacher uses a variety of instructional strategies and roles to facilitate learning and to help students become independent thinkers and problem-solvers who use higher-order thinking in the classroom and the real world.

Competency 009: The teacher uses a variety of instructional materials and resources (including human and technological resources) to support individual and group learning.

Competency 010: The teacher uses processes of informal and formal assessment to understand individual learners, monitor instructional effectiveness, and shape instruction.

Competency 011: The teacher structures and manages the learning environment to maintain a classroom climate that promotes the lifelong pursuit of learning and encourages cooperation, leadership, and mutual respect.

Domain III—Understanding the Teaching Environment

Competency 012: The teacher is a reflective practitioner who knows how to promote his or her own professional growth and can work cooperatively with other professionals in the system to create a school culture that enhances learning and encourages positive change.

Competency 013: The teacher knows how to foster strong school-home relationships that support student achievement of desired learning outcomes.

Competency 014: The teacher understands how the school relates to the larger community and knows strategies for making interactions between school and community mutually supportive and beneficial.

Competency 015: The teacher understands requirements, expectations, and constraints associated with teaching in Texas and can apply this understanding in a variety of contexts.

Don't panic! You will not be asked direct questions about the competencies, nor will you even be asked to tell which competency applies in a particular situation when you take the Professional Development ExCET. Nevertheless, a strong understanding of the competencies is essential for successful performance on the test. The competencies are broad statements of skills, knowledge, and understanding that you need in order to be an effective classroom teacher in Texas. You should read them carefully to familiarize yourself with the specific knowledge you will need to demonstrate on the test. You should reflect on them, so that you understand their meanings and can apply the terms and concepts used in them to actual teaching situations. This book is designed to help you learn to do that.

Format of the Professional Development ExCET

Each Professional Development ExCET consists of 90 multiple-choice questions. Each test question requires the test taker to choose among four answer choices labeled A, B, C, or D. The test taker must mark his or her answer choices on a separate answer sheet. The 90 test questions are grouped into Teacher Decision Sets of related questions. Each Decision Set begins with a "stimulus," a short descriptive paragraph about a classroom situation, followed by two or more questions. Then more information is presented in the form of another stimulus which leads to additional questions, and so on. Typically, a Decision Set will have two or more stimuli for six to fifteen questions. The classroom situations described in the decision sets may indicate a particular content area (for example, mathematics); however, knowledge of that content area will not be necessary in order for you to answer the question correctly. Content-specific knowledge is *not* tested on the professional development tests; so don't worry if the stimulus mentions a subject area that you feel insecure about. Answer the question based on your knowledge of what a teacher would do *regardless of the content area*. The entire test consists of the 90 four-option questions divided into six to eight Teacher Decision Sets.

Scoring of the Professional Development ExCET

The Professional Development ExCET tests are scored electronically. Ten of the test items do not count, because they are being tested for use on future tests—but you will not know which 10. Only 80 items are used to determine your score on the test. The State Board for Educator Certification has set 70 as the minimum passing standard for the tests. Currently (in 1999) to reach the passing standard, you must answer correctly a minimum of 70 percent of the 80 test items that count; that is, you must get 56 of the 80 test items correct in order to receive a passing score. Your score is based on the number of questions answered correctly. There is no penalty for incorrect answers.

About This Book

This book is organized around the professional development competencies. It includes a thorough review of the knowledge base related to each competency and two full-length tests of 90 questions each for each of the two professional development tests. The answers are keyed to the competencies, with explanations supported by educational theory of effective practice. Upon completion of this book, not only will you be better prepared to take the Professional Development ExCET, but you will be a better prepared Texas public school teacher.

CHAPTER 3

HOW SHOULD YOU USE THIS BOOK?

Learn How to Study for the Test

Do not be overwhelmed by the task of preparing for the professional development ExCET. The test is challenging, but you can do well with smart preparation. Developing effective study skills will help you prepare adequately. Here are some suggestions for developing a successful study plan.

1. **Write a study plan.** Make a calendar and plan what you will do to review, how long it will take, and exactly when you will review. Putting your plan in writing is like your own personal guarantee of success.

2. **Select a time for studying.** Set aside a certain time for studying, and decide that, for this period, studying for the ExCET has priority over all other activities. You will learn faster and retain more if you study over an extended period of time—preferably three to four months in short daily sessions—than if you try to cram for a few days before the test.

3. **Choose a place to study.** Locate a comfortable place that is free of distractions and undue noise so that you can concentrate. The place you choose should be set aside for studying, so that when you are there, you expect to study. Ideally, you will have adequate lighting and a room temperature that is not too warm or too cold. Try to have all the necessary study aids (paper, pens, textbooks, notes, and so on) nearby, so that you do not have to interrupt your studying to go get something you need.

4. **Use this book wisely.** Read through the list of competencies for the professional development tests to get a general picture of what the tests cover. Then take the appropriate diagnostic test to help you discover your strengths and weaknesses. Make a list of the competency areas you had problems with. Review the competencies and knowledge-base material and review the explanations for the questions you missed. When you have finished your review, which should include the material in this book along with your college textbooks, your class notes, and other resource materials you have gathered (see Appendix F for suggested resource material), take the practice test in this book. Analyze the results of the practice test and review competency areas in which you are still weak.

5. **Concentrate when you study.** Don't let yourself be diverted by thoughts of other things or outside distractions. Ask friends not to call you during your study time. Do not try to watch television or listen to loud, distracting music while studying. On the other hand, for some students,

too much quiet is distracting. If you are in this category and feel listening to music helps your concentration, then select music that does not interrupt your thought patterns. Monitor yourself by making a check mark on a separate sheet of paper whenever your concentration wanders. Work on reducing the number of check marks you record each study session. If you begin to feel drowsy, get up and move around. If you get hungry, have a light snack.

6. Take notes. Take notes as you study, using your own words to express ideas. Leave ample room in the left margin so that you can revise or make comments when you review your notes. Extract key ideas and write them in the left margin to use as study cues later on. You may want to make index cards or create a computerized database to aid you in memorizing key ideas. Go over your note cards, or review the database, periodically to refresh your memory about key ideas.

7. Plan to master the competencies. Developing a strong understanding of the professional development competencies is essential to successful performance on the Professional Development ExCET. The reason is that the test is based on these competencies and is designed to ensure that individuals who become teachers in Texas can recognize and apply these "best practices" of classroom instruction. Try to relate the competencies to your own experiences so that they will be more meaningful to you. Use the study material in Chapter 4 to give yourself the edge of knowing and being able to apply the competencies.

8. Relate the review material to state standards. You cannot expect to reach the level of understanding necessary for successful application, evaluation, and synthesis of concepts by reading casually through the review material. Make sure you understand the authors' explanations and can discuss the material in various ways or use it in a different situation. As you read, try to connect the explanations of appropriate teacher behaviors to the fifteen Professional Development ExCET competencies and to the five Learner-Centered Proficiencies for Texas Teachers (see Appendix E)—learner-centered knowledge, learner-centered instruction, equity in excellence for all learners, learner-centered communication, and learner-centered professional development.

9. Plan to review. Set aside certain days to review material you have already studied. This will reinforce what you have learned and identify material you may need to restudy.

10. Don't make excuses. Studying for the ExCET must be a priority. It will require a lot of time and a conscientious commitment on your part. Think of it as a job that you must do. In reality, studying for the ExCET is one of the most important jobs you will ever do. The outcome of the test can determine your future career opportunities. Do not avoid studying for it by making excuses or procrastinating.

11. Organize a study group, if possible. A good way of learning and reinforcing the material is to discuss it with others. If possible, set up a regular time to study with one or more classmates or friends. Ask questions among yourselves to discover new insights. Seeing the material from the perspectives of others will help you to formulate your understanding of it better.

12. Do not schedule more than two tests on the same test date. Even though you can register for as many as four tests on the same test date, most students should not take four ExCET tests in one day. By the time you get to the last test, you are usually too exhausted to be mentally alert. If the last test you take is the professional development ExCET, you may find yourself unable to think at the level necessary to choose correctly among the answer choices. You should spread the tests out over two or more test dates so that you will have more time in which to take each test.

Learn What to Do Before the Test

There are several things you can do to prepare yourself for the day of the test.

1. Make sure you know where the test center is located, how to get there, and how to enter the building.

2. Make dependable arrangements to get to the test center in plenty of time. If you plan to go by car, find out where to park.

3. Avoid consuming alcoholic beverages or taking nonprescription drugs during the days before the test. The use of such products may impair your mental alertness on the day of the test.

4. The day before the test, gather together the materials that you will need: your admission ticket, two forms of identification (including one that is government-issued with a recent photograph), several sharpened No. 2 pencils, a simple twist-type pencil sharpener (so that you need not waste time walking back and forth to a pencil sharpener if your point breaks), a good eraser, an accurate watch (so that you can pace yourself during the test) and, if desired, some mints (for a quick energy boost if you get hungry or tired.

5. The night before the test, spend a short time (no more than an hour) reviewing the competencies. Then relax for the rest of the evening by doing something you enjoy.

6. Go to bed in time for a good night's rest.

7. On the day of the test, get up early so that you do not have to rush to get ready and to reach the test center.

8. Dress comfortably in clothes you have worn before. Unless the weather is extremely hot, wear layers of clothing that can be removed so that you can adapt to fluctuations in the room temperature at the test center.

9. Eat a light, balanced breakfast.

10. Arrive at the test center no later than 7:30 AM for the morning session or 1:30 PM for the afternoon session.

11. When you receive the test, take several deep, slow breaths, exhaling slowly while mentally visualizing yourself performing successfully on the test before you begin. Do not get upset if you feel nervous. Most of the people taking the test with you will be experiencing some measure of anxiety. During the test, try to remain as calm as possible. Stop periodically and take several deep, slow breaths, exhaling slowly, to help you relax. This is your big day, the day you have been waiting and preparing for. Now is your chance to show what you can do. Go for it!

Learn Test-Taking Strategies

1. Follow directions. Throughout the test, follow all directions carefully, including the oral directions of the test administrator and the written directions in the test booklet. The test booklet will contain general directions for individual test questions or groups of test questions. If you do not understand something in the directions, do not hesitate to ask the test administrator for assistance.

2. Pace yourself. The morning session officially begins at 8:00 AM and ends at 1:00 PM The afternoon session officially begins at 2:00 PM and ends at 7:00 PM. You have five hours in the test session. You may allocate your time as you need. Because you control the allocation of time, however, it is important that you move through the test at a steady pace. The test consists of 90 multiple-choice items, which will be grouped into Teacher Decision Sets. As you begin the test, skim through the booklet to see how many Decision Sets it contains. Then mentally divide your time accordingly. You should also gauge an approximate halfway point that you expect to reach by the end of two and one-half hours. Mark this point and the expected time of arrival at the top of the booklet. Work as rapidly as you can without being careless, *but do not rush.* (There are no extra points for finishing first.) Use your watch to check the time occasionally.

3. Try to answer the questions in order. Skipping around through the examination can waste valuable time and may cause mistakes on your answer sheet.

4. Do not allow a question to immobilize you. If a question is taking too much time, place a question mark next to it in your test booklet (*not* on the answer sheet) and make your best guess on the answer sheet. If you have time at the end of the test, go back and review that question. Try to keep the number of such question marks to less than 10.

5. Read each question entirely. Do not skim the directions in an effort to save time; you may misread important words and select the wrong answer. Try to determine which competency is the primary focus of the question. The answer must relate to that competency (for instance, this question focuses on classroom management). If the question is complex or wordy, restate it in your own words. Leave out information that you don't need to answer the question.

6. Don't read too much into a question. Stick with the stimulus. You should not assume that something is going on or will happen unless it is clearly and plainly stated in the description of the classroom situation.

7. Eliminate as many wrong answers as you can. Read all the answer choices. One of them is the correct answer. Think of it—you do not have to come up with the right answer from scratch. The right answer is there before your eyes. You simply must select it from the four choices given. To help you do that, eliminate any choices that you know are incorrect. Be especially on the watch for answer choices that express ideas that you agree with, but that are too off-topic (do not relate to the focus of the question) to apply to the situation being described. If two choices, in essence, duplicate each other, eliminate both of them—there can be only one best choice. In your test booklet, lightly cross out the choices you have eliminated so that you do not waste time rereading them. After you have eliminated a choice, do not go back to it. Put a question mark beside a choice you are unsure about. Try to eliminate at least two answer choices. Read and evaluate all choices that you have not eliminated, **reread the question** (don't skip doing this!), and then select the most reasonable answer. Remember that the test questions call for the "best answer." Sometimes two answers may seem correct, but one answer is slightly better than the other. To decide which to choose, look for (a) a global response that includes correct ideas from other answer choices (but is not a duplicate of any of them), (b) a response choice that more precisely answers the question than the other choice, or (c) a response consistent with logic and past experience.

8. Answer all the test questions. Your score is based on the number of questions you answer correctly. *You are not penalized for a wrong answer.* If you do not know an answer, eliminate as many choices as you can, then guess.

9. Change answers only if you have good reason for doing so. It is not wise to change answers based on a hunch or a whim.

10. Write in the test booklet. You are allowed to write in the test booklet. Take advantage of this by circling or underlining key words or phrases and crossing out answer choices you've eliminated. Remember, though, to mark *all* your answer choices on the separate answer document. Answers to questions recorded only in the test booklet will not be scored.

11. Mark your answer sheet carefully. The tests are scored electronically. You are responsible for proper completion of your answer sheet to ensure accurate scoring. You may want to record your answers in batches of several questions, rather than to go back and forth between the test booklet and the answer sheet as you proceed through the test. Record your answers in the margin of the test booklet before transferring them to your answer sheet. Carefully and completely fill in the space corresponding to the answer you select for each question. Mark only one answer for each question. Be sure to mark each answer in the row with the same number as the question. If you skip a question, also skip the corresponding number on your answer sheet. If you change an answer, be sure to erase the old answer completely before marking the new one. Also erase any stray marks on the answer document because these may be misinterpreted by the electronic scoring machine.

12. Keep your cool. During the test, try to remain as calm as possible. Stop periodically and take several deep, slow breaths, exhaling slowly, to help you relax. Do not be upset if the student next to you finishes, gets up, and leaves before you do. Keep your mind focused on the task at hand—completing your exam. Trust yourself. You should not expect to know the correct response to every question on the exam. Think only of doing your personal best.

13. Practice these strategies. As you work through the diagnostic and practice tests provided in this book, consciously use the strategies suggested in this section as preparation for the actual ExCET. Use a watch to get a sense of how fast you can complete the test without making careless errors. Remember: The better prepared you are, the more confident you will be on the day of the test.

Plan a Study Program

When you read through the list of competencies covered on the professional development ExCET, you may feel overwhelmed by the task of preparing for the test. Ideally, you will spend three to four months reviewing for the ExCET so that you will have ample time to "overlearn" the material. To help you organize and budget your time, set up a specific time schedule. Try to set aside approximately two hours for each session. If you complete one session per day (including weekends), it should take you about five to six weeks to work through the review and practice provided in this book.

If your test date is coming up soon, you may need to extend your study time per day or omit sections of the book that cover material you feel you already know fairly well.

Take the diagnostic test before you begin your study program. Carefully study the answer explanations for *all* the questions, not just the ones you missed, because some of your correct responses may have been arrived at incorrectly or by guessing.

Plan your study program so that you concentrate first on competency areas in which you are weak. Systematically read each chapter in the review sections.

When you complete the study program, take the practice test. Carefully study the answer explanations for *all* the questions, and review again any topics in which you need additional practice.

If you have only a few days in which to get ready for the test, the following 15-hour modified review plan may be the best study strategy for you:

First: Take the diagnostic test. (2½ hours)

Second: Go over the diagnostic test answer explanations. (3½ hours)

Third: Study Chapter 4—Master the Competencies. (3 hours)

Fourth: Take the practice test. (2½ hours)

Fifth: Go over the practice test answer explanations. (3½ hours)

Learn About the Types of Question Formats

Part Two of this book contains two full-length professional development diagnostic tests—one for the elementary level and one for the secondary level. Each test has the same number and type of question that you will find on the actual professional development ExCET. Before you take the diagnostic test for your level, you should know about the "best," "likely," "most likely," and "first" that you will see often on the test, and the two main formats in which test items are presented: single-response questions and multiple-response questions.

Stem Types

There are two types of stems, each asking for a different kind of answer:

- *True response stems.* The correct option will be something that is true (for instance, something the teacher *should do*).
- *False response stems.* The correct option will be something that is *not* true (for example, something the teacher *should not do*).

Priority-Setting Questions

The stems for the ExCET questions will usually ask you to select the item among the responses that

- best illustrates, best describes, etc.;
- is a likely purpose, is a likely result, etc.;
- is most likely the purpose, is most likely to happen, etc.; or
- is the first step, is the best first step.

When you have to pick the "best" response, there will probably be other appropriate answers, but you must select the one that is the "best" of all of them.

When you have to pick a "likely" response, there will be only one appropriate answer choice which is "likely" and the rest of the choices will be unlikely.

When you have to pick the "most likely" response, there may be other likely answers, but you must select the one that is "most likely."

When you have to pick the "first step" or the "best first step," all of the answer choices will (usually) be appropriate things to do, but you need to pick the one that should be done "first."

Single-Response Questions

Most of the questions on the professional development ExCET tests require a single response, which the test taker will select from among the answer choices—A, B, C, or D—listed below the question. Following is an example of this type of question.

Ms. Jones likes to actively involve her third grade students in the learning process. During a follow-up discussion after groups experimented with magnets, she asks, "Why did the magnet attract some things and not others?" Sam and Mary have their hands waving in the air before she is finished. Ms. Jones says, "I'll give everyone a few minutes to think about the question." Then she repeats it. After a few minutes of watching the students' faces, she asks different ones if they have an answer. By posing the question to the whole class before calling on individual students, Ms. Jones is *most* likely attempting to promote learning by:

    A. encouraging students to be creative problem solvers.
    B. providing students with clear learning expectations.
    C. ignoring over-anxious students so that they do not monopolize class discussion time.
    D. encouraging more students to respond.

The best strategy to use when answering a single-response question is to read the stimulus and question stem carefully. Think about what aspect of the classroom situation is under discussion in the question and which competency is its primary focus. Then read each answer choice, trying to eliminate any that are clearly incorrect or implausible based on the information provided in the stimulus and on your knowledge about the relevant competency and principles and concepts that relate to the pedagogy of the situation. In the test booklet, lightly cross out the choices you eliminate.

The question is asking about Ms. Jones' *likely* purpose in using a particular questioning strategy. Thus, its primary focus is Competency 007: *The teacher uses effective verbal, nonverbal, and media communication techniques to shape the classroom into a community of learners engaged in active inquiry, collaborative exploration, and supportive instruction.* Eliminate A because Ms. Jones is processing what happened in the experiment, not asking the students to problem solve. Eliminate B because Ms. Jones is not conveying learning expectations. Eliminate C because the stimulus provided the information that Ms. Jones wants to actively involve her students in the learning process. Ignoring over-anxious learners would leave them out of the learning process. The understandings and skills expressed in Competency 007 indicate that the teacher should foster effective, constructive, and purposeful communication in the classroom. Choice D is consistent with this competency. Asking a question first and then calling a student's name is an effective method teachers can use to keep all students mentally involved in the learning process. When the question comes before the student's name, all students are given the opportunity to think and process their answers because the teacher has not yet identified the student who will be asked to respond. Research shows that asking the question first increases the number of responses and elicits more correct and longer responses. Choice D is the correct response.

Multiple-Response Questions

Some questions on the professional development ExCET tests have a question stem followed by a set of responses numbered with Roman numerals. The test taker is given answer choices—A, B, C, or D—that offer combinations of the Roman numeral responses. Following is an example of this type of question.

Mr. Williams, a geography teacher, begins a thematic unit on "The Environment." He enlists the help of his students in determining topics and procedures for investigations. He believes it is important for students to make some decisions related to their interests and to how to go about solving problems. Mr. Williams' classroom approach is *most* likely intended to achieve which of the following?

I.   He wants to increase students' intrinsic motivation.
II. He wants to provide an opportunity for students to interact with each other.
III. He wants to positively affect students' self-motivation.
IV. He wants to provide an opportunity for students to practice democratic decision making.

A. I and II only
B. I and III only
C. II and III only
D. I, III, and IV only

Using a two-step process is the best approach when answering a multiple response question. As a first step you should identify Roman numeral responses you are sure are correct and eliminate any Roman numeral responses that are clearly incorrect or implausible. Read the stimulus and question stem carefully. Then read each Roman numeral choice, put a check next to any you feel are correct, and lightly cross out any that you are sure should be eliminated. Next, lightly cross out an answer choice if it *does not include* a Roman numeral you felt was correct, or if it *includes* a Roman numeral you eliminated.

Mr. Williams is allowing students to have choices in their learning and giving students control over their learning experiences, techniques associated with motivating students. Thus, the primary focus of this question is Competency 005: *The teacher understands how motivation affects group and individual behavior and learning and can apply this understanding to promote learning.* You must decide upon the *most* likely answer choice. Mr. Williams is building an educational environment that is respectful of the student and encourages student participation in decision making. According to motivational theory, allowing students to have choices in the design of their education experiences will have a positive impact on intrinsic motivation (I) and self-motivation (III). The answer choice must include Roman numerals I and III. Put a check beside answer choices B and D. Cross out Roman numeral IV because the stimulus does not indicate that students will be involved in democratic decision making. Cross out answer choice D. Therefore, choice B is the correct response.

Don't forget that aside from drawing on the educational preparation that you've had to get yourself to this point, you also need to use plain common sense when taking the ExCET. Read the items carefully and subject the answer choices to a good dose of down-to-earth thinking. Watch especially for answer choices that express ideas that you agree with but are too far from the topic to apply to the situation being described.

You will benefit greatly from this preparation manual. By using the recommendations in this book as you complete your study program, you will be prepared to walk into the testing room with confidence. Good luck on the test and on your new career as a teacher!

CHAPTER 4

MASTER THE 15 COMPETENCIES

Introduction

The *ExCET Preparation Manual* for the professional development tests lists the 15 professional development competencies, each followed by a descriptive, explanatory paragraph. This chapter will analyze each competency. Developing a strong understanding of the professional development competencies is essential to successful performance on the Professional Development ExCET. The reason is that the test is based on these competencies and is designed to ensure that individuals who become teachers in Texas can recognize and apply these "best practices" of classroom instruction. The competencies cover the pedagogical and professional knowledge and skills that all teachers are expected to have acquired in their teacher preparation programs. Undoubtedly, you have applied these skills and knowledge during your student teaching or internship experience. Notwithstanding this practical experience, you must take the time to study the competencies and connect them to classroom situations. Doing so should greatly improve your score on the Professional Development ExCET.

Words to Know

Certain common words are used frequently throughout the entire set of competencies. If you do not know what these words mean in an educational context, they can be "stopper words" for you on the ExCET. The first step in mastering the competencies is to make sure none of the verbs are "stopper verbs" for you. The following lists suggest simplified synonyms that you can substitute for the verbs when you encounter them on the ExCET. In some cases, the synonyms fall short of communicating the full meaning of the verb, but the basic idea is retained.

Stopper Verbs

- Verbs that mean to *know* or *grasp* (a concept):
  be aware (of): The teacher *is aware of* the multiplicity of roles that teachers may be called upon to assume. (Competency 015)
  recognize: The teacher *recognizes* the importance of maintaining ongoing parent-teacher communication with students' families. (Competency 013)
  understand: The teacher *understands* the relationship between careful planning and student success in the classroom. (Competency 006)

- Verbs that mean to *care about* (and respond positively to):
  appreciate: The teacher *appreciates* the cultural dimensions of communication. (Competency 007)
  respect: The teacher *respects* differences. (Competency 003)

- Verbs that mean to *use:*
  apply: The teacher *applies* knowledge of human development to design instruction. (Competency 001)
  employ: The teacher *employs* a variety of formal and informal assessment techniques. (Competency 010)

- Verbs that mean to *help* or *cause* (something to happen or increase):
  encourage: The teacher *encourages* students to communicate effectively in a variety of contexts. (Competency 007)
  enhance: The teacher knows how to *enhance* learning for all students through the appropriate use of instructional materials and resources learning. (Competency 009)
  facilitate: The teacher *facilitates* a positive social and emotional atmosphere in the classroom. (Competency 011)
  foster: The teacher knows how to take advantage of community strengths and resources to *foster* student growth. (Competency 014)
  nurture: The teacher uses an understanding of human developmental processes to *nurture* student growth. (Competency 001)
  promote: The teacher is a reflective practitioner who knows how to *promote* his or her own professional growth. (Competency 012)
  support: The teacher uses a variety of instructional materials and resources to *support* individual and group learning. (Competency 009)

- Verbs that mean to *make* or *set up* (something):
  construct: The teacher knows how to select or *construct* and use assessment instruments for various purposes. (Competency 010)
  create: The teacher knows how to *create* a learning environment that takes advantage of positive factors and minimizes negative factors. (Competency 002)
  design: The teacher can *design* instruction to facilitate learning in different situations. (Competency 004)
  devise: The teacher knows how to work cooperatively with parents to *devise* strategies for use at home and in the classroom. (Competency 013)
  establish: The teacher is able to *establish* a relationship of trust with parents or guardians from diverse backgrounds. (Competency 013)
  structure: The teacher *structures* and manages the learning environment. (Competency 011)

- Verbs that mean to *change* (something):
  adjust: The teacher constantly monitors and *adjusts* strategies in response to learner feedback. (Competency 008)
  affect: The teacher knows how motivation *affects* group and individual behavior and learning. (Competency 005)
  influence: The teacher understands factors inside and outside the classroom that *influence* students' perceptions of their own worth and potential. (Competency 002)

modify: The teacher employs a variety of formal and informal assessment techniques to *modify* instructional delivery. (Competency 010)

vary: The teacher can *vary* his or her role in the instructional process. (Competency 008)

- Verbs that mean to *think about* (something and respond to it):

  consider: The teacher *considers* environmental factors that may affect learning in designing a supportive and responsive classroom community. (Competency 002)

  take account of: In designing instruction, the teacher *takes account of* factors relevant to instructional planning. (Competency 006)

- Verbs that mean to *get* or *reach* (something):

  acquire: The teacher helps students *acquire* strategies and skills that will be useful to them in the real world. (Competency 008)

  achieve: The teacher chooses lessons and activities that help students *achieve* an in-depth understanding. (Competency 006)

  accomplish: The teacher chooses lessons and activities that help students acquire the will to set and *accomplish* their own long- and short-term goals. (Competency 006)

  develop: The teacher understands how students *develop* knowledge and skills. (Competency 004)

- Additional verbs to know:

  celebrate: to make known with honor or praise

  diminish: to decrease

  engage: to keep busy

  ensure: to make sure

  explore: to find out about

  impart: to tell or make known

  implement: to carry out

  maintain: to keep up

  manage: to control

  maximize: to make as large as possible

  minimize: to make as small as possible

  model: to be an example of

  monitor: to oversee

  pursue: to seek

  reflect: to show

  respond: to answer or react to

  stimulate: to awaken

Although verbs are the main words that commonly appear throughout the competencies, some other words may keep you from understanding fully.

Other Stopper Words

factor: an element that has an effect or impact on something else.

Example. In designing instruction, the teacher takes account of *factors* relevant to instructional planning. (Competency 006)

principles: the basic underlying assumptions; fundamental rules or standards.
Example. The teacher understands *principles*, procedures, advantages, and limitations associated with various instructional strategies. (Competency 008)
Example. The teacher understands basic *principles* of conducting parent-teacher conferences. (Competency 013)

purposeful: personally meaningful; has a purpose constructed from within.
Example. The teacher knows how to foster *purposeful* communication by and among all students in the class. (Competency 007)

Analyses of the Competencies

Domain I Understanding Learners—What you should know about learners

Competency 001: The teacher uses an understanding of human developmental processes to nurture student growth through developmentally appropriate instruction.

The teacher recognizes that students' developmental characteristics affect what and how they learn and that effective decision making about instructional content and methods takes into account individual students' level of development in the various domains (e.g., cognitive, social, emotional, aesthetic). The teacher is aware of expected developmental progressions and ranges of individual variation in each domain, knows how to foster growth in each domain, and understands how development in any one domain may affect performance in other domains. The teacher applies knowledge of human development to design instruction that helps students at various developmental levels make connections between their current skills and understandings and those that are new to them.

Analysis: This competency deals with **developmentally appropriate instruction.** To decide whether this competency is the primary focus of an ExCET question, look for ideas related to how children develop and what instructional strategies/activities are most appropriate for the various levels of development. Key ideas for this competency are:

- human developmental processes—series of changes that students go through as they mature
- expected developmental progressions—the different stages you expect students to go through as they mature
- developmentally appropriate instruction—instruction that is geared to the mental, social, emotional, and/or physical readiness of the student
- students' developmental characteristics—what students are like at different stages of their development
- students' level of development—where students are in their readiness to learn
- domains of development—the different areas in which children

develop as they grow older: cognitive (mental), social (relationships with others), emotional (one's feelings), and aesthetic (what one finds pleasing)

7 • developmental progressions—the sequence of advances that students go through as they mature

8 • ranges of individual variation—the differences (developmentally) within a group of students, especially at a particular chronological age

Competency 002: The teacher considers environmental factors that may affect learning in designing a supportive and responsive classroom community that promotes all students' learning and self-esteem.

The teacher understands how various external factors (e.g., conflict within students' families, peer relationships, gang- or drug-related community problems, malnutrition) may affect students' lives and their performance in school and knows how to create a learning environment that takes advantage of positive factors and minimizes the effects of negative factors. The teacher recognizes signs of stress in students (e.g., a sudden drop in grades, an increase in aggressiveness) and knows how to respond appropriately to help students deal with stress. The teacher understands factors inside and outside the classroom that influence students' perceptions of their own worth and potential (e.g., grouping practices, parent and teacher expectations, prior experiences in school), recognizes the effects of these perceptions on learning, and knows how to plan instruction to enhance all students' self-esteem and to create an environment in which all students feel safe, accepted, competent, and productive.

Analysis: This competency deals with **students' self-esteem.** To decide whether this competency is the primary focus of an ExCET question, look for ideas related to making students feel safe, accepted, competent, and productive in the classroom. Key ideas for this competency are:

1 • environmental factors—elements inside or outside of school that affect students' ability to learn

2 • supportive—encouraging and helpful, with low levels of threat

3 • responsive—shows consideration for learners' unique needs and characteristics

4 • students' self-esteem—students' perceptions of their own worth and potential; can be affected by factors in and out of school (for instance, grouping practices, parent and teacher expectations, prior experiences in school)

5 • external factors—elements outside of school that affect students' ability to learn

6 • learning environment—the surrounding conditions in which instruction takes place

7 • negative factors—factors (for example, conflict within students' families, peer relationships, gang- or drug-related community problems, malnutrition, stress) that interfere with student learning

8 • positive factors—factors (for instance, parental involvement, good nutrition) that facilitate student learning

Competency 003: The teacher appreciates human diversity, recognizing how diversity in the classroom and the community may affect learning and creating a classroom environment in which both the diversity of groups and the uniqueness of individuals are recognized and celebrated.

The teacher is aware that each student brings to the classroom a constellation of personal and social characteristics related to a variety of factors such as ethnicity, gender, language background, exceptionality, etc. The teacher recognizes the instructional implications of student diversity and knows how to turn the diversity within and beyond the classroom to advantage by creating an environment that nurtures a sense of community, respects differences, fosters learning, and enhances students' understanding of the society in which they live.

Analysis: This competency deals with **diversity.** To decide whether this competency is the primary focus of an ExCET question, look for instructional strategies/activities that respect and celebrate both the diversity of groups and the uniqueness of individuals. Key ideas for this competency are:

- human diversity—the differences in terms of various personal (for instance, race, ethnicity, gender, exceptionality) and social characteristics (such as socioeconomic status, religion) among people
- classroom environment—the atmosphere surrounding classroom interactions (for example, nurturing a sense of community, being respectful of differences, fostering learning)
- diversity of groups—the differences by groups of students (for instance, by gender, by ethnicity, by socioeconomic status)
- uniqueness of individuals—the special and particular characteristics of students as individuals (for example, learning styles, handicapping conditions, gender expectations, cultural backgrounds, potential for at-risk indicators, age levels)
- constellation of personal and social characteristics—the varied characteristics of students
- ethnicity—a cultural sense of identity shared by a group of people
- gender—male or female
- language background—prior language experience
- exceptionality—a condition such as a sensory deficit, physical handicap, mental retardation, behavioral disorder, communication disorder, special learning disability, gift, talent, being developmentally delayed, abused, or neglected
- instructional implications of student diversity—the need for instructional materials and strategies/activities to reflect a knowledge of and support for the varied characteristics of students (for example, learning styles, handicapping conditions, gender expectations, cultural backgrounds, potential for at-risk indicators, age level)
- sense of community—an awareness of belonging to, being accepted by, and having a responsibility toward the collective group of students in the class

Competency 004: The teacher understands how learning occurs and can apply this understanding to design and implement effective instruction.

The teacher understands how students develop knowledge and skills and recognizes instructional strategies that promote student learning (e.g., linking new information to old, fostering a view of learning as a purposeful pursuit, promoting a sense of responsibility for one's own learning). The teacher is aware of factors that affect learning (e.g., individual talents, learning styles, teaching styles, prior learning experiences) and can design instruction to facilitate learning in different situations and to help students learn how to learn and to monitor their own performance.

Analysis: This competency deals with **how learning occurs.** To decide whether this competency is the primary focus of an ExCET question, look for ideas related to ways to teach based on knowing how students learn. Key terms for this competency are:

- instructional strategies that promote student learning—ways to deliver instruction that increase student learning
- linking new information to old—helping students make connections between new learning and what they already know
- fostering a view of learning as a purposeful pursuit—helping students to see that learning is something people do because it is personally meaningful to them
- promoting a sense of responsibility for one's own learning—making students more self-directed/self-initiated
- individual talents—special abilities
- learning styles—the different ways of processing information
- teaching styles—the different ways of delivering instruction
- prior learning experiences—student's past history of learning

Competency 005: The teacher understands how motivation affects group and individual behavior and learning and can apply this understanding to promote student learning.

The teacher understands the importance of motivation to learning, knows how to help students become self-motivated, and is able to recognize factors and situations that are likely to promote or diminish motivation. The teacher is aware of the characteristics and effects of intrinsic and extrinsic motivation and knows how to use a variety of techniques (e.g., relating lessons to students' personal interests, allowing students to have choices in their learning, giving students control over their learning experiences, leading individual or groups of students to ask questions and pursue problems that are meaningful to them) to engage students in learning activities and to help them develop the motivation to achieve.

Analysis: This competency deals with **motivation.** To decide whether this competency is the primary focus of an ExCET question, look for instructional strategies/activities that help students develop the motivation to achieve. Key ideas for this competency are:

- motivation—the willingness or drive to accomplish something
- self-motivated—motivated from within oneself without need of outside influence
- intrinsic motivation—an internal source of motivation that may be triggered in students by relating lessons to students' personal

interests, allowing students to have choices in their learning, giving students control over their learning experiences, leading individual or groups of students to ask questions and pursue problems that are meaningful to them

4 • extrinsic motivation—motivation created by events or rewards (for instance, stickers, stars, praise) outside the individual

Domain II Enhancing Student Achievement—What you should know about how to teach

Competency 006: The teacher uses planning processes to design outcome-oriented learning experiences that foster understanding and encourage self-directed thinking and learning in both individual and collaborative settings.

The teacher understands the relationship between careful planning and student success in the classroom. In designing instruction the teacher takes account of factors relevant to instructional planning (e.g., learners' backgrounds, desired learner outcomes, content of instruction, integrated curriculum, input from students, available materials and resources, time and space constraints). The teacher chooses lessons and activities that reflect the principles of effective instruction and that help students achieve an in-depth understanding and acquire the will to set and accomplish their own long-term and short-term goals. The teacher makes use of collaborative processes (e.g., working with other teachers) in planning instruction and in designing individual and group activities.

Analysis: This competency deals with **planning**. To decide whether this competency is the primary focus of an ExCET question, look for ideas related to designing and planning instruction, both in individual and in group settings.

1 • planning processes—the acts involved in planning (for instance, selecting objectives)

2 • outcome-oriented learning experiences—instructional strategies/activities meant to achieve clearly defined outcomes

3 • self-directed thinking—thinking that is guided by one's own self

4 • self-directed learning—learning that is guided by one's own self

5 • individual settings—students working alone

6 • collaborative settings—students working with others (for instance, cooperative learning groups)

7 • factors relevant to instructional planning—elements that are important to consider when planning instruction

8 • learners' backgrounds—what you know about the learners

9 • desired learner outcomes—what you want your students to learn

10 • content of instruction—what you teach

11 • integrated curriculum—a curriculum that makes connections between and among various disciplines

12 • input from students—information gathered from students

13 • available materials and resources—what you have to work with (for example, computers, CD-ROM, videodiscs, primary documents and artifacts, audiovisual equipment, manipulatives, local experts)

14 • time and space constraints—the limits on the time and space you
    have
15 • principles of effective instruction—principles consistent with learner-
    centered instruction in which students are active, successful
    participants
16 • (student's) long-term goals—what the student wants to accomplish in
    the future
17 • (student's) short-term goals—what the student wants to accomplish
    right away
18 • collaborative processes—working with others (for instance, working
    with other teachers)

Competency 007: The teacher uses effective verbal, nonverbal, and
    media communication techniques to shape the classroom into a
    community of learners engaged in active inquiry, collaborative
    exploration, and supportive interactions.

The teacher understands that communication takes place verbally,
nonverbally, and through the use of media. Using a variety of modes and
tools of communication, the teacher imparts expectations and ideas to
create a climate of trust, respect, support, and inquiry. The teacher models
effective communication strategies (e.g., monitoring the effects of
messages, being a reflective listener, simplifying and restating, being
sensitive to nonverbal cues given and received) and encourages students
to communicate effectively in a variety of contexts. The teacher is a
thoughtful questioner who asks questions that elicit different levels of
thinking and recognizes that different ways of questioning achieve
different purposes (e.g., promoting risk taking and problem solving,
facilitating factual recall, encouraging divergent thinking, stimulating
curiosity). The teacher appreciates the cultural dimensions of
communication and knows how to foster effective, constructive, and
purposeful communication by and among all students in the class.

Analysis: This competency deals with **communication.** To decide
whether this competency is the primary focus of an ExCET question, look
for ideas related to verbal, nonverbal, and media communication
techniques. Key ideas for this competency are:

1 • verbal communication—spoken or written messages
2 • nonverbal communication—unspoken messages communicated
    through facial expressions (for example, smiling, scowling), eye
    contact, body language (for example, nodding, leaning toward a
    student), touching, patting on the back, displaying students' work
3 • media communication—the transmission of information via overhead
    transparencies, newspapers, magazines, radio, television, videodiscs,
    CD-ROM, and so on
4 • community of learners—a unified group of learners in which all are
    contributing toward the destination of learning; a learning community
    where students can learn alone and together in a safe and challenging
    environment
5 • active inquiry—lively investigation and problem solving in pursuit of
    answers to questions
6 • collaborative exploration—investigating and exploring with others

7 • supportive interactions—ways of acting toward one another that encourage and help each other

8 • effective communication strategies—ways of communicating that work well (for instance, monitoring the effects of messages, being a reflective listener, simplifying and restating, being sensitive to nonverbal cues given and received)

9 • thoughtful questioner—someone who asks questions that elicit different levels of thinking (who considers Bloom's taxonomy) and recognizes that different ways of questioning achieve different purposes (for example, promoting risk taking and problem solving, facilitating factual recall, encouraging divergent thinking, stimulating curiosity)

10 • cultural dimensions of communication—the aspects of culture that influence communication

Competency 008: The teacher uses a variety of instructional strategies and roles to facilitate learning and to help students become independent thinkers and problem solvers who use higher-order thinking in the classroom and the real world.

The teacher uses an array of instructional strategies to actively engage students in learning, and constantly monitors and adjusts strategies in response to learner feedback. The teacher understands principles, procedures, advantages, and limitations associated with various instructional strategies (e.g., interdisciplinary instruction, cooperative learning, discovery learning) and appropriately chooses among alternative strategies to achieve different purposes and meet different needs. The teacher can vary his or her role in the instructional process (e.g., instructor, facilitator, coach, audience) in relation to the content and purposes of instruction and the levels of need and independence of the students. The teacher knows how to make instruction relevant to students' own needs and purposes and helps students acquire strategies and skills (including higher-order thinking skills, such as comparison, analysis, evaluation) that will be useful to them in the real world.

Analysis: This competency deals with **instructional strategies.** To decide whether this competency is the primary focus of an ExCET question, look for instructional strategies/activities related to helping students become independent thinkers and problem solvers who use higher-order thinking. Key ideas for this competency are:

1 • instructional strategies—method or means by which instruction is delivered (such as lecture, simulation, hands-on activity)

2 • independent thinkers—those whose thinking is not controlled by others

3 • problem solvers—those who can apply knowledge and skills to produce a result

4 • higher-order thinking—thinking at the higher levels of Bloom's taxonomy (for example, comparison, analysis, synthesis, evaluation)

5 • interdisciplinary instruction—instruction that makes connections between and among various disciplines

6 • cooperative learning—a teaching strategy in which students work together on assigned tasks and are rewarded on the basis of the

success of the group; in so doing, they take responsibility for their own learning as well as for that of their classmates

7 • discovery learning—a teaching strategy in which the teacher creates situations in which students can learn on their own; learning proceeds in this sequence: identification of a problem, development of hypotheses, testing of hypotheses, arrival at conclusions

8 • teacher's role in the instructional process—role teacher assumes (such as instructor, facilitator, coach, audience)

Competency 009: The teacher uses a variety of instructional materials and resources (including human and technological resources) to support individual and group learning.

The teacher knows how to enhance learning for all students through the appropriate use of instructional materials and resources (e.g., computers, CD-ROM, videodiscs, primary documents and artifacts, AV equipment, manipulatives, local experts) and helps students understand the role of technology as a learning tool. The teacher evaluates the effectiveness of specific materials and resources for particular situations and purposes; selects appropriate materials and resources to address individual students' strengths and needs, learning styles, preferred modalities, and interests; understands the value of using multiple resources in instruction; and can manage the logistics of individual and collaborative use of limited materials and resources.

Analysis: This competency deals with **materials and resources.** To decide whether this competency is the primary focus of an ExCET question, look for ideas related to how to use instructional materials and resources—especially technology—to enhance student learning. Key ideas for this competency are:

1 • instructional materials and resources—human and technological resources (for instance, computers, CD-ROM, videodiscs, primary documents and artifacts, audiovisual equipment, manipulatives, local experts) that can be used in instruction

2 • learning style—one's orientation for approaching learning tasks and processing information in certain ways

3 • preferred modality—the predominant way a student takes in information through the five primary senses (see, hear, smell, taste, touch)

4 • interests—what engages one's time and thoughts

5 • logistics—the details of handling something that has to be moved around (either physically or figuratively)

Competency 010: The teacher uses processes of informal and formal assessment to understand individual learners, monitor instructional effectiveness, and shape instruction.

The teacher understand the importance of ongoing assessment as an instructional tool and employs a variety of formal and informal assessment techniques (e.g., observation, portfolio, teacher-made classroom test, student self-assessment, peer assessment, standardized test) to enhance his or her knowledge of learners, monitor students' progress in achieving outcomes, and modify instructional delivery. The teacher is aware of the characteristics, uses, advantages, and limitations of different types of assessments; understands assessment-related issues such as those related to bias, reliability, validity, and grading; and knows how to select or construct and use assessment instruments for various purposes.

Analysis: This competency deals with **assessment.** To decide whether this competency is the primary focus of an ExCET question, look for ideas related to how to select or construct and use assessment instruments for various purposes. Key ideas for this competency are:

- assessment—a process in which data about students' performance is collected
  Note: Assessment is *not* a synonym for evaluation. Evaluation is the process of making a *judgment* (for instance, regarding effectiveness of a program) after critically examining assessment data and other relevant information.
- informal assessment—unofficial, casual gathering of data about students (for example, casual observation)
- formal assessment—official gathering of data about students (such as observation checklist, portfolio, teacher-made classroom test, student self-assessment, peer assessment, standardized test)
- monitor instructional effectiveness—observe students to determine whether they understand
- shape instruction—modify instruction (to meet student needs)
- bias—a term applied to a test that is slanted in favor of a particular group
- reliability—the degree to which a test consistently measures what it measures
- validity—the degree to which a test measures what it is supposed to measure

Competency 011: The teacher structures and manages the learning environment to maintain a classroom climate that promotes the lifelong pursuit of learning and encourages cooperation, leadership, and mutual respect.

The teacher knows how to promote student ownership of and membership in a smoothly functioning learning community whose members are responsible, cooperative, purposeful, and mutually supportive. The teacher facilitates a positive social and emotional atmosphere in the classroom, establishes and maintains standards of behavior, manages routines and transitions, maximizes the amount of class time spent in learning, and creates a physical setting that is conducive to the achievement of various goals.

Analysis: This competency deals with **classroom management.** To decide whether this competency is the primary focus of an ExCET question, look for ideas related to managing the behavior of the students in the class. Key ideas for this competency are:

- learning environment—the surrounding conditions in which instruction takes place
- classroom climate—the atmosphere or mood (warm or hostile, supportive or threatening, accepting or ridiculing) surrounding classroom interactions
- smoothly functioning learning community—a unified group of

learners whose members are responsible, cooperative, purposeful, and mutually supportive

Domain III Understanding the Teaching Environment—What you should know about being a teacher

Competency 012: The teacher is a reflective practitioner who knows how to promote his or her own professional growth and can work cooperatively with other professionals in the system to create a school culture that enhances learning and encourages positive change.

The teacher understands the importance of reflection and self-evaluation and recognizes personal factors (e.g., self-concept, attitudes toward authority, biases, sense of mission) that affect one's role as a teacher and the nature of one's interpersonal relationships with students. The teacher recognizes that he or she is a member of a learning community and knows how to work effectively with all members of that community (e.g., planning a new curriculum, working across disciplines, assessing school effectiveness, implementing site-based management plans). The teacher actively seeks out opportunities to grow professionally; knows how to use different sources of support, information, and guidance (e.g., mentor, principal, professional journals and organizations, inservice training programs) to enhance his or her own professional skills and knowledge; and is aware of the value of technology in promoting efficient time use and professional growth.

Analysis: This competency deals with **professionalism.** To decide whether this competency is the primary focus of an ExCET question, look for ideas related to a teacher's enhancing his or her own professional skills and knowledge and working with colleagues and other professionals. Key ideas for this competency are:

- reflective practitioner—a teacher who systematically reflects on his or her performance in the classroom and development as a teacher
- professional growth—the process of improving one's professional skills and knowledge
- school culture—the learned, shared, and transmitted norms of the school
- reflection and self-evaluation—rethinking and reevaluating values and practices
- interpersonal relationships—relationships between individuals
- learning community—teachers become leaders and leaders become teachers to work together to achieve the school's mission
- mentor (teacher)—an experienced teacher who acts as an advisor and guide to a less experienced teacher

Competency 013: The teacher knows how to foster strong school-home relationships that support student achievement of desired learning outcomes.

The teacher is able to establish a relationship of trust with parents or guardians from diverse backgrounds and to develop effective parent-teacher partnerships that foster all students' learning and well-being. The teacher recognizes the importance of maintaining ongoing parent-teacher communication, is aware of factors that may facilitate or impede communication with students' families, and understands basic principles of conducting parent-teacher conferences (e.g., beginning and ending on a positive note, avoiding technical jargon) and knows how to work cooperatively with parents to devise strategies for use at home and in the classroom.

Analysis: This competency deals with **school-home relationships.** To decide whether this competency is the primary focus of an ExCET question, look for ideas related to teachers working with parents or guardians. Key ideas for this competency are:

- school-home relationship—the mutual dealings between the school and parents or guardians
- parent-teacher partnerships—the joining of parents and teachers to work together to support student achievement of desired learning outcomes
- basic principles of conducting parent-teacher conferences—what works when conducting parent-teacher conferences (for instance, beginning and ending on a positive note, avoiding technical jargon)

Competency 014: The teacher understands how the school relates to the larger community and knows strategies for making interactions between school and community mutually supportive and beneficial.

The teacher is aware of the significance of the school-community relationship and understands the value of working with local citizens to establish strong and positive ties between the school and the community. The teacher knows how to take advantage of community strengths and resources to foster student growth. In addition, the teacher is aware of problems facing the community (e.g., drugs, gangs, racism, crime, unemployment, poverty), understands how these problems may affect students' lives and learning, and is aware of resources and strategies that can help students cope with community problems.

Analysis: This competency deals with **school-community relationships.** To decide whether this competency is the primary focus of an ExCET question, look for ideas related to teachers working with the community. Key ideas for this competency are:

- school-community relationship—the mutual dealings between the school and the community
- problems facing the community—sources of trouble in a community (for instance, drugs, gangs, racism, crime, unemployment, poverty)

Competency 015: The teacher understands requirements, expectations, and constraints associated with teaching in Texas, and can apply this understanding in a variety of contexts.

The teacher is familiar with the various expectations (e.g., those of school boards, principals, colleagues, parents, students) and constraints (e.g., legal requirements, ethical responsibilities) placed on members of the teaching profession and is aware of the multiplicity of roles that teachers may be called upon to assume (e.g., instructor, resource person, problem solver, curriculum developer, school spokesperson). The teacher understands the laws and guidelines relevant to education (e.g., those related to civil rights, special needs, confidentiality, child abuse) and ensures that his or her decisions and actions are in compliance with legal and ethical requirements and the legitimate interests of others. The teacher understands the structure of the Texas education system, recognizes types of authority and decision-making structures within the system (e.g., centralized systems, site-based management), and knows how to work within the system to address issues and make decisions appropriately.

Analysis: This competency deals with **ethical, legal, and professional standards.** To decide whether this competency is the primary focus of an ExCET question, look for ideas related to teachers working within the system to address issues and make decisions appropriately. Key ideas for this competency are:

- requirements—what teachers must do
- expectations—what stakeholders expect of teachers (for example, school boards, principals, colleagues, parents, students)
- constraints—policies, operating procedures, laws and guidelines (federal, state, district, and campus) that direct what teachers can/should do (for instance, legal requirements, ethical responsibilities)
- multiplicity of roles—the varied professional roles of a teacher (such as instructor, resource person, problem solver, curriculum developer, school spokesperson)
- laws and guidelines relevant to education—laws and guidelines (federal, state, district, and campus) that educators must adhere to (for example, those related to civil rights, special needs, confidentiality, child abuse)
- to be in compliance—to adhere to
- centralized systems—systems in which decision making is concentrated in the central office
- site-based management—school-level (campus) governance that has been mandated by state legislation; mandates input from the community, parents, teachers, and administration on topics concerning the students followed by consensus decision making

"Good Practices" Suggested by the Competencies

General ideas pervading the competencies suggest that "good practices" involve the following:

Learner-Centered Instructional Strategies/Activities

- Student-centered learning experiences (for instance, related to the interests and varied characteristics of students)
- Developmentally appropriate instruction

- Teachers who support learners' intellectual, social, and personal development
- Multiculturism and equity; celebration of likenesses and differences among individuals; cross-cultural experiences; attitudes that foster unity
- Learning experiences that fit the different approaches to learning of diverse learners (that is, learning styles)
- Instructional variety
- Students being given control over their learning experiences
- Teachers who are responsive to student input
- Meaningful and purposeful learning based on prior knowledge
- Connections—relating subject matter to other content areas and the real world
- A positive, supportive, respectful, risk-free classroom environment— a place in which all students feel safe, accepted, competent, and productive
- Success for all

Challenging and Active Instruction

- Students as active, successful learners
- Students as self-directed/self-initiated learners
- Students as open-minded, inquiring learners (for example, understanding different points of views, valuing others' opinions)
- Instructional activities that are hands-on and use concrete materials (such as models or manipulatives)
- Use of open-ended problems and problem-solving projects
- Students making conjectures and conducting investigations
- Students collecting and organizing data
- Students engaged in meaningful tasks
- Students engaged in actual or authentic problem-solving situations
- Requiring students to justify their thinking
- Students using higher-order and critical thinking skills—that is, apply, analyze, synthesize, problem solve, evaluate
- Students putting together information to come up with new ideas or understandings—that is, being creative thinkers
- Teachers in various roles—instructor, facilitator, coach

Collaboration

- Collaborative learning, planning, and supportive interaction in the classroom
- Learning environments that encourage social interaction, active engagement in learning, and self-motivation

Effective Communication

- Teachers who use effective verbal and nonverbal communication
- Written teacher communication that is appropriate and accurate

- Teachers who are reflective listeners—listening with feeling as well as with cognition
- Teachers who are thoughtful questioners—using appropriate questioning to challenge students; considering Bloom's taxonomy
- Teachers who seek and value students' questions and point of view
- Teachers who encourage students to engage in dialogue, both with the teacher and with one another

Effective Monitoring and Assessment

- Monitoring and assessment responsive to students' varied needs and characteristics
- Teachers who give specific, constructive, and timely feedback
- Assessment aligned with instruction
- Variety of assessment techniques (for instance, teacher observation, student exhibitions, student portfolios)
- Student assessment as an ongoing process, interwoven with teaching
- Student self-assessment
- Teachers who provide opportunities for relearning and reassessment

Effective Classroom Management

- Teachers who are courteous and respectful
- Teachers who maximize academic learning time
- Teachers who use the least intrusive intervention to stop or redirect inappropriate behavior
- Teachers whose intervention techniques ensure that the dignity of the student, even the seriously disruptive student, is preserved
- Teachers who encourage self-discipline and self-management
- Teachers who create a safe and orderly environment

Professionalism

- Teacher self-reflection
- Teacher collaboration with colleagues and other professionals
- An appreciation of lifelong learning (for instance, teacher actively seeks out professional development opportunities)
- Teachers who work with parents and the community
- Teachers who follow ethical, legal, and professional standards
- Teachers who are knowledgeable of recent developments and issues

"Poor Practices" to Avoid as Response Choice

When taking the ExCET, you should avoid response choices that suggest teachers should

- teach by telling; be dispensers of knowledge
- teach isolated topics
- use low-level learning objectives

- use worksheets
- use timelines (unless the stated purpose is to learn facts and dates)
- emphasize rote memorization of rules and/or rote practice
- use rote activities and/or rote drill and practice
- emphasize one answer and one method
- use questions that require only yes-or-no responses
- fail to acknowledge the varied characteristics of students
- fail to encourage students who are reluctant or are having problems
- be inconsistent, unfair, or treat students inequitably
- use coercion, sarcasm, or ridicule
- use harsh, negative, nonspecific feedback
- test for the sole purpose of assigning grades

How to Use the Material in This Chapter to Answer ExCET Questions

You should review the 15 competencies regularly until you have a good recall of the key ideas that apply to each competency. When you read an ExCET question, you should immediately begin deciding what competency is the primary focus of the question. Do this by looking for aspects of the stimulus or question that relate to key ideas of the competencies. Once you are confident you have identified the relevant competency, if possible, eliminate answer choices that do not apply to that competency—particularly, eliminate those answer choices that contain key ideas from other competencies. A number of the questions on the ExCET will have key ideas from competencies other than the relevant competency as distractors (incorrect answer choices). An edge that you will have when you take the ExCET is that these questions will be easier for you because you can readily eliminate distractors based on your knowledge of the competencies' key ideas. After eliminating as many distractors as you can in this manner, select the answer choice that is most consistent with educational theory of effective practice related to the relevant competency. Now give it a try.

Sample Questions

1. Mr. Josephsen, a fifth-grade social studies teacher, is teaching a unit on free enterprise. The class is talking about the guest speaker they had yesterday who told them how she started her own business. During the discussion, Kyle asks, "Could we start a business?" The rest of the class chimes in with, "Yeah, yeah, could we, Mr. Josephsen?" Mr. Josephsen reminds the class of what their guest told them about how difficult it is to run a business. In chorus, the class assures him they are willing to work hard. Mr. Josephsen then explains to them that if they are truly serious about this, many decisions must be made. He poses two questions to the class: "What kind of business will you establish?" and "How will you go about it?" The students begin talking and sharing their ideas. Yolandra suggests that the students work in groups to do some research and come up with some answers to these questions.

During the class discussion, Mr. Josephsen demonstrates his understanding of the importance of motivation to learning *primarily* by

    A. encouraging students to communicate effectively in a variety of contexts.
    B. creating a classroom environment in which students have control over their learning experiences.
    C. fostering a view of learning as a purposeful pursuit.
    D. promoting student ownership in a smoothly functioning learning community.

This stem of the question tells you that this question deals with **motivation.** Thus, the primary focus of the question is Competency 005: *The teacher understands how motivation affects group and individual behavior and learning and can apply this understanding to promote student learning.* Eliminate A because it is a key idea found in Competency 007 and relates to **communication.** Eliminate C because it is a key idea found in Competency 004 and relates to **how learning occurs.** Eliminate D because it is a key idea found in Competency 011 and relates to **classroom management.** Mr. Josephsen understands that intrinsic motivation is enhanced when students are allowed to have control over their learning experiences. This is a key idea found in Competency 005 **(motivation).** Choice B is the correct response.

2. During the first week of school, Ms. Alexander, who teaches geometry, has her class of 22 students participate in a geometry "scavenger hunt." Each student is given a picture of a geometry figure for which they are to find an example in the school building or school yard. On the back of the picture, they are to draw a rough sketch of the example they find. Ms. Alexander gives the students a 45-minute time limit to find all the items that she distributes. She encourages them to work as a team and help each other. If they finish the scavenger hunt within the allotted time, the class will be rewarded with a pizza party on the following Friday. The *most* likely reason for Ms. Alexander's scavenger hunt activity during the first week of school is

    A. to foster a view of learning as a purposeful pursuit.
    B. to encourage students to assume responsibility for their own learning.
    C. to relate lessons to students' personal interests.
    D. to promote student ownership in a smoothly functioning learning community.

When you read the stimulus, two aspects that should catch your attention is that Ms. Alexander's scavenger-hunt activity is conducted during the *first week* of school, and that she encourages the students to *work as a team and help each other* during the scavenger hunt. Teachers typically plan activities during the first week of school that will help their classrooms become places where learning can occur—where students are responsible, cooperative, purposeful, and mutually supportive. These ideas are related to **classroom management.** Thus, the primary focus of this question is Competency 011: *The teacher structures and manages the learning environment to maintain a classroom climate that promotes* *the lifelong pursuit of learning and encourages cooperation, leadership, and mutual respect.* Eliminate A and B because they are key ideas found in Competency 004 and relate to **how learning occurs.** Eliminate C because it is a key idea found in Competency 005 and relates to **motivation.** Ms. Alexander encourages the students to work as a team and help each other during the scavenger hunt. Clearly, during this *first* week of school, she wants to promote student ownership in a smoothly functioning learning community. Choice D is the correct response.

A Caveat

In general, the strategy of identifying the competency when you read the question will be very helpful to you in achieving success on the ExCET. Notwithstanding, you may not always be able to identify the competency correctly when you first read the question; and, further, occasionally the question may use language or wording that causes you to misidentify the competency. You need to be prepared to shift gears and think through the problem when (or if) this occurs. Another caution is that the competencies are not independent of each other—many times they overlap. For example, when teachers are **planning** (Competency 006), they must consider **instructional strategies** (Competency 008). Therefore, it may occur, for example, that two competencies apply to a single ExCET question, so even if you decide that one of them *best* applies, you are likely to need to use ideas from both competencies to answer such a question. Also, not every question on the ExCET will have distractors that are key ideas from other competencies. The review material provided in Chapters 7–9 and in the Appendixes should be most helpful when you need to eliminate distractors based on educational theory of effective practice. The main point is **don't get bogged down because you're trying to figure out the competency**—just reread the question and the answer choices and work through the problem.

Sample Questions

1. When Mr. Luna is developing his classroom management plan, which of the following is *most* important for him to consider?

   A. his educational philosophy.
   B. his knowledge of the students' behavior the previous year.
   C. the classroom management plan of the teacher next door.
   D. the appropriateness of his classroom management plan to his students' grade level.

Upon first reading, this question appears to deal with **classroom management.** However, the only two answer choices that are clearly related to this competency are B and C, both of which are not educationally sound. You are left to choose between A and D. This is a priority-setting question—you must select the answer choice that is *most* important to the task at hand. Choose D because you know that this is very important, and you don't know enough about Mr. Luna's educational philosophy to determine whether it would be consistent with doing this. Since you know that D deals with **developmentally appropriate instruction,** you now know that the primary focus of this question is Competency 001: *The teacher uses an understanding of human developmental processes to nurture student growth through developmentally appropriate instruction.* It is important that Mr. Luna consider the developmental characteristics of his students, so that he will be realistic in his expectations of behavior for this age group. Choice D is the correct response.

2. Ms. Garcia has been using a whole-group setting in her eighth-grade math class. After reading *Cooperative Learning in Mathematics: A Handbook for Teachers*, she decides to try letting her students work in small groups. When organizing her students into cooperative learning groups, Ms. Garcia ensures that the groups are diverse in ability, gender, ethnicity, and social class. Grouping students this way is *most* likely to benefit students by

    I.   enhancing students' understanding of prejudice.
    II. fostering positive feelings among students from different groups.
    III. enhancing interpersonal relationships.
    IV. increasing competition among different groups in the class.

    A. I and II only
    B. I, II, and III only
    C. II and III only
    D. II, III, and IV only

This question deals with both **diversity** (Ms. Garcia's grouping practice considers the diversity of her students) and **instructional strategies** (Ms. Garcia is using cooperative learning groups to deliver instruction). Thus, the primary focus of this question is either Competency 003 or Competency 008. Glancing at the Roman numeral choices, you can see that most deal with the effects of cooperative learning strategies. Thus, most educators familiar with the competencies would suggest that the primary focus of this question is Competency 008: *The teacher uses a variety of instructional strategies and roles to facilitate learning and to help students become independent thinkers and problem solvers who use higher-order thinking in the classroom and the real world.* Even though Competency 008 best applies, you also may have to use an understanding of key ideas related to diversity, which are discussed under Competency 003 in the review material in Chapter 7 to answer the question. Eliminate Roman I because in the stimulus prejudice is not mentioned as something that students are likely to encounter. Eliminate A and B. Eliminate Roman IV because competition is usually decreased when cooperative learning strategies are used. Eliminate D. Research indicates that teachers should organize students in groups that are diverse in ability, gender, ethnicity, and socioeconomic status. Such groupings foster positive feelings among students from different groups and enhance interpersonal relationships. Choice C is the correct response.

    These two questions underscore the importance of thinking carefully and thoughtfully through the test. There is no substitute for intelligent, critical thinking when you are taking the ExCET.

It's time for you to assess yourself by taking the diagnostic test that corresponds to the level at which you are planning to teach—elementary (Chapter 5) or secondary (Chapter 6). If you are seeking all-level certification, you may take either the elementary or the secondary test.

PART TWO

Assess Yourself

A DIAGNOSTIC ELEMENTARY PROFESSIONAL DEVELOPMENT TEST

Diagnostic Test Directions

The test consists of 90 multiple-choice questions with four answer choices. Read each question carefully and choose the ONE best answer. Mark your answer on the answer sheet (see page 421) beside the number that matches the question number. Completely fill in the space that has the same letter as the answer you have selected.

Sample Question

1. Austin is the capital of what state?
    A. Arkansas
    B. California
    C. Tennessee
    D. Texas

Austin is the capital of Texas. Choice D is the correct response. You would mark your answer beside question number 1 on the answer sheet and you would fill in the space corresponding to the letter D as follows:

1. (A) (B) (C) ●

Mark only one answer for each question. If you change an answer, completely erase the old answer before marking the new one. You should answer all the questions since *you are not penalized for a wrong answer.*

You will have approximately five hours to complete the test. You may go back and forth through the test as you desire. When you have completed the test, turn to the answer key and answer explanations at the end of the test to check your answers.

SET 1 BEGINS HERE

Mr. Arnold is a sixth-grade teacher. He and his students have been involved in a social studies unit on "free enterprise." The class is talking about the guest speaker they had yesterday who told them how she started her own business. During the discussion, Maria asks, "Could we start a business?" The rest of the class chimes in with, "Yeah, yeah, could we, Mr. Arnold?" Mr. Arnold reminds the class of what their guest told them about how much hard work was involved. In chorus, the class assures him they are willing to accept the responsibility. The teacher then tries to explain to them that if they are truly serious about this, there are many decisions that must be made. Mr. Arnold poses several questions to the group. "What kind of business will you establish?" and "How will you go about it?" He also reminds the students that the class has no money and asks them how they plan to set up a business with no money. The students begin talking and sharing some of their ideas. Jason suggests the students work in groups to come up with some answers to these questions. The students also decide to seek permission from the appropriate school authorities to attend a noon meeting of the local chamber of commerce to learn more about businesses in town.

1. In a school that is practicing site-based management, who would be included in making a decision about the students' request?

   I. school board members
   II. superintendent
   III. principal
   IV. campus school-community committee

   A. I only
   B. II only
   C. III and IV only
   D. II, III, and IV only

2. Mr. Arnold's likely purpose for the questions he posed for the group to consider is:

   A. to offer students an opportunity to develop their research skills in a collaborative group setting.
   B. to offer students encouragement in pursuing their own individual interests in a group setting.
   C. to offer students an opportunity to engage in critical thinking and problem solving.
   D. to offer the students an opportunity to use previous knowledge in a collaborative setting.

3. Allowing students to plan and start up their own business is *most* likely to

   I. encourage independent and creative thinking.
   II. promote the development of cross-cultural experiences.
   III. encourage acquisition of paper-and-pencil computation skills.
   IV. deepen insights and understandings relative to the real world of business.

   A. I and III only
   B. I and IV only
   C. II and III only
   D. III and IV only

4. By encouraging students to pursue their idea of the business venture, Mr. Arnold demonstrates his understanding of motivational theory *primarily* by:

    A. encouraging students to communicate effectively in a variety of contexts.
    B. allowing students a measure of control over their learning experiences.
    C. linking new learning to prior knowledge.
    D. promoting student ownership in a smoothly functioning learning community.

5. Once Mr. Arnold decides to let the students engage in the business venture, he should be prepared to:

    I. assume a variety of roles as needed.
    II. assign specific roles to the students.
    III. help the students resolve personality differences.
    IV. direct student plans for presentation of the project outcomes to interested school personnel and parents.

    A. I and IV only
    B. II, III, and IV only
    C. I, II, and III only
    D. I, II, III, and IV

Mr. Arnold's students realize they will need money to rent the necessary equipment and buy the supplies to get the business started. Mr. Arnold tells them that a bank would want to know their plans for the business before it would give them a loan. The class decides to plan everything in detail and to keep complete records. Heather suggests they invite someone from the bank to come and explain the procedures involved in applying for a loan.

6. Inviting a local business such as a bank to participate in a school project is an example of:

    I. providing opportunities for school-community collaboration.
    II. helping the community to realize that schools are capable of helping students learn.
    III. raising students' awareness and understanding of resources in the community.
    IV. promoting positive public relations between the community and the school.

    A. I and II only
    B. I and IV only
    C. II and III only
    D. I, III, and IV only

7. Which of the following types of computer applications would be best for the class to use for keeping the inventory records for their business?

    A. database
    B. graphing
    C. simulation
    D. spreadsheet

8. After the class secures a loan from the bank, Mr. Arnold suggests they write a letter thanking the bank executives. His *primary* instructional purpose for this activity is to allow students at this grade level to:

    A. communicate the bond between the school and community.
    B. practice their reading and writing skills.
    C. practice socially correct behavior.
    D. recognize the value of establishing positive community relations.

Finally, after much planning and hard work, the class is ready to open their business selling after-school snacks. Although Mr. Arnold appreciates the educational merits of the class project, he is concerned that parents may see it as mere entertainment that takes students away from their serious studies. However, the students are enthusiastic as they prepare to assume their roles and get involved in their business venture.

9. A major rationale for using a project such as this, where the students participate in a real-world project, is which of the following?

    A. It will contribute to the development of the students' basic skills.
    B. It will enhance the students' sense of community service.
    C. It will encourage students to actively seek out knowledge.
    D. It will require less time than expository teaching methods.

10. Which of the following strategies should Mr. Arnold use with parents?

    A. He should explain the project to the parents, but emphasize that it is a students-only project.
    B. He should recruit parent volunteers to help with the project.
    C. He should avoid involving business leaders who are also parents of his students.
    D. He should explain to parents that it would be best if they not discuss the project with other community members.

11. One day a heated discussion among some of the students occurred. The "workers" were unhappy with the "management." Which of the following should Mr. Arnold do as a *first* step in solving this conflict?

    A. Instruct the students to put aside their differences and continue as usual.
    B. Have each group list its grievances and see if a compromise can be reached.
    C. Explain to the students that unless they can work together, there will be no business.
    D. Suggest that the students exchange places for a few days.

12. Mr. Arnold asks the students to determine whether or not the business was successful and to reflect on their roles and participation. Which of the following is a benefit of having students do this assignment?

    A. It will allow Mr. Arnold to evaluate the students' mastery of the social studies objectives for the unit.
    B. It will promote self-assessment and self-evaluation on the part of the student.
    C. It will promote a healthy competitive spirit among the students.
    D. It will allow Mr. Arnold to identify those students who exhibited leadership skills.

SET 1 ENDS HERE

SET 2 BEGINS HERE

Ms. Garcia is a new teacher who has been trying to teach creative writing to her fourth-grade class. She recently assigns a writing assignment on "What I Did During Summer Vacation" to the class and is disappointed and frustrated when most of the papers she receives are dull and uninteresting. She discusses her dismay with her colleague, Ms. Rivas, who also has given her fourth-grade class a writing assignment. When Ms. Rivas shows Ms. Garcia the papers she has collected from her class, Ms. Garcia is impressed that most of Ms. Rivas' students have written imaginative, creative papers. She asks Ms. Rivas how she motivates her students to write so well. Ms. Rivas responds that she first encourages students to write on topics that they are interested in or care about. She has the students work together in small groups to help each other plan essays, critique each other's drafts, help each other with editing, and finally produce final versions to be turned in.

13. What is Ms. Rivas using to enhance motivation?

   I.   reward/punishment method
   II. self-motivation
   III. group dynamics
   IV. reverse psychology

   A. I, II, and III only
   B. II and III only
   C. II and IV only
   D. I and IV only

14. Ms. Rivas' likely purpose in allowing the students in the small groups to critique each other's papers is which of the following?

   A. The brighter students can correct the other students' mistakes before the papers have to be graded.
   B. The students can compare themselves to one another.
   C. The students can learn from each other.
   D. The students can assess their own strengths and weaknesses.

15. While her students are working in their small groups, Ms. Rivas should:

   A. avoid listening in on the groups' discussions.
   B. ignore any misbehavior that goes on within a group.
   C. monitor each group.
   D. sit at her desk and answer questions only when asked.

Ms. Garcia has been using a whole-group setting; now, after visiting with Ms. Rivas, Ms. Garcia decides to try letting her students work in small groups.

16. When planning lessons, which of the following are changes that using small-group work will be likely to involve?

   I.   eliminating the need for teacher presentations to convey information and skills before students work together
   II. having a system for appointing the highest-achieving students as group leaders
   III. requiring developing students' social skills for working in small groups
   IV. requiring that the group task be well organized

   A. I and II only
   B. I, II, and III only
   C. II, III, and IV only
   D. III and IV only

17. Ms. Garcia's decision to consult Ms. Rivas *best* illustrates which of the following principles?

   A. Teachers need to understand the importance of being reflective practitioners.
   B. Teachers should actively engage in group processes to make decisions.
   C. Teachers should know how to support student achievement of desired learning outcomes.
   D. Teachers need to stay abreast of current knowledge and practices.

18. Before starting a new writing activity using small groups, Ms. Garcia decides, upon the advice of Ms. Rivas, that she should assign her students to specific groups. When making the assignments, she ensures that the groups are diverse in gender, ethnicity, and ability level. Grouping students this way benefits students because it is likely to:

   A. help students learn to deal with prejudice.
   B. promote Ms. Garcia's professional growth.
   C. nurture a sense of community in the classroom.
   D. enhance students' ability to be thoughtful questioners.

19. After students complete the writing activity, Ms. Garcia displays the finished writing samples on the wall outside her classroom. This *best* illustrates that Ms. Garcia:

   A. understands factors that influence students' self-worth.
   B. knows how to apply knowledge of human development to promote student learning.
   C. knows how to enhance the learning for all students through the appropriate use of instructional materials.
   D. understands the importance of formative assessment.

SET 2 ENDS HERE

SET 3 BEGINS HERE

> Woodview is an old historic town. When a large oil company wants to drill on the site of the old university building, the town becomes embroiled in a bitter controversy over whether or not to allow the drilling. Mr. Bentley decides he will use the controversy as the basis for a discussion in his fifth-grade social studies class. He poses the following question to the class: "Should preservation of historic landmarks stand in the way of economic development?"

20. Mr. Bentley's question is *most* likely posed for the purpose of:

    A. encouraging students to recall factual information.
    B. providing students with clues to his personal opinions about the controversy.
    C. checking students' understanding of the nature of the controversy.
    D. providing a framework for engaging students in active inquiry.

21. Most likely, the main purpose that Mr. Bentley uses a class discussion about the community controversy is to:

    A. provide a means for students to practice public speaking skills.
    B. let students learn to collaborate to solve problems.
    C. engage students in higher-order thinking in an authentic context.
    D. minimize the negative effects of community problems on student performance.

22. Before beginning the class discussion, it is important that Mr. Bentley:

    A. know which students to call upon.
    B. let the students choose sides of the issue first.
    C. give his opinion on the issue in order to set the tone for the discussion.
    D. make sure the students are somewhat familiar with the issue.

23. What are students likely to learn from the class discussion?

    A. The old university building has little historical value.
    B. Accurate information is critical for effective communication.
    C. Community problems can be solved through thoughtful discussion.
    D. Working with others can lead to better and quicker solutions to problems.

24. The class discussion over the town controversy brings to the classroom:

    A. an outside conflict that serves only to distract from the learning process.
    B. the use of an external factor as a tool to promote student motivation.
    C. an opportunity for students to have choices in their learning.
    D. an understanding of how the school relates to the larger community.

25. A class discussion would be *most* appropriate when:

    A. the lesson involves objectives at the knowledge level of Bloom's taxonomy.
    B. the lesson involves objectives in the affective domain.
    C. students are younger or less mature.
    D. the topic has simple concepts that students will react to in similar ways.

26. During the class discussion Mr. Bentley's primary role should be:

    A. a judge.
    B. a critic.
    C. an arbitrator.
    D. a moderator.

Mr. Bentley wants to help his students develop their critical thinking skills, so he asks a lot of questions during each class. Typically his questions are similar to the following:

"What is the longest river in the U.S.?"

"How can you check your answer?"

"When was the Vietnam War?"

27. To improve his questioning technique, Mr. Bentley should do which of the following?

   A. Ask more divergent questions.
   B. Ask more questions that have only "yes" or "no" answers.
   C. Ask more convergent questions.
   D. Ask more focusing questions.

28. If Mr. Bentley is typical of most teachers, which of the following is *most* likely?

   A. He will direct more questions to female students.
   B. He will direct easier questions to male students.
   C. He will direct about the same number of questions to both male and female students.
   D. He will direct more questions to male students.

29. To improve participation in and the quality of the discussions in class, Mr. Bentley should:

   I. ask the question before identifying a student by name.
   II. use who? what? where? and when? questions only.
   III. wait at least three seconds before calling on a student.
   IV. recognize only those students with hands raised.

   A. I and III only
   B. I and IV only
   C. II and IV only
   D. II, III, and IV only

Mr. Bentley brings to class a large-scale map of the city. As a class activity, he invites the students to come up one by one and show on the map the approximate location of their home. During the class activity, Melissa, who has returned after being absent from school for several days, appears to be trying to draw attention to herself. She twists and turns and taps her pencil on her desk.

30. Which intervention should Mr. Bentley use *first* with Melissa?

   A. Say, "Melissa," and shake his head disapprovingly when she looks at him.
   B. Look sternly at Melissa, but continue with the lesson.
   C. Ask Melissa, "Will you come show us on the map where you live?"
   D. Stop the lesson and send Melissa to the office.

31. The next day, Melissa's mother, Ms. Nethery, calls and asks to meet with Mr. Bentley after school about Melissa's grades, since Melissa missed several assignments when she was absent. Mr. Bentley agrees to meet with Ms. Nethery as soon as school is out. During the parent-teacher conference with Ms. Nethery, one thing that Mr. Bentley should *not* do is:

   A. offer Ms. Nethery refreshments.
   B. tell Ms. Nethery that he thinks Melissa is an underachiever.
   C. show Ms. Nethery Melissa's grades up to that point.
   D. paraphrase Ms. Nethery's comments for clarity.

For a social studies unit on government, Mr. Bentley designs his lesson plans around the theme of "civic ideas and practices." To begin the unit, he has the students discuss in small groups what they think being a "good citizen" means. Then he asks that students each write about a time they saw another student be a good citizen somewhere in the school—in the classroom, in the cafeteria, on the playground, and so on.

32. Mr. Bentley's decision to use a thematic approach *best* demonstrates his understanding of the importance of:

   A. helping students to understand relationships within a discipline.
   B. selecting developmentally appropriate instructional strategies.
   C. nurturing a sense of community in the classroom.
   D. enhancing students' ability to apply knowledge in various contexts.

33. Having students write about a time they saw someone being a good citizen is most likely to enhance their understanding of "civic ideas and practices" by:

   A. helping students to focus on significant events in their lives.
   B. encouraging students to learn from each other.
   C. helping students relate the content to their lives and experiences.
   D. enhancing students' ability to be reflective listeners.

SET 3 ENDS HERE

> Ms. Curl, a new third-grade teacher, is enthusiastic about her first year. She looks forward to meeting her students and has many plans for them. The first day of class, Ms. Curl introduces herself and shares with the students some of her ideas for the classroom. She tells the students she wants them to keep both a language arts and a mathematics portfolio, which will be sent home with them at the end of each grading period.

34. As a new teacher, Ms. Curl needs to be aware of which of the following?

    A. During the first few days of school, teachers need to teach students specific procedures for how to line up, ask for help, and so forth.
    B. To avoid problems later on in the year, teachers need to establish a disciplined climate in their classrooms by using frequent time-outs during the first few days of school.
    C. During the first few days of school, classroom management will be easier if the teacher works with individual students to explain classroom rules and procedures.
    D. Early on, teachers need to establish a warm and caring environment by ignoring misbehavior unless it disrupts the flow of the lesson.

35. Ms. Curl wants to make sure she begins the year in the right way. An activity that she should probably *not* do on the first day of class is:

    A. break students into small groups and discuss school rules and procedures separately with each group.
    B. go over school rules and procedures in a whole-group setting.
    C. respond immediately to stop any misbehavior.
    D. use simple, enjoyable tasks for the first lesson.

36. Ms. Curl is likely to know that the *primary* purpose of having students develop portfolios is which of the following?

    A. documentation if a question should arise concerning grades
    B. enhancement of the teacher's knowledge of the learners
    C. student self-assessment
    D. peer assessment

Since she is a first-year teacher, Ms. Curl knows it is crucial that a classroom management plan that includes a system of rules and procedures for classroom interactions needs to be in place at the beginning of the school year. Through the use of brainstorming and discussion, she and the students make up a list of class rules that they post in the classroom.

37. When developing her classroom management plan, which of the following is *most* important for Ms. Curl to consider?

    A. her educational philosophy
    B. the behavioral reports from the previous year
    C. the classroom management plan of the teacher next door
    D. the appropriateness of the plan for her students' grade level

38. The rules for Ms. Curl's classroom are posted as depicted below:

CLASS RULES
Rule 1. Be respectful of others.
Rule 2. Work quietly.
Rule 3. Do not run indoors.
Rule 4. Complete your work.

    Which rule should be restated in a more appropriate format?

    A. Rule 1
    B. Rule 2
    C. Rule 3
    D. Rule 4

In Ms. Curl's classroom, the students have all been assigned to one of five reading groups according to reading ability. As she met with each reading group for the first time, she asked the students to write down some important topics they wished to read about in class. She then took the lists and designed that group's reading lessons around the topics proposed by the students in the group.

39. Which of the following is likely to happen as a result of Ms. Curl's using five ability groups?

    A. Ms. Curl will have increased behavior management problems because she will have to focus her attention on one group at a time, leaving the students in the other four groups without direct supervision.
    B. Ms. Curl's high-ability students will have an increased opportunity to become more accepting of their low-achieving classmates because they will not be held back by them in the reading groups.
    C. All of Ms. Curl's students will experience achievement gains since ability grouping will allow them to experience an accelerated curriculum and advanced instruction.
    D. Ms. Curl will experience a decreased opportunity to allow high-ability students to move ahead at a faster pace because of the competitive structure that results with ability grouping.

40. What was Ms. Curl's motivational purpose in selecting reading topics from student-generated lists?

    A. to adapt instruction to emerging needs
    B. to allow students to have choices in their learning
    C. to encourage students to communicate effectively
    D. to help students achieve an in-depth understanding of their long-term goals

41. By involving students in selecting their own reading topics, Ms. Curl is likely to be attempting to:

    A. enhance the self-esteem of the students.
    B. give the students experience in teamwork.
    C. improve the students' organizational skills.
    D. satisfy the need in students for a stable, routine, and predictable environment.

Despite her use of student-generated reading topics, Ms. Curl continually has trouble keeping the students in the low-ability reading group interested and motivated to learn to read. One day, Leaia asks, "Can we skip reading today?" When Ms. Curl asks why, the students chorus, "We don't like reading."

42. Which of the following would *most* likely benefit the low-ability reading group students?

    I.   Ms. Curl should encourage the students to take responsibity for their own learning.
    II. Ms. Curl should give concrete examples of abstract concepts.
    III. Ms. Curl should make sure the students receive feedback from their peers.
    IV. Ms. Curl should demand less work and effort from the low-ability reading group.

    A. I, II, and III only
    B. I and II only
    C. II and III only
    D. II and IV only

43. Ms. Curl wants to increase the amount of time her students are actively engaged in reading. The *most* effective strategy would probably be to:

    A. increase the length of time she reads aloud to the reading groups.
    B. give weekly quizzes on the vocabulary words from the reading lessons.
    C. post a "Do Not Disturb" sign on the classroom door during reading time.
    D. require students to read chorally together.

44. During a recent whole-group reading lesson, most of the students are very attentive and interested, with the exception of Juan, who is rolling a small ball on his desk. What would be the *best* approach for Ms. Curl to use with Juan?

    A. She should ignore Juan's off-task behavior completely so as not to lose the momentum of the reading lesson.
    B. She should walk by Juan's desk and unobtrusively take the ball without interrupting the discussion.
    C. She should stop the lesson, take the ball, and reprimand Juan in a quiet voice.
    D. She should walk to Juan's desk, take the ball, and hold it up for the rest of the class to see.

45. At midsemester, Ms. Curl asks the students to write down what they like least about reading class. This type of assessment is called a:

    A. summative evaluation.
    B. formative evaluation.
    C. norm-referenced evaluation.
    D. criterion-referenced evaluation.

Ms. Curl has been planning a field trip for the science unit that she is almost ready to initiate. She would like to take her third-grade class on a nature walk, but she is hesitant to do so because she has a Down syndrome student, Laura, who has been mainstreamed into her classroom. Ms. Curl would like Laura to participate in the class activities, including the field trip; however, she knows very little about Laura's disability, although she feels Laura can join in.

46. Ms. Curl is aware that the admission, review, and dismissal (ARD) committee determined that, for Laura, Ms. Curl's classroom met the criterion of "least restrictive environment." Least restrictive environment means that:

    A. a student's classroom environment should be appropriate to his or her level of disability.
    B. special educators should have the full responsibility for tailoring the school environment to a student's needs.
    C. all children should be able to participate in regular school activities, regardless of disability.
    D. disabled children should attend special schools.

47. In determining and addressing Laura's educational needs relative to the field trip, it is *most* important that Ms. Curl:

    A. pair Laura with a capable classmate who can help her when she goes on the field trip.
    B. respond appropriately to Laura's unique individual needs.
    C. ask the special education teacher to accompany Laura on the field trip.
    D. exclude Laura from the field trip since it may be too stressful for her.

48. In arranging and conducting the field trip, Ms. Curl should be aware that she has a *legal* obligation to:

    A. obtain written permission from all parents and guardians to take their children on the field trip.
    B. obtain written permission from only the parents or guardian of Laura to take her on the field trip.
    C. send written notes to parents and guardians informing them of the TAAS objectives for the field trip.
    D. send written notes to only the parents or guardian of Laura informing them of the TAAS objectives for the field trip.

SET 4 ENDS HERE

SET 5 BEGINS HERE

> Ms. Cartwright has been hired as a seventh-grade teacher at Southpoint Middle School, located in a town whose population of 25,000 falls mainly in the lower-to-middle socioeconomic class. Ms. Cartwright holds high expectations for all her students, although a number of them did poorly in elementary school.

49. By holding high expectations for all her students, Ms. Cartwright is likely to find that:

A. students to some degree live up to the expectations that teachers hold for them.
B. teacher expectations are more powerful than parental or peer pressure.
C. teacher expectations have no impact on academic achievement.
D. high teacher expectations create anxiety in low-ability students and cause achievement to decline.

50. Although Southpoint Middle School is located in a lower-to-middle-class town, the values of the school will tend to reflect:

A. upper-class values.
B. middle-class values.
C. lower-class values.
D. the values of the majority of students who attend.

51. As Ms. Cartwright was leaving the parking lot one afternoon, she overheard a lower-income mother talking to her child. Ms. Cartwright was reminded that lower-socioeconomic-class parents are more likely than middle-or upper-socioeconomic-class parents to:

A. use expressive language.
B. use commands.
C. use questions.
D. take their child's perspective.

52. Frequently, Ms. Cartwright uses questioning strategies in her classes in which she will call only on students who raise their hands to respond. This method of recognizing students for response is:

A. limited, because students who don't volunteer will miss an opportunity to actively participate in the lesson.
B. positive, because it keeps the teacher from having to call on low-ability students who may not know the correct answer and will be embarrassed by being called on.
C. more effective than calling on students using a random process.
D. more effective than other questioning strategies because volunteers give a higher proportion of correct responses.

After several weeks of school, Ms. Cartwright finds that the children from the lower socioeconomic backgrounds have difficulty achieving at the same level as the other children. Ms. Cartwright consults the curriculum supervisor because she wants to increase the achievement of the many lower-socioeconomic-class children in her class.

53. Which of the following will the curriculum supervisor likely advise Ms. Cartwright to consider using?

    A. immediate rewards
    B. independent projects
    C. competitive reward structures
    D. individual seatwork

54. The curriculum supervisor might also remind Ms. Cartwright that children from low socioeconomic backgrounds, on average:

    A. do as well in school as other children.
    B. do about as well as other children.
    C. do poorly in school.
    D. enter school behind other children but eventually close the gap in high school.

55. Ms. Cartwright is concerned by the lower-socioeconomic-class students' lack of interest and enthusiasm in mathematics. The curriculum supervisor will likely advise her that an assessment approach she might use to motivate these students toward earning better math grades is:

    A. grading on the basis of improvement for a short period.
    B. using a lower grading standard.
    C. giving a lot of short, quick quizzes on the basic skills.
    D. eliminating math homework for this group of students.

56. The curriculum supervisor suggests further that Ms. Cartwright use a task analysis in planning the next mathematics lesson. The advantage of using this process is:

    A. gaining increased awareness of the subskills students need for mastering more complex skills.
    B. seeing firsthand the importance of planning effective objectives.
    C. allowing students to make important decisions about what they should and should not attend to.
    D. encouraging students to work and learn independently.

The ethnic demographics of Southpoint Middle School show that 55 percent of the student body is Anglo-American, 30 percent African-American, and 15 percent Hispanic-American. Ms. Cartwright has convinced the site-based team on her campus to approach the principal about promoting multicultural education in their school.

57. Which of the following practices would be consistent with the goals of multicultural education?

  I. directly confronting racism
  II. encouraging teachers to evaluate their views about cultural diversity
  III. acknowledging and building on cultural differences
  IV. using literature that depicts main characters striving to develop bicultural identities

  A. I and III only
  B. II and IV only
  C. I, II, and III only
  D. I, II, III, and IV

58. Ms. Cartwright's classes are ethnically mixed. To increase social harmony among her students, she should:

  A. use one-to-one activities such as tutoring.
  B. avoid discussing racial or ethnic relations with the class.
  C. use competitive games and contests.
  D. establish within-class ability groups in selected subjects.

59. Ms. Cartwright and the school counselor have been discussing gender differences in the classroom. With regard to gender differences, Ms. Cartwright should:

  A. make allowances for gender differences by allowing students freedom to pursue their own interests.
  B. use more masculine-oriented modeling to increase females' assertiveness.
  C. treat male and female students similarly whenever appropriate.
  D. have more activities where boys and girls are grouped separately.

60. Ms. Cartwright has been reviewing legislation related to inclusion. When she looks at PL 94-142, she is reminded that this law obligates each state to:

  A. give federal support to arrangements made by local jurisdictions.
  B. provide a free and appropriate public education for all disabled children.
  C. integrate all disabled children into regular classrooms.
  D. ensure that mildly disabled children are mainstreamed into regular classrooms.

SET 5 ENDS HERE

SET 6 BEGINS HERE

In a team meeting, Mr. Manzano, a new second-grade teacher at Santa Rosa Elementary School, is discussing with his team members what he is planning to do in the coming year. He tells them that he wants to foster critical thinking and enhance problem-solving skills in his students, so he has decided to use inquiry and discovery learning with cooperative learning groups in his classroom.

61. The teaching strategies that Mr. Mazano has decided to use will *most* likely:

    A. provide more structure.
    B. sequence instruction.
    C. establish group morale.
    D. foster independent learning.

62. When teaching a lesson on magnets in science, which of the following would Mr. Manzano likely do?

    A. Show the whole class different kinds of magnets and demonstrate their properties.
    B. In small groups, have the students take turns reading aloud from their science books about magnets.
    C. Have the students experiment with magnets in cooperative learning groups.
    D. In cooperative learning groups, have the students do worksheets on the different types of magnets and their properties.

63. Which of the following strategies would be *least* desirable for Mr. Manzano to use in mathematics?

    A. He should encourage students to suspend judgment about the best solution when initially faced with the problem.
    B. He should allow more time for problems requiring creative skills than for analytical problems.
    C. He should establish a teacher-centered classroom environment.
    D. He should teach students strategies for approaching situations requiring problem-solving skills.

64. Which of the following would be likely to enhance critical thinking in Mr. Manzano's class?

    I. He should teach for deeper understanding of content.
    II. He should encourage students to discuss their problem solutions with each other.
    III. He should require students to justify the reasoning behind their conclusions.
    IV. He should help students develop metacognitive strategies.

    A. I and III only
    B. I and IV only
    C. II, III, and IV only
    D. I, II, III, and IV

65. Mr. Manzano's class has a wide range of achievement levels. Which of the following *best* reflects current research regarding grouping practices?

    A. Grouping students according to ability level works best for all students.
    B. Homogeneous grouping of slow learners and heterogeneous grouping for the other students in the class work best.
    C. Using whole-group instruction only works best.
    D. Heterogeneous grouping of all the students works best for most situations.

66. In mathematics, Mr. Manzano assigns the following problem:

    Write a word problem that can be solved with the following number sentence: $28-16=12$.

    Which of the following is likely the *primary* purpose for this assignment?

    A. It will improve the students' understanding of mathematical principles.
    B. It will reinforce the students' basic addition and subtraction skills.
    C. It will help students learn that most math problems have one right answer.
    D. It will enhance students' appreciation of the application of mathematics to real-world problem solving.

67. Because he is using innovative teaching methods, Mr. Manzano is concerned about his students' performance on the TAAS test. Mr. Manzano could *best* meet this concern by:

    A. setting aside part of the day for TAAS study.
    B. making sure the TEKS for his grade level are included in his curriculum.
    C. including more drill and practice lessons over TAAS objectives.
    D. making sure the students always use their textbooks.

Mr. Manzano served on an ARD committee to review the academic progress of Harriet, who scores on-level on achievement tests but who is hearing-impaired. The IEP developed by the ARD committee specifies that Harriet be placed in Mr. Manzano's classroom. Mr. Manzano does not have training in special education, so he is concerned about the inclusion of Harriet in his classroom. He decides to attend professional development training on teaching special education students as soon as an opportunity arises.

68. In addition to the classroom teacher, Mr. Manzano, who else legally might have served on Harriet's ARD committee?

    I.   Harriet's parents or guardian
    II. a special education teacher
    III. a speech and hearing teacher
    IV. the principal

    A. I and II only
    B. I, II, and IV only
    C. I, III, and IV only
    D. I, II, III, and IV

69. A type of service generally not provided for special education students under federal law is:

    A. payment for prescription drugs.
    B. extended time for test taking.
    C. computer access.
    D. homework monitoring.

70. Mr. Manzano's probable purpose for participating in staff development is:

    A. to be a risk taker and innovator.
    B. to participate in collaborative decision making.
    C. to demonstrate that he has clearly defined goals.
    D. to enhance his own professional skills and knowledge.

71. In the professional development training, which of the following will Mr. Manzano likely be informed that he should *not* do?

    A. Use a preferential seating arrangement for Harriet.
    B. Make sure the rest of Harriet's classmates are aware of the nature and seriousness of Harriet's disability.
    C. Modify assignments and/or tests for Harriet.
    D. Use multisensory techniques and demonstrations.

72. The professional development training Mr. Heeney attended stressed that teachers need to know the legal rights of parents of a child with disabilities. Mr. Heeney is likely to have learned that, with regard to ARD committee meetings, the rights of parents of a child with disabilities include:

    I.   the right to written notice of scheduled meetings at least five school days before the meeting.
    II. the right to bring an attorney to the meeting.
    III. the right to have an interpreter if the parents' primary language is other than English.
    IV. the right to audiotape-record the meeting as long as all attending are informed about it.

    A. I and III only
    B. I, III, and IV only
    C. III and IV only
    D. I, II, III, and IV

73. During one lesson Mr. Manzano indicates to Harriet that she is to answer his question and waits patiently for her to respond. How would you evaluate this approach to the student?

    A. Negative, because it could embarrass Harriet in front of the rest of the class.
    B. Negative, because it communicates negative expectations about Harriet.
    C. Positive, because it communicates positive expectations about Harriet.
    D. Positive, because it communicates to all the students that Mr. Manzano is in charge.

Jimmy is an exceptionally bright student who writes very well but seldom completes his work, makes fun of class activities, and, generally, behaves disruptively. Clearly, Jimmy enjoys being the class clown. Whenever he disrupts the class, Mr. Manzano gives Jimmy time-out, isolating him in a separate part of the classroom out of view of his peers.

74. How would you evaluate Mr. Manzano's strategy for dealing with Jimmy's misbehavior?

   A. The strategy is appropriate since it deprives Jimmy of his audience.
   B. The strategy is inappropriate since Jimmy will continue to misbehave in his new location.
   C. The strategy is inappropriate since Jimmy will receive the class's sympathy.
   D. The strategy is appropriate since it uses a reward system.

75. The best strategy to reduce off-task behavior is:

   A. making the lesson more interesting.
   B. using moderate punishment such as time-out.
   C. making the lessons more difficult.
   D. discussing the problem with individual students.

76. Jimmy's father visits the school to complain about a lower-than-expected grade Jimmy received in science because he did not complete some homework assignments. Which of the following approaches would be appropriate for Mr. Manzano to use with this parent?

   A. He should explain to the parent that Jimmy can do better work since he is obviously a bright student.
   B. He should explain to the parent that the other students do well under his grading policy, so he sees no reason to change Jimmy's grade.
   C. He should explain to the parent that Jimmy's problem is most likely related to his behavior problems in class.
   D. He should explain his grading policy to the parent and show samples of incomplete work.

SET 6 ENDS HERE

Ms. Voigtel, a fifth-grade teacher, is very concerned because the students in her class are disruptive and unmotivated. Her class is a heterogeneous mixture of ability levels and interests. After the first two weeks of school, she holds a class meeting in which she asks, "What is wrong?" Joe Don responds, "How can we complete our work when we do not understand what it is that you ask us to do day in and day out?" Kathryn raises her hand and says, "When I do understand the assignment, it is usually boring: read the book and complete the worksheet. Why can't we work together on some of our assignments?"

77. Ms. Voigtel could increase motivation to learn in her classroom by:

I.   selecting content that is relevant to the students' lives.
II. encouraging students to assist in planning instructional activities.
III. making sure students know what to do and how to do it.
IV. using simulations and role playing.

A. I, II, and III only
B. I, II, and IV only
C. II, III, and IV only
D. I, II, III, and IV

78. Ms. Voigtel's decision to hold a class meeting to deal with the disruptive behavior illustrates her understanding that:

A. she is a member of a learning community and knows how to work effectively with all members of that community.
B. she knows the importance of promoting student ownership in a smoothly functioning learning community.
C. she must impart expectations and ideas to create a climate of trust.
D. she must help students become self-motivated.

79. When reviewing her discipline management plan, Ms. Voigtel should focus on two important concerns:

A. consistency and fairness.
B. isolation and suspension.
C. threat and fear.
D. detention hall and suspension.

80. Ms. Voigtel wants to obtain information about her students' strengths and weaknesses in subject areas. The *most* appropriate assessment approach for her to use is to:

A. administer end-of-unit matching tests.
B. administer diagnostic tests.
C. administer comprehensive true-false tests.
D. administer norm-referenced tests.

81. In order to increase the achievement of her students who are doing poorly, Ms. Voigtel should *first* consider:

A. a competitive reward structure.
B. immediate feedback.
C. giving praise at fixed intervals.
D. giving praise on an intermittent schedule.

82. Based on Kathryn's request, Ms. Voigtel agrees to implement some cooperative learning activities in her classroom. It is very important that she include two *essential* components, namely:

    A. appointed team leaders and flexible membership.
    B. individual accountability and group assessment.
    C. improvement points and tangible rewards.
    D. baseline scores and ability grouping.

83. When Ms. Voigtel uses cooperative learning activities, she groups heterogeneously, based on students' abilities. For other activities, she groups her students on the basis of ability level and assigns independent activities to the more capable students, while using direct instruction with the less capable groups of students. This teacher's behavior *best* illustrates:

    A. adapting instruction to the characteristics of the learner.
    B. matching teaching strategies to the type of learning task.
    C. using effective classroom management.
    D. matching student characteristics to the learning objective.

84. With the implementation of cooperative learning, the achievement of Ms. Voigtel's students improves. However, she is concerned that although Jonathan is well behaved, he consistently performs poorly in class. Jonathan's behavior is *most* consistent with that of a student who:

    A. is severely mentally retarded.
    B. has an attention deficit disorder.
    C. is emotionally disturbed.
    D. has a learning disability.

At the end of the first six weeks, Ms. Voigtel has her first parent-teacher conference of the year. She meets with Dekolvin's parents about their concern that his grades are low. Ms. Voigtel wants Dekolvin's parents to be thoroughly informed of their child's progress, so she spends most of the thirty minutes that the conference lasts explaining what Dekolvin is learning in school and showing samples of his work. When the parents leave, Ms. Voigtel feels the conference has not been successful. Later that same day, Ms. Voigtel receives a telephone call from Leslie's father. He wants to come after school to discuss his daughter's school work. During the after-school conference, Leslie's father tells Ms. Voigtel that his daughter is not being properly challenged with the work Ms. Voigtel has been giving her. He says that Leslie is a bright and gifted child who should be in the Gifted/Talented program.

85. Which of the following would have *most* improved Ms. Voigtel's conference with Dekolvin's parents?

A. She should have included Dekolvin in the conference.
B. During the conference, she should have paused and encouraged the parents to talk.
C. She should have provided the parents with an outline of her comments.
D. She should not have done anything differently.

86. Which of the following would be an appropriate way for Ms. Voigtel to respond to Leslie's parent?

A. Show him some of Leslie's work and explain that Leslie is very bright, but not gifted.
B. Explain the Gifted/Talented program to him and agree to initiate screening procedures.
C. Suggest that he needs to discuss his concerns with the principal.
D. Thank him for his interest, but politely explain that she is the person most qualified to make instructional decisions regarding Leslie.

87. The counselor and Ms. Voigtel have conflicting opinions about an at-risk student, Jaime, who has some marginal reading difficulties. The problem is whether or not Jaime should be given a higher-than-earned grade on the basis of attitude and effort. To resolve this problem, Ms. Voigtel meets with the counselor and listens to her concerns. Ms. Voigtel's decision to meet with the counselor is an example of a teacher recognizing:

A. the relationship between careful planning and student success in the classroom.
B. that students' developmental characteristics affect what and how they learn.
C. that she is a member of a learning community and should work with all members in that community.
D. that understanding laws and guidelines relevant to education is critical when dealing with other professionals.

Although Ms. Voigtel is not a new teacher, the principal feels she can benefit by having a mentor teacher, Ms. Harper, this year. Now that Ms. Voigtel is settled into her classroom, she realizes that it is only the end of the first six weeks of school and she has run out of enrichment activities for her class. When Ms. Voigtel asks Ms. Harper for help with ideas, Ms. Harper suggests that Ms. Voigtel set up some learning centers in her room.

88. Learning centers that will be of *most* benefit to Ms. Voigtel's class should:

    I.   meet the varied characteristics of the students.
    II. be designed for students to work in isolation, away from their peers.
    III. include carefully designed and easy-to-read worksheets.
    IV. be self-contained—all materials needed are contained within the center.

    A. I and III only
    B. I and IV only
    C. II and III only
    D. I, III, and IV only

89. When Ms. Voigtel was checking attendance on Monday, a student asked why Billy was always absent on Mondays. Upon checking her records, Ms. Voigtel finds this has been true several times. She also discovers that Billy's grades have been steadily dropping. Later, she recalls that last week she had seen bruises on Billy's arms and he had acted very withdrawn. She suspects he is experiencing abuse at home. She asks Ms. Harper for advice on what to do. Ms. Harper should tell Ms. Voigtel to:

    A. set up a conference with the parents to see if her suspicions are true.
    B. discuss her suspicions with some of Billy's friends.
    C. notify the proper legal authorities at once and let them check into the situation.
    D. wait a while longer and observe Billy to see if she is correct in her suspicions.

90. At the end of the school year, Ms. Harper is helping Ms. Voigtel plan for the beginning of the coming school year. Ms. Voigtel has selected a cooperative learning group activity to use on the first class day as a means to get acquainted with her students and for the students to get to know one another. She is very excited about this idea because she is aware of the many positive benefits of cooperative learning. Which of the following recommendations should Ms. Harper make to Ms. Voigtel?

    A. Ms. Voigtel should have students follow up with written reports of the group activity.
    B. Ms. Voigtel should monitor the social interactions of the students while they are working in their groups.
    C. Ms. Voigtel should have the students evaluate each other's level of participation in the group activity.
    D. Ms. Voigtel should replace the group activity with a simpler, more relaxing type of activity that involves the whole class.

SET 7 ENDS HERE

Answer Key

Item Number	Correct Answer	Competency
1	C	015
2	C	007
3	B	008
4	B	005
5	C	008
6	D	014
7	D	009
8	C	001
9	C	008
10	B	013
11	B	011
12	B	010
13	B	005
14	C	006
15	C	011
16	D	006
17	A	012
18	C	003
19	A	002
20	D	007
21	C	006
22	D	004
23	B	007
24	B	005
25	B	006
26	D	008
27	A	007
28	D	003
29	A	007

30	B	011
31	B	013
32	A	006
33	C	004
34	A	011
35	A	011
36	C	010
37	D	001
38	C	011
39	A	008
40	B	005
41	A	002
42	A	003
43	C	011
44	B	011
45	B	010
46	A	015
47	B	015
48	A	015
49	A	002
50	B	002
51	B	002
52	A	007
53	A	003
54	C	002
55	A	010
56	A	006
57	D	003
58	A	003
59	C	003
60	B	015

61	D	008
62	C	008
63	C	008
64	D	008
65	D	008
66	A	006
67	B	006
68	D	015
69	A	015
70	D	012
71	B	015
72	D	015
73	C	007
74	A	011
75	A	011
76	D	013
77	D	005
78	B	011
79	A	011
80	B	010
81	B	003
82	B	008
83	A	008
84	D	003
85	B	013
86	B	013
87	C	012
88	B	006
89	C	015
90	D	008

Answer Explanations

1. **C** This question deals with campus decision making, which relates to **ethical, legal, and professional standards.** Thus, its primary focus is Competency 015: *The teacher understands requirements, expectations, and constraints associated with teaching in Texas, and can apply this understanding in a variety of contexts.* Teachers should understand and recognize the levels of authority and important decision-making structures within the school system and know how to work within the system to make appropriate decisions regarding students. In 1991, HB 2885 established site-based decision making, which directed local school districts to decentralize decision making. Eliminate Roman I and II because on campuses practicing site-based decision making, decisions regarding student field trips are made at the campus level, without the necessity of consulting the superintendent or the school board. Eliminate A, B, and D. Choice C is the correct response.

2. **C** This question asks about Mr. Arnold's questioning techniques, which relates to **communication.** Thus, its primary focus is Competency 007: *The teacher uses effective verbal, nonverbal, and media communication techniques to shape the classroom into a community of learners engaged in active inquiry, collaborative exploration, and supportive interactions.* Eliminate A because the students are "brainstorming" in response to Mr. Arnold's question, not researching. Eliminate B because Mr. Arnold is encouraging the class to work together as a team, not individually. Eliminate D because Mr. Arnold did not ask the students about what they already know about setting up a business. Mr. Arnold is a thoughtful questioner who is asking higher-order questions that elicit critical thinking and promote problem solving. Choice C is the correct response.

3. **B** This question deals with **instructional strategies.** Thus, its primary focus is Competency 008: *The teacher uses a variety of instructional strategies and roles to facilitate learning and to help students become independent thinkers and problem solvers who use higher-order thinking in the classroom and the real world.* Eliminate Roman II because it is not supported by the stimulus and, besides, it relates to **diversity** (Competency 003). Eliminate C. Eliminate Roman III because it is not supported by the stimulus. Eliminate A and D. Mr. Arnold uses the idea of setting up a class business as a means to structure the learning environment to encourage students to think independently and creatively. By assuming the roles and responsibilities associated with a real business, the students are likely to gain deeper insights and understandings of the business world. Choice B is the correct response.

4. **B**　This question deals with **motivation.** Thus, its primary focus is Competency 005: *The teacher understands how motivation affects group and individual behavior and learning and can apply this understanding to promote student learning.* Eliminate A because it relates to **communication** (Competency 007). Eliminate C because it relates to **how learning occurs** (Competency 004). Eliminate D because it relates to **classroom management** (Competency 011). Mr. Arnold understands that intrinsic motivation is enhanced when students are allowed to have control over their learning experiences. This is a key idea found in Competency 005 **(motivation).** Choice B is the correct response.

5. **C**　This question deals with **instructional strategies.** Thus, its primary focus is Competency 008: *The teacher uses a variety of instructional strategies and roles to facilitate learning and to help students become independent thinkers and problem solvers who use higher-order thinking in the classroom and the real world.* Eliminate Roman IV because it is teacher-directed, rather than student-centered. Eliminate A, B, and D. Mr. Arnold should know that, as with other learning activities, he can expect successes and failures during the class project. His role will be critical, and he will find himself playing a variety of nondirective roles, as needed. In addition, real-world projects require careful planning and monitoring, including the assignment of specific roles to students and the resolution of personality differences that often arise. Choice C is the correct response.

6. **D**　This question deals with the **school-community relationship.** Thus, its primary focus is Competency 014: *The teacher understands how the school relates to the larger community and knows strategies for making interactions between school and community mutually supportive and beneficial.* Eliminate Roman II because most likely the students would be learning from the bank visitor, not from the school. Eliminate A and C. Educating young people is the responsibility of everyone in the community. By involving a local bank in a school project, collaboration and positive public relations between the community and the school are promoted. Additionally, learning from the bank personnel will raise students' awareness and understanding of community resources. Choice B is the correct response.

7. **D**　This question asks about technology, which comes under **materials and resources.** Thus, its primary focus is Competency 009: *The teacher uses a variety of instructional materials and resources (including human and technological resources) to support individual and group learning.* Eliminate A because databases do not have the range of computational features needed for inventories. Eliminate B and C because graphing and computer simulations are inappropriate for keeping inventory records. A spreadsheet is used to arrange information and formulas into rows

and columns, like a ledger or worksheet for a business. Choice D is the correct response.

8. **C**   The question stem indicates that Mr. Arnold is concerned with appropriate activities for sixth-grade students—he is concerned with **developmentally appropriate instruction.** Thus, the primary focus of this question is Competency 001: *The teacher uses an understanding of human developmental processes to nurture student growth through developmentally appropriate instruction.* Eliminate A because it relates to **communication** (Competency 007). Eliminate B because the students will not be practicing their reading skills, per se. Eliminate D because it relates to **school-community relationships** (Competency 014). Mr. Arnold is likely to be aware that most students at this grade level are in the "good boy/nice girl" stage of moral development, where doing what others expect is morally correct. He is helping them learn the rules and conventions about what people should do in interactions with each other by having them learn and practice socially acceptable behavior while they are growing up, so that the behavior is likely to continue into adulthood. Choice C is the correct response.

9. **C**   This question deals with **instructional strategies.** Thus, its primary focus is Competency 008: *The teacher uses a variety of instructional strategies and roles to facilitate learning and to help students become independent thinkers and problem solvers who use higher-order thinking in the classroom and the real world.* Eliminate A because the students will be involved in higher-order levels of cognitive learning, rather than concentrating on basic skills. Eliminate B because it relates to **school-community relationships** (Competency 014). Eliminate D because real-world projects usually require more time than expository (teacher-telling) methods. The rationale for using a real-world project is the belief that the students will actively seek out knowledge, rather than waiting to be told what they are supposed to know, as often happens when expository teaching methods are used. Choice C is the correct response.

10. **B**   This question deals with **school-home relationships.** Thus, its primary focus is Competency 013: *The teacher knows how to foster strong school-home relationships that support student achievement of desired learning outcomes.* Eliminate A and C because they are in conflict with the competency that encourages involving parents. Eliminate D because it puts the parents in an awkward position. Students whose parents are actively involved in their schooling achieve more than other students. The teacher should work toward establishing strong ties between the parents and the school. Choice B is the correct response.

11. **B**   This question deals with **classroom management.** Thus, its primary focus is Competency 011: *The teacher structures and manages the learning environment to maintain a classroom*

climate that promotes the lifelong pursuit of learning and encourages cooperation, leadership, and mutual respect. Eliminate A because it is teacher-directed and authoritarian. Eliminate C because this measure would be viewed as threatening the students. Eliminate D because this strategy might help the problem, but it should not be Mr. Arnold's *first* step. Mr. Arnold knows how to promote student membership in a smoothly functioning learning community and to facilitate a positive social and emotional atmosphere in the classroom. Conflict is an inevitable feature of all social relations. The first step Mr. Arnold should take is to help the students define the conflict by having them list their grievances to see if a compromise can be reached. Choice B is the correct response.

12. **B** This question deals with **assessment.** Thus, its primary focus is Competency 010: *The teacher uses processes of informal and formal assessment to understand individual learners, monitor instructional effectiveness, and shape instruction.* Eliminate A because the students are evaluating, not Mr. Arnold. Eliminate C because this would not be considered a benefit. Eliminate D because there is no reason to expect a connection between the students' self-reflections and their leadership skills. When students participate in self-assessment and self-evaluation, they are using critical, higher-order thinking skills, engaging in the highest level of Bloom's taxonomy of educational objectives. Choice B is the correct response.

13. **B** This question deals with **motivation.** Thus, its primary focus is Competency 005: *The teacher understands how motivation affects group and individual behavior and learning and can apply this understanding to promote learning.* Eliminate Roman I because it relates to discipline—**classroom management** (Competency 011). Eliminate A and D. Eliminate Roman IV because Ms. Rivas is not wanting the students to do the opposite of what she's asked them to do. Eliminate C. Ms. Rivas enhances self-motivation (Roman II) by allowing students to have choices in their learning and by relating lessons to their personal interests. In addition, she understands that when students work in groups, they are likely to encourage and help each other (Roman III), which enhances motivation. Choice B is the correct response.

14. **C** This question deals with **planning.** Thus, its primary focus is Competency 006: *The teacher uses planning processes to design outcome-oriented learning experiences that foster understanding and encourage self-directed thinking and learning in both individual and collaborative settings.* Eliminate A because it is likely to have a negative impact on the lower-ability students. Eliminate B because it fosters competition. Eliminate D because it is not supported by the stimulus—there is no indication the students will be doing this. When planning writing activities, Ms. Rivas understands the benefits of collaboration. She knows that

when students work together they experience positive interdependence; promote each other's learning by helping, sharing, and encouraging one another; and explain, discuss, and teach each other. As a result, the quality of the students' writing samples is likely to be enhanced. Choice C is the correct response.

15. **C** This question relates both to **instructional strategies** (Ms. Rivas is using small groups) and **classroom management** (What should Ms. Rivas do to promote effective group work?). Glancing at the answer choices, you can see that most relate to **classroom management.** Thus, the primary focus of this question is Competency 011: *The teacher structures and manages the learning environment to maintain a classroom climate that promotes the lifelong pursuit of learning and encourages cooperation, leadership, and mutual respect.* Eliminate A and D because they conflict with effective classroom management procedures that emphasize teachers should constantly monitor what is going on in class. Eliminate B because effective classroom managers are quick to respond to and stop or redirect inappropriate behavior. Ms. Rivas understands the important role the teacher must assume when using a collaborative setting. The teacher should monitor each group and give feedback on the learning task and group skills. Choice C is the correct response.

16. **D** This question deals with **planning.** Thus, its primary focus is Competency 006: *The teacher uses planning processes to design outcome-oriented learning experiences that foster understanding and encourage self-directed thinking and learning in both individual and collaborative settings.* Eliminate Roman I because some topics may require Ms. Garcia to present new information or teach skills before students work in groups. Eliminate A and B. Eliminate Roman II because it sends a negative message to average- and low-ability students. Eliminate C. It is important that Ms. Garcia understand the relationship between careful planning and student success in the classroom. Research indicates that small-group activities can increase student achievement more than traditional lessons if students are well prepared to work in small groups and the group task is well organized. Choice D is the correct response.

17. **A** This question deals with **professionalism.** Thus, its primary focus is Competency 012: *The teacher is a reflective practitioner who knows how to promote his or her own professional growth and can work cooperatively with other professionals in the system to create a school culture that enhances learning and encourages positive change.* Eliminate B because Ms. Garcia did not make her decision in a group setting. Eliminate C and D because they do not relate to this question—neither the stimulus nor this question contain the ideas expressed in these answer choices. Ms. Garcia understands the importance of reflection and self-evaluation. She recognizes that she is a member of a learning community and actively seeks out other professionals as resources to enhance her

professional skills and knowledge. Choice A is the correct response.

18. **C** This question deals with **diversity.** Thus, its primary focus is Competency 003: *The teacher appreciates human diversity, recognizing how diversity in the classroom and the community may affect learning and creating a classroom environment in which both the diversity of groups and the uniqueness of individuals are recognized and celebrated.* Eliminate A because in the stimulus, there is no indication that the students will be exposed to prejudice. (Don't read too much into a question.) Eliminate B because it relates to **professionalism** (Competency 012). Eliminate D because it relates to **communication** (Competency 007). Ms. Garcia demonstrates that she knows how to turn the diversity in her classroom to advantage. By creating diverse learning groups that must work together, she is fostering communication and collaboration among students and promoting their understanding of each other. These interactions will nurture a sense of community in the classroom. Choice C is the correct response.

19. **A** When Ms. Garcia displays students' work, she makes students feel accepted, competent, and productive—this positively affects **students' self-esteem.** Thus, the primary focus of this question is Competency 002: *The teacher considers environmental factors that may affect learning in designing a supportive and responsive classroom community that promotes all students' learning and self-esteem.* Eliminate B because it relates to **developmentally appropriate instruction** (Competency 001). Eliminate C because it relates to **materials and resources** (Competency 009). Eliminate D because it relates to **assessment** (Competency 010). By creating a classroom environment in which students feel accepted, competent, and productive, Ms. Garcia demonstrates that she understands factors that positively influence students' self-worth (Competency 002). Choice A is the correct response.

20. **D** This question deals with both **planning** (Mr. Bentley is using his question as the focus of his lesson) and **communication** (what is the purpose of Mr. Bentley's question?). Glancing at the answer choices, you can see that most relate to purposes for questioning— **communication.** Thus, the primary focus of this question is Competency 007: *The teacher uses effective verbal, nonverbal, and media communication techniques to shape the classroom into a community of learners engaged in active inquiry, collaborative exploration, and supportive interactions.* Eliminate A because Mr. Bentley's question is one that should elicit divergent thinking, not factual recall. Eliminate B because teachers should encourage students to be independent thinkers and, thus, not give them hints about what to think. Eliminate C because Mr. Bentley's question isn't asking about what the students already know about the

controversy. Mr. Bentley's question is designed to create a climate of inquiry. He does not have a single right answer to this question in mind, but rather wants students to explore and develop their own ideas about the topic. His question is meant to provide a framework for engaging students in active inquiry during the ensuing class discussion. Choice D is the correct response.

21. **C** This question deals with **planning.** Thus, its primary focus is Competency 006: *The teacher uses planning processes to design outcome-oriented learning experiences that foster understanding and encourage self-directed thinking and learning in both individual and collaborative settings.* This is a priority-setting question—you will have to decide which of the responses is *most* likely. Eliminate A because it relates to **communication.** Eliminate B because it is not supported by the stimulus—the students are discussing a problem, not solving one. Eliminate D because it deals with an environmental factor (the town controversy) that may negatively affect student performance, which falls under **students' self-esteem** (Competency 002). Although the discussion will provide opportunities for students to talk during class and may minimize the negative effects of community problems in the classroom, facilitating higher-order thinking is most likely Mr. Arnold's main purpose. Choice C is the correct response.

22. **D** This question deals with **how students learn.** Thus, its primary focus is Competency 004: *The teacher understands how learning occurs and can apply this understanding to design and implement effective instruction.* Eliminate A because teachers should plan to involve all students in the learning activity. Eliminate B and C because both tend to discourage independent thinking. Mr. Bentley understands how students develop knowledge and skills. He knows that before beginning a discussion in which students will be expected to take a position and defend it, it is important that they have an adequate knowledge of the topic. Choice D is the correct response.

23. **B** This question deals with both **communication** (the students engage in a discussion) and **assessment** (what did the students learn?). Glancing at the answer choices, you can see that they do not deal with **assessment** issues, so the primary focus of this question is Competency 007: *The teacher uses effective verbal, nonverbal, and media communication techniques to shape the classroom into a community of learners engaged in active inquiry, collaborative exploration, and supportive interactions.* Eliminate A because a discussion is unlikely to lead to an absolute conclusion, since no undisputed facts are provided. Eliminate C and D because the students are discussing a problem, not solving it. During the discussion, Mr. Bentley should monitor the effects of messages, simplifying and restating when necessary, and encouraging the students to communicate effectively. He should

emphasize to the students that the critical elements of verbal communication are accuracy of language, accuracy of information, standardization of language, and clearly defined expectations. Choice B is the correct response.

24. **B** This question deals with factors that influence student learning—an idea that occurs in Competency 002 **(students' self-esteem)** and Competency 005 **(motivation).** Glancing at the answer choices is not much help in deciding which of these is the primary focus, so don't make a decision yet. Eliminate A because it is not supported by the stimulus—no indication that the controversy was a distraction. Eliminate C because it is not supported by the stimulus—students are not given choices. Eliminate D because it relates to **school-community relationships** (Competency 014). Since you know that B deals with **motivation,** you now know that the primary focus of this question is Competency 005: *The teacher understands how motivation affects group and individual behavior and learning and can apply this understanding to promote student learning.* Mr. Bentley understands the importance of motivation to learning and is able to recognize factors and situations that are likely to promote motivation. He uses an external factor (that is, the community controversy) as a tool to engage students in active learning and to help motivate them to learn. Choice B is the correct response.

25. **B** This question deals with **planning.** Thus, its primary focus is Competency 006: *The teacher uses planning processes to design outcome-oriented learning experiences that foster understanding and encourage self-directed thinking and learning in both individual and collaborative settings.* Eliminate A because objectives consistent with a student discussion are at the higher levels of Bloom's taxonomy, not at the lower, knowledge level. Eliminate B because younger or less mature students may not have the necessary prior knowledge to enter productively into a discussion. Eliminate D because discussions should generate a variety of divergent ideas. Educational research has established that group discussion in which students publicly commit themselves is effective at changing individuals' attitudes. Since attitudes fall in the affective domain, choice B is the correct response.

26. **D** This question deals with instructional strategies. Thus, its primary focus is Competency 008: *The teacher uses a variety of instructional strategies and roles to facilitate learning and to help students become independent thinkers and problem solvers who use higher-order thinking in the classroom and the real world.* In a class discussion, the ideas should be drawn from the students, so Eliminate A, B, and C because Mr. Bentley's acting as judge, critic, or arbitrator—dominant roles—would be likely to discourage students from expressing their ideas. Mr. Bentley knows when to vary his role in the instructional process in relation to the content

and purposes of instruction and the levels of need and independence of the students. He wants the ideas to be drawn from the students, so he assumes the nondirective role of moderator, rather than playing a dominant role during the lesson. Choice D is the correct response.

27. **A** This question deals with questioning, which comes under **communication.** Thus, its primary focus is Competency 007: *The teacher uses effective verbal, nonverbal, and media communication techniques to shape the classroom into a community of learners engaged in active inquiry, collaborative exploration, and supportive interactions.* Eliminate B, C, and D because these question types require one right answer or solution, thus eliciting only lower-level thinking skills. Divergent questions (for instance, Can you explain? Why do you think that happened?) allow for multiple solutions, eliciting higher-order and critical thinking skills. To develop students' critical and creative thinking skills, Mr. Bentley should be using Bloom's taxonomy by asking more higher-order divergent questions. Choice A is the correct response.

28. **D** This question deals with **diversity.** Thus, its primary focus is Competency 003: *The teacher appreciates human diversity, recognizing how diversity in the classroom and the community may affect learning and creating a classroom environment in which both the diversity of groups and the uniqueness of individuals are recognized and celebrated.* Eliminate A, B, and C because they are in conflict with research findings. Numerous research investigations have shown that most teachers, regardless of their gender, unconsciously direct more questions to male students than to female students. Choice D is the correct response.

29. **A** This question deals with **communication.** Thus, its primary focus is Competency 007: *The teacher uses effective verbal, nonverbal, and media communication techniques to shape the classroom into a community of learners engaged in active inquiry, collaborative exploration, and supportive interactions.* Eliminate Roman II because the quality of the discussion will not be improved with these lower-level question types. Eliminate C and D. Eliminate Roman IV because this works against participation. Eliminate B. Asking a question *first* and *then* calling a student's name is an effective method teachers can use to keep all students mentally involved in the learning process (Roman I). When the question comes before the student's name, all students are given the opportunity to think and process their answers because the teacher has not yet identified the student who will be asked to respond. Research shows that asking the question first increases the number of responses as well as eliciting more correct and longer responses. Sufficient wait time, the length of time a teacher waits for a student to answer a question before giving up, is also important for quality instruction (Roman III). Research has found that teachers who wait

at least three seconds before giving up on students obtain more participation and better learning results. Choice A is the correct response.

30. **B**   This question deals with **classroom management.** Thus, its primary focus is Competency 011: *The teacher structures and manages the learning environment to maintain a classroom climate that promotes the lifelong pursuit of learning and encourages cooperation, leadership, and mutual respect.* Mr. Bentley should be aware of the need to maintain focus in the classroom. Mr. Bentley's *first* intervention should be the least intrusive. Eliminate A, C, and, D because they interrupt the flow of the lesson. Mr. Bentley should try nonverbal interventions, like a stern gaze, before moving to more intrusive measures. Choice B is the correct response.

31. **B**   This question deals with **school-home relationships.** Thus, its primary focus is Competency 013: *The teacher knows how to foster strong school-home relationships that support student achievement of desired learning outcomes.* Eliminate A because it is a good idea to offer parents refreshments, especially if it's late in the day. Eliminate C because Ms. Nethery has a legal right to see Melissa's grades. Eliminate D because paraphrasing parents' comments can avoid misunderstandings or miscommunications, especially when dealing with parents whose home language is other than English. Teachers should avoid diagnosing a parent's child without the proper credentials to do so. Choice B is the correct response.

32. **A**   This question deals with **planning.** Thus, its primary focus is Competency 006: *The teacher uses planning processes to design outcome-oriented learning experiences that foster understanding and encourage self-directed thinking and learning in both individual and collaborative settings.* Eliminate B because it relates to **developmentally appropriate instruction** (Competency 001). Eliminate C because it relates to **diversity** (Competency 003). Eliminate D because it is not supported by the stimulus as clearly as is choice A. By designing a unit around "civic ideas and practices," Mr. Bentley will be giving students the opportunity to learn about relationships within this central theme of social studies. Choice A is the correct response.

33. **C**   This question deals with **how learning occurs.** Thus, its primary focus is Competency 004: *The teacher understands how learning occurs and can apply this understanding to design and implement effective instruction.* Eliminate D because it relates to **communication** (Competency 007). Eliminate A and B because neither the stimulus nor the question stem contain the ideas expressed in these answer choices. Understanding is enhanced when content is related to students' lives and experiences. Choice C is the correct response.

34. **A** This question deals with **classroom management.** Thus, its primary focus is Competency 011: *The teacher structures and manages the learning environment to maintain a classroom climate that promotes the lifelong pursuit of learning and encourages cooperation, leadership, and mutual respect.* Eliminate B because it is not consistent with establishing a positive social and emotional atmosphere in the classroom. Eliminate C because during the first days of school, effective classroom managers are involved with the whole class. Eliminate D because effective classroom managers respond immediately to stop any misbehavior. The first days of school are critical in establishing classroom order. During the first days of school, effective classroom managers spend much of the time teaching students specific classroom procedures. Choice A is the correct response.

35. **A** This question deals with **classroom management.** Thus, its primary focus is Competency 011: *The teacher structures and manages the learning environment to maintain a climate that promotes the lifelong pursuit of learning and encourages cooperation, leadership, and mutual respect.* Ms. Curl should know how to promote student membership in a smoothly functioning learning community and to facilitate a positive social and emotional atmosphere in the classroom. She should be aware that, according to research, effective classroom managers initially are involved with the whole class; have clear, specific plans for introducing rules and procedures; use simple, enjoyable tasks; and respond immediately to stop any misbehavior. Choices B, C, and D are consistent with these guidelines. Choice A is the correct response, since Ms. Curl should *not* break students into groups on the first day.

36. **C** This question deals with **assessment.** Thus, its primary focus is Competency 010: *The teacher uses processes of informal and formal assessment to understand individual learners, monitor instructional effectiveness, and shape instruction.* This is a priority-setting question—you must select the *primary* purpose. Eliminate A and B because portfolios can be used for these purposes, but neither of these is the *primary* purpose for using portfolios. Eliminate D because peer assessment is not a purpose for using portfolios. A portfolio is a purposeful collection of the student's work to evidence his or her learning. Keeping a portfolio is one of the best ways for students to engage in the evaluation of themselves. Choice C is the correct response.

37. **D** Upon first reading, this question appears to deal with **classroom management.** However, the only two answer choices that are clearly related to classroom management are B and C, both of which are not educationally sound. You are left to choose between A and D. This is a priority-setting question—you must select the answer choice that is *most* important to the task at hand. Choose D because you know that this is very important, and you don't know

enough about Ms. Curl's educational philosophy to determine whether it would be consistent with doing this. Since you know that D deals with **developmentally appropriate instruction,** you now know the primary focus of this question is Competency 001: *The teacher uses an understanding of human developmental processes to nurture student growth through developmentally appropriate instruction.* It is important that Ms. Curl consider the developmental characteristics of her students, so that she will be realistic in her expectations of behavior for this age group. Choice D is the correct response.

38. **C** This question deals with **classroom management.** Thus, its primary focus is Competency 011: *The teacher structures and manages the learning environment to maintain a classroom climate that promotes the lifelong pursuit of learning and encourages cooperation, leadership, and mutual respect.* Classroom rules should be stated in positive terms. Choices A, B, and C are consistent with this guideline. Using negative terms often results in students' exhibiting the undesirable behavior that you want them to avoid. Rule 3 should be reworded to say, perhaps, "Walk, when indoors." Choice C is the correct response.

39. **A** This question deals with **instructional strategies.** Thus, its primary focus is Competency 008: *The teacher uses a variety of instructional strategies and roles to facilitate learning and to help students become independent thinkers and problem solvers who use higher-order thinking in the classroom and the real world.* Eliminate B because research indicates that within-class ability grouping widens the gap between high-ability and low-ability students—thus, it is unlikely that the high-ability students will become more accepting of the low-ability students. Eliminate C because numerous experts contend that ability grouping is detrimental to low achievers because they often get locked into a low-level curriculum. Eliminate D because a competitive structure should not prohibit students from moving ahead at a faster pace. Ms. Curl should be aware that behavior management problems may arise when within-class ability grouping is used because other students are expected to work independently while the teacher works with a particular group. Ms. Curl will have to make sure the rest of the class has an assignment they understand and can do while she gives attention to a particular group. Choice A is the correct response.

40. **B** This question deals with **motivation.** Thus, its primary focus is Competency 005: *The teacher understands how motivation affects group and individual behavior and learning and can apply this understanding to promote student learning.* Eliminate A because it relates to **instructional strategies** (Competency 008). Eliminate C because it relates to **communication** (Competency 007). Eliminate D because it relates to **planning** (Competency 006). Ms. Curl understands the importance of motivation to learning and is

aware of the characteristics and effects of intrinsic and extrinsic motivation. She knows how to use a variety of techniques, such as allowing students to have choices in their learning, to engage students in learning activities, and to help them develop the motivation to achieve. Choice B is the correct response.

41. **A** Upon first reading, this question appears to deal with **motivation** (Ms. Curl is giving students choices in their learning). However, none of the answer choices are directly related to **motivation.** Eliminate B and C because they are not supported by the stimulus. The students did not work in teams (A), nor are you told that they used organizational skills when generating the reading topics lists (B). Now, you must select between A and D. Both of these responses relate to **students' self-esteem.** Thus, you now know that the primary focus of this question is Competency 002: *The teacher considers environmental factors that may affect learning in designing a supportive and responsive classroom community that promotes all students' learning and self-esteem.* Eliminate D because giving choices in reading topics will not necessarily provide a stable, routine, and predictable environment. Ms. Curl understands Maslow's Hierarchy of Human Needs and recognizes the importance of establishing a supportive and responsive classroom community. She knows that using a student's ideas will help that student feel recognized and accepted, thus enhancing the student's self-esteem. Choice A is the correct response.

42. **A** This question deals with **diversity.** Thus, its primary focus is Competency 003: *The teacher appreciates human diversity, recognizing how diversity in the classroom and the community may affect learning and creating a classroom environment in which both the diversity of groups and the uniqueness of individuals are recognized and celebrated.* Eliminate Roman IV because all students should be challenged to learn, even students in the low-ability group. Eliminate D. It is very important that students learn very early that they are responsible for their own learning (Roman I). Ms. Curl can help these students to be more successful in reading comprehension by giving concrete examples of abstract concepts (Roman II). Also, receiving feedback from their peers will help to motivate the students. Students are usually concerned about performing well in front of their peers even though they may not be motivated by a teacher (Roman III). Choice A is the correct response.

43. **C** This question deals with **classroom management.** Thus, its primary focus is Competency 011: *The teacher structures and manages the learning environment to maintain a classroom climate that promotes the lifelong pursuit of learning and encourages cooperation, leadership, and mutual respect.* This is a priority-setting question—you must select the answer choice that is *most* effective. It is important for Ms. Curl to maximize the amount of class time spent in learning. Eliminate A, B, and D because their

effectiveness is diminished when class is interrupted. She should be aware that one important source of lost instructional time is interruptions. Interruptions not only cut into instructional time; they also break momentum. Ms. Curl should post a "Do Not Disturb" sign on the classroom door during reading time to avoid interruptions. Choice C is the correct response.

44. **B**   This question deals with **classroom management.** Thus, its primary focus is Competency 011: *The teacher structures and manages the learning environment to maintain a classroom climate that promotes the lifelong pursuit of learning and encourages cooperation, leadership, and mutual respect.* This is a priority-setting question—you must select the answer choice that is the *best* approach for Ms. Curl to use with Juan. Ms. Curl should understand the importance of establishing and maintaining standards of behavior, while maximizing the amount of class time spent in learning. Eliminate A because effective classroom managers respond immediately to stop or redirect any misbehavior. Eliminate C because educational research suggests that teachers should follow the principle that misbehaviors should be corrected using the simplest intervention that will work while avoiding unnecessary disruption of the lesson. Eliminate D because it is an inappropriate teacher behavior—when disciplining, the dignity of the student must be preserved. Ms. Curl should walk by Juan's desk and unobtrusively take the ball because this action stops the misbehavior without stopping the lesson. Choice B is the correct response.

45. **B**   This question assesses Competency 010: *The teacher uses processes of informal and formal assessment to understand individual learners, monitor instructional effectiveness, and shape instruction.* Eliminate A because summative assessment is assessment that follows instruction and occurs at the end of a unit, semester, and so forth. Eliminate C because norm-referenced assessment refers to the use of standardized tests that focus on a comparison of a student's score to those of other students. Eliminate D because criterion-referenced assessment refers to the use of tests that are designed to measure mastery of specific skills. Norm- and criterion-referenced tests are formal assessments. Formative assessment is designed to acquire feedback before the end of a unit, semester, and so forth. It is used to guide the content and pace of lessons. Ms. Curl is using an informal assessment to acquire information before the end of the semester. Choice B is the correct response.

46. **A**   This question deals with **ethical, legal, and professional standards.** Thus, its primary focus is Competency 015: *The teacher understands requirements, expectations, and constraints associated with teaching in Texas, and can apply this understanding in a variety of contexts.* According to the Individuals with Disabilities Education Act (IDEA; formerly

PL 94-142), placement in the "least restrictive environment" means placement of the student in the regular classroom to the maximum extent appropriate. Eliminate B because the burden of providing an appropriate environment should not be placed entirely upon the special education teachers. Eliminate C because it is not always in the best interest of the disabled student to participate in regular school activities. By law, the ARD committee must place the student in a classroom with his or her peers, unless the student's disability is so severe that education in a regular classroom setting cannot be achieved satisfactorily. Eliminate D because it conflicts with the law for students who can function in a regular classroom setting. Choice A is the correct response.

47. **B** This question deals with **ethical, legal, and professional standards.** Thus, its primary focus is Competency 015: *The teacher understands requirements, expectations, and constraints associated with teaching in Texas, and can apply this understanding in a variety of contexts.* This is a priority-setting question—you must select the answer choice that is most important for Ms. Curl to do. Eliminate C as inappropriate, since asking the special education teacher to go on the field trip is likely to be an imposition for that teacher. According to IDEA, each student with disabilities must have an Individualized Education Program (IEP) designed to meet his or her unique individual needs. As Laura's teacher, Ms. Curl is required by law to comply with Laura's IEP. Eliminate A and D because these are measures Ms. Curl could possibly take, but they may be inappropriate or even illegal depending on Laura's unique individual needs as specified in her IEP. Thus, in determining and addressing Laura's educational needs pertaining to the field trip, it is *most* important that Ms. Curl respond appropriately (and in compliance with Laura's IEP) to Laura's unique individual needs. Choice B is the correct response.

48. **A** This question deals with **ethical, legal, and professional standards.** Thus, its primary focus is Competency 015: *The teacher understands requirements, expectations, and constraints associated with teaching in Texas, and can apply this understanding in a variety of contexts.* Eliminate C and D because the teacher has no legal obligation to inform parents about TAAS objectives. Eliminate B because teachers are legally obligated to obtain written permission from all parents and guardians of their students, not just from parents or guardians of the special education students. Choice A is the correct response.

49. **A** This question deals with **students' self-esteem.** Thus, its primary focus is Competency 002: *The teacher considers environmental factors that may affect learning in designing a supportive and responsive classroom community that promotes all students' learning and self-esteem.* Eliminate B because research indicates that for young adolescents, peer influence replaces adult influence. Eliminate C because teacher expectations affect student self-

concept and motivation, which, in turn, affect academic achievement. Eliminate D because anxiety in small doses can improve academic achievement, as long as students are not held to an unrealistic level of expectation. Ms. Cartwright is likely to be aware of what is known as the "self-fulfilling prophecy," which predicts that, with time, a student's behavior and achievement will conform more closely to the expectations the teacher has for that student. Choice A is the correct response.

50. **B**   This question relates to environmental factors that may affect **students' self-esteem** and thus affect learning. Therefore, its primary focus is Competency 002: *The teacher considers environmental factors that may affect learning in designing a supportive and responsive classroom community that promotes all students' learning and self-esteem.* According to research, most schools in the United States reflect middle-class values; therefore, students from the lower socioeconomic class are frequently disadvantaged because their culture may promote behavior and values that are inconsistent with the middle-class values at school. It is important for Ms. Cartwright to understand this, so that she can create an environment in which all her students feel safe, accepted, and capable of achieving. Choice B is the correct response.

51. **B**   This question deals with an environmental factor (socioeconomic status) that affects students' learning, which falls under **students' self-esteem.** Thus, its primary focus is Competency 002: *The teacher considers environmental factors that may affect learning in designing a supportive and responsive classroom community that promotes all students' learning and self-esteem.* According to research, lower-socioeconomic-class parents are more likely to use commands in conversing with their children, whereas middle-class parents are more likely to use expressive language. Children who are accustomed to responding to commands may not be as well prepared to respond to the language of middle-class teachers, which is typically expressive. Choice B is the correct response.

52. **A**   This question deals with **communication.** Thus, its primary focus is Competency 007: *The teacher uses effective verbal, nonverbal, and media communication techniques to shape the classroom into a community of learners engaged in active inquiry, collaborative exploration, and supportive interactions.* Eliminate B because teachers should provide appropriate and nonthreatening opportunities for all students to be involved in the lesson, even those who sometimes are reluctant to do so. Eliminate C because an effective method of calling on students is to use a random process, so that all participate and are kept attentive during the teaching act. Eliminate D because allowing volunteers to dominate the lesson will establish a classroom climate where some students will be likely to assume a passive role during classroom discourse; further, the teacher will not be able to adequately assess whether those not participating are learning. Ms. Cartwright's strategy is

limited because students who don't volunteer will miss the opportunity to actively participate in the lesson. Choice A is the correct response.

53. **A** This question deals with both **diversity** (How do students from different socioeconomic levels differ?) and an environmental factor (socioeconomic status) that influences learning (Ms. Cartwright wants to increase the achievement of the students), which is related to **students' self-esteem.** Glancing at the answer choices, you can see that you are going to have to know what works best with lower-socioeconomic-status students in order to decide among the answer choices—so you need to know characteristics of the learner. Thus, the primary focus of this question is Competency 003: *The teacher appreciates human diversity, recognizing how diversity in the classroom and the community may affect learning and creating a classroom environment in which both the diversity of groups and the uniqueness of individuals are recognized and celebrated.* Ms. Cartwright should consider immediate rewards (Choice A). Slavin explains that children from lower-socioeconomic-status backgrounds are less likely to respond to delayed reinforcement (more adapted to immediate gratification), less willing to compete (Eliminate C), and more oriented toward cooperation with other children (Eliminate B and D) and individualized contact with the teacher than middle-class students. Choice A is the correct response.

54. **C** This question deals with both **diversity** (How do students from different socioeconomic levels differ?) and an environmental factor (socioeconomic status) that influences learning (Ms. Cartwright wants to increase the achievement of the students), which relates to **students' self-esteem.** Glancing at the answer choices, you can see that they deal with the performance of the lower-socioeconomic-status students. Thus, you will need to know how socioeconomic status affects learning. Thus, the primary focus of this question is Competency 002: *The teacher considers environmental factors that may affect learning in designing a supportive and responsive classroom community that promotes all students' learning and self-esteem.* Eliminate A, B, and D because these responses are inconsistent with research findings indicating that, on average, children from lower-socioeconomic-class backgrounds are less likely to achieve as well in school as children from middle-class backgrounds. Regarding the difficulties for children from lower-socioeconomic-class backgrounds, Slavin explains that these children (on average) are less likely to be as well prepared when entering school and their upbringings emphasize behaviors and values different from those (such as individuality and future time orientation) expected of them in schools. Further, researchers have found that middle-class teachers often have low expectations for low-socioeconomic-class students, which is likely to influence those students' perception of their own worth and potential and, in turn, may result in low achievement for

these students. Slavin makes the point that teachers should be aware that children from other than mainstream, middle-class backgrounds are often at a disadvantage in the typical school environment, and the teachers should make efforts to recognize the potential of these students to achieve. Choice C is the correct response.

55. **A**   This question deals with both **assessment** (Which assessment approach does the curriculum supervisor recommend?) and **motivation** (The assessment approach should motivate students to earn better grades). Glancing at the answer choices, you can see that they mostly deal with **assessment,** so the primary focus of this question is Competency 010: *The teacher uses processes of informal and formal assessment to understand individual learners, monitor instructional effectiveness, and shape instruction.* Eliminate B and D because these approaches would be likely to have a negative impact on how the students think about themselves. Eliminate C because drill and practice on basic skills is likely to result in increased lack of interest and enthusiasm on the part of the students. Ms. Cartwright should consider grading based on improvement for a short period. This is likely to increase motivation and interest by making it possible for all students, regardless of ability, to succeed. Choice A is the correct response.

56. **A**   This question deals with **planning.** Thus, its primary focus is Competency 006: *The teacher uses planning processes to design outcome-oriented learning experiences that foster understanding and encourage self-directed thinking and learning in both individual and collaborative settings.* Task analysis requires the teacher to analyze a task to determine the exact steps a student must go through to successfully complete it. Eliminate B because using task analysis is a part of planning effective objectives, since it allows the teacher to determine if a lesson objective is at an appropriate level of difficulty; however, additional criteria must be considered as well (for instance, the type of learning desired— cognitive, affective, psychomotor). Eliminate C and D because task analysis is something the teacher does, not the students. The benefit of performing a task analysis for each lesson is that the teacher will be able to determine the prerequisite skills needed in order that students can master more complex skills. Choice A is the correct response.

57. **D**   This question deals with **diversity.** Thus, its primary focus is Competency 003: *The teacher appreciates human diversity, recognizing how diversity in the classroom and the community may affect learning and creating a classroom environment in which both the diversity of groups and the uniqueness of individuals are recognized and celebrated.* Creating an environment that respects and confirms the dignity of students as human beings is essential in meeting the needs of diverse students. As when dealing with other inappropriate behavior, teachers should

respond immediately to expressions of racism (Roman I). To avoid stereotypical expectations, teachers should evaluate their views about cultural diversity (Roman II). Acknowledging and building on cultural differences allow teachers to plan accordingly (Roman III). Literature that validates the struggle to develop a bicultural identity celebrates and values individual differences and similarities (Roman IV). Choice D is the correct response.

58. **A** This question deals with **diversity.** Thus, its primary focus is Competency 003: *The teacher appreciates human diversity, recognizing how diversity in the classroom and the community may affect learning and creating a classroom environment in which both the diversity of groups and the uniqueness of individuals are recognized and celebrated.* Eliminate B because failure to discuss ethnic issues openly may allow conflicts between ethnic groups to develop, so probably would not contribute to group harmony. Eliminate C and D because competitive games or ability groups might result in group disharmony. Ms. Cartwright should use one-to-one activities, such as tutoring, because they allow students to get to know each other and to cooperate with one another and, thus, contribute to harmonious relations among the students. Choice A is the correct response.

59. **C** This question deals with **diversity.** Thus, its primary focus is Competency 003: *The teacher appreciates human diversity, recognizing how diversity in the classroom and the community may affect learning and creating a classroom environment in which both the diversity of groups and the uniqueness of individuals are recognized and celebrated.* Eliminate A because students may pursue interests traditionally associated with their gender to avoid being ridiculed by their classmates. Eliminate B because it promotes sex-role stereotyping. Eliminate D because gender differences are likely to increase when boys and girls are grouped separately. Teachers should avoid differential treatment of boys and girls in class by treating male and female students similarly, whenever appropriate. Choice C is the correct response.

60. **B** This question deals with **ethical, legal, and professional standards.** Thus, its primary focus is Competency 015: *The teacher understands requirements, expectations, and constraints associated with teaching in Texas, and can apply this understanding in a variety of contexts.* It is appropriate for Ms. Cartwright to make sure she has a clear understanding of the laws applying to the students with special needs who come to her classroom. Eliminate A, C, and D because these measures are not mandated in PL 94-142. Public Law 94-142, the Education for All Handicapped Children Act of 1975, subsequently revised and now known as the Individuals with Disabilities Education Act (IDEA), obligates each state to provide free and appropriate public education for all children. Choice B is the correct response.

61. **D** This question deals with **instructional strategies.** Thus, its primary focus is Competency 008: *The teacher uses a variety of instructional strategies and roles to facilitate learning and to help students become independent thinkers and problem solvers who use higher-order thinking in the classroom and the real world.* This is a priority-setting question—you must select the *most* likely answer choice. Eliminate A, B, and C because these may occur, but would not necessarily result from inquiry training, discovery learning, and cooperative learning. Mr. Manzano's plans will be likely to help foster independent learning, since the teaching strategies he has decided to use will give the students more responsibility for their own learning and each other's learning. Choice D is the correct response.

62. **C** This question deals with **instructional strategies.** Thus, its primary focus is Competency 008: *The teacher uses a variety of instructional strategies and roles to facilitate learning and to help students become independent thinkers and problem solvers who use higher-order thinking in the classroom and the real world.* The stimulus tells us that Mr. Manzano wants to use inquiry and discovery learning with cooperative learning groups to foster higher-order thinking and enhance problem-solving skills. Eliminate A because it is teacher-directed with students as passive learners. Eliminate B because the students who are listening are passive participants. Eliminate D because worksheets address low-level cognitive objectives (that is, facts, knowledge). Mr. Manzano is likely to know that allowing the students to discover properties of magnets in a cooperative group setting will help them to develop a deeper understanding of the scientific principles involved. Choice C is the correct response.

63. **C** This question deals with **instructional strategies.** Thus, its primary focus is Competency 008: *The teacher uses a variety of instructional strategies and roles to facilitate learning and to help students become independent thinkers and problem solvers who use higher-order thinking in the classroom and the real world.* This is a priority-setting question—you must select the *least* desirable answer choice. Choices A, B, and D are consistent with good teaching practices that encourage self-directed thinking and learning. Mr. Manzano should be aware that establishing a teacher-centered classroom environment would be likely to result in less risk taking and higher-level thinking and discourage active inquiry. Choice C is the correct response.

64. **D** This question assesses Competency 008: *The teacher uses a variety of instructional strategies and roles to facilitate learning and to help students become independent thinkers and problem solvers who use higher-order thinking in the classroom and the real world.* Critical thinking is the mental process of acquiring information, then evaluating it to reach a logical conclusion. To promote critical thinking in his classroom Mr. Manzano should

teach for deeper understanding of content because thinking critically and deeper understanding of content are inseparable (Roman I); encourage students to discuss their problem solutions with each other because this will help them clarify their thinking (Roman II); requiring students to justify the reasoning behind their conclusions because this will force students to critically analyze their and each other's thinking (Roman III); and helping students develop metacognitive strategies because when students receive instruction and guidance in how to become aware of their own thinking processes (metacognition), they become better critical thinkers. Choice D is the correct response.

65. **D** This question deals with grouping practices, which come under **instructional strategies.** Thus, the primary focus of this question is Competency 008: *The teacher uses a variety of instructional strategies and roles to facilitate learning and to help students become independent thinkers and problem solvers who use higher-order thinking in the classroom and the real world.* This is a priority-setting question—you must select the best answer choice. Eliminate A and B because ability grouping may negatively affect the attitudes, achievement, and opportunities of low-ability students. Eliminate C because it disagrees with research indicating that students benefit from working in small groups. Some evidence suggests that high-ability learners may gain from ability grouping, but removing them from interaction with their peers may be problematic. Most authorities agree that heterogeneous grouping benefits all students. This does not mean that high-ability students should have to learn and work at the same pace as lower-ability students, nor does it mean that they should not be given opportunities to work alone or cooperatively with other high achievers. Choice D is the correct response.

66. **A** This question deals with **planning.** Thus, its primary focus is Competency 006: *The teacher uses planning processes to design outcome-oriented learning experiences that foster understanding and encourage self-directed thinking and learning in both individual and collaborative settings.* This is a priority-setting question—you must select Mr. Manzano's *primary* purpose. The stimulus tells us that Mr. Manzano wants to foster critical thinking and enhance problem-solving skills. Eliminate B because this may occur, but it is probably not Mr. Manzano's primary purpose, since basic skills involve lower-level thinking. Eliminate C because there are many correct solutions for the assignment. Eliminate D because it is not supported by the stimulus—mathematics is not being applied in the real world. The stimulus tells us that Mr. Manzano wants to foster critical thinking and enhance problem-solving skills. In designing instruction, teachers should choose lessons and activities that help students achieve an in-depth understanding of the content material. Posing open-ended assignments that have many correct solutions requires students to apply their reasoning powers in addition to using their knowledge of basic skills.

Mr. Manzano knows that allowing the students to figure out for themselves what will work for this problem will help them to develop a deeper understanding of the mathematical principles involved. Choice A is the correct response.

67. **B** This question deals with **planning.** Thus, its primary focus is Competency 006: *The teacher uses planning processes to design outcome-oriented learning experiences that foster understanding and encourage self-directed thinking and learning in both individual and collaborative settings.* Eliminate C since drill and practice should be deemphasized in the math classroom. Eliminate D because reliance on the textbook can stifle the teacher's interactions with the students. Eliminate A because Mr. Manzano may do that, but it is most important that he make sure the Texas Essential Knowledge and Skills (TEKS)—upon which the TAAS is based—are included in his curriculum. Choice B is the correct response.

68. **D** This question deals with **ethical, legal, and professional standards.** Thus, its primary focus is Competency 015: *The teacher understands requirements, expectations, and constraints associated with teaching in Texas, and can apply this understanding in a variety of contexts.* The comprehensive special education elements assigned by law to be administered by the Texas Education Agency (TEA) include an admissions, review, and dismissal (ARD) committee that designs the Individualized Education Program (IEP) for the disabled student. The Individuals with Disabilities Education Act Amendments of 1997 specify that the ARD committees must include the parents (or guardians) of the child, at least one regular education teacher of the child (provided the child is participating in a regular education classroom), at least one special education teacher of the child, a representative of the school who is qualified to provide or supervise the provision of special services (which may be the principal), someone who can interpret evaluation results, and other individuals who may be of help in designing an Individualized Education Program (IEP) for the student. Choice D is the correct response.

69. **A** This question deals with **ethical, legal, and professional standards.** Thus, its primary focus is Competency 015: *The teacher understands requirements, expectations, and constraints associated with teaching in Texas, and can apply this understanding in a variety of contexts.* Under the Individuals with Disabilities Education Act and Section 504 of the Rehabilitation Act of 1973, many types of "supplementary aids and services," such as extended time for test taking, computer access, homework monitoring, and many other services, are available for special education students; however, available medical services are for "diagnostic and evaluative purposes only," so payment for prescription drugs would not be an included service. Choice A is the correct response.

70. **D** This question deals with **professionalism.** Thus, its primary focus is Competency 012: *The teacher is a reflective practitioner who knows how to promote his or her own professional growth and can work cooperatively with other professionals in the system to create a school culture that enhances learning and encourages positive change.* Eliminate A and C because the stimulus provides no reason to assume that Mr. Manzano wants to be a risk taker or innovator or to demonstrate that he has clearly defined goals by participating in the inservice. Eliminate B because it is not supported by the stimulus—there is no indication Mr. Manzano will participate in collaborative decision making during the inservice. Mr. Manzano's concern about having Harriet in his class precipitated his decision to participate in staff development, so his likely purpose was to enhance his own professional skills and knowledge regarding teaching special education students. Mr. Manzano is aware of his professional obligation to seek out opportunities to grow professionally. Choice D is the correct response.

71. **B** This question deals with **ethical, legal, and professional standards.** Thus, its primary focus is Competency 015: *The teacher understands requirements, expectations, and constraints associated with teaching in Texas, and can apply this understanding in a variety of contexts.* Accommodations that teachers may make for disabled students include preferential seating, modification of assignments and/or tests, and use of multisensory techniques and demonstrations. According to the Americans with Disabilities Act of 1994, disabled students should not be singled out as disabled in front of their classmates. Choice B is the correct response.

72. **D** This question deals with **ethical, legal, and professional standards.** Thus, its primary focus is Competency 015: *The teacher understands requirements, expectations, and constraints associated with teaching in Texas, and can apply this understanding in a variety of contexts.* The Individuals with Disabilities Education Act Amendments of 1997 (IDEA 97) has strengthened the rights of parents who have a child with a disability in school. With regard to ARD committee meetings, parents have the right to written notice of scheduled meetings at least five school days before the meeting (Roman I), the right to bring an attorney to the meeting (Roman II), the right to have an interpreter if the parents' primary language is other than English (Roman III), and the right to audiotape-record the meeting as long as all attending are informed about it (Roman IV). Choice D is the correct response.

73. **C** This question deals with wait time, which comes under **communication.** Thus, its primary focus is Competency 007: *The teacher uses effective verbal, nonverbal, and media communication techniques to shape the classroom into a community of learners engaged in active inquiry, collaborative exploration, and supportive interactions.* Eliminate A, B, and D

because they disagree with the opinions of experts that teachers should wait for students to respond. Mr. Manzano is aware that exceptional students add to the diversity of the classroom. He knows that waiting for Harriet to respond sends a message of expectation and acceptance of Harriet to the class. Choice C is the correct response.

74. **A** This question deals with **classroom management.** Thus, its primary focus is Competency 011: *The teacher structures and manages the learning environment to maintain a classroom climate that promotes the lifelong pursuit of learning and encourages cooperation, leadership, and mutual respect.* Eliminate B and C, as they disagree with the opinion of experts that recommend time-out as appropriate. Eliminate D because no rewards are used. Mr. Manzano is aware that time out may be especially effective for students whose misbehavior is motivated by desire for attention from one's peers. Choice A is the correct response.

75. **A** This question deals with **classroom management.** Thus, its primary focus is Competency 011: *The teacher structures and manages the learning environment to maintain a classroom climate that promotes the lifelong pursuit of learning and encourages cooperation, leadership, and mutual respect.* This is a priority-setting question—you must select the *best* strategy. Choices B, C, and D may work, but Mr. Manzano should know that the *best* way to prevent off-task behavior is to teach lessons that are so interesting and engaging to students that they will pay attention and not get off-task. Choice A is the correct response.

76. **D** This question assesses Competency 013: *The teacher knows how to foster strong school-home relationships that support student achievement of desired learning outcomes.* Successful parent-teacher conferences can be the key that enhances the student's growth and promotes learning. Eliminate A and C because teachers should avoid diagnosing students to parents. Eliminate B because Mr. Manzano should not discuss the other students' performance with Jimmy's father. Mr. Manzano needs to explain his grading policy and show samples of incomplete work. He needs to emphasize that he expects students to be responsible and turn in work that is complete. Choice D is the correct response.

77. **D** This question deals with **motivation.** Thus, its primary focus is Competency 005: *The teacher understands how motivation affects group and individual behavior and learning and can apply this understanding to promote student learning.* In heterogeneously grouped classes, Ms. Voigtel must be able to provide instruction for students with a wide range of interests. The students should be provided with some options with regard to interests and types of activities. She can increase motivation to learn by selecting content that is relevant to the students' lives (Roman I), encouraging students to assist in planning instructional activities (Roman II),

making sure students know what to do and how to do it (Roman III), and using simulations and role playing (Roman IV). Choice D is the correct response.

78. **B** This question deals with **classroom management.** Thus, its primary focus is Competency 011: *The teacher structures and manages the learning environment to maintain a classroom climate that promotes the lifelong pursuit of learning and encourages cooperation, leadership, and mutual respect.* This question deals with **classroom management.** Eliminate A because it relates to **professionalism** (Competency 012). Eliminate C because it relates to **communication** (Competency 007). Eliminate D because it relates to **motivation** (Competency 005). Ms. Voigtel probably knows that providing an opportunity for the students to recognize the problem and suggest solutions is likely to promote ownership in a smoothly functioning learning community (Competency 011). Choice B is the correct response.

79. **A** This question deals with **classroom management.** Thus, its primary focus is Competency 011: *The teacher structures and manages the learning environment to maintain a classroom climate that promotes the lifelong pursuit of learning and encourages cooperation, leadership, and mutual respect.* Eliminate B, C, and D because they are punitive and threatening approaches to discipline and should not be Ms. Voigtel's main focus. While reviewing her plan, Ms. Voigtel realizes that she spent more time focusing on the number of consequences of inappropriate behavior than on evaluating the management plan for consistency and fairness. Usually when students view a discipline management plan as fair and is implemented consistently, mutual respect is the resulting behavior. Choice A is the correct response.

80. **B** This question deals with **assessment.** Thus, its primary focus is Competency 010: *The teacher uses processes of informal and formal assessment to understand individual learners, monitor instructional effectiveness, and shape instruction.* This is a priority-setting question; you must decide which of the answer choices is *most* appropriate. Eliminate A and C because these tests usually do not provide sufficient information about the students' abilities for diagnostic purposes. Eliminate D because norm-referenced tests may not provide diagnostic information. Diagnostic tests provide teachers with specific information about students' abilities relative to subject matter subskills. They are effective tools for assessing students' strengths and weaknesses. Choice B is the correct response.

81. **B** This question deals with **motivation.** Thus, its primary focus is Competency 005: *The teacher understands how motivation affects group and individual behavior and learning and can apply this understanding to promote student learning.* This is a priority-setting question—you must determine what Ms. Voigtel should do

first. Students who are failing need to experience some degree of success. Eliminate A because a competitive reward schedule may have a negative effect on the students who are doing poorly—they may give up. Eliminate C and D because scheduled praise will likely be viewed as insincere by the students. Ms. Voigtel should design activities that will enable students to receive immediate feedback. There is a positive correlation between the motivation to learn and academic achievement when feedback immediately follows student performance. Choice B is the correct response.

82. **B** This question deals with **instructional strategies.** Thus, its primary focus is Competency 008: *The teacher uses a variety of instructional strategies and roles to facilitate learning and to help students become independent thinkers and problem solvers who use higher-order thinking in the classroom and the real world.* Eliminate A and C because appointed leaders, flexible membership, improvement points, and tangible rewards may be incorporated into cooperative learning activities, but none of these are "essential" components. Eliminate D because most experts on cooperative learning recommend heterogeneous (mixed-ability) grouping, not ability grouping. Effective cooperative learning activities should be designed to ensure that each member of the groups is accountable for his or her learning (individual accountability) as well as contributing to the success of the group (group assessment). Therefore, Ms. Voigtel must design cooperative learning activities with both components in mind to make sure that not just the higher achievers are motivated to perform well. Choice B is the correct response.

83. **A** This question deals with **instructional strategies.** Thus, its primary focus is Competency 008: *The teacher uses a variety of instructional strategies and roles to facilitate learning and to help students become independent thinkers and problem solvers who use higher-order thinking in the classroom and the real world.* This is a priority-setting question—you must select the *best* answer choice. Eliminate C because it relates to Competency 011 **(classroom management).** Eliminate B and D because they focus on the learning task and not the learner—they are not learner-centered. Ms. Voigtel takes account of factors relevant to instructional planning, such as the varied characteristics of the learners in her classrooms. She recognizes the importance of adapting instruction to meet the needs of the more able learners, as well as the needs of the less able learners. Choice A is the correct response.

84. **D** This question deals with **diversity.** Thus, its primary focus is Competency 003: *The teacher appreciates human diversity, recognizing how diversity in the classroom and the community may affect learning and creating a classroom environment in which both the diversity of groups and the uniqueness of individuals are recognized and celebrated.* Eliminate B and C because Jonathan is well behaved—not likely to have an attention

deficit disorder (ADD) or be emotionally disturbed. Eliminate A because severely mentally retarded children usually are not placed in the regular classroom. Children who have a learning disability but are not emotionally disturbed or have ADD tend to be quiet and well behaved. Choice D is the correct response.

85. **B** This question deals with **school-home relationships.** Thus, its primary focus is Competency 013: *The teacher knows how to foster strong school-home relationships that support student achievement of desired learning outcomes.* This is a priority-setting question—you must select which answer choice would have *most* improved the conference. Eliminate A, C, and D because Ms. Voigtel's main problem was that she talked too much and did not get to hear much from Dekolvin's parents. Frequently, parents are intimidated by parent-teacher conferences; often, they are concerned that they may say something that is embarrassing or will cause harm to their child. Therefore, they will accept one-way communication unless the teacher makes an effort to involve them in the discussion. Choice B is the correct response.

86. **B** This question deals with **school-home relationships.** Thus, its primary focus is Competency 013: *The teacher knows how to foster strong school-home relationships that support student achievement of desired learning outcomes.* Eliminate A because teachers should avoid diagnosing students to parents. Eliminate C and D because they are too abrupt. Ms. Voigtel recognizes the importance of maintaining ongoing parent-teacher communication and understands strategies for promoting effective communication. Listening to the concerns of Leslie's father and showing that she takes them seriously by acting on them in an appropriate manner will foster positive school-home relations. Choice B is the correct response.

87. **C** This question deals with **professionalism.** Thus, its primary focus is Competency 012: *The teacher is a reflective practitioner who knows how to promote his or her own professional growth and can work cooperatively with other professionals in the system to create a school culture that enhances learning and encourages positive change.* This question deals with **professionalism.** Eliminate A because it relates to **planning** (Competency 006). Eliminate B because it relates to **developmentally appropriate instruction** (Competency 001). Eliminate D because it relates to **ethical, legal, and professional standards** (Competency 15). Ms. Voigtel should understand that she is a member of a learning community and should know how to work effectively with *all* members of that community (Competency 012). Choice C is the correct response.

88. **B** This question deals with **planning.** Thus, its primary focus is Competency 006: *The teacher uses planning processes to design outcome-oriented learning experiences that foster understanding*

*and encourage self-directed thinking and learning in both
individual and collaborative settings.* Eliminate Roman II because
most students benefit more from working in collaboration with
others. Eliminate C. Eliminate Roman III because centers should
involve "hands-on" activities, not worksheets (a "poor practice").
Eliminate A and D. Centers should meet the varied characteristics
of the students (Roman I) and students should not have to get up to
go get materials once they are working in a center (Roman IV).
Choice B is the correct response.

89. **C** This question deals with **ethical, legal, and professional
standards.** Thus, its primary focus is Competency 015: *The teacher
understands requirements, expectations, and constraints
associated with teaching in Texas, and can apply this
understanding in a variety of contexts.* According to Texas Family
Code 261.101, Ms. Voigtel must report suspected child abuse to
appropriate legal authorities within 48 hours (eliminate D) of first
suspecting the abuse. She should not discuss her suspicions with
Billy's parents (eliminate A) or his friends (eliminate B). Knowing
failure to report is a Class B misdemeanor. Choice C is the correct
response.

90. **D** This question deals with cooperative learning, which comes under
instructional strategies, so, at first, you will think this question
relates to Competency 008. However, when you read the answer
choices, you see that A, B, and C *all* relate to instructional strategies
and *all* would be appropriate measures for Ms. Voigtel to take. How
can this be? It is not a priority-setting question, so you are not asked
to decide which is the *best* answer choice. This dilemma tells you
that you need to reread the question and read *all* the answer choices
carefully. This question is an example of what you were warned
about at the end of Chapter 4—that you may not always be able to
identify the competency correctly when you first read the question;
further, sometimes the question may use language or wording that
causes you to misidentify the competency. You need to be prepared
to shift gears and think through the problem when (or if) this
occurs. When you read D, you should recognize that it is consistent
with effective **classroom management** practices. Thus, the primary
focus of this question is actually Competency 011: *The teacher
structures and manages the learning environment to maintain a
classroom climate that promotes the lifelong pursuit of learning
and encourages cooperation, leadership, and mutual respect.* As an
experienced teacher, Ms. Harper should be aware that according to
research, effective classroom managers are initially involved with
the whole class; have clear, specific plans for introducing rules and
procedures; use simple, enjoyable tasks; and respond immediately to
stop any misbehavior. Therefore, Ms. Voigtel should not break
students into groups on the first day. Choice D is the correct
response.

CHAPTER 6

A DIAGNOSTIC SECONDARY PROFESSIONAL DEVELOPMENT TEST

Diagnostic Test Directions

The test consists of 90 multiple-choice questions with four answer choices. Read each question carefully and choose the ONE best answer. Mark your answer on the answer sheet (see page 423) beside the number that matches the question number. Completely fill in the space that has the same letter as the answer you have selected.

Sample Question

1. Austin is the capital of what state?
    A. Arkansas
    B. California
    C. Tennessee
    D. Texas

Austin is the capital of Texas. Choice D is the correct response. You would mark your answer beside question number 1 on the answer sheet and you would fill in the space corresponding to the letter D as follows:

1. Ⓐ Ⓑ Ⓒ ●

Mark only one answer for each question. If you change an answer, completely erase the old answer before marking the new one. You should answer all the questions since *you are not penalized for a wrong answer.*

You will have approximately five hours to complete the test. You may go back and forth through the test as you desire. When you have completed the test, turn to the answer key and answer explanations at the end of the test to check your answers.

SET 1 BEGINS HERE

> Ms. Solomon is a first-year history teacher at Fairview High School, located in a primarily low-to-middle-socioeconomic-class town with a population of 30,000. The ethnic demographics of Fairview show that 75 percent of the student body is Anglo-American, 20 percent African-American, and 5 percent Hispanic-American. All the history classes are heterogeneously grouped according to academic ability.

1. Ms. Solomon has observed a difference in the achievement of the low-socioeconomic-class students and the middle-class students. Her observation is related to the finding of studies that show that students from low socioeconomic backgrounds usually:

   A. do better in school than children from middle-class backgrounds.
   B. do about as well as children from middle-class backgrounds.
   C. do more poorly in school than children from middle-class backgrounds.
   D. enter school behind children from middle-class backgrounds but eventually close the gap in high school.

2. Since she is a first-year teacher, Ms. Solomon has been assigned an experienced, successful teacher, Mr. Hernandez, as a mentor. Ms. Solomon asks Mr. Hernandez for advice on how to increase the achievement of the students from low socioeconomic backgrounds. Mr. Hernandez is likely to advise her to consider:

   A. independent projects.
   B. competitive reward structures.
   C. individual seat work.
   D. immediate rewards.

3. Mr. Hernandez also suggests that Ms. Solomon initiate a task analysis in planning the next lesson. An advantage of using this process is:

   A. gaining increased awareness of the subskills students need for mastering more complex skills.
   B. allowing students to make important decisions about what they should and should not attend to.
   C. seeing firsthand the importance of planning effective objectives.
   D. encouraging students to work and learn independently.

4. Ms. Solomon tells Mr. Hernandez she is also concerned about the students' lack of interest and enthusiasm in history class. Which of the following would Mr. Hernandez most likely recommend as a means of assessment to motivate Ms. Solomon's students toward earning better grades in history?

   A. reducing the number of tests given
   B. grading on the basis of improvement for a short period
   C. giving feedback several weeks after the test is taken
   D. using a lower standard for grading

5. Mr. Hernandez notes during his observation of Ms. Solomon's class that she uses questioning strategies in which she calls only on students who raise their hands to respond. He is likely to explain to Ms. Solomon that this method of recognizing students for responses is:

   A. positive, because it avoids having to call on shy students who do not know the answer and may experience embarrassment in front of the whole class.
   B. more effective than calling on students using a random process.
   C. limited, because students who don't volunteer may miss an opportunity to be actively engaged in the lesson.
   D. positive, because volunteers give a higher proportion of correct responses from which all may benefit.

Mr. Hernandez has been working with at-risk students for the past five years. Ms. Solomon is aware that many of her students can be classified as at-risk students—slower learners who generally fall between regular and special education—who typically function below grade level. Mr. Hernandez tells Ms. Solomon that teacher expectations are an important factor when working with at-risk students.

6. Which of the following is likely to be effective for communicating high expectations to at-risk students?

   I. accepting and praising all work
   II. encouraging or requiring an oral response to questions
   III. allowing sufficient wait time for student answers
   IV. expressing expectations directly

   A. I, II, and IV only
   B. II and III only
   C. III and IV only
   D. II, III, and IV only

7. Mr. Hernandez tells Ms. Solomon that most at-risk students would benefit from an instructional approach that considers their learning styles. Learning style is:

   A. an indication of one's intelligence.
   B. unchangeable.
   C. different from individual to individual.
   D. strictly biological.

Ms. Solomon assumes that all students who function below grade level are served by special education. She consults Mr. Hernandez about these slower learners who are in regular education but who seem to have "fallen between the cracks" when it comes to special services.

8. Since Mr. Hernandez is more experienced in working with slower learners, he will likely know which of the following?

    I.   Slower learners are classified as "learning disabled" and therefore qualify for special education under IDEA.
    II. Special education classes would better serve slower learners.
    III. Most slower learners do not meet the definition of "child with a disability" under IDEA.
    IV. The needs of slower learners could possibly be addressed under Section 504 of the Rehabilitation Act of 1973.

    A. I and II only
    B. I, II, and III only
    C. III only
    D. III and IV only

9. A significant discrepancy between learning ability and academic achievement is *best* described as:

    A. mental retardation.
    B. a learning disability.
    C. emotionally disturbed.
    D. autism.

Ms. Solomon tells Mr. Hernandez that some ethnic clashes on campus have spilled over into her classroom, impacting the classroom climate in a negative manner.

10. Mr. Hernandez is likely to recommend which of the following practices to improve Ms. Solomon's classroom climate?

    A. Avoid discussing racial or ethnic relations with the class.
    B. Use one-on-one activities such as tutoring.
    C. Use competitive games and contests.
    D. Establish between-class ability groups in selected subjects.

11. Ms. Solomon has convinced the school's campus council to approach the principal about promoting multiculturalism in the school. A practice that would *not* be consistent with the goals of multicultural education is one:

    A. emphasizing the establishment of special pull-out programs to serve limited English proficiency students.
    B. encouraging teachers to evaluate their views about cultural diversity.
    C. directly confronting racism.
    D. using a variety of teaching methods rather than concentrating on those that work best for most students.

12. Ms. Solomon is considering implementing a more culturally diverse approach to the study of history in her class. Ms. Solomon and Mr. Hernandez are likely to agree that an effective *first* step to enhance teaching while appreciating cultural diversity would be which of the following?

   A. She should persuade the principal to hold a campus-wide diversity awareness week.

   B. She should spend some time in self-reflection to examine her own attitudes and beliefs about other cultural groups.

   C. She should examine the books she is currently using for bias and stereotyping of cultural groups.

   D. She should administer an interest inventory to her students to aid in her selection of appropriate supplementary reading material.

13. Ms. Solomon recognizes that appreciation of diversity also involves attention to gender differences in the classroom. With regard to this issue, it is most important that Ms. Solomon:

   A. make allowances for gender differences by giving students freedom to pursue their own interests.

   B. treat males and females similarly whenever appropriate.

   C. use more masculine-oriented modeling to increase females' assertiveness.

   D. have more activities where males and female students are grouped separately so that female students do not feel pressured.

SET 1 ENDS HERE

SET 2 BEGINS HERE

During inservice training before the first day of classes, Ms. Lazarine, an eighth-grade health teacher, attends a cooperative learning workshop. She is excited about implementing cooperative learning strategies in her classroom during the school year and is busy planning group activities that she can use with her students.

14. Which of the following is an essential component of cooperative learning that Ms. Lazarine is likely to have learned in the inservice workshop?

   A. Using cooperative learning activities frees the teacher from monitoring student work.
   B. When using cooperative learning activities, students' rewards should be interdependently determined.
   C. Cooperative learning activities free the teacher from having to use strict grading policies.
   D. When using cooperative learning, group size should not be predetermined.

15. Another essential component of cooperative learning Ms. Lazarine should include is:

   A. appointed team leaders.
   B. individual accountability.
   C. tangible rewards.
   D. baseline scores.

16. Ms. Lazarine should also be aware that two common problems associated with cooperative learning are:

   I.   inadequate teacher training
   II. inadequate student training
   III. lack of student achievement
   IV. too much noise in the classroom

   A. I and II only
   B. I and IV only
   C. II and III only
   D. II and IV only

17. In the cooperate learning workshop she attended, Ms. Lazarine likely learned that a major motivational reason cooperative learning produces positive instructional results is because of:

   A. the cooperative incentive structure.
   B. the mode's inherent appeal to teachers.
   C. the competitive task structure.
   D. the homogeneous nature of the groups.

18. Research regarding the use of cooperative learning with gifted students says that:

   A. it is ineffective, and should not be used with gifted students in any setting.
   B. its effectiveness for gifted students has been challenged, although its benefits for low-achieving students is recognized.
   C. it is highly effective for the remainder of the class, and gifted students should be put in charge of groups.
   D. it is highly effective, and should be the exclusive mode of learning in a mixed class of gifted and regular students.

Ms. Lazarine is a member of an instructional team that meets on a regular basis. The team members tell Ms. Lazarine that when they use cooperative learning activities, students are grouped heterogeneously; however, when reviewing basic skills, they incorporate ability grouping for their regular students and assign independent activities for the high-achieving students.

19. This process is an example of:

   A. adapting instruction to the characteristics of the learner.
   B. matching teaching strategies to the type of learning task.
   C. using effective classroom management.
   D. matching student characteristics to the learning objective.

20. In one of the meetings of the instructional team, Ms. Lazarine asks for advice about the appropriate use of media. The more experienced members of the team will likely tell Ms. Lazarine that it is effective to:

   I.   use media to fill in on Fridays, before holidays, or times that would otherwise be wasted.
   II. specify the learning objectives involved when using media.
   III. debrief students after the use of the media materials.
   IV. hold students accountable for learning from the media materials used.

   A. I, II, and IV only
   B. II and III only
   C. III and IV only
   D. II, III, and IV only

21. Mr. Lockett, a new teacher who is a member of Ms. Lazarine's instructional team, is planning the physical arrangement of his room. He will most likely be advised to do which of the following?

   A. Seat the students in the "action zone" to ensure their participation.
   B. Seat low-achieving students near each other so he can work more easily with them.
   C. Keep frequently used supplies and materials readily accessible.
   D. Seat students who are behavioral problems near the teacher's desk.

22. The use of instructional teams *best* illustrates which of the following principles?

   A. Teachers should communicate the mission of the school to colleagues to create an environment that supports innovation and risk taking.
   B. If teachers are to learn from each other, they must interact within a cooperative context.
   C. Schools are loosely coupled organizations in which teachers function far more independently than interdependently.
   D. Teachers should work with colleagues to establish strong and positive ties between the school and the community.

As a health teacher, Ms. Lazarine must discuss the typical sequence of physical development in adolescence. She is aware that the timing and rate at which puberty occurs vary widely. These differences mean that some of Ms. Lazarine's students may be completely mature, while others at the same age have not begun puberty.

23. Ms. Lazarine is likely to be aware that late-maturing boys:

    A. have less self-confidence than early maturers.
    B. get along better with their families than early maturers.
    C. are treated as older than their age by adults.
    D. are better coordinated than early maturers.

24. Ms. Lazarine also is likely to be aware that early-maturing girls:

    A. may develop precocious heterosexual interests.
    B. are at a distinct social disadvantage over late maturers toward the end of middle school.
    C. have poorer adjustment throughout adolescence than late maturers.
    D. have higher self-esteem than early-maturing boys.

25. When Ms. Lazarine sends three-week progress reports home, one-third of her students are failing. She wonders if physiological needs may be playing a role in her students' lack of academic achievement. Which of the following *best* describes the role of physiological needs in students' academic performance?

    A. Physiological needs have no relationship to academic performance.
    B. A student with unmet physiological needs may show little interest in academic performance.
    C. Those with unmet physiological needs should be referred to a physician.
    D. Students with unmet physiological needs are likely to avoid failure in relationships with others.

26. As a health teacher, Ms. Lazarine is likely to be aware that nutritional deficiencies during adolescence are:

    A. more common among girls than boys.
    B. common, but unimportant to health.
    C. rarely encountered.
    D. found only among the poor.

SET 2 ENDS HERE

SET 3 BEGINS HERE

Mr. Cooper, a second-year English teacher at Stephens High School, taught tenth-grade honors English last year. This year, his teaching assignment includes one regular tenth-grade class, mixed-ability grouped, and three honors English classes. Mr. Cooper starts out using the same strategies and holding the same expectations for all of his classes. He tells his mentor, Ms. Lehmann, that he is very concerned because the students in his regular class are disruptive and unmotivated, and many are failing. Ms. Lehmann suggests that since this is the fourth week of school, Mr. Cooper should consider having a class meeting with the students in his regular class. When Mr. Cooper holds the class meeting and asks, "What is wrong?" Rayford replies, "How do you expect us to be quiet and how can you expect us to complete our work when most of us do not understand the assignments you give us?" Mae raises her hand and says, "I understand the assignments, but they are so boring, the same thing day in and day out: read the chapters and complete the worksheet. Why can't we work together on some of our assignments?"

27. Mr. Cooper discusses with Ms. Lehmann the students' comments made during the class meeting. Ms. Lehmann is likely to remind Mr. Cooper that since he teaches different ability levels, he should remember that research on teacher expectations reveals which of the following?

    A. Teachers often demand less from low achievers than from high achievers.
    B. Teacher expectations have no effect on student achievement.
    C. Teachers often demand too much from low achievers.
    D. Research regarding teacher expectations is too inconclusive to merit specific conclusions.

28. Ms. Lehmann might also suggest that Mr. Cooper could use which of the following to accommodate the wide range of student abilities in his regular class?

    I. Feature topics identified as interesting to students.
    II. Plan instructional alternatives for high-ability students.
    III. Allow uninterested students to pursue different topics.
    IV. Individualize instruction.

    A. I and II only
    B. I, II, and III only
    C. I, II, and IV only
    D. I, II, III, and IV

29. For the coming six weeks, Mr. Cooper has decided to use ability groups within his regular classes. Which of the following is likely to happen as a result of Mr. Cooper's using ability groups?

    A. increased behavior management problems.
    B. increased compliance by students with classroom rules.
    C. increased engaged learning time.
    D. increased achievement among average- and low-ability students.

30. Mr. Cooper and Ms. Lehmann have agreed that his course syllabus in English needs revising. They determine that his course syllabus needs to be strengthened in the area of critical thinking skills. Which of the following should Mr. Cooper do to promote the development of critical thinking skills?

    I. He should teach for deeper understanding of content.
    II. He should establish a controlled, teacher-centered classroom.
    III. He should require students to justify the reasoning behind their conclusions.
    IV. He should help students develop metacognitive strategies.

    A. I and II only
    B. I and III only
    C. II and III only
    D. I, III, and IV only

Mr. Cooper is still concerned about the students' behavior in his regular class. He discusses the problem of off-task and disruptive student behavior with Ms. Lehmann. Mr. Cooper assures his mentor that he holds high expectations for all of his students. He describes his usual class routine as checking the roll and giving a short explanation of the day's activities. After the explanation, he distributes a worksheet of about fifty drill and practice activities on grammar for the students to work on in class.

31. The likely reason for the students' off-task behavior in Mr. Cooper's class is:

    A. large class size.
    B. long engagement in repetitive and boring tasks.
    C. high academic expectations for average students.
    D. teacher presentations given with only moderate enthusiasm.

32. Mr. Cooper should remember that the *best* guard against disruptive behavior is:

    A. a well-planned lesson.
    B. a principal who will support the teacher.
    C. a teacher who is physically larger and stronger that the students.
    D. corporal punishment.

33. In addition to the off-task behavior, Mr. Cooper also confides to Ms. Lehmann that many of his students appear bored and apathetic during the lessons. Ms. Lehmann is *most* likely to suggest that, to increase student attention, Mr. Cooper should:

A. relate the lessons to the needs and interests of the students.
B. use moderate punishment such as time-out when students are not paying attention.
C. praise by name the students who pay attention.
D. discuss the problem with individual students.

34. Rayford, who spoke up during the class meeting, enjoys being the class clown. Ms. Lehmann suggests that Mr. Cooper should isolate Rayford; therefore, he will avoid letting Rayford's peers reinforce his disruptive behavior. Ms. Lehmann's suggestion may be described as:

A. inappropriate, since Rayford will continue to misbehave outside of class.
B. inappropriate, because Rayford will receive sympathy from his peers.
C. appropriate, because it deprives Rayford of his audience.
D. appropriate, because it will increase Rayford's group status.

At the end of the semester, Mr. Cooper and Ms. Lehmann review his discipline management plan. During this process, Mr. Cooper realizes that when he designed his plan, he focused primarily on the consequences for inappropriate behavior.

35. Ms. Lehmann is likely to remind Mr. Cooper the *most* effective type of discipline for the secondary classroom is one that emphasizes:

A. assertive behavior.
B. submissive behavior.
C. self-discipline.
D. authoritarian discipline.

36. Ms. Lehmann is likely to suggest that Mr. Cooper should possibly focus on which of the following in revising his discipline management plan?

A. isolation and suspension
B. consistency and fairness
C. threat and fear
D. detention hall and suspension

SET 3 ENDS HERE

SET 4 BEGINS HERE

> Mr. Heeney is a beginning tenth-grade social studies teacher at North Heights High School. He is faced with the problem of a difference between his philosophy and that of his principal regarding a conducive learning climate. His principal, Ms. Chew, believes that a classroom has to be completely quiet and orderly at all times for learning to occur, and that direct instruction should be used as the primary teaching strategy. Although Mr. Heeney concurs that orderliness is important, he uses cooperative learning groups and games and simulations that sometimes elevate the noise level in the classroom.

37. The *best* approach for Mr. Heeney to use to build a positive working relationship with his principal would be to:

  A. invite the principal to visit his class to observe his teaching methods and their effects.
  B. make sure the principal does not visit his class, so that she won't be disturbed by his classroom methods.
  C. send memos to the principal regarding his students' progress.
  D. organize parents to send a petition supporting his teaching methods to the principal and superintendent.

38. Mr. Heeney plans to use some inquiry and discovery methods, cooperative learning, and laboratory assignments in the coming week. Mr. Heeney's *primary* motivation for selecting these teaching strategies is to provide:

  A. ways to create variety.
  B. ways to establish routine.
  C. ways to establish group morale.
  D. ways to develop critical-thinking skills.

39. When Ms. Chew visits Mr. Heeney's class, she commends him for having such high time-on-task in his classroom. Which of the following would have motivated high time-on-task *most* effectively?

  A. He provided good explanations in response to student needs.
  B. He experimented with different management systems.
  C. He understood the importance of time.
  D. He conveyed the importance of learning and the value of the academic task to the students.

At the end of the first six weeks of class, Mr. Heeney realizes it is necessary for him to communicate with his students' parents. He wants to make sure that each student's parents are thoroughly informed of their child's progress, but he is also aware that misunderstandings may occur.

40. Of the following, the *best* technique for clearing up misunderstandings when talking with parents is to:

    A. convey correct information to them.
    B. tell them honestly that they are distorting what you are saying.
    C. ask them to listen carefully.
    D. ask them to repeat to you their understanding of what has been said.

41. One morning Mr. Heeney is preparing for his first teacher-parent conference of the day. During a conference with parents the day before, Mr. Heeney realized that he had spoken for most of the thirty minutes, and he knows that the conference was not effective. Based on this information, what should Mr. Heeney consider doing differently this time?

    A. Include the student in the conference.
    B. Pause and encourage the parents to respond and offer suggestions during the conference.
    C. Provide the parents with an outline of his comments and suggestions for improving their child's achievement.
    D. Eliminate his opening remarks.

42. Communication with a parent about a student's progress:

    A. should be used only when a student is experiencing problems.
    B. should be used only on an emergency basis.
    C. should emphasize parental responsibility for changing the student's behavior.
    D. should be used for all students.

43. Mr. Heeney answers a knock on his classroom door to find an irate parent. Mr. Heeney is annoyed that his lesson has been interrupted. The *best* approach for Mr. Heeney to use with the parent is to:

    A. express his annoyance.
    B. conduct a parent-teacher conference at that moment.
    C. give the parent a solution to the problem.
    D. remain unemotional.

Mr. Heeney serves on an ARD committee that determines that a student, Yvonne, who is speech and hearing impaired, should be mainstreamed into his class. Although she has multiple disabilities, Yvonne is capable of functioning in the regular classroom environment. The ARD committee determines that Mr. Heeney's classroom meets the criterion of "least restrictive environment."

44. "Least restrictive environment" means that:

    A. a student's classroom environment should be appropriate to his or her level of disability, neither more nor less restrictive.
    B. special educators should have the full responsibility for tailoring the school environment to a student's needs.
    C. all children should be able to participate in regular school activities, regardless of disability.
    D. disabled children should attend special schools.

45. In addition to the classroom teacher, who else could legally serve on Yvonne's ARD committee?

    I.   Yvonne's parents or guardian
    II. a special education teacher
    III. a speech and hearing teacher
    IV. the principal

    A. I and IV only
    B. I, II, and III only
    C. II, III, and IV only
    D. I, II, III, and IV

46. Although he served on Yvonne's ARD committee, Mr. Heeney still feels unsure about his professional and legal responsibilities in meeting her needs. Which of the following would *not* be an appropriate measure for Mr. Heeney to take?

    A. Report Yvonne's progress to her parents as often as he reports to the parents of the other students in the class.
    B. Have a tutor work with Yvonne in the library, so that she will have a quiet setting more conducive to learning.
    C. Provide opportunities for Yvonne to interact with other hearing-impaired students.
    D. Help Yvonne work and interact with other students in the class.

47. To better prepare himself as Yvonne's teacher, Mr. Heeney attends professional development training on PL 105-17, the Individuals with Disabilities Education Act Amendments of 1997 (IDEA 97). He is likely to learn that with regard to ARD committee meetings, the rights of parents of a child with disabilities include:

    I.   the right to written notice of scheduled meetings at least five school days before the meeting.
    II. the right to bring an attorney to the meeting.
    III. the right to have an interpreter if the parents' primary language is other than English.
    IV. the right to audiotape-record the meeting as long as all attending are informed about it.

    A. I and III only
    B. I, III, and IV only
    C. III and IV only
    D. I, II, III, and IV

48. Mr. Heeney's decision to attend the professional development training on IDEA 97 *best* illustrates which of the following principles?

   A. Teachers should be risk takers and innovators.
   B. Teachers should participate in collaborative decision making.
   C. Teachers should demonstrate that they have clearly defined goals.
   D. Teachers should enhance their professional skills and knowledge.

49. Mr. Heeney calls on Yvonne and waits patiently for her to answer. He continues to wait even though she has difficulty responding. How would you evaluate this approach to the student?

   A. ineffective, because it places the student and teacher in a power struggle
   B. effective, because it communicates positive expectations to the class about Yvonne
   C. effective, because it communicates negative expectations to the class about Yvonne
   D. effective, because it establishes Mr. Heeney's authority

50. Mr. Heeney asks Ms. Chew whether the school is going to implement a full inclusion program. She responds, "There are many advocates of full inclusion, but I am unsure when the district will consider implementing a comprehensive program." Full inclusion refers to:

   A. the selective placement of special education students in one or more regular education classes.
   B. hiring only teachers who are certified in special education.
   C. keeping disabled students in separate classes for all or part of the day.
   D. having all special education students, regardless of disability or severity, in a regular classroom full-time.

SET 4 ENDS HERE

SET 5 BEGINS HERE

Pleasantview is an old historic town. When a large oil company wants to drill on the site of the old university building, the town becomes embroiled in a bitter controversy over whether or not to allow the drilling. Mr. Juarez, the twelfth-grade civics teacher, decides to use the controversy as the basis for a class discussion. He feels the students will learn a lot about politics and how city governments operate during the discussion. He poses the following question to the class:

Should preservation of historic landmarks stand in the way of economic development?

51. Mr. Juarez's question is likely to be *most* useful for:

A. encouraging students to recall factual information.

B. providing students with clues about his personal opinions about the controversy.

C. providing a framework for engaging students in active inquiry.

D. checking students' understanding of the nature of the controversy.

52. Before beginning the class discussion, it is important that Mr. Juarez:

A. know which students to call upon.

B. let the students choose sides on the issue first.

C. give his opinion on the issue in order to set the tone for the discussion.

D. make sure the students are somewhat familiar with the issues.

53. Mr. Juarez's primary purpose for using a class discussion is to:

A. provide a medium for students to practice public speaking in class.

B. let students learn to collaborate to solve problems.

C. engage students in higher-order thinking in a real-world context.

D. minimize the negative effects of community problems in the classroom.

Mr. Juarez wants to create a climate in the classroom that facilitates student interaction and participation. He realizes there are many factors to consider if his class discussion will be successful in promoting student learning.

54. Which of the following seating arrangements would work *best* for the whole-class discussion that Mr. Juarez has planned?

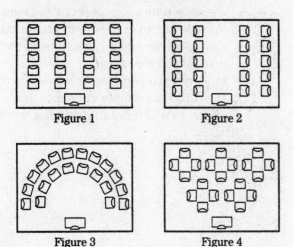

Figure 1   Figure 2

Figure 3   Figure 4

A. Figure 1
B. Figure 2
C. Figure 3
D. Figure 4

55. As Mr. Juarez plans his questions for the discussion, he should consider which of the following?

A. Effective teachers ask more when?, where?, how?, and what? questions.
B. Effective teachers ask more divergent questions.
C. Effective teachers ask more convergent questions.
D. There is no relationship between teacher questioning and teacher effectiveness.

56. Mr. Juarez realizes that wait time is important, yet he often finds it difficult to apply the recommended three-second wait time for students' responses to questions. According to experts, which of the following is probably the *main* reason for this?

A. The teacher fears that silence might disturb the momentum of the lesson.
B. There is a strong norm in American culture against silence.
C. The teacher fears that silence might lead to student misbehavior.
D. The teacher fears student achievement will suffer.

57. Mr. Juarez realizes the role he chooses to play during the class discussion can have an impact on the level and quality of participation of the students. During the class discussion Mr. Juarez's primary role should be as:

A. a judge.
B. a moderator.
C. a critic.
D. an arbitrator.

58. Mr. Juarez wants to keep disruptive behavior to a minimum during the class discussion to maintain the momentum of the lesson. He hopes that if he reinforces desirable behavior, the students will be less likely to misbehave. All of the following are actions that may reinforce desired behavior during a lesson *except*:

A. ignoring minor distractions.
B. praising effectively.
C. smiling at students who look attentive.
D. cueing good behavior.

After the class discussion, the students tell Mr. Juarez how much they enjoyed it and that they learned a lot. They tell him that they want to have other class discussions on "real-life" issues in the future. Mr. Juarez is pleased to hear their comments because he had not been sure how the students would respond to the discussion.

59. The class discussion over the town controversy brought to the classroom:

    A. an outside conflict that served only to distract from what the students should be learning.
    B. the use of an external factor as a tool to promote student learning.
    C. an opportunity for students to have choices in their learning.
    D. an understanding of how the school relates to the larger community.

60. Students *most* likely learned from the class discussion that:

    A. the old university building has great historical value.
    B. community leaders can serve as role models for students.
    C. working with others can lead to better and quicker solutions to problems.
    D. accuracy of information is a critical element of verbal communication.

61. A class discussion would be *most* appropriate when:

    A. the lesson involves objectives at the knowledge level of Bloom's taxonomy.
    B. the lesson involves objectives in the affective domain.
    C. students are younger or less mature.
    D. the topic has simple concepts that students will react to in similar ways.

SET 5 ENDS HERE

SET 6 BEGINS HERE

Ms. Webb teaches a microcomputer applications class. There are twenty-five students in the class: seventeen freshmen, five sophomores, two juniors, and one senior. On the first day, Ms. Webb asks the students to complete a questionnaire about their previous computer experience. When she reads through their responses after class, she finds that her students vary considerably in their previous computer training, from those who, literally, have never turned on a computer to those who have computers at home and have had extensive experience.

62. Ms. Webb's decision to obtain information about her students' prior computer experience is *best* explained by which of the following?

   A. She knows that identifying problem students early is a basic skill that successful teachers must possess.
   B. She needs to provide the students with feedback about their progress in her class.
   C. She needs information that will help her design appropriate learning activities for her students.
   D. She wants to check on established levels of achievement for grading purposes.

63. Which of the following is Ms. Webb using to obtain information about her students?

   A. formative assessment
   B. summative assessment
   C. achievement assessment
   D. diagnostic assessment

64. Which of the following would probably be an *ineffective* instructional strategy for Ms. Webb to use?

   A. whole-group demonstration
   B. individualized instruction
   C. peer tutoring
   D. laboratory application

After several weeks of class, Ms. Webb has become concerned because Julie, the one senior in her class, has become a discipline problem. Julie nearly always comes late to class. As far as Ms. Webb can ascertain from talking to other teachers, Julie has plenty of time to get from their classes to hers. Furthermore, Julie repeatedly talks socially to the two freshmen girls who sit on either side of her during class. Ms. Webb reviews Julie's responses on the first-day questionnaire, which indicates that Julie has extensive experience and ability in the use of computers.

65. Which of the following should Ms. Webb do *first* to try to reduce Julie's tardiness?

    A. Deduct points from Julie's six-weeks' grade.
    B. Give Julie extra work to complete.
    C. Discuss the problem with Julie individually.
    D. Draw the class's attention to Julie when she arrives late.

66. Ms. Webb decides that one approach she could use to reduce Julie's misbehavior in class is to ask Julie to serve as a peer-tutor for some of Julie's less experienced younger peers. How would you evaluate this strategy?

    A. ineffective, because the class will likely think Julie is the teacher's pet
    B. ineffective, because Julie will likely continue to misbehave while tutoring
    C. effective, because Julie will likely be given an opportunity to act as a group leader
    D. effective, because Julie's behavior will likely improve.

67. Research on the effects of peer tutoring on learning indicates that:

    A. the results are much the same regardless of the expertise of the tutor.
    B. the tutors benefit, but the tutees do not.
    C. achievement of both the tutors and the tutees increases.
    D. neither tutors nor tutees benefit significantly, but achievement motivation increases for both.

68. Ms. Webb is concerned about the age difference between Julie and some of the freshmen and sophomore students that Julie will be helping. Which of the following should Ms. Webb know about cross-age tutoring compared to same-age tutoring?

    A. Research indicates that cross-age tutoring is less popular among students.
    B. Cross-age tutoring is more often recommended by researchers.
    C. Cross-age tutoring is easier to implement in classroom settings.
    D. Cross-age tutoring is less effective for learning.

69. After a week as a peer-tutor, Julie tells Ms. Webb that Pierre, a low-achieving freshman student Julie has been working with, does not even try to finish his assignments. Ms. Webb checks Pierre's records and finds he scored at the 80th percentile overall on his most recent battery of achievement tests. It is always the case that a student who scores at the 80th percentile has:

    A. scored the same as or better than 80 percent of a norm group.
    B. scored better than 20 percent of a norm group.
    C. correctly answered 80 percent of the test questions.
    D. correctly answered 20 percent of the test questions.

70. The *most* appropriate strategy for Ms. Webb to use with Pierre would be to:

    A. reduce the difficulty of the material that he has to learn.
    B. establish a systematic reinforcement schedule for his completed work.
    C. extend the deadlines for his completion of lessons.
    D. reduce the amount of material that he has to learn.

Fridays are a special day in Ms. Webb's class. Every Friday, the students get to learn about how to use the Internet. Ms. Webb has been teaching her students how to send and receive e-mail messages and how to access information resources. Ms. Webb has also arranged for professors at a nearby university to serve as "experts" to whom her students can electronically pose academic or technical questions. Both the students and the professors have been enthusiastic about the arrangement.

71. The arrangement with the professors *best* illustrates which of the following?

   A. Teachers should create a learning environment in which taking risks and sharing new ideas are supported and encouraged.
   B. Teachers should use technological and other resources to facilitate continual professional growth.
   C. Teachers should know how to take advantage of community strengths and resources to promote student achievement.
   D. Teachers should understand the value of technology in promoting efficient use of class time.

72. At midsemester, Ms. Webb submits a questionnaire to the students in which she asks them what they liked least about the class. This type of assessment is called a:

   A. summative assessment.
   B. formative assessment.
   C. norm-referenced assessment.
   D. criterion-referenced assessment.

Many of the students respond on the midsemester questionnaire that what they enjoyed least about the class is "not getting to spend enough time on the 'Net.'" Based on this feedback, Ms. Webb decides to involve the students in a telecommunications project. With the assistance of the university experts who have been helping her students, Ms. Webb is able to initiate an Internet project between a high school English class in Japan and her computer class. The students from the two countries will communicate with each other via e-mail messages.

73. Ms. Webb's decision to modify the curriculum in response to student feedback will *most* likely accomplish which of the following?

   A. It will satisfy the need in students for a stable, routine, and predictable environment.
   B. It will encourage students to use self-reflection in the learning process.
   C. It will encourage learning and promote student success.
   D. It will prompt students to assess their understanding of long-term instructional goals.

74. Which of the following are likely to be benefits of involving students in the telecommunications project with Japan?

   I. It will provide an opportunity for the students from both countries to learn of each other's culture and way of life.
   II. It will increase the interactivity of the classroom and thereby improve learning.
   III. It will promote community recognition that American schools can meet the academic needs of Japanese students.
   IV. It will promote innovation and educational excellence in Texas.

   A. I and II only
   B. II and IV only
   C. I, II, and IV only
   D. I, II, III, and IV

When a devastating earthquake occurs in Japan, Ms. Webb's students are very worried about their e-mail friends in Japan. Telephone lines in Japan are down, so they wait with great apprehension with Ms. Webb for an e-mail message about the condition of the high school where the Japanese students go to school. When the message that the school is still standing and all the students are okay comes across the screen, Ms. Webb's students shout with relief and joy. They immediately send off e-mail messages of concern and condolences to the Japanese students, but they want to do more. "Let's collect money in the community for the quake victims, Ms. Webb," they suggest. Ms. Webb agrees to help the students do this.

75. Even though telephone lines are down in Japan, Ms. Webb's students are still able to receive and send messages to their Japanese friends via the Internet. Ms. Webb will *most* likely use this situation as an opportunity to convey to students:

   A. the importance of technology as a learning tool.

   B. the importance of establishing a positive social climate in the classroom.

   C. the power of informal networks to enhance learning.

   D. the power and utility of technology.

76. In a school that is practicing site-based management, who would be included in making the decision to allow Ms. Webb's students to proceed in collecting money for the Japanese quake victims?

   I. the school board
   II. the superintendent
   III. the principal
   IV. the campus school-community committee

   A. I and II only
   B. I and IV only
   C. II and III only
   D. III and IV only

77. Which of the following will be the *most* likely result of allowing students to collect money in the community to help the Japanese quake victims?

   A. It will explain the educational goals of the school to the broader community.

   B. It will provide an opportunity for the community to gain an understanding of problems facing Japanese schools.

   C. It will prompt community recognition that schools encourage students to have a sense of social responsibility.

   D. It will assure community members that schools can be counted on to help solve problems in the real world.

Since many of the other faculty at her school also have computers, Ms. Webb asks the principal if she might conduct an inservice workshop for the teachers. The principal agrees and schedules Ms. Webb's workshop for the next inservice day.

78. Conducting the workshop *best* illustrates which of the following?

    A. Ms. Webb uses technology to explain and enhance the mission of the school.
    B. Ms. Webb actively engages in an exchange of ideas with colleagues to establish a successful learning community.
    C. Ms. Webb knows and uses community resources to promote professional growth.
    D. As a member of a collaborative team, Ms. Webb uses group processes to make decisions and solve problems.

79. During the workshop, a member of the mathematics faculty consults Ms. Webb about using computer-aided instruction (CAI) in mathematics. Which of the following should Ms. Webb tell this teacher is the most important *first* step in instituting effective CAI?

    A. Purchase additional hardware.
    B. Ability group the students.
    C. Evaluate appropriate software.
    D. Take a refresher course in programming.

80. During the workshop, the art teacher tells Ms. Webb that she has been using a popular computer graphics software package in her classes and her students thoroughly enjoy it; however, she has discovered that the school does not own any licensed copies of the software. What action, if any, should Ms. Webb advise this teacher to take?

    A. Tell her to immediately remove all copies of the software from the computers in her classroom.
    B. Tell her to continue to use the software, but contact the manufacturer about obtaining licensed copies.
    C. Tell her to continue to use the software, but contact the district technology specialist and discuss the problem.
    D. Tell her to continue to use the software and say nothing.

SET 6 ENDS HERE

SET 7 BEGINS HERE

Mr. Kim teaches health/physical education at Richard Paul Middle School. While students are engaged in team activities, Mr. Kim overhears two sixth-graders, Jimmy and Tyrone, talking. Jimmy tells Tyrone, "I need some crack. I just finished my last hit." Mr. Kim asks Jimmy and Tyrone to stay after class. Following is an excerpt from their discussion.

Mr. Kim: "Jimmy, I wanted to talk to you about what you said about needing some crack. I've noticed that you have been uninterested in the activities in class lately, and I was wondering what was going on. Now, I know what the problem is—you are a 'crackhead.'"

Jimmy: "Mr. Kim, you got it all wrong. I was just mouthing off to Tyrone. I don't do no drugs."

Tyrone: "That's right, Mr. Kim, I knew he was just kidding. Jimmy doesn't mess with that stuff."

Mr. Kim: "I am not so sure. Some of your other teachers have told me that your grades have dropped a lot since school started, Jimmy. Aren't you failing math and English this six weeks?"

Jimmy: "Well, I am not doing real good in school right now, but it's not because of drugs. You gotta believe me, Mr. Kim."

Mr. Kim: "Well, you two need to go on to your next class. I'll talk to you later."

81. Mr. Kim's handling of this situation is:

   I.   inappropriate, because Mr. Kim has jumped to conclusions about Jimmy.
   II. inappropriate, because it will probably cause resentment and mistrust toward Mr. Kim.
   III. appropriate, because it will make Tyrone aware of possible consequences of drug use.
   IV. appropriate, because it will probably stop Jimmy's drug use.

   A. I only
   B. I and II only
   C. III only
   D. III and IV only

82. Instead of confronting the two boys after class, which of the following would have been the *most* appropriate strategy for Mr. Kim to do regarding Jimmy?

   A. Immediately report Jimmy to the authorities.
   B. Call Jimmy's parents and tell them about his comment on drug use.
   C. Discuss his concerns about Jimmy with the school counselor.
   D. Question the other students to obtain more information about Jimmy's drug use.

83. When Mr. Kim discussed Jimmy's grades in front of Tyrone, his actions were:

   A. inappropriate, because the drug problem was more important.
   B. inappropriate, because he violated Jimmy's rights of privacy.
   C. appropriate, because Jimmy's behavior will likely change as a result.
   D. appropriate, because peer pressure from Tyrone toward Jimmy to do better will likely result.

Mr. Kim is aware of the alarming rate of drug use among students in middle school. He decides to revise the two-week unit he had planned to teach in health class on drug abuse. He feels this particular unit is a very important part of the curriculum, and he wants to feel confident that it will help increase the students' understanding of the dangerous effects of drug abuse. Through the Texas Safe and Drug-Free Schools and Communities (SDFSC) program, which has been recognized as a national model, Mr. Kim obtains resource materials to use in the unit, including lesson plans, videos, titles, and interactive Web-site addresses that stress the hazards of minors' illegal use of drugs. He also plans to invite well-known dynamic guest speakers to visit the class to talk with students about the social pressures that sometimes lead to drug use.

84. Mr. Kim's decision to obtain materials through the Texas SDFSC program *best* illustrates which of the following?

   A. The teacher knows how to capitalize on strong school-community relationships to support desired student outcomes.
   B. The teacher knows how to work cooperatively with community leaders to achieve desired student behavior.
   C. The teacher is aware of the resources and strategies that can help schools cope with community problems.
   D. The teacher knows how to make the broader community aware of problems facing the school community.

85. *Most* likely Mr. Kim's lessons for the unit will be designed to:

   A. enhance students' understanding of the society in which we live.
   B. enhance students' ability to memorize and recall factual information.
   C. enhance students' independent thinking and decision-making skills.
   D. enhance students' ability to apply information learned.

86. On the first day of teaching the unit on drug abuse, Mr. Kim walks into class and puts the following transparency on the overhead projector:

   > ALCOHOL
   > TOBACCO
   > MARIJUANA
   > COCAINE
   > HEROIN
   > DO THESE SUBSTANCES
   > HAVE ANYTHING IN COMMON?
   > WHY OR WHY NOT?

   This instructional step is *best* described as which of the following?

   A. focus
   B. reteaching
   C. guided practice
   D. closure

87. Next, Mr. Kim shows a video on the dangers of drug use and ways students can avoid being drawn into trying drugs. During the showing of the video, Mr. Kim stops the tape periodically and asks "How would you handle that situation?" This strategy *best* illustrates which of the following?

    A. Effective teachers foster a view of learning as a purposeful pursuit.
    B. Students stay on task when they are aware they are monitored.
    C. Teachers' efforts to maintain classroom discipline correlate with student engagement.
    D. Effective teachers emphasize the value and importance of the learning activity.

88. During the presentation of a guest speaker, Sabrina makes a loud, rude comment. Mr. Kim is unable to make eye contact with Sabrina, so he quickly passes her a note directing her to not speak out again. Sabrina remains quiet for the rest of the presentation. Mr. Kim's actions *best* illustrate which of the following?

    I. Effective teachers use a variety of verbal and nonverbal signals to stop inappropriate behaviors.
    II. Excessive behavior correction may result in increased off-task behaviors.
    III. Effective teachers give the rationale for appropriate behaviors.
    IV. Effective teachers are quick to respond and stop disruptive behaviors.

    A. I and II only
    B. I and IV only
    C. II and III only
    D. III and IV only

Mr. Kim decides to have his students spend several days working in cooperative learning groups to research and make reports on the effects of drugs on the human physiology using a list of interactive Web sites recommended by the SDFSC. He assigns the students to one of five groups: alcohol, tobacco, marijuana, cocaine, and heroin. Each group will prepare a presentation on the effects of the drug on five major organs: the heart, brain, liver, lungs, and central nervous system.

89. This teaching approach *best* reflects Mr. Kim's understanding that:

   A. students should be given opportunities to communicate health-related ideas using a variety of different media.
   B. students should be given opportunities to apply health-related concepts in a real-world situation.
   C. students should be given opportunities to understand the role of technology as a learning tool.
   D. students should be given opportunities to appreciate the cultural impartiality of technology.

90. As part of the Safe and Drug-Free Schools and Communities program at Richard Paul Middle School, Mr. Kim works with community members in the neighborhood around the school to organize volunteers to take time each day to walk children to and from school. This action *best* illustrates that Mr. Kim understands:

   A. the value of working with local citizens to establish strong ties between the school and the community.
   B. the value of strategies that are mutually supportive and beneficial to the school and the community.
   C. the value of taking advantage of community strengths and resources to solve the school's problems.
   D. the value of establishing a relationship of trust with parents.

SET 7 ENDS HERE

Answer Key

Item Number	Correct Answer	Competency
1	C	002
2	D	003
3	A	006
4	B	010
5	C	007
6	D	002
7	C	004
8	D	015
9	B	015
10	B	003
11	A	003
12	B	003
13	B	003
14	B	008
15	B	008
16	A	008
17	A	005
18	B	008
19	A	006
20	D	009
21	C	011
22	B	012
23	A	001
24	A	001
25	B	002
26	A	001
27	A	002
28	D	008
29	A	008

30	D	008
31	B	011
32	A	011
33	A	005
34	C	011
35	C	011
36	B	011
37	A	012
38	D	006
39	D	005
40	A	013
41	B	013
42	D	013
43	D	013
44	A	015
45	D	015
46	B	015
47	D	015
48	D	012
49	B	007
50	D	015
51	C	007
52	D	004
53	C	006
54	C	011
55	B	007
56	B	007
57	B	008
58	A	005
59	B	005
60	D	007

61	B	006
62	C	004
63	A	010
64	A	008
65	C	011
66	D	011
67	C	002
68	B	008
69	A	010
70	B	005
71	C	014
72	B	010
73	C	006
74	C	009
75	D	009
76	D	015
77	C	014
78	B	012
79	C	009
80	A	015
81	B	002
82	C	012
83	B	015
84	C	006
85	C	006
86	A	006
87	D	004
88	B	011
89	C	009
90	B	014

Answer Explanations

1. **C** This question relates to environmental factors that may impact **students' self-esteem** and thus impact learning. Therefore, its primary focus is Competency 002: *The teacher considers environmental factors that may affect learning in designing a supportive and responsive classroom community that promotes all students' learning and self-esteem.* Eliminate A, B, and D because these responses are inconsistent with research findings that indicate, on average, that children from lower-socioeconomic-class backgrounds are less likely to achieve as well in school as children from middle-class backgrounds. Regarding the difficulties for children from lower-socioeconomic-class backgrounds, Slavin explains that these children (on average) are less likely to be as well prepared when entering school and their upbringings emphasize behaviors and values different from those (such as individuality and future time orientation) expected of them in schools. Further, researchers have found that middle-class teachers often have low expectations for low-socioeconomic-class students, which is likely to influence those students' perception of their own worth and potential and, in turn, may result in low achievement for these students. Slavin makes the point that teachers should be aware that children from other than mainstream, middle-class backgrounds are often at a disadvantage in the typical school environment, and the teachers should make efforts to recognize the potential of these students to achieve. Choice C is the correct response.

2. **D** This question deals both with **diversity** (How do students from different socioeconomic levels differ?) and an environmental factor (socioeconomic status) that influences learning (Ms. Solomon wants to increase the achievement of the students), which is related to **students' self-esteem.** Glancing at the answer choices, you can see that you are going to have to know what works best with lower-socioeconomic-status students in order to decide among the answer choices—so you need to know characteristics of the learner. Thus, the primary focus of this question is Competency 003: *The teacher appreciates human diversity, recognizing how diversity in the classroom and the community may affect learning and creating a classroom environment in which both the diversity of groups and the uniqueness of individuals are recognized and celebrated.* Ms. Solomon should consider immediate rewards (Choice D). Slavin explains that children from lower-socioeconomic-status backgrounds are less likely to respond to delayed reinforcement (more adapted to immediate gratification), less willing to compete (eliminate B), and more oriented toward cooperation with other children (eliminate A and C) and individualized contact with the teacher than middle-class students. Choice D is the correct response.

3. **A** The question deals with **planning.** Thus, its primary focus is Competency 006: *The teacher uses planning processes to design outcome-oriented learning experiences that foster understanding and encourage self-directed thinking and learning in both individual and collaborative settings.* Task analysis requires the teacher to analyze a task to determine the exact steps a student must go through to successfully complete it. Eliminate B and D because task analysis is something the teacher does, not the students. Eliminate C because using task analysis is a part of planning effective objectives, since it allows the teacher to determine if a lesson objective is at an appropriate level of difficulty; however, additional criteria must be considered as well (for instance, the type of learning desired—cognitive, affective, psychomotor). The benefit of performing a task analysis for each lesson is that the teacher will be able to determine the prerequisite skills needed in order that students can master more complex skills. Choice A is the correct response.

4. **B** This question deals with both **assessment** (Which assessment approach does Mr. Hernandez recommend?) and **motivation** (The assessment approach should motivate students to earn better grades). Glancing at the answer choices, you can see that they mostly deal with **assessment,** so the primary focus of this question is Competency 010: *The teacher uses processes of informal and formal assessment to understand individual learners, monitor instructional effectiveness, and shape instruction.* Eliminate A and D because these approaches are likely to have a negative impact on how the students think about themselves. Eliminate C because feedback is more effective and more meaningful when it occurs immediately after testing. Ms. Solomon should consider grading based on improvement for a short period. This is likely to increase motivation and interest by making it possible for all students, regardless of ability, to succeed. Choice B is the correct response.

5. **C** This question deals with **communication.** Thus, its primary focus is Competency 007: *The teacher uses effective verbal, nonverbal, and media communication techniques to shape the classroom into a community of learners engaged in active inquiry, collaborative exploration, and supportive interactions.* Eliminate A because teachers should provide appropriate and nonthreatening opportunities for all students to be involved in the lesson, even those who sometimes are reluctant to do so. Eliminate B because an effective method of calling on students is to use a random process, so that all participate and are kept attentive during the teaching act. Eliminate D because allowing volunteers to dominate the lesson will establish a classroom climate where some students will be likely to assume a passive role during classroom discourse; further, the teacher will not be able to adequately assess whether those not participating are learning. Ms. Solomon's strategy is limited because students who don't volunteer will miss the

opportunity to actively participate in the lesson. Choice C is the correct response.

6. **D** This question deals with **students' self-esteem.** Thus, its primary focus is Competency 002: *The teacher considers environmental factors that may affect learning in designing a supportive and responsive classroom community that promotes all students' learning and self-esteem.* "At risk" describes a student with socioeconomic challenges, limited-English proficiency, cultural diversity, poverty, race, or teen pregnancy, which may place them at a disadvantage in achieving academic, social, or career goals. Such students are deemed "at risk" of failing, dropping out, or "falling through the cracks" at school. Teachers should understand factors inside the classroom, such as teacher expectations, that influence these students' perceptions of their own worth and potential. Eliminate Roman I because praise serves to inform students of what they are doing right; therefore, it is critical that the praise be given for right answers and appropriate behavior. Especially with at-risk students, accepting and praising all work will not be effective in facilitating learning and will send a confused message about teacher expectations. Eliminate A. Roman II, III, and IV represent consensus in educational research and theory about maximizing teaching and learning for all students, but especially in working with at-risk students. Teachers should encourage such students to express themselves orally (Roman II) because of the need for schools to provide opportunities for development of effective oral communication skills, which is often lacking in the home environment of at-risk students. Because disengagement is problematic with at-risk students, the teacher must provide a confidence-building environment, including giving them sufficient wait time Roman (III) and expressing expectations clearly and directly (Roman IV). Choice D is the correct response.

7. **C** This question deals with **how learning occurs.** Thus, its primary focus is Competency 004: *The teacher understands how learning occurs and can apply this understanding to design and implement effective instruction.* Learning style is the manner in which an individual perceives and processes information in learning situations. Researchers agree that every person has an individual learning style (Choice C) and that learning style is an indicator not of intelligence but rather of how a person learns (eliminate A), that learning-style strengths may change over time and with training (eliminate B), and that although certain learning style characteristics are biological in nature, others are developed through experience (eliminate D). Knowledge of learning-style theory can assist teachers in designing educational conditions in which most students are likely to learn. Identifying learning styles as a basis for providing responsive instruction is essential to educators today as they meet diverse student populations. Choice C is the correct response.

8. **D** This question deals with **ethical, legal, and professional standards.** Thus, its primary focus is Competency 015: *The teacher understands requirements, expectations, and constraints associated with teaching in Texas, and can apply this understanding in a variety of contexts.* Eliminate Roman I because, for the majority of slower learners, the discrepancy between performance and potential is not severe enough to warrant a classification of "learning disabled" that would qualify them for special education services. Eliminate A and B. This also eliminates Roman II, which conflicts with research findings that indicate slower learners are better served in regular classrooms where they can learn with and from other students. Most slower learners do not meet the definition of "child with a disability" under IDEA (formerly PL 94-142), which enumerates specific disabilities, such as mental retardation and hearing, speech, and visual impairments (Roman III)—although some may have their needs addressed under Section 504 of the 1973 Rehabilitation Act (Roman IV), which defines being disabled more broadly, to include such conditions as Attention Deficit Disorder (ADD) and dyslexia. Choice D is the correct response.

9. **B** This question deals with **ethical, legal, and professional standards.** Thus, its primary focus is Competency 015: *The teacher understands requirements, expectations, and constraints associated with teaching in Texas, and can apply this understanding in a variety of contexts.* A learning disability is a significant discrepancy between learning ability and academic achievement (Choice A). A learning disability is a learning disorder in one or more of the processes required in using and understanding written or spoken material. The disorder may be evident in compromised ability to speak, think, read, write, spell, listen, or do mathematical operations. Such disorders usually include conditions of dyslexia, perceptual difficulties, and aphasia. Normally not included are learning problems representative of traditional special education categories: blind (or partially sighted), deaf, physically disabled, or mentally retarded (eliminate A); emotionally disturbed (eliminate C); and autism (Choice D). Choice B is the correct response.

10. **B** This question deals with **diversity.** Thus, its primary focus is Competency 003: *The teacher appreciates human diversity, recognizing how diversity in the classroom and the community may affect learning and creating a classroom environment in which both the diversity of groups and the uniqueness of individuals are recognized and celebrated.* Eliminate A because failure to discuss ethnic issues openly may allow conflicts between ethnic groups to continue, so would be unlikely to improve the classroom climate. Eliminate C and D because competitive games or ability groups might add to racial tension. Ms. Solomon should use one-on-one activities, such as tutoring, because they allow

students to get to know each other and to learn to cooperate with one another. Choice B is the correct response.

11. **A** This question deals with **diversity.** Thus, its primary focus is Competency 003: *The teacher appreciates human diversity, recognizing how diversity in the classroom and the community may affect learning and creating a classroom environment in which both the diversity of groups and the uniqueness of individuals are recognized and celebrated.* Creating an environment that respects and confirms the dignity of students as human beings is essential in meeting the needs of diverse students. Teachers should reflect on their own values, stereotypes, and prejudices and how these might be affecting their interactions with students (eliminate B). As when dealing with other inappropriate behavior, teachers should respond immediately to expressions of racism (eliminate C). Teachers should recognize the instructional implications of diversity by using a variety of teaching methods that reflect a belief in "success for all" students, rather than concentrating on teaching methods that work best for "most students" (eliminate D). The principal should not consider the establishment of special classes to serve disabled students because multiculturalism means valuing and including all students, regardless of their differences. Students with special needs, including those with limited English proficiency, should not be segregated unless they cannot function in a regular classroom. Choice A is the correct response.

12. **B** This question deals with **diversity.** Thus, its primary focus is Competency 003: *The teacher appreciates human diversity, recognizing how diversity in the classroom and the community may affect learning and creating a classroom environment in which both the diversity of groups and the uniqueness of individuals are recognized and celebrated.* This is a priority-setting question—you must decide what Ms. Solomon should do *first.* Eliminate A because it may send the message that recognizing and celebrating differences need receive attention only during that period. Indeed, research findings indicate that such measures may be too brief or superficial and, as a result, are unlikely to improve cross-group harmony. Choice B is related to **professionalism** (teacher self-reflection), but don't eliminate it, because it is also related to **diversity** (beliefs and attitudes about other cultural groups), so it could be the correct answer choice. Choices C and D are measures Ms. Solomon might take to implement a more culturally diverse curriculum; however, your knowledge of effective multicultural practices should tell you that before proceeding with her plans, Ms. Solomon should *first* examine her own personal beliefs and feelings about other cultural groups. Many teachers are unaware of their own biases and prejudices. Effective teachers reflect on their own values, stereotypes, and prejudices and how these might be affecting their decisions in the classroom. Choice B is the correct response.

13. **B** This question deals with **diversity.** Thus, its primary focus is Competency 003: *The teacher appreciates human diversity, recognizing how diversity in the classroom and the community may affect learning and creating a classroom environment in which both the diversity of groups and the uniqueness of individuals are recognized and celebrated.* Eliminate A because students may pursue interests traditionally associated with their gender to avoid being ridiculed by their classmates. Eliminate C because it promotes sex-role stereotyping. Eliminate D because gender differences are likely to increase when boys and girls are grouped separately. Teachers should avoid differential treatment of boys and girls in class by treating male and female students similarly, whenever appropriate. Gender differences are increased through biases, stereotyping, and differential treatment of boys and girls in class. Choice B is the correct response.

14. **B** This question deals with **instructional strategies.** Thus, its primary focus is Competency 008: *The teacher uses a variety of instructional strategies and roles to facilitate learning and to help students become independent thinkers and problem solvers who use higher-order thinking in the classroom and the real world.* Teachers should understand principles, procedures, advantages, and limitations associated with various instructional strategies (such as cooperative learning). Teachers should closely monitor student work (eliminate A), adhere to strict grading policies (eliminate C), and determine group size (eliminate D) before assigning students to groups. When cooperative learning is used, rewards for students are based on group performance, so students "sink or swim" together interdependently. Recent research underscores that such practices have a positive impact on student behavior and academic achievement. Choice B is the correct choice.

15. **B** This question deals with **instructional strategies.** Thus, its primary focus is Competency 008: *The teacher uses a variety of instructional strategies and roles to facilitate learning and to help students become independent thinkers and problem solvers who use higher-order thinking in the classroom and the real world.* Eliminate A, C, and D, because appointing team leaders, giving tangible rewards, and establishing baseline scores for group members are practices that might be used in a cooperative learning setting, but these are not considered "essential" components. Effective cooperative learning activities should be designed to ensure that each member of the group is accountable for his or her learning as well as for contributing to the success of the group. Therefore, Ms. Lazarine must design cooperative learning activities and monitor them in such a way that she is satisfied that each member makes a meaningful contribution to the group's activities and is responsible for his or her learning at the same time. In addition, by ensuring individual accountability, she can guard

against higher achievers (and their parents) feeling that "lazy" students are getting a "free ride." Choice B is the correct response.

16. **A** This question deals with **instructional strategies.** Thus, its primary focus is Competency 008: *The teacher uses a variety of instructional strategies and roles to facilitate learning and to help students become independent thinkers and problem solvers who use higher-order thinking in the classroom and the real world.* Teachers should understand principles, procedures, advantages, and limitations associated with various instructional strategies (such as cooperative learning). Eliminate Roman III because research strongly supports the positive outcomes for students when cooperative learning is used. Eliminate C. Eliminate Roman IV because increased noise may occur when cooperative learning is used, but effective classroom managers teach students how to use their "one-foot" voices to keep the noise to an acceptable level. Eliminate B and D. It is important to realize that placing students in a learning group and expecting them to cooperate and successfully work together (without careful and thoughtful planning by the teacher beforehand) is unrealistic and is likely to lead to disappointing results. Teachers require adequate training (Roman I) in order for cooperative learning to be implemented successfully, and students must be taught the interpersonal skills needed for high-quality small-group work (Roman II). Choice A is the correct response.

17. **A** This question deals with **motivation.** Thus, its primary focus is Competency 005: *The teacher understands how motivation affects group and individual behavior and learning and can apply this understanding to promote student learning.* Eliminate B because it is off-topic—whether or not it is appealing to teachers does not affect student motivation. Eliminate C because cooperative learning emphasizes group accomplishments, not competition. Eliminate D because effective cooperative learning groups should be heterogeneous in membership. The positive interdependence that is an essential component of cooperative learning is a strong motivational incentive for the students. Students perceive that it is to their advantage if others students in their group learn and to their disadvantage if others in their group do poorly. Also, a group incentive structure allows all students, even those who usually perform poorly, an opportunity to succeed, which can be highly motivating for these students. Choice A is the correct response.

18. **B** This question deals with **instructional strategies.** Thus, its primary focus is Competency 008: *The teacher uses a variety of instructional strategies and roles to facilitate learning and to help students become independent thinkers and problem solvers who use higher-order thinking in the classroom and the real world.* Teachers should understand principles, procedures, advantages, and limitations associated with various instructional strategies (for instance, cooperative learning). Eliminate A because gifted students

can benefit from cooperative learning groups since they are working toward group success, rather than individual achievement, and hence feel less isolated. Also, it is a way for all students, including the gifted students, to learn essential interpersonal life skills and to develop the ability to work collaboratively—a skill now greatly in demand in the workplace. Eliminate C because teachers should not use cooperative learning groups to meet the needs of gifted students by putting them in charge of groups, since the average- and low-ability students may be overpowered by such an arrangement. Eliminate D because, in general, teachers should use a variety of instructional strategies. Critics of the use of cooperative learning strategies with gifted students argue that high-achieving students are penalized by working in heterogeneous cooperative learning groups, but acknowledge the benefits of such groups for low-achieving students. They complain that high achievers feel used and frustrated by low achievers who are not motivated to perform well. Other researchers, such as Johnson and Johnson, contend that high-achieving students learn as much in cooperatively structured classes as they do in traditional classes; further, they benefit socially from the opportunity to work collaboratively and help others. Nevertheless, high achievers should also be given opportunities to work cooperatively with other high achievers or on independent projects. Choice B is the correct response.

19. **A** This question deals with **planning.** Thus, its primary focus is Competency 006: *The teacher uses planning processes to design outcome-oriented learning experiences that foster understanding and encourage self-directed thinking and learning in both individual and collaborative settings.* Eliminate C because it relates to Competency 011 (**classroom management**). Eliminate B and D because they focus on the learning task and not the learner— they are not learner-centered. In designing instruction, Ms. Lazarine's team members take account of factors relevant to instructional planning, such as the varied characteristics of the learners in their classrooms. They recognize the importance of adapting instruction to meet the needs of the more able learners, as well as the needs of the less able learners. Choice A is the correct response.

20. **D** This question deals with **materials and resources.** Thus, its primary focus is Competency 009: *The teacher uses a variety of instructional materials and resources (including human and technological resources) to support individual and group learning.* Eliminate Roman I because the teacher should be aware that media need to be integrated into the curriculum, not used to "fill in" on off days. Eliminate A. When teachers use media, they should follow the routine practices that apply to any teaching approach, including specifying the learning objectives (Roman II), debriefing students after the use of the media materials (Roman III), and holding students accountable for learning from the media materials used (Roman IV). Choice D is the correct response.

21. **C** This question deals with **classroom management.** Thus, its primary focus is Competency 011: *The teacher structures and manages the learning environment to maintain a classroom climate that promotes the lifelong pursuit of learning and encourages cooperation, leadership, and mutual respect.* Eliminate A because "action zone" applies to a situation where students are seated in rows, which may not serve the instructional purpose of the lesson. Eliminate B and D because these practices are in conflict with providing a supportive and responsive classroom climate that promotes students' self-esteem. The teacher should facilitate a positive social and emotional atmosphere in the classroom and create a physical setting that is conducive to the achievement of various goals. Classroom control is easiest to maintain when supplies and materials are located in places that require minimal foot traffic. Mr. Lockett should be aware that keeping frequently used supplies and materials readily accessible minimizes disturbances in the classroom. Choice C is the correct response.

22. **B** This question deals with **professionalism.** Thus, its primary focus is Competency 012: *The teacher is a reflective practitioner who knows how to promote his or her own professional growth and can work cooperatively with other professionals in the system to create a school culture that enhances learning and encourages positive change.* The teachers in the instructional team recognize that they are members of a learning community and know how to work effectively with each other. Eliminate D because it relates to **school-community relationships** (Competency 14). Eliminate A because it is not supported by the stimulus, which does not address communicating the mission of the school or creating a supportive and risk-taking environment as activities associated with Mr. Lockett's instructional team. Eliminate C because it conflicts with Competency 12, which emphasizes that teachers are members of a learning community. Traditionally, teachers have not been effective in working cooperatively with peers. They have been systematically isolated from one another during most of the school day. By implementing the use of instructional teams that meet regularly to discuss concerns and plan together, this school is affording the teachers an opportunity to learn from each other and thereby enhance instruction. Choice B is the correct response.

23. **A** This question deals with **developmentally appropriate instruction.** Thus, its primary focus is Competency 001: *The teacher uses an understanding of human developmental processes to nurture student growth through developmentally appropriate instruction.* Researchers have long been interested in the differences between adolescents who enter puberty early and those who enter it late. Early-maturing boys are large for their age and

better coordinated than late-maturing boys (eliminate D). Because of the noticeable differences in body size and physical ability, late-maturing boys suffer socially induced inferiority and are often treated as younger than their age by adults (eliminate C). They develop negative self-perceptions and self-concepts (Choice A) and are more likely to have conflicts with their parents (eliminate B). Choice A is the correct response.

24. **A** This question deals with **developmentally appropriate instruction.** Thus, its primary focus is Competency 001: *The teacher uses an understanding of human developmental processes to nurture student growth through developmentally appropriate instruction.* Researchers have long been interested in the differences between adolescents who enter puberty early and those who enter it late. The onset of puberty in girls tends to have a negative effect when it occurs in elementary school. The first to mature are likely to experience discomfort because they stand out from the less mature majority. Eliminate B and C because, by the time a girl is in middle school, she no longer feels self-conscious about her mature appearance. Eliminate D because researchers have noted that early-maturing females score lower on measures of self-esteem than early-maturing males do. Early maturation often results in a precocious interest in boys. Choice A is the correct response.

25. **B** This question deals with physiological needs that fall under **students' self-esteem.** Thus, its primary focus is Competency 002: *The teacher considers environmental factors that may affect learning in designing a supportive and responsive classroom community that promotes all students' learning and self-esteem.* Teachers should understand how various external factors may affect students' lives and their performance in school. According to Maslow's theory, all human beings have certain needs that must be met. These needs are listed in a hierarchy as follows: *physiological,* such as food and shelter; *safety,* such as security and order; *belongingness and love,* such as affection and affiliations with others; *esteem,* such as self-respect, worthiness, and gaining approval and recognition; *self-actualization,* such as self-fulfillment and personal achievement. According to Maslow's theory, physiological needs such as hunger, thirst, and bodily comforts are the strongest needs because, if deprived, a person could or would die. Eliminate A because, for example, a hungry child is unlikely to be ready to learn. Eliminate C because some unmet physiological needs can be met, for example, through school programs such as those established under Chapter I (formerly Title I) of the Elementary and Secondary Act of 1965 that serve economically underprivileged children. Eliminate D because it relates to belongingness and love needs, not physiological needs. According to Maslow's theory, physiological needs must be at least partially satisfied before a person will try to satisfy higher needs related to learning, such as esteem and self-actualization. A student with

unmet physiological needs (such as one who is hungry or feels ill) is likely to have little psychological energy to put into learning. Choice B is the correct response.

26. **A** The question deals with **developmentally appropriate instruction.** Thus, its primary focus is Competency 001: *The teacher uses an understanding of human development processes to nurture student growth through developmentally appropriate instruction.* Eliminate B and C because they are not supported by research. Eliminate D because nutritional deficiencies, such as anorexia and bulimia, transcend socioeconomic boundaries. Most studies of nutrition during adolescence show that adolescent girls have nutritional deficiencies more often than boys—mainly because girls eat less and diet more. Choice A is the correct response.

27. **A** This question deals with teacher expectations, which falls under **students' self-esteem.** Thus, its primary focus is Competency 002: *The teacher considers environmental factors that may affect learning in designing a supportive and responsive classroom community that promotes all students' learning and self-esteem.* Eliminate B and D because they are not consistent with research findings regarding the impact of teacher expectations on self-worth and academic achievement. Eliminate C because it contradicts research findings that low achievers are often stereotyped by teachers as being less capable than high achievers because the teachers do not believe they can learn. Mr. Cooper is teaching three classes composed of high-ability students only and one composed of mixed-ability students. Therefore, when he moves from a high-ability group to the mixed-ability group, it is essential that he be conscious of both his verbal and his nonverbal behaviors because, according to Good and Brophy, he may have a tendency to have lower expectations for the students in the regular classroom, especially those who are low achievers. This, in turn, may have a significant impact on student self-worth and achievement. Choice A is the correct response.

28. **D** This question deals with **instructional strategies.** Thus, its primary focus is Competency 008: *The teacher uses a variety of instructional strategies and roles to facilitate learning and to help students become independent thinkers and problem solvers who use higher-order thinking in the classroom and the real world.* In Mr. Cooper's regular class, he must be able to provide instruction for students with a wide range of interests. He might accomplish this by featuring topics that students have identified as interesting (Roman I), planning instructional alternatives for high-ability students (Roman II), allowing uninterested students to pursue different topics (Roman III), and/or individualizing instruction (Roman IV). Choice D is the correct response.

29. **A** This question deals with **instructional strategies.** Thus, its primary focus is Competency 008: *The teacher uses a variety of instructional strategies and roles to facilitate learning and to help students become independent thinkers and problem solvers who use higher-order thinking in the classroom and the real world.* Choice A deals with **classroom management;** suppose you eliminate it. Eliminate D because research suggests that ability grouping may actually reduce achievement levels among average- and low-ability learners. Eliminate B and C because increased student compliance with classroom rules and increased engaged learning time are unlikely outcomes of using ability groups, unless the teacher is proactive in structuring and managing the learning environment to minimize off-task behavior and noncompliance with rules. You've eliminated all the answer choices, so what should you do? Reread the problem and the answer choices. Your knowledge of grouping practices should tell you that B, C, and D are definitely incorrect, so the correct answer choice must be A. You should not have eliminated it because it deals with **classroom management** *with regard to ability grouping.* Mr. Cooper should be aware that behavior management problems may arise when ability grouping is used, because other students are expected to work independently while the teacher works with a particular group. Mr. Cooper will have to make sure that the rest of the students know and follow guidelines for appropriate behavior when he is working with an individual group of students, and that they have an assignment they understand and can do while he gives attention to the group. Choice A is the correct response.

30. **D** This question deals with **instructional strategies.** Thus, its primary focus is Competency 008: *The teacher uses a variety of instructional strategies and roles to facilitate learning and to help students become independent thinkers and problem solvers who use higher-order thinking in the classroom and the real world.* Critical thinking is the mental process of acquiring information, then evaluating it to reach a logical conclusion. Eliminate Roman II because Ms. Lehmann would be likely to know that critical thinkers should be provided with opportunities to assume responsibility for their own learning and to become independent thinkers, which would most likely not occur in a teacher-centered classroom climate. Eliminate A and C. To promote critical thinking in his classroom, Mr. Cooper should teach for deeper understanding of content because deeper understanding of content and thinking critically are inseparable (Roman I), require students to justify the reasoning behind their conclusions because this will force students to critically analyze their and other's thinking (Roman III), and help students develop metacognitive strategies because when students receive instruction and guidance in how to become aware of their own thinking processes (metacognition), they become better critical thinkers (Roman IV). Choice D is the correct response.

31. **B** This question deals with **classroom management.** Thus, its primary focus is Competency 011: *The teacher structures and manages the learning environment to maintain a classroom climate that promotes the lifelong pursuit of learning and encourages cooperation, leadership, and mutual respect.* Eliminate A because it is not supported by the stimulus—you are not told that Mr. Cooper's class is "large." Eliminate C because it relates to **students' self-esteem** (Competency 002)—anyway, high teacher expectations usually increase student motivation to be involved. Eliminate D because it is not supported by the stimulus, which does not tell you about Mr. Cooper's presentations. Mr. Cooper needs to know that varying the content of lessons and using a variety of materials and approaches can help prevent off-task behavior. Choice B is the correct response.

32. **A** This question deals with **classroom management.** Thus, its primary focus is Competency 011: *The teacher structures and manages the learning environment to maintain a classroom climate that promotes the lifelong pursuit of learning and encourages cooperation, leadership, and mutual respect.* A well-planned lesson can decrease disruptive behavior. Eliminate B because it refers to the relationship between the teacher and the principal, which is related to **professionalism** (Competency 12). Eliminate C because the size of the teacher should not be a factor in effective classroom management. Eliminate D because corporal punishment is a violent, dehumanizing, and ineffective means of discipline that goes against the purposes of our educational system. The most important element affecting classroom behavior is the teacher's ability to plan interesting lessons that will increase the amount of time students spend actually learning and decrease boredom. Choice A is the correct response.

33. **A** This question deals with **motivation.** Thus, its primary focus is Competency 005: *The teacher understands how motivation affects group and individual behavior and learning and can apply this understanding to promote student learning.* This is a priority-setting question—you must decide which is the *most* likely answer choice. Mr. Cooper's problem is that students are not interested in the lesson. Eliminate B because time-out removes the student from the class activities, which is likely to decrease interest. Teachers should know how to effectively use students' interests to increase motivation. Teachers should capitalize on the students' interests and prior experiences. Generally, students pay closer attention and become more involved when the topics relate directly to their experiences and interests. Eliminate C and D because these are measures that Mr. Cooper might take, but they would not be as effective as that recommended in Choice A. Choice A is the correct response.

34. **C** This question deals with **classroom management.** Thus, its
primary focus is Competency 011: *The teacher structures and
manages the learning environment to maintain a classroom
climate that promotes the lifelong pursuit of learning and
encourages cooperation, leadership, and mutual respect.*
Eliminate A because it is not supported by the stimulus—you do
not know that Rayford will be removed from the classroom (do not
read too much into a question!). Eliminate B and D because
research does not support that either of these is likely to happen.
By isolating Rayford, Mr. Cooper will be depriving him of his
audience. The strategy is appropriate because it appears that
Rayford is motivated to misbehave in order to receive attention
from his peers. Choice C is the correct response.

35. **C** This question deals with **classroom management.** Thus, its
primary focus is Competency 011: *The teacher structures and
manages the learning environment to maintain a classroom
climate that promotes the lifelong pursuit of learning and
encourages cooperation, leadership, and mutual respect.* This is a
priority-setting question—you must decide which is the *most*
effective discipline strategy. Eliminate A, B, and D because
assertive discipline, submissive behavior, and authoritarian
discipline are models based on the premise that student behavior
must be controlled by the teacher. Teachers who create the proper
classroom atmosphere encourage students to develop control of
their own behavior. Self-discipline is an effective secondary
classroom management goal because it makes students responsible
for their own behavior. However, in order for this system to work,
students need to be convinced that it is in their best interest to
conform to the teacher's and school's expectations. Choice C is the
correct response.

36. **B** This question deals with **classroom management.** Thus, its
primary focus is Competency 011: *The teacher structures and
manages the learning environment to maintain a classroom
climate that promotes the lifelong pursuit of learning and
encourages cooperation, leadership, and mutual respect.*
Eliminate A, C, and D because they are punitive and threatening
approaches to discipline and should not be Mr. Cooper's main
focus. While reviewing his plan, Mr. Cooper realized that he focused
primarily on the number of consequences of inappropriate
behavior, rather than on consistency and fairness; and, therefore,
his plan was ineffective. He essentially created a self-fulfilling
prophecy in which the students live up to his low expectations of
them. Ms. Lehmann is aware that when students view a discipline
management plan as fair and it is implemented consistently, mutual
respect usually results. Choice B is the correct response.

37. **A** This question deals with **professionalism.** Thus, its primary focus
is Competency 012: *The teacher is a reflective practitioner who
knows how to promote his or her own professional growth and*

can work cooperatively with other professionals in the system to create a school culture that enhances learning and encourages positive change. Eliminate B and D because they are unprofessional and inappropriate. Eliminate C because it involves a one-way communication (Mr. Heeney to the principal), which would be less likely to build a positive relationship between Mr. Heeney and the principal than Choice A. Currently, principals are accustomed to "walk-throughs" (unannounced visits). So, Mr. Heeney should invite his principal to stop by and observe his classes during cooperative learning activities, games, or simulations on numerous occasions. Choice A is the correct response.

38. **D** This question deals with **planning.** Thus, its primary focus is Competency 006: *The teacher uses planning processes to design outcome-oriented learning experiences that foster understanding and encourage self-directed thinking and learning in both individual and collaborative settings.* This is a priority-setting question—you have to decide which answer choice is Mr. Heeney's *primary* motivation. Eliminate A because, although using these various methods does provide variety, this is unlikely to be Mr. Heeney's primary motivation for selecting these particular strategies, since the instructional purpose of the strategies should be his main concern. Eliminate B because it relates to **classroom management** (Competency 011). Eliminate C because it relates to **students' self-esteem** (Competency 002). Mr. Heeney is likely to understand principles, procedures, advantages, and limitations associated with various instructional strategies and to choose from among them to achieve different purposes. Inquiry and discovery methods, cooperative learning, and laboratory assignments are effective ways to help students develop critical thinking skills. This is obviously Mr. Heeney's primary motivation for selecting these particular strategies. Choice D is the correct response.

39. **D** This question deals with **motivation.** Thus, its primary focus is Competency 005: *The teacher understands how motivation affects group and individual behavior and learning and can apply this understanding to promote student learning.* This is a priority-setting question—you must decide which response would have been *most* effective for motivating students to stay on-task. Eliminate A because teachers should prepare students in advance for the task, rather than explaining during the task, although they should not refuse to assist students who need additional explanation. Eliminate B because it relates to **classroom management.** Eliminate C because it is about Mr. Heeney, not about what motivates students. Mr. Heeney no doubt knows the importance of maximizing the amount of class time students are actively engaged in learning and is aware that students' interest in and desire to complete classroom tasks can be enhanced by making sure the students recognize the importance and value of the

academic task, thereby triggering their intrinsic motivation. Choice D is the correct response.

40. **A** This question deals with **school-home relationships.** Thus, its primary focus is Competency 013: *The teacher knows how to foster strong school-home relationships that support student achievement of desired learning outcomes.* Eliminate B, C, and D because they "talk down" to the parent, conveying an attitude of superiority on the part of the teacher. Effective communication with parents is very important. Mr. Heeney should know that the critical elements of verbal communication are accuracy of language, accuracy of information, standardization of language, and clearly defined expectations. Conveying correct information is the most effective technique for clearing up misunderstandings that may occur. Choice A is the correct response.

41. **B** This question deals with **school-home relationships.** Thus, its primary focus is Competency 013: *The teacher knows how to foster strong school-home relationships that support student achievement of desired learning outcomes.* The probable reason Mr. Heeney's parent-teacher conference on the previous day was not effective is that he did not provide sufficient opportunity for parental input. Frequently, parents are intimidated by parent-teacher conferences, and they are concerned that they may say something that is embarrassing or will cause harm to their child. Therefore, they will accept one-way communication, unless the teacher makes an effort to involve them in the conversation. During the conference, Mr. Heeney should pause and encourage the parents to respond and offer suggestions. Eliminate A and C because they do not address the problem that occurred in the previous conference. Eliminate D because it won't necessarily lead to increased parental input. Choice B is the correct response.

42. **D** This question deals with **school-home relationships.** Thus, its primary focus is Competency 013: *The teacher knows how to foster strong school-home relationships that support student achievement of desired learning outcomes.* Eliminate A and B because contact with parents should be ongoing and systematic, rather than reactive to problems or emergencies. Eliminate C because student behavior is a shared student-parent-teacher responsibility. The person with the most opportunities to build a positive parent-school relationship is the classroom teacher. Teachers can be effective public relations agents by building a solid partnership with the parents of their students. Positive telephone calls and letters throughout the year to all parents telling of class happenings and their children's achievement will be most welcome and appreciated. Choice D is the correct response.

43. **D** This question deals with **school-home relationships.** Thus, its primary focus is Competency 013: *The teacher knows how to foster strong school-home relationships that support student*

achievement of desired learning outcomes. Eliminate A because it is unprofessional and inappropriate teacher behavior. Eliminate B because parent-teacher conferences should be planned and scheduled in advance and should not interrupt ongoing instruction. Eliminate C because the problem should be resolved collaboratively and be given sufficient time for thought. The person with the most opportunities to build a positive parent-school relationship is the classroom teacher. When communicating with a parent, even when the parent has appeared unexpectedly and disrupted a lesson, the teacher should maintain self-control and remain unemotional. Choice D is the correct response.

44. **A** This question assesses Competency 015: *The teacher understands requirements, expectations, and constraints associated with teaching in Texas, and can apply this understanding in a variety of contexts.* Teachers should have a clear understanding of the laws applying to the students who come to the class with special needs. According to IDEA (formerly PL 94-142), which went into effect in 1977, placement in the "least restrictive environment" means placement of the student in the regular classroom to the maximum extent appropriate. Eliminate B because the burden of providing an appropriate environment should not be placed entirely upon the special education teachers. Eliminate C because it is not always in the best interest of the disabled student to participate in regular school activities. Mr. Heeney should be aware that by law, the ARD committee must place the student in a classroom with his or her peers, unless the student's disability is so severe that education in a regular classroom setting cannot be achieved satisfactorily. Eliminate D because it conflicts with the law for students who can function in a regular classroom setting. Choice A is the correct response.

45. **D** This question deals with **ethical, legal, and professional standards.** Thus, its primary focus is Competency 015: *The teacher understands requirements, expectations, and constraints associated with teaching in Texas, and can apply this understanding in a variety of contexts.* The teacher understands and recognizes the levels of authority and important decision-making structures within the school system and knows how to work within the system to make appropriate decisions regarding students. The comprehensive special education elements assigned by law to be administered by the Texas Education Agency (TEA) include an admission, review, and dismissal (ARD) committee. The Individuals with Disabilities Education Act Amendments of 1997 specifies that the ARD committees must include but are not limited to the parents (or guardians) of the child, at least one regular education teacher of the child (provided the child is participating in a regular education classroom), at least one special education teacher (or, where appropriate, special education provider) of the child, a representative of the school who is qualified to provide or supervise the provision of special services

(which may be the principal), someone who can interpret evaluation results, and other individuals who may be of help in designing an Individualized Education Program (IEP) for the student. Choice D is the correct response.

46. **B** This question deals with **ethical, legal, and professional standards.** Thus, its primary focus is Competency 015: *The teacher understands requirements, expectations, and constraints associated with teaching in Texas, and can apply this understanding in a variety of contexts.* Eliminate A because Mr. Heeney is required by IDEA to report Yvonne's progress to her parents as often as he reports to the parents of other students in the class. Eliminate C because according to TEC 29.305, if practicable, the school must provide opportunities for Yvonne to be educated "in the company of" other hearing-impaired students. Eliminate D because IDEA requires that special education students whose "placement" is in the regular education classroom must have opportunities to interact with their nondisabled classmates. Mr. Heeney should not remove Yvonne to another setting away from the regular classroom—such as the library—because that would violate Yvonne's IEP, which states that her placement is in Mr. Heeney's classroom. Only Yvonne's ARD committee can change her placement; Mr. Heeney does not have the legal authority to do so by himself. Choice B is the correct response.

47. **D** This question deals with **ethical, legal, and professional standards.** Thus, its primary focus is Competency 015: *The teacher understands requirements, expectations, and constraints associated with teaching in Texas, and can apply this understanding in a variety of contexts.* IDEA 97 has strengthened the rights of parents who have a child with a disability in school. With regard to ARD committee meetings, parents have the right to written notice of scheduled meetings at least five school days before the meeting (Roman I), the right to bring an attorney to the meeting (Roman II), the right to have an interpreter if the parents' primary language is other than English (Roman III), and the right to audiotape-record the meeting as long as all attending are informed about it (Roman IV). Choice D is the correct response.

48. **D** This question deals with **professionalism.** Thus, its primary focus is Competency 012: *The teacher is a reflective practitioner who knows how to promote his or her own professional growth and can work cooperatively with other professionals in the system to create a school culture that enhances learning and encourages positive change.* Eliminate A and C because the stimulus provides no reason to assume Mr. Heeney wants to be a risk taker or innovator or to demonstrate that he has clearly defined goals by participating in the inservice. Eliminate B because it is not supported by the stimulus—there is no indication Mr. Heeney will participate in collaborative decision making during the inservice. Mr. Heeney is aware of his professional obligation to seek out

opportunities to grow professionally. Mr. Heeney is seeking out an opportunity to grow professionally and to enhance his own professional skills and knowledge. Choice D is the correct response.

49. **B** This question deals with **communication.** Thus, its primary focus is Competency 007: *The teacher uses effective verbal, nonverbal, and media communication techniques to shape the classroom into a community of learners engaged in active inquiry, collaborative exploration, and supportive interactions.* Eliminate A and C because by giving Yvonne sufficient wait time, Mr. Heeney is sending a positive message to Yvonne—that he values her input in the class. By continuing to wait, he is providing Yvonne with adequate wait time since he no doubt recognizes that her speech impairment may slow her response. Eliminate D because it relates to **classroom management** (Competency 011). By waiting patiently for Yvonne to respond, Mr. Heeney sends a message to the class that he values her response. Choice B is the correct response.

50. **D** This question deals with **ethical, legal, and professional standards.** Thus, its primary focus is Competency 015: *The teacher understands requirements, expectations, and constraints associated with teaching in Texas, and can apply this understanding in a variety of contexts.* Teachers should be aware of terminology associated with the teaching profession. Eliminate A because selectively placing special education students in one or more regular education classes is usually referred to as "mainstreaming." Eliminate B because the term *inclusion* is not about the certification of the teachers. Eliminate C because this is linked to traditional forms of special education service delivery, where students were removed or "pulled out" of regular education classes for all or part of the day. Full inclusion means that all special education students, regardless of disability or severity, will be in a regular classroom/program full-time. All services must be taken to the child in that setting. Choice D is the correct response.

51. **C** This question deals with **communication.** Thus, its primary focus is Competency 007: *The teacher uses effective verbal, nonverbal, and media communication techniques to shape the classroom into a community of learners engaged in active inquiry, collaborative exploration, and supportive interactions.* This is a priority-setting question—you will have to decide which of the responses is *most* useful. Eliminate A because Mr. Juarez's question is one that should elicit divergent thinking, not factual recall. Eliminate B because teachers should encourage students to be independent thinkers and, thus, not give them hints about what to think. Eliminate D because Mr. Juarez's question isn't asking about what the students already know about the controversy. Mr. Juarez's question is designed to create a climate of inquiry. He does not have a single right answer to the question in mind, but rather wants students to explore and develop their own ideas about the topic.

His question is meant to provide a framework for engaging students in active inquiry during the ensuing class discussion. Choice C is the correct response.

52. **D** This question deals with **how learning occurs.** Thus, its primary focus is Competency 004: *The teacher understands how learning occurs and can apply this understanding to design and implement effective instruction.* Eliminate A because teachers should plan to involve all students in the learning activity. Eliminate B and C because both tend to discourage independent thinking. Mr. Juarez understands how students develop knowledge and skills. He knows that before beginning a discussion in which students will be expected to take a position and defend it, it is important that they have an adequate knowledge of the topic. Choice D is the correct response.

53. **C** This question deals with **planning.** Thus, its primary focus is Competency 006: *The teacher uses planning processes to design outcome-oriented learning experiences that foster understanding and encourage self-directed thinking and learning in both individual and collaborative settings.* This is a priority-setting question—you must decide which of the answer choices is Mr. Juarez's *primary* purpose. Eliminate A because it relates to **communication** (Competency 007). Eliminate B because it is not supported by the stimulus—the students are discussing a problem, not solving one. Eliminate D because it relates to **students' self-esteem** (Competency 002)—the controversy is an outside factor that may have a negative effect in the classroom. Mr. Juarez uses a class discussion as a means to foster understanding and encourage higher-order thinking. Although the discussion will provide opportunities for students to talk during class and may minimize the negative effects of community problems in the classroom, facilitating higher-order thinking is the main purpose. Choice C is the correct response.

54. **C** This question deals with **classroom management.** Thus, its primary focus is Competency 011: *The teacher structures and manages the learning environment to maintain a climate that promotes the lifelong pursuit of learning and encourages cooperation, leadership, and mutual respect.* Mr. Juarez should know how to promote student membership in a smoothly functioning learning community and to facilitate a positive social and emotional atmosphere in the classroom that encourages class participation. This is a priority-setting question—you must select the *best* seating arrangement. Seating students in rows, as in Figure 1 (A) and Figure 2 (B), will limit student participation. When students are seated in rows, students sitting near the front and center of the room are likely to speak more freely than students seated elsewhere; further, with these arrangements, students seated in the back of the row may lose interest. Seating the students in a U-shape, as in Figure 3, will facilitate student interaction during the

whole-group discussion, since students will be able to see each other and the teacher face to face, will feel more involved in the activity, and can be accessed more readily by the teacher. Seating students in clusters, as in Figure 4 (D), is a useful arrangement for group activities, but would not be the best seating arrangement for a whole-group discussion. The correct response is Choice C.

55. **B** This question deals with **communication.** Thus, its primary focus is Competency 007: *The teacher uses effective verbal, nonverbal, and media communication techniques to shape the classroom into a community of learners engaged in active inquiry, collaborative exploration, and supportive interactions.* Research suggests that effective teachers encourage and promote critical thinking and problem solving. They are thoughtful questioners who know how to elicit different levels of thinking by careful selection of appropriate questions. Eliminate A and C because when? where? how? and what? questions and convergent (closed-response) questions elicit lower-level thinking—knowledge and comprehension—and do not encourage or promote critical thinking and problem solving. Eliminate D because it is not supported by research findings. By asking more divergent (open-ended) questions, the teacher stimulates the students to think more critically, which helps them clarify their understandings and construct their own knowledge. Choice B is the correct response.

56. **B** This question deals with **communication.** Thus, its primary focus is Competency 007: *The teacher uses effective verbal, nonverbal, and media communication techniques to shape the classroom into a community of learners engaged in active inquiry, collaborative exploration, and supportive interactions.* This is a priority-setting question—you have to select the answer choice that is the *main* reason. Research regarding wait time indicates that the desire to avoid silence, a cultural norm in our society, can cause a teacher to become very uncomfortable and unable to wait three seconds or more for students' responses, even though waiting for students to respond communicates positive expectations for them and results in more thoughtful responses, thereby enhancing achievement. Choices A, C, and D are possible reasons teachers may find the three-second wait time difficult to implement, but research indicates that the cultural norm against silence is the strongest factor working against sufficient wait time. Choice B is the correct response.

57. **B** This question deals with **instructional strategies.** Thus, its primary focus is Competency 008: *The teacher uses a variety of instructional strategies and roles to facilitate learning and to help students become independent thinkers and problem solvers who use higher-order thinking in the classroom and the real world.* In a class discussion, the ideas should be drawn from the students, so Eliminate A, C, and D because Mr. Juarez's acting as judge, critic, or arbitrator—dominant roles—would be likely to discourage students

from expressing their ideas. Mr. Juarez should know when to vary his role in the instructional process in relation to the content and purposes of instruction and the levels of need and independence of the students. Since he wants the ideas to be drawn from the students, he should assume the nondirective role of moderator, rather than playing a dominant role during the lesson. Choice B is the correct response.

58. **A** This question deals with **motivation.** Thus, its primary focus is Competency 005: *The teacher understands how motivation affects group and individual behavior and learning and can apply this understanding to promote student learning.* Mr. Juarez understands the power of effective reinforcement. Eliminate B, C, and D because by praising effectively (Choice B), smiling at students who look attentive (Choice C), and cueing good behavior (Choice D), Mr. Juarez will reinforce desirable behaviors, and thus motivate students to continue the good behaviors. Ignoring minor distractions is not a form of reinforcement because the teacher is taking no action. Choice A is the correct response.

59. **B** This question does not give enough information for you to decide the competency initially. You will have to read the answer choices and select which one is consistent with effective educational practice. Eliminate A because it is not supported by the stimulus—there is no indication that the controversy was a distraction. Eliminate C and D because they are not supported by the stimulus—you are not told that the students were given choices (C) or that the class discussed the school's relationship to the community (D). Choice B deals with **motivation.** Thus, you now know that the primary focus of this question is Competency 005: *The teacher understands how motivation affects group and individual behavior and learning and can apply this understanding to promote student learning.* Mr. Bentley understands the importance of motivation to learning and is able to recognize factors and situations that are likely to promote motivation. He uses an external factor (that is, the community controversy) as a tool to engage students in active learning and to help motivate them to learn. Choice B is the correct response.

60. **D** This question deals with both **communication** (the students engage in a discussion) and **assessment** (what did the students learn?). Glancing at the answer choices, you can see that they do not deal with **assessment** issues, so the primary focus of this question is Competency 007: *The teacher uses effective verbal, nonverbal, and media communication techniques to shape the classroom into a community of learners engaged in active inquiry, collaborative exploration, and supportive interactions.* Eliminate A because a discussion is unlikely to lead to an absolute conclusion since few, if any, facts are provided. Eliminate B because it is not supported by the stimulus—there is no mention of community leaders as role models. Eliminate C because the

students are discussing a problem, not solving it. During the discussion, Mr. Juarez should monitor the effects of messages, simplifying and restating when necessary, and encouraging the students to communicate effectively. He should emphasize to the students that the critical elements of verbal communication are accuracy of language, accuracy of information, standardization of language, and clearly defined expectations. Choice D is the correct response.

61. **B** This question deals with **planning.** Thus, its primary focus is Competency 006: *The teacher uses planning processes to design outcome-oriented learning experiences that foster understanding and encourage self-directed thinking and learning in both individual and collaborative settings.* This is a priority-setting question—you must select the response that is *most* appropriate. Eliminate A because objectives consistent with a student discussion are at the higher levels of Bloom's taxonomy, not at the lower, knowledge level. Eliminate C because younger or less mature students may not have the necessary prior knowledge to enter productively into a discussion. Eliminate D because discussions should generate a variety of divergent ideas. Educational research has established that group discussion in which students publicly commit themselves is effective in changing individuals' attitudes. Since attitudes fall in the affective domain, Choice B is the correct response.

62. **C** This question deals with **how learning occurs.** Thus, its primary focus is Competency 004: *The teacher understands how learning occurs and can apply this understanding to design and implement effective instruction.* This is a priority-setting question—you must select the *best* response. Eliminate A because it is not supported by the stimulus—there is no indication that Ms. Webb considers the wide range of computer expertise in her class to be a problem (don't read too much into a question!). Eliminate B and D because they relate to **assessment** (Competency 010). Ms. Webb is aware that prior learning experiences affect learning, so she uses the questionnaire to obtain information that will help her design lesson activities geared to the various levels of ability of her students. Choice C is the correct response.

63. **A** This question deals with **assessment.** Thus, its primary focus is Competency 010: *The teacher uses processes of informal and formal assessment to understand individual learners, monitor instructional effectiveness, and shape instruction.* Teachers should be knowledgeable of the uses and limitations of different types of assessments. Eliminate B because *summative* assessment occurs at the end of an instructional experience (for example, unit, semester, year), *not* before. Eliminate C because Ms. Webb's questionnaire is not designed to measure achievement, but is an informal assessment of students' prior knowledge. *Formative* assessment is assessment that takes place both before and during

the learning process. It is used to guide the content and pace of lessons and may take various forms (such as informal survey, diagnostic instrument, pretest, or ungraded skills checklist). Eliminate D because *diagnostic* assessment is a formative assessment procedure that uses carefully designed (formal) instruments to pinpoint each student's individual strengths and weaknesses. Ms. Webb's questionnaire is an informal survey that will not yield such specific data; still, it is a form of formative assessment. Choice A is the correct response.

64. **A**   This question deals with **instructional strategies.** Thus, its primary focus is Competency 008: *The teacher uses a variety of instructional strategies and roles to facilitate learning and to help students become independent thinkers and problem solvers who use higher-order thinking in the classroom and the real world.* Ms. Webb should understand the advantages and limitations associated with various instructional strategies. To make instruction effective for all her students, Ms. Webb needs to take into account their diverse needs. Individualized instruction (Choice B), peer tutoring (Choice C), and laboratory application (Choice D) allow an opportunity for the teacher to accommodate the levels of need and independence of the students, so that instruction is more effective. Since her students vary widely in experiences and abilities, whole-group demonstration would most likely be ineffective because it will not accommodate individual student differences. The demonstration might be too advanced for some students and too easy for others. Choice A is the correct response.

65. **C**   This question deals with **classroom management.** Thus, its primary focus is Competency 011: *The teacher structures and manages the learning environment to maintain a climate that promotes the lifelong pursuit of learning and encourages cooperation, leadership, and mutual respect.* This is a priority-setting question—you must decide what Ms. Webb should do *first.* Ms. Webb should know how to promote student membership in a smoothly functioning learning community and to facilitate a positive social and emotional atmosphere in the classroom. Eliminate A and B because they are punitive approaches to discipline and, if taken, should be only as a last resort. Eliminate D because it is an inappropriate teacher behavior—when dealing with a discipline problem, the student's dignity must be preserved. In dealing with Julie's tendency to be tardy, Ms. Webb should keep in mind that in order to solve the problem, she needs to understand the problem. Julie is the most direct and accessible source of information about the problem; so the *first* step for Ms. Webb to take is to talk with Julie to determine her awareness of the problem, the meaning that it holds for her, and how they can reach a mutual solution to the problem. Choice C is the correct response.

66. **D** This question deals with **classroom management.** Thus, its primary focus is Competency 011: *The teacher structures and manages the learning environment to maintain a classroom climate that promotes the lifelong pursuit of learning and encourages cooperation, leadership, and mutual respect.* Eliminate A because, despite obstacles such as a negative reaction from the class, research provides extensive evidence supporting the use of peer and cross-age tutoring and its positive outcomes. Eliminate B because peer tutoring is recommended as a way to deal with misbehaving students, which suggests that Julie's behavior is likely to improve. Eliminate C because it is not supported by the stimulus—there is no indication that Ms. Webb will be assigning students to groups. Researchers have identified benefits that accrue to peer tutors, including improvement in social behaviors and classroom discipline. Indeed, peer tutoring is recommended as a way to deal with misbehaving students, so Julie's behavior will probably improve if she becomes a peer tutor. Choice D is the correct response.

67. **C** This question deals with **students' self-esteem.** Thus, its primary focus is Competency 002: *The teacher considers environmental factors that may affect learning in designing a supportive and responsive classroom that promotes all students' learning and self-esteem.* Eliminate A, B, and D because they disagree with research findings. Teachers who are aware of the influence of peers on students' social and intellectual development can take advantage of this factor by using peer tutoring. Research investigating the effects of peer tutoring on student achievement has found that, in general, the achievement of both tutors and tutees increases. Choice C is the correct response.

68. **B** This question deals with **instructional strategies.** Thus, its primary focus is Competency 008: *The teacher uses a variety of instructional strategies and roles to facilitate learning and to help students become independent thinkers and problem solvers who use higher-order thinking in the classroom and the real world.* Eliminate A, C, and D because they disagree with research findings. Ms. Webb should be aware that most often it is recommended that tutors and tutees be separated by two to three grade levels. Slavin suggests that this is partly because students may look up to an older student and accept him or her as a tutor, but might resent a same-age classmate appointed to tutor them. Choice B is the correct response.

69. **A** This question deals with **assessment.** Thus, its primary focus is Competency 010: *The teacher uses processes of informal and formal assessment to understand individual learners, monitor instructional effectiveness, and shape instruction.* Eliminate B, C, and D because they are inconsistent with the definition of *percentile.* For standardized tests, percentile scores are scores that reflect a student's standing relative to a norm group. The 80th

percentile is the score that is the same or better than 80 percent of the scores of the norm group. Choice A is the correct response.

70. **B** This question deals with **motivation.** Thus, the primary focus of this question is Competency 005: *The teacher understands how motivation affects group and individual behavior and learning and can apply this understanding to promote student learning.* This is a priority-setting question—you have to select the *most* appropriate strategy. Eliminate A, C, and D because they reflect a lower performance standard for Pierre, which sends a negative message to him regarding Ms. Webb's opinion of his capabilities— and thus conflict with Competency 002, which says teachers should have high expectations of students. Based on Pierre's achievement results, Ms. Webb probably feels that Pierre is capable of better performance in her class. She can influence Pierre's desire or perseverance to learn by using specific strategies to motivate him to learn. If Ms. Webb establishes a systematic reinforcement schedule for Pierre's completed work, after a while he will find that doing the work pays off in ability to understand what is going on in class and in better grades. These natural reinforcers are likely to motivate him to continue to be successful. Choice B is the correct response.

71. **C** This question deals with **school-community relationships.** Thus, its primary focus is Competency 014: *The teacher understands how the school relates to the larger community and knows strategies for making interactions between school and community mutually supportive and beneficial.* This is a priority-setting question—you have to select the *best* response. Eliminate A because it relates to **classroom management** (Competency 011). Eliminate B because it relates to **professionalism** (Competency 012). Eliminate D because it relates to **materials and resources** (Competency 009). Ms. Webb is aware of the significance of the school-community relationship and understands the value of establishing partnerships with other community entities. She has devised a way to take advantage of the strengths and resources of the nearby university to promote the academic achievement of her students. Choice C is the correct response.

72. **B** This question deals with **assessment.** Thus, its primary focus is Competency 010: *The teacher uses processes of informal and formal assessment to understand individual learners, monitor instructional effectiveness, and shape instruction.* Eliminate A because summative assessment is assessment that follows instruction and occurs at the end of a unit, semester, and so forth. Eliminate C because norm-reference assessment refers to the use of standardized tests that focus on a comparison of a student's score to those of other students. Eliminate D because criterion-referenced assessment refers to the use of tests that are designed to measure mastery of specific skills. Norm- and criterion-referenced tests are formal assessments. Formative assessment is designed to

acquire feedback before the end of a unit, semester, and so forth. It is used to guide the content and pace of lessons. Ms. Webb is using an informal assessment to acquire information before the end of the semester. Choice B is the correct response.

73. **C** This question deals with **planning.** Thus, its primary focus is Competency 006: *The teacher uses planning processes to design outcome-oriented learning experiences that foster understanding and encourage self-directed thinking and learning in both individual and collaborative settings.* Eliminate A because it is related to Maslow's Hierarchy of Human Needs, which deals with **students' self-esteem** (Competency 002). Eliminate B because it relates to **how learning occurs** (Competency 004). Eliminate D because it is off-topic. Ms. Webb understands factors relevant to instructional planning, such as desired learner outcomes that encourage learning and promote student success in the classroom. Choice C is the correct response.

74. **C** This question deals with technology, which comes under **materials and resources.** Thus, its primary focus is Competency 009: *The teacher uses a variety of instructional materials and resources (including human and technological resources) to support individual and group learning.* Eliminate Roman III because there is no reason to suppose the project would or should promote community recognition that American schools can meet the academic needs of Japanese students. Eliminate D. By exchanging information about each other through e-mail, the students from both countries will have an opportunity to learn about each other's culture and way of life (Roman I). Further, the interactivity that the project will evoke in the classroom is likely to lead to increased learning in Ms. Webb's class (Roman II). Finally, the telecommunications project is likely to promote innovation and educational excellence in Texas (Roman IV) by serving as a model for other schools. Choice C is the correct response.

75. **D** This question deals with technology, which comes under **materials and resources.** Thus, its primary focus is Competency 009: *The teacher uses a variety of instructional materials and resources (including human and technological resources) to support individual and group learning.* This is a priority-setting question— you have to select the response that is *most* likely. Eliminate B because it relates to **classroom management** (Competency 011). Eliminate A and C because they are not supported by the question stem, which focuses on the reliability of e-mail—instead, they focus on technology as a learning tool. Ms. Webb understands the value of using technology. She is likely to use the situation as an opportunity to convey to students the power and utility of technology. Choice D is the correct response.

76. **D** This question deals with **ethical, legal, and professional standards.** Thus, its primary focus is Competency 015: *The teacher understands requirements, expectations, and constraints associated with teaching in Texas, and can apply this understanding in a variety of contexts.* Teachers should understand and recognize the levels of authority and important decision-making structures within the school system and know how to work within the system to make appropriate decisions regarding students. In 1991, HB 2885 *established site-based decision making,* which directed local school districts to decentralize decision making. Eliminate Roman I and II because on campuses practicing site-based decision making, decisions regarding student fund-raising projects are made at the campus level, without the necessity of consulting the school board or the superintendent. Eliminate A, B, and C. Choice D is the correct response.

77. **C** This question deals with **school-community relationships.** Thus, its primary focus is Competency 014: *The teacher understands how the school relates to the larger community and knows strategies for making interactions between school and community mutually supportive and beneficial.* This is a priority-setting question—you must select the response that is *most* likely. Eliminate A because you would not expect the project to explain educational goals. Eliminate B because a natural disaster, such as an earthquake, would not lead to understanding about problems in Japan's schools. Eliminate D because the earthquake is a natural disaster, not a problem to be solved. Ms. Webb should be aware of the school-community relationship and understand the value of a project like this in promoting community recognition of the school in encouraging students to care about and help others, thereby promoting a sense of social responsibility in the students. Choice C is the correct response.

78. **B** This question deals with **professionalism.** Thus, its primary focus is Competency 012: *The teacher is a reflective practitioner who knows how to promote his or her own professional growth and can work cooperatively with other professionals in the system to create a school culture that enhances learning and encourages positive change.* Eliminate A, B, and C because they are not supported by the stimulus—there is no indication that Ms. Webb will be explaining the mission of the school, using community resources, or making decisions and solving problems when conducting the workshop. Ms. Webb understands that all professionals have an obligation to work cooperatively with each other for the improvement and advancement of professional growth. The workshop will give Ms. Webb an opportunity to engage in an exchange of ideas with her colleagues to establish a successful learning community. Choice B is the correct response.

79. **C** This question deals with technology, which comes under **materials and resources.** Thus, its primary focus is Competency 009: *The teacher uses a variety of instructional materials and resources (including human and technological resources) to support individual and group learning.* This is a priority-setting question— you must select the answer choice that Ms. Webb should do *first.* Eliminate B because it relates to **instructional strategies** (Competency 008). Eliminate A because it may or may not be necessary to purchase additional software. Eliminate D because teachers can use computer-assisted instruction (CAI) software without knowing programming. Ms. Webb knows that learning can be enhanced through the appropriate use of multiple resources in instruction. The idea behind CAI is to use the computer as a tutor; however, not all the software on the market is good. Ms. Webb needs to heed the caveat "Buyer beware!" and evaluate the software before using it. Choice C is the correct response.

80. **A** This question deals with **ethical, legal, and professional standards.** Thus, its primary focus is Competency 015: *The teacher understands requirements, expectations, and constraints associated with teaching in Texas, and can apply this understanding in a variety of contexts.* Eliminate B, C, and D because they are inconsistent with Ms. Webb's ethical and legal responsibilities. Ms. Webb should be aware that using unlicensed software is illegal. She should tell the teacher to immediately remove all copies of the software from the computers. The teacher should follow Principle I of the Code of Ethics and Standard Practices of Texas Educators, which states that "the educator should endeavor to maintain the dignity of the profession by respecting and obeying the law, demonstrating personal integrity, and exemplifying honesty." Choice A is the correct response.

81. **B** This question deals with **students' self-esteem.** Thus, its primary focus is Competency 002: *The teacher considers environmental factors that may affect learning in designing a supportive and responsive classroom community that promotes all students' learning and self-esteem.* Mr. Kim should be aware of the importance of developing positive relationships with his students. Teachers should be supportive of students and create an environment in which all students feel safe, accepted, confident, and productive. Eliminate Roman III because Mr. Kim's behavior is inappropriate, so is likely to have a negative effect on Tyrone. Eliminate C and D. Obviously, Mr. Kim has jumped to conclusions about Jimmy (Roman I) that are likely to cause Jimmy and possibly Tyrone to mistrust and resent him (Roman II). Choice B is the correct response.

82. **C** Upon first reading, this question seems to deal with **ethical, legal, and professional standards** (Competency 015). Go with that for the moment. The only answer choice that clearly relates to Competency 015 is D, but you should eliminate D because talking to

other students about Jimmy would be a violation of Jimmy's privacy. Eliminate A because Mr. Kim is assuming Jimmy is guilty of drug use when he may not be. Eliminate B because if Jimmy is telling the truth, Mr. Kim may unnecessarily alarm Jimmy's parents. Instead of confronting the boys after class, Mr. Kim should have discussed his concerns with the school counselor (C). Thus, you now know that this question assesses Competency 012: *The teacher is a reflective practitioner who knows how to promote his or her own professional growth and can work cooperatively with other professionals in the system to create a school culture that enhances learning and encourages positive change.* Teachers should recognize they are part of a community of professionals dedicated to helping students. They should understand and know how to work effectively with all members of the school to solve problems that arise. Choice C is the correct response.

83. **B** This question deals with **ethical, legal, and professional standards.** Thus, its primary focus is Competency 015: *The teacher understands requirements, expectations, and constraints associated with teaching in Texas, and can apply this understanding in a variety of contexts.* Eliminate A because obeying ethical, legal, and professional standards takes precedence over other considerations. Eliminate C and D because Mr. Kim's behavior was inappropriate. Mr. Kim needs to be aware of Principle IV of the Texas Code of Ethics and Standard Practices for Texas Educators, which states, "The educator should not reveal confidential information concerning students unless disclosure serves professional services or is required by law." Choice B is the correct response.

84. **C** This question deals with **planning.** Thus, its primary focus is Competency 006: *The teacher uses planning processes to design outcome-oriented learning experiences that foster understanding and encourage self-directed thinking and learning in both individual and collaborative settings.* Eliminate A, B, and D because they are off the topic of the question stem, which focuses on Mr. Kim's decision to obtain materials from the Texas SDRSC program. Mr. Kim is aware of the problems drug use will cause the school and his community. He understands how these problems may affect students' lives and learning and is aware of resources and strategies that can help with the problems. Choice C is the correct response.

85. **C** This question deals with **planning.** Thus, its primary focus is Competency 006: *The teacher uses planning processes to design outcome-oriented learning experiences that foster understanding and encourage self-directed thinking and learning in both individual and collaborative settings.* This is a priority-setting question—you must select the response that is *most* likely. Eliminate A because it is not supported by the stimulus—Mr. Kim's unit is focused on drug use, not on society, in general. Mr. Kim is

aware that students will be more likely to avoid drug use if they are able to think for themselves and make informed, intelligent decisions. Eliminate B and D because although these may be additional outcomes, most likely Mr. Kim's lessons will be designed to enhance students' independent thinking and decision-making skills. Choice C is the correct response.

86. **A** This question assesses Competency 006: *The teacher uses planning processes to design outcome-oriented learning experiences that foster understanding and encourage self-directed thinking and learning in both individual and collaborative settings.* Eliminate B because *reteaching* occurs after the teacher recognizes that the students need additional instruction, not as an introduction to a lesson. Eliminate B because *guided practice* occurs when the students are practicing previously taught learning activities under the guidance of the teacher. Eliminate D because *closure* occurs at the end of a lesson. Mr. Kim understands that an effective lesson begins by engaging the students' interest. He uses the transparency to get the attention of the students and focus that attention on the lesson topic that is to follow. This component of a lesson is called a *focus.* Choice A is the correct response.

87. **D** This question deals with **how learning occurs.** Thus, its primary focus is Competency 004: *The teacher understands how learning occurs and can apply this understanding to design and implement effective instruction.* This is a priority-setting question—you must select the *best* response. Eliminate B because it relates to **classroom management** (Competency 011)—Mr. Kim is involving the students, not simply monitoring them. Eliminate C because it relates to **classroom management.** Eliminate D because it is not supported by the stimulus—Mr. Kim is asking for input, not conveying information. Mr. Kim knows that students learn best when what they are learning becomes personally meaningful to them. By asking the students to respond to his question, they process the information on a personal level, which fosters a view of learning as a purposeful pursuit. Choice D is the correct response.

88. **B** This question deals with **classroom management.** Thus, its primary focus is Competency 011: *The teacher structures and manages the learning environment to maintain a climate that promotes the lifelong pursuit of learning and encourages cooperation, leadership, and mutual respect.* Eliminate Roman II because sending a note to a student is not an excessive correction. Eliminate A and C. Eliminate Roman III because it is not supported by the stimulus—Mr. Kim did not provide Sabrina with a rationale. Eliminate D. In his handling of this situation, Mr. Kim demonstrates that he knows how to facilitate a positive social and emotional atmosphere in the classroom and establish and maintain standards of behavior. He is quick to respond to the disruptive behavior

(Roman IV), but uses a verbal signal (Roman I) to stop it. Choice B is the correct response.

89. **C**   This question is about technology, which relates to **materials and resources.** Thus, it's primary focus is Competency 009: *The teacher uses a variety of instructional materials and resources (including human and technological resources) to support individual and group learning.* Eliminate A, B, and D because they are not supported by the stimulus—don't read too much into a question. You are not told that the students will be using a variety of media to do their research and reports (A); you know only that they will be using the Internet. Obtaining information from the Internet and writing a report is not an example of applying knowledge in a real-world context (B). There is no indication that the students will experience the cultural impartiality of technology as they use the Internet. Mr. Kim knows how to enhance learning for his students through the appropriate use of technology. Researching on the Internet will promote students' appreciation of the Internet as a resource for learning and will help them understand the role of technology as a learning tool. Choice C is the correct response.

90. **B**   This question deals with the **school-community relationship.** Thus, its primary focus is Competency 014: *The teacher understands how the school relates to the larger community and knows strategies for making interactions between school and community mutually supportive and beneficial.* This is a priority-setting question—you must select the *best* answer choice. Eliminate D because it relates to the **school-parent relationship** (Competency 013). Eliminate A because it is not supported by the stimulus—the focus of the volunteer "walkers" program is child safety, not strengthening school-community ties. Eliminate C because although the volunteers may help decrease drugs and violence problems for the school, it is unlikely that one strategy will solve the problems. Because child safety is a concern of the entire community, the volunteer "walkers" program is a strategy that is mutually beneficial to the school and the community. Choice A is the correct response.

PART THREE

Review and Practice

CHAPTER 7

DOMAIN I—UNDERSTANDING LEARNERS

Competency 001

The teacher uses an understanding of human developmental processes to nurture student growth through developmentally appropriate instruction.

As students mature, they progress through cognitive, psychosocial, and physical developmental stages. Effective teachers recognize that students' developmental characteristics affect their performance in school, and design instruction that is responsive to the varied characteristics of students in their classrooms.

Piaget believed that intellectual growth involves two fundamental processes: *assimilation* and *accommodation*. Assimilation involves meshing new experiences into existing mental structures, which Piaget called *schema*. Accommodation requires creating new schema to fit the new data or information. When children encounter new data or information, they experience *disequilibrium* until they can either assimilate or accommodate it and thus achieve equilibrium. Piaget believed that disequilibrium is an unnatural state and that all learners seek equilibrium through either assimilation or accommodation.

Piaget spent a lifetime observing children and the way they think in learning situations. He concluded that children do not think like adults, nor do they see the world as adults do. According to Piaget, cognition, or thinking, is an active and interactive process that develops in stages. The stages are invariable but the ages of children entering them may vary.

His first stage, *sensorimotor*, begins at birth and continues until about age two. During this stage, learning is through the senses and motor development. Children learn to distinguish themselves from the external world. They discover the beginning of independence through cause and effect and learn that objects exist even when they are not visible.

During the *preoperational* stage, from ages two to seven, children are highly imaginative and they love games of "pretend." Vocabulary develops rapidly, children can classify according to one property, and they are very egocentric (self-centered). Symbolic thinking develops during this stage. This period is also characterized by what children cannot do—conserve.

Conservation is the cognitive ability to understand that quantity remains the same even though the shape may have changed.

In Piaget's third stage, *concrete operations*, ages seven to eleven, children begin to conserve. This means they recognize that number, length, quantity, mass, area, weight, and volume of objects has not necessarily changed even though the appearance of these objects may have changed. This involves the mental operation of *reversibility*. Children are now able to apply logical thought to concrete objects and can sort objects into multiple categories. They can now understand the need for rules and abide by them.

The last stage of development, *formal operations*, begins at about age eleven and continues to adulthood. Adolescents who reach this stage begin to think more easily about abstract concepts, things they cannot touch or see. They can develop hypotheses, organize information, test hypotheses, and solve problems. They can also make generalizations, think about the thinking of others, and reflect on their own thinking. However, for most young adolescents Piaget's concrete operations stage is predominant, although frequently an adolescent functions at the concrete operations stage for some topics (such as mathematical problem solving) and the formal stage for other topics (such as civil rights). Teachers should not assume that all adolescents are at the same stage developmentally or that an individual student functions at the same level in all situations. Whether all people achieve formal operational thinking at this or any other stage is still a major question.

Kohlberg studied the way children (and adults) reason about rules that govern their moral behavior. After conducting a long series of studies with children and adults, Kohlberg found that moral development occurs in a specific sequence of stages, regardless of culture. He identified six stages of moral growth, which he grouped into the following three levels:

Preconventional Level (Age birth to 9 years)	Conventional Level (Age 10 to 15 years)	Postconventional Level (Age 16 to adulthood)
Stage 1: *Punishment-Obedience Orientation.* Rules are obeyed to avoid punishment.	Stage 3: *Good Boy–Nice Girl Orientation.* Good behavior is doing what others expect and whatever is approved by them. Peer acceptance is needed.	Stage 5: *Social Contract Orientation.* What's right is defined in terms of standards that have been agreed upon by the whole society. Rules are subject to change if outdated.
Stage 2: *Instrumental-Relativist Orientation.* What's right is whatever satisfies one's own needs and occasionally the needs of others.	Stage 4: *Law-Order Orientation.* Good behavior is doing one's duty, respecting authority, and obeying the laws of society.	Stage 6: *Universal Ethical Principle.* What's right is a decision of one's conscience according to ethical principles. Ethical principles are abstract concepts such as justice, equality, and the dignity of all people.

Erik Erikson developed a life-cycle conception of personality development. According to him, people go through a series of major crises as they proceed through life. At each stage there is a critical social crisis. How the individual reacts to each future crisis is determined by earlier development and by adjustment to social experiences.

Trust versus Mistrust (Birth to 18 months): During this first stage, an infant whose basic physical needs are met and who feels loved and secure will develop feelings of trust. Otherwise, the seeds of mistrust will be firmly planted.

Autonomy versus Doubt (18 months to 3 years): During the second stage, children should be allowed to explore, make simple choices, and learn to control themselves as autonomy is experienced. Otherwise, feelings of self-doubt will prevail.

Initiative versus Guilt (3 to 6 years): Children need to develop a sense of personal identity. It is important that they have opportunities to initiate activities and engage in real and make-believe play. Nurturing and reinforcing children's male or female identities at this stage will help build a firm foundation for the next stages and diminish feelings of guilt.

Industry versus Inferiority (6 to 12 years): Numerous skills are acquired at this stage and children seemingly cannot learn fast enough. If they experience satisfaction and success with the completion of tasks they are assigned or initiate, they will feel good about themselves and develop a sense of industry rather than inferiority.

Identity versus Role Confusion (12 to 18 years): The changes that take place during this stage of adolescence bring about a major shift in personal development. This is the time of transition from childhood to adulthood when adolescents are developing a sense of identity. When they are able to know themselves, they have a sense of who they are and are comfortable with their own identity. If this does not happen, then a sense of role confusion can result.

Intimacy versus Isolation (young adulthood): This is the period when young adults are able to make a commitment to another person, to a cause, or to a career. They are able to give a sense of direction to their lives. Otherwise, they feel isolated from the rest of the world.

Generativity versus Self-absorption (middle adulthood): Concern with future generations and child rearing is the main focus of this stage. People should continue to grow in this stage and become less selfish; if they don't, stagnation sets in and they become self-absorbed or self-indulgent, caring for no one.

Integrity versus Despair (late adulthood): Those who reach the final stage find themselves looking back on their lives with a feeling of satisfaction or with a sense of despair about how life turned out for them—or somewhere in between these two conditions. Coming to terms with one's life and accepting one's failures as well as successes lead to ego integrity. Anguishing over lost opportunities and dreading poor health and death lead to despair.

Physical development of children proceeds from head to toe in what is called a *cephalocaudal* progression. This means motor ability develops from the top down. Infants are first able to control their heads, then their shoulders, and arms, and, finally, their legs and feet. While this is taking place, growth and motor ability are also developing in a *proximodistal* progression, from the central axis of the body outward. Trunk and shoulder movements occur before separate arm movements. Hand and finger control comes last. For a summary, see the following chart:

Physical Development Chart

Ages 3–4	Ages 5–7	Ages 8–10	Ages 11–13
1. Increased skill in large muscle coordination; girls ahead of boys	1. Girls ahead of boys in development and physical achievement	1. Increased importance of physical skills in influencing status and self-concept	1. Onset of adolescent growth spurt for boys
2. Increased speed, coordination, and motor skills	2. Small muscle and eye hand coordination developing	2. Girls taller, stronger, and more skillful in small muscle coordination	2. Peak growth spurt for girls; awkwardness in girls typical
3. High physical energy level	3. Increased skill in handling tools and materials	3. Continued high physical energy level	3. Pubescent stage for girls
4. Ability to dress and undress self	4. Ability to draw a recognizable human figure	4. Onset of adolescent growth spurt for girls	4. Improved motor development and coordination for boys
5. Ability to walk up and down stairs—alternating feet	5. Continued high physical energy	5. Quiet growth period for boys	5. Boys ahead of girls in physical achievement
	6. Necessary physical skills for playing games		

Adolescents sometimes have problems because of the physical changes in their bodies and appearance at puberty. Also, the timing of puberty varies widely, which often affects how adolescents feel about themselves. No matter whether they are early or late maturers, they may become self-conscious about being "different." Some adolescents may be completely physically mature before others of the same age have begun puberty. Research indicates that early maturation for boys is an advantage. Early maturing boys are larger and perform better athletically. Because of the difference in size and athletic ability, late-maturing boys experience low self-esteem and poor self-image. Girls who experience the onset of puberty in elementary school tend to experience difficulties and feel uncomfortable because they are different from the less mature majority. By the late middle-school years, early-maturing girls have become comfortable with their pubertal changes and are more at ease than are later maturers. Early-maturing girls sometimes develop a precocious interest in boys, which may cause some anxiety for parents.

Adolescents are trying to adjust socially and find their own identity at the same time. Girls often become overly concerned with their body image. They have a tendency to eat less and diet more than boys. Most studies of nutrition during adolescence show that adolescent girls have nutritional deficiencies more often than do boys.

According to the National Middle School Association (NMSA), young adolescents need social and emotional support to succeed as students. Based on the opinion of experts such as Dorman and Scales, the NMSA suggests that young adolescents have seven key developmental needs: the need for self-exploration, the need for positive social interaction with both adults and peers, the need for a diversity of experiences, the need for meaningful participation in society, the need for physical activity, the need for competence and achievement, and the need for structure and clear limits. Children in this age group are in the beginning stages of developing their self-concept and identity. This stage of psychosocial development is a time of self-exploration in which self-esteem and self-confidence fluctuate. Adolescents are more concerned about their peer group than with teachers, parents, or other adults in their lives. Teachers can take advantage of this by having students work together on well-defined tasks. Teachers must also be alert to the concern that the increased peer pressure experienced by young adolescents may lead to experimentation with tobacco, alcohol, drugs, and sex.

Additionally, Kellough and Kellough identified characteristics that are common among adolescents, including:

- Curious
- Academic achievement not a priority
- Interested in learning to solve real-life problems
- Concerned about physical appearance
- Face responsibility for sexual behavior before full emotional and social maturity has occurred
- Experience different rates of maturity
- Easily offended and sensitive to criticism
- Inconsistent in their behavior
- Moody, restless, lack self-esteem
- Optimistic and hopeful
- Vulnerable, naive
- Capable of exaggerations
- Emerging sense of humor
- Act out unusual or drastic behavior (that is, daring, argumentative)
- May appear confused and frightened at new school
- Very loyal to peer-group values
- Often rebellious toward parents
- Socially at risk
- Challenge authority
- Need love and acceptance
- Strive to define sex roles
- Idealistic
- Have difficulties with moral and ethical issues

Competency 002

The teacher considers environmental factors that may affect learning in designing a supportive and responsive classroom community that promotes all students' learning and self-esteem.

Classrooms should be inviting, attractive places where students feel comfortable and welcome. An atmosphere of caring and warmth can be created with attractive, stimulating bulletin boards and a few green plants. Some teachers like an area rug in a corner, a claw-footed bathtub to denote a "special" section of the room, a rocking chair or bean bag chair, and maybe a lamp or two. Numerous books, magazines, and games are also useful in creating a feeling of pride and ownership in "our" classroom. A teacher who creates such an environment is providing a learning atmosphere that encourages and motivates students to be successful, thus creating good feelings of self-worth. That teacher is also meeting some important needs of the students.

According to Maslow, all human beings have certain needs that must be met. These needs are listed in a hierarchy as follows:

1. *Physiological,* such as food and shelter

2. *Safety,* such as security and order

3. *Belongingness and love,* such as affection and affiliation with others

4. *Esteem,* such as self-respect, worthiness, and gaining approval and recognition

5. *Self-Actualization,* such as self-fulfillment and personal achievement

The hungry child or the child who is worried about a family problem such as divorce or illness will obviously not be attentive in the classroom.

Teacher expectations also influence student achievement. Teachers who have high expectations have students who actually perform better. This is often referred to as the *self-fulfilling prophecy.* Teachers who expect students to be successful have confidence in their students' abilities and treat them accordingly. The students believe in themselves and are able to achieve.

Attributions are the causes students assign to their successes or failures. The following four attributions are used most frequently: ability ("I'm just not smart"), effort ("I tried really hard"), task difficulty ("That test was impossible"), or luck ("I guessed right"). *Locus of control* is the degree to which students feel that events they experience are under their own control (internal control), rather than under the control of other people or forces outside of themselves (external control). Researchers believe that students will be more likely to engage in learning activities when they attribute success or failure to things they can control like their own effort, or lack of it, rather than to forces over which they have little or no control, such as their ability, luck, or outside forces. Teachers should help students, especially at-risk learners, link their successes to something they did to contribute to the success. When this occurs, the students develop self-efficacy and the confidence that they have the power within themselves to be successful.

Teachers who are aware of the influence of peers on students' social and intellectual development can take advantage of this factor by using *peer tutoring*, that is, by having students help each other learn by teaching each other. The principal types of peer tutoring are *same-age tutoring*, where the tutor is about the same age as the tutee, and *cross-age tutoring*, where the tutor is older than the tutee. Greenwood, Carta, and Hall noted three commonly cited benefits of peer tutoring: improvement in achievement, improvement in social behaviors and classroom discipline, and improvement in peer relations. Slavin reported that cross-age tutoring is more often recommended by researchers than same-age tutoring. He suggested that this is partly because students may look up to an older student and accept them as a tutor, but might resent a same-age classmate appointed to tutor them.

Children enter school with a variety of personal and social characteristics. Teachers need to be aware that various factors may affect students' lives and, thus, their behavior and achievement in school. Teachers need to know how to exploit the potential of the positive factors and diminish the impact of the negative factors that affect student performance.

Good and Brophy described ways teachers vary in their behavior toward students they perceive to be high- or low-achievers:

- seat high-achievers across from and down the middle of the room
- seat low-achievers far from the teacher
- seat low-achievers near each other in a group
- give fewer nonverbal cues to low-achievers during instruction (smile less often, maintain less eye contact, etc.)
- call on high-achievers much more frequently than low-achievers
- use longer wait time for responses from high-achievers
- fail to stay with low-achievers when they attempt a response
- criticize low-achievers more frequently for incorrect responses
- praise high-achievers more frequently for correct public responses
- praise low-achievers more frequently for inadequate public responses
- provide low-achievers with less frequent and, when given, less specific feedback regarding their responses
- demand less work and effort from low-achievers
- interrupt performance of low-achievers more frequently
- talk negatively about low-achievers more frequently
- punish off-task behavior of low-achievers and more frequently ignore it in high-achievers

Researchers have found a number of additional factors that influence how teachers perceive students. They warn that these potential sources of bias may cause disparate teacher expectations. For example,

- socioeconomic status (SES)—lower expectations for lower SES students
- gender—lower expectations for elementary boys because of their slower maturation; lower expectations for older girls because of sex-role stereotyping
- ethnicity—lower expectations for some minorities, higher for others
- previous academic performance/standardized test scores—lower expectations for low performers because of the belief they don't have the ability to learn

- outward appearance—lower expectations for students who wear out-of-style or inexpensive clothing or who have poor grooming habits
- speech patterns—lower expectations for students who use poor grammar or have accents that make them difficult to understand
- neatness—lower expectations for students who have poor handwriting, turn in messy work, or are disorganized
- behavior—lower expectations for students with records of misbehavior
- readiness—lower expectations for late maturers or inexperienced students because of the belief that they will be unable to learn
- seat location—lower expectations for students seated on the sides or in the back of the room
- negative teacher talk—lower expectations for students who are talked about as having low ability by other teachers or the principal
- tracking—lower expectations for lower track students
- halo effect—expectations based on one characteristic of a student: lower if characteristic is negative; higher, if characteristic is positive
- school location—lower expectations for rural or inner-city students, higher for surburban students

In speaking of socioeconomic status (SES), Slavin contends that, in the United States, the culture of our schools reflects mainstream, middle-class values. Researchers have found that middle SES teachers often have low expectations for low SES students, which, in turn, may result in low achievement for these students. Indeed, on average, children from lower SES backgrounds are less likely to achieve as well in school as children from middle SES backgrounds. Slavin makes the point that teachers should be aware that children from other than mainstream, middle-class backgrounds are often at a disadvantage in the typical school environment.

Slavin explains that these children (on average) are less likely to be as well-prepared when entering school, and their upbringings often emphasize behaviors and values different from those (such as individuality and future time orientation) expected of them in schools. They are less likely to respond to delayed reinforcement, less willing to compete, and more oriented toward cooperation with other children and individualized contact with the teacher. Even the way parents of lower SES children communicate with their children tends to differ from that of middle SES parents. Lower SES mothers generally give more commands and less clear directions.

Grouping practices can also affect students' perceptions of themselves and their own worth. Most experts agree that grouping based on diagnostic information related to specific subjects like math or reading can be beneficial for students, particularly if regrouping as students progress takes place frequently. However, teachers should use ability grouping cautiously. A Carnegie Foundation report, *An Imperiled Generation*, summarized the harmful effects of ability grouping. The report concluded that such grouping has a devastating impact on how teachers think about students and how students think about themselves. Research findings indicate that grouping by ability results in academic benefit for higher-ability students, but has a negative effect on academic performance for low-ability students. The harmful effects of ability grouping for low-ability students are pronounced, including low expectations for their achievement and behavior, less instruction time resulting in less learning, less opportunity to experience higher-level topics, and lowered self-esteem, all of which have a stigmatizing effect on these students. These findings are particularly disturbing when one considers that low-socioeconomic children tend to score below average on the types of assessments that are often used to assign students to ability groups. If the ability grouping system is very rigid, not providing for frequent reassessment of students and regrouping, poor and minority students are likely to be tracked into an inferior educational experience. In contrast, positive results can accrue for low-achieving students placed in mixed-ability cooperative learning groups, including improved self-image and willingness to learn, in part because they receive group assistance and support, and, not insignificantly, because they are allowed to experience a more challenging curriculum. Nonetheless, teachers should monitor group interactions to ensure that students with high academic ability are not treated more favorably by the group as a whole than are the low-ability students in the group, and that all students are expected to contribute to group success.

Of course, differences among students are not absolute and irrefutable and should not be used by teachers to stereotype students. Often, teachers are unaware of unwarranted lower (or higher) expectations they may have for particular students. This is one of the reasons it is important for teachers, as professional practitioners, to engage in self-reflection. Teachers need to examine critically and honestly their own classroom behaviors to assess whether they inadvertently may be displaying different expectation levels for students whose performance capabilities are similar. The importance of recognizing student differences is so that teachers can make every effort to provide opportunities for success for all students in their classrooms. It is vitally important that teachers deal with all children in such a way that each feels safe, accepted, and capable of achieving.

Competency 003

The teacher appreciates human diversity, recognizing how diversity in the classroom and the community may affect learning and creating a classroom environment in which both the diversity of groups and the uniqueness of individuals are recognized and celebrated.

If you look in any public school in Texas, you will find a mixture of students who differ in many ways. Differences such as cognitive, gender, cultural, linguistic, and social are always present (See Competencies 001, 002, and 004). These are characteristics over which a student has little or no control. Although diversity is inevitable and should be celebrated, it can be very challenging for the classroom teacher to help students develop behaviors and attitudes appropriate for survival in the general society while, at the same time, fostering appreciation for unique cultural behaviors and attitudes.

Teachers should be careful not to view students whose behaviors are different from those of the predominant social group as less worthy or less capable. The first step a teacher needs to take is to examine his or her own views and feelings about cultural differences. We all have biases, so it takes a concentrated effort to avoid stereotypical expectations. To meet this challenge teachers can begin by developing good teacher-student relationships. Teachers need to develop an awareness of practices common in various cultures, so that when children behave in a manner consistent with their culture, the behavior will not be misinterpreted. Nevertheless, teachers should discuss with students that some behaviors are acceptable at home but not at school.

Teachers must realize that they themselves are the essential factor in a multicultural environment because they set the climate for learning. It is of paramount importance for teachers to embrace the attitude that if the materials are suitable and presented on the appropriate level, all students can learn. Whether children achieve is contingent on whether they have self-esteem and are confident in their own ability and on whether their teachers believe they can succeed.

Creating an environment that respects and confirms the dignity of students as human beings is essential in meeting the needs of diverse students. Teachers must be aware of cultural and sexual stereotypes and should avoid behavior that pigeonholes students. Rather, teachers must promote learning for all students.

In her review of the research (available at www.nwrel.org/scpd/sirs/8/topsyn7.html), Kathleen Cotton found that effective teachers of culturally diverse classes:

- Reflect on their own values, stereotypes, and prejudices and how these might be affecting their interactions with children and parents
- Engage in staff development activities that can expose and reduce biases and increase skill in working with diverse populations
- Arrange their classrooms for movement and active learning
- Interact one-to-one with each child at least once daily
- Communicate high expectations for the performance of all students
- Give praise and encouragement
- Communicate affection for and closeness with students through verbal and nonverbal means, such as humor, soliciting student opinion, self-disclosure, eye contact, close proximity, and smiling
- Avoid public charting of achievement data
- Give children responsibility for taking care of materials, decorating, greeting visitors, and so on
- Treat all students equally and fairly
- Have classrooms that reflect the ethnic heritage and background of all the children in the classroom
- Form flexible reading groups
- Make use of cooperative learning groups that are culturally heterogeneous and teach students skills for working in these groups
- Offer learning activities congruent with the cultural and individual learning styles and strengths of students
- Teach students social skills related to getting along well together
- Conduct many learning activities that are not graded
- Include some student-selected activities

- Provide accurate information about cultural groups through straightforward discussions of race, ethnicity, and other cultural differences
- Teach about both cross-cultural similarities and cross-cultural differences
- Learn a few words of the language and general background information about the religious backgrounds, customs, traditions, holidays, festivals, practices, and so on of students and incorporate this information into learning experiences for them
- Use a variety of materials rather than relying only on the information in textbooks
- Review materials for cultural biases and stereotypes and remove biased items from the curriculum
- Take issue with culturally demeaning statements, jokes, graffiti, and so on
- Use racial or other intercultural incidents as a springboard for providing information and skills to avoid such incidents
- Engage parent involvement
- Demonstrate interest in and respect for the family's culture when interacting with parents
- Find out as much as they can about each child's experiences and family situation that can help them to understand and meet the child's needs

Some suggestions for teachers are the following:

1. Remember that cultural diversity in our schools and society can be recognized and appreciated without denunciation of Western values and cultural traditions.

2. Recognize that there are as many differences within a group as there are between groups.

3. Remember there is a positive correlation between teacher expectations and academic performance.

4. Remember to hold high expectations for students, regardless of ethnicity, gender, or exceptionality.

5. Remember that self-esteem and academic achievement go hand in hand.

6. Remember there is no one approach to meeting the educational needs of all children in a multicultural classroom.

7. Remember multiculturalism is not a "minority thing"; it includes us all.

8. Remember that human understanding is a lifetime endeavor.

Furthermore, numerous research studies consistently support the idea that each student learns differently. When students are taught through the methods each prefers, they do better (see Competency 004). Teachers should be aware of student differences and be willing to examine their own teaching styles in order to modify classroom practices and procedures to optimize the learning situation for all students. Considering the diverse demographic characteristics of the students in most Texas classrooms, this recommended strategy may be particularly useful in spotting learning problems and enhancing the overall performance of Texas school children. Teachers should respond flexibly and creatively to students' needs. They should provide varied environments within the classroom and use multisensory resources in the delivery of instruction.

Competency 004

The teacher understands how learning occurs and can apply this understanding to design and implement effective instruction.

When designing instruction, teachers need a strong knowledge base of how students learn. Numerous studies have been conducted on the factors that affect learning. The implications of the research are that teachers should help students make connections between past and present learning experiences, foster a view of learning as a personally meaningful pursuit, promote a sense of responsibility for one's own learning, and encourage experimentation and reasoning.

The view of learning that incorporates these features has come to be known as *constructivism*. Evolving from the works of John Dewey, Jean Piaget, Lev Vygotsky, and other proponents of child-centered methods, constructivism is a learner-centered approach to teaching that emphasizes teaching for understanding, predicated on the concept that students construct knowledge by making connections between past and present learning experiences. Teachers must provide a learning environment that provides experiences from which the learner can construct meaning based on what the learner already knows. Constructivist teachers help learners to reinvent their knowledge, thus creating new understandings. To develop understanding about a concept, students need to see the "whole" picture and also need to be able to break it down into its various parts. Constructivist teachers take a whole-to-parts approach, with the content organized around broad concepts. When the students break down a concept into parts, they can understand how the parts fit together because they know what the whole looks like.

Constructivist learning encourages students to think, to consider carefully, to make decisions, and to reflect. Students are actively engaged in seeking answers to questions and solutions to actual or authentic problems. They reflect on and communicate their ideas as a regular part of instruction and are provided with opportunities to discover principles on their own. Student autonomy and initiative are encouraged. Learning is negotiated between the teacher and the students. This results in decreasing the number of activities controlled by the teacher, thus empowering the students to assume responsibility for their own learning.

Researchers such as Rita and Kenneth Dunn have suggested that effective teachers should consider the learning styles of their students in order to facilitate academic achievement. *Learning style* is the manner in which an individual perceives and processes information in learning situations. Knowledge of learning style theory can assist teachers in designing educational conditions in which most students are likely to learn. According to the Dunns' research, classrooms can be designed to either stimulate or inhibit learning for students based on their individual learning style needs: quiet versus sound, bright versus soft lighting, warm versus cool temperature, formal versus informal seating designs, and so on.

Educators usually refer to the predominant way a student takes in information through the five primary senses (see, hear, smell, taste, touch) as *sensory modality strength*. Students who prefer to learn by seeing or reading something are *visual* learners; students who learn best by listening are *auditory* learners; and students who prefer to learn by touching objects, by feeling shapes and textures, and by moving things around are *tactile/kinesthetic* learners. Some students have a single modality strength (visual, auditory, tactile/kinesthetic), while others have combination, or mixed, modalities. Children with mixed modality strengths usually are able to process information efficiently no matter how it is presented. In contrast, children with a single modality strength may experience difficulties when instruction is presented outside the scope of that modality strength. It is generally known that most elementary school children learn best through tactile or kinesthetic experiences. Middle and secondary school teachers should be aware that most of the students they teach also tend to prefer and to learn best by being physically involved in their learning experiences. Sitting and listening is difficult for these students; therefore, these teachers should consider limiting their use of the lecture method in presenting instruction. As students mature, however, their dependence on the tactile/kinesthetic modality decreases. Many students in the upper high school grades are visual learners who can read easily and rapidly and can visualize what they are reading. Most students eventually learn to adjust when the instructional material is not consistent with their modality preference. Notwithstanding, most educators agree that planning for those learners who are visual, auditory, tactile/kinesthetic, or a combination of these is critical if teachers are to help all learners be successful (see Appendix B for guidelines).

The concept of *brain hemisphericity* is closely linked to the work on student learning modality. Each hemisphere of the brain is associated with certain thinking traits, and therefore certain learning styles. Considerable research has been done that supports the notion that people who are left-brain-dominant learn in different ways than do right-brain-dominant people. The terms *left/right, analytic/global*, and *inductive/deductive* are often used interchangeably to describe learners. *Left/analytic/inductive* learners respond to verbal instruction; process thought logically; think from part to whole; depend on words and language for meaning; prefer lessons that proceed in a step-by-step logical order, where details build on one another; and prefer well-structured assignments. *Right/global/ inductive* learners respond to visual and kinesthetic instruction, process thought holistically, see patterns and relationships, think from whole to part, prefer to see the "big picture" before exploring the small details, depend on images and pictures for meaning, and can work on several parts of a task at the same time. Each of us is a whole-brained person, but, usually, with a preference for receiving information through either the left or right hemisphere. Neither preference is in any way superior to the other, although instruction in most public schools in America typically favors the left-brain-dominant student.

Witkin's work on *field independence-field dependence* closely parallels brain hemisphericity findings. According to Witkin, *field-independent* learners have the ability to perceive objects without being influenced by the background; are passive in social situations; tend to be less influenced by their peers; and tend to study in programs requiring analytical, abstract, impersonal spheres, such as electronics, engineering, and mathematics. In contrast, *field-dependent* learners have the ability to perceive objects as a whole rather than as individual parts, tend to have difficulty separating out specific parts from a situation or pattern; tend to see relational and inferential concepts; tend to be active in social situations; tend to be more influenced by suggestion and to reach consensus in discussion groups more readily than field independents; and tend to study in programs requiring interpersonal, nonscientific orientation, such as history and literature and the helping professions.

Howard Gardner proposed the theory of multiple intelligences. He suggested that humans have seven intelligences:

- *Verbal/linguistic intelligence*—the ability to use and produce words
- *Logical-mathematical intelligence*—the ability to do math, recognize patterns, and problem-solve
- *Visual/spatial intelligence*—the ability to form images and pictures in the mind
- *Body/kinesthetic intelligence*—the ability to use the body in physical activities
- *Interpersonal intelligence*—the ability to work cooperatively with other people
- *Musical/rhythmic intelligence*—the ability to recognize musical and rhythmic patterns and sounds
- *Intrapersonal intelligence*—the ability to know oneself

Teachers whose practices reflect the research on multiple intelligences learn to look at learners from seven different viewpoints. They recognize that students have less anxiety and can learn better when the learning task is congruent with their strengths and abilities. For example, in social studies, verbal/linguistic learners would prefer to debate about a historical event, while body/kinesthetic learners would prefer to act it out.

Kagan's work on *reflectivity-impulsivity* concluded that individuals are consistent in the way they process information and the speed with which they do it. *Impulsive* students tend to work and make decisions quickly. They respond to situations with the first thought that occurs to them, often finishing assignments and tests before everyone else. *Reflective* students ponder all the alternatives carefully before responding, working carefully and deliberately. Impulsive students tend to concentrate on speed, while reflective students concentrate more on accuracy.

If all students are to be successful, teachers must understand that students learn in different ways, while teachers often teach the way they were taught. Nevertheless, there are critics who suggest that teachers should disregard students' learning styles and that children should learn to adapt to the teacher's style. These critics seem to be disregarding the research that indicates that certain learning style characteristics are biological in nature and that, in the short run, learning styles are remarkably resistant to change. Perhaps the most reasonable approach for teachers to use is to recognize that some students' behaviors are manifestations of the students' learning styles (such as needing to see the big picture before focusing on details) and should not automatically be viewed negatively; to cater to individual styles as much as possible, particularly at first; to use a mix of teaching styles so that students with different learning styles will have an opportunity to learn in their preferred style at least occasionally; and to teach students how to function in situations when the teaching style does not match their own learning style.

To make instruction effective for all students, the teacher needs to take into account their diverse needs. It is not unusual for teachers to have a wide range of ability levels in their classrooms. Excessive use of whole-group instruction or demonstration in such classrooms may be ineffective because it does not accommodate individual student differences. The instruction might be too advanced for some students and too easy for others.

Teachers need to be aware of the characteristics of both high-ability and low-ability learners. According to Gallagher, teacher identification of high-ability, or *intellectually gifted*, students has been flawed. Their identification is determined by how well the child fits the "perfect" student model (that is, performs well in school, behaves well, turns in work on time, etc.). They often overlook large numbers of intellectually superior children because these children may not be performing well in school. In reality, the percentage of gifted students who perform below their ability level is high. Albert Einstein, Thomas Edison, and Winston Churchill are good examples of students who likely would not have been identified as gifted by their teachers. High-ability students are ready for fast-paced, very abstract instruction and learn better in less structured environments. Effective teachers recognize that high-ability students need opportunities to work alone and also with other high-ability students.

Low-ability learners, or "*at risk*" students, are most often found among students who test just below average in intelligence. These slower learners are the students who often "fall through the cracks" between special education and regular education. These students are not incapable of learning, but they are (usually) concrete thinkers who need structured environments. Effective teachers present materials, assignments, and directions in small, sequential steps when teaching at-risk students.

Responsive teachers accommodate for the varied characteristics of the students in their classrooms, thus enabling more students to succeed. In addition, it is important to remember that students can assume some responsibility for their own learning. Teachers who actively involve their students in the learning process are helping them to develop this responsibility.

Competency 005

The teacher understands how motivation affects group and individual behavior and learning and can apply this understanding to promote student learning.

All human beings are born with a natural curiosity and desire to learn. Unfortunately, many students show little or no excitement about school learning. A primary objective of an effective teacher is to stimulate in pupils the desire, or *motivation*, to learn. *Motivation* is the willingness of a student to engage in learning. (See Appendix B for guidelines.) Teachers are challenged to tap into students' innate urges to learn by using teaching strategies that influence students' motivation. Research on motivation has focused on topics such as *intrinsic* and *extrinsic motivation, reinforcement,* and *achievement motivation.*

Sometimes a student wants to learn something just for the sake of learning it. We say this student wants to learn because of *intrinsic motivation:* The desire to learn originates within the student and stems from the student's intellectual curiosity, attitudes, beliefs, and needs regarding the learning task. Teachers who try to make learning relevant to students' lives and help them see why learning is important will often find that students become intrinsically motivated to learn. If desire to learn does not arise from within the student, the teacher may need to use *extrinsic motivation* in the form of external rewards or incentives to get them to engage in learning. In extrinsic motivation, the emphasis is on external factors that students find desirable. Teachers who reward students with stickers or stars, granting of free time, or special treats are using extrinsic motivation.

Along with the effective use of intrinsic and extrinsic motivation, the appropriate use of *reinforcement,* the recognition and rewarding of students' good behavior, is a long-recognized and essential skill for classroom teachers. The idea is that students' accomplishments should be rewarded not only with good grades but also with other rewards: verbal praise (see Appendix B for guidelines), public recognition (such as public displays of good work), tangible rewards (such as stickers, stars, stamps), extra privileges, and so forth. The basic principle of reinforcement is that students will continue good behaviors that are reinforced and discontinue undesirable behaviors when they are not reinforced. Most teachers prefer to use *positive reinforcement,* in the form of things given to students, rather than *negative reinforcement,* which is removal from an unpleasant situation (such as release from having to stay in after school if the student behaves appropriately). Do not confuse negative reinforcement with *punishment,* which is a negative consequence, such as detention. Teachers need to use reinforcers that are perceived as desirable by students. For example, elementary students may enjoy getting stickers as rewards, but high school students would prefer free time or getting to see a movie for their good behavior. Teachers should use reinforcement to inform students about what they are doing right. It should be given contingent on specific student behaviors and should be awarded in such a way that it helps to develop intrinsic motivation and other natural outcomes of desirable student performance. When properly used, reinforcement helps students appreciate their successes, develops positive self-concepts, and increases motivation for additional learning. It is a powerful tool that teachers can use to motivate students and increase good behaviors. Nevertheless, teachers should also remember that a great deal of reinforcement occurs inside students when they do something well, whether they receive recognition or reward from the teacher or not. The satisfaction and accomplishment that students feel for success in school and gaining the respect of their teachers and peers are potent reinforcements.

Unfortunately, what motivates a student today may not motivate that student tomorrow and what motivates one student may not motivate another. Teachers continually strive to find different ways of providing extrinsic motivation through creating a classroom atmosphere that is attractive and stimulating and through the use of tangible reinforcers.

The development of students' intrinsic desire to learn is the real goal of teachers but the use of external rewards may be the best means to achieve this goal, especially in the beginning stages. Structuring the learning environment so that students will have opportunities to work together, make decisions, and solve problems that are relevant to them will help students become intrinsically motivated.

Achievement motivation is the tendency to strive for success and to choose goal-oriented, success/failure activities. Students high in achievement motivation want and expect to succeed, and when they fail, they try harder. In some cases, students may have a strong desire to achieve, but they may be more controlled by the need to maintain a positive self-image, so they seek achievement by avoiding failure. Failure avoiders tend to choose either very easy or very difficult tasks, the reasoning being that they will likely succeed at the easy task; and if they fail at the difficult task, they can attribute the failure to the difficulty level of the task, rather than to their own lack of ability.

Teachers should let students know that teachers notice when students do their best. They should offer praise and encouragement for right answers and appropriate behavior. Learning activities should seem worthwhile and interesting. Students should be encouraged to participate in the planning of instructional activities so that they feel their opinions are valued and respected. Content should be tied to students' previous experiences and students should know why the content is important. Students should know what to do and how to do it, and teachers should set standards so students will know when they are doing well.

Teachers' behavior and demeanor in the classroom can also affect student motivation. Kindsvatter, Wilen, and Ishler suggested that highly motivating teachers are enthusiastic, energetic, exciting, and stimulating. When such teachers introduce lessons, they focus students' attention on the learning activity, communicate clearly the purposes of activities, and stimulate students to get involved. During lessons, they move around the classroom, vary voice level and quality, use instructional variety, change pace during the lesson, and use gestures (such as okay signs), facial expressions (such as smiles), body movements (such as nods), and other nonverbal signals to create a presence in the classroom that excites students to learn. In addition, their questioning techniques are student-oriented and nonevaluative.

Practice Questions on Domain I

Ms. Lee, a kindergarten teacher, overhears two of the boys in her class arguing over which one is going to marry her. She is not upset and does not reprimand them because she realizes this behavior is to be expected. This teacher's behavior *best* reflects her knowledge and consideration of:

    A. students' developmental processes.
    B. the importance of developing positive self-esteem.

C. allowing students to practice self-discipline.

D. teaching students to solve their own problems.

Essentially, this question assesses your ability to recognize the relevant competency. Because the question deals with the psychosocial development of young children, which falls under **developmentally appropriate instruction,** the primary focus of the question is Competency 001: *The teacher uses an understanding of human developmental processes to nurture student growth through developmentally appropriate instruction.* Thus, Choice A is the correct response. This teacher recognizes individual students' levels of social and emotional development. According to Erikson, during the Initiative versus Guilt stage, children develop a sense of their male or female identities. It is quite common for boys to want to marry their mother or teacher and for girls to want to marry their father.

Mr. Williams, a geography teacher, is planning a thematic unit on "The Environment." He plans to enlist the help of his students in determining topics and procedures for investigations. He believes it is important for students to make some decisions related to their interests and how to go about solving problems. Mr. Williams' approach to planning *best* demonstrates his understanding that motivation to learn can be enhanced when:

I. students are allowed to pursue problems that are meaningful to them.

II. students are allowed to discover principles on their own.

III. students are allowed to have choices in their learning.

IV. students are provided with opportunities to practice democratic decision making.

A. I and II only

B. I and III only

C. II and III only

D. III and IV only

This question deals with **motivation.** Thus, the primary focus of this question is Competency 005: *The teacher understands how motivation affects group and individual behavior and learning and can apply this understanding to promote learning.* Eliminate Roman II because the stimulus does not state that the students will be discovering principles on their own (remember, don't read too much into a question). Eliminate choices A and C. Eliminate Roman IV because the stimulus does not state that decisions will be made democratically, only that students will be assisting in the decision making (again, stick to the stimulus). Eliminate Choice D. Mr. Williams is building an educational environment that is respectful of the student and encourages student participation in decision making. According to motivational theory, allowing students to have choices in the design of their education experiences (the students help in determining topics and procedures) and allowing students to pursue problems that are meaningful to them (the students help in determining topics that will be investigated) will have a positive impact on intrinsic motivation. Choice B is the correct response.

CHAPTER 8

DOMAIN II—ENHANCING STUDENT ACHIEVEMENT

Competency 006

The teacher uses planning processes to design outcome-oriented learning experiences that foster understanding and encourage self-directed thinking and learning in both individual and collaborative settings.

Research studies have identified certain characteristics that are essential for effective teaching. They found that effective teachers are clear about instructional goals and accept responsibility for student learning; choose, adapt, and use materials effectively; have a firm command of subject matter and teaching strategies; motivate students by communicating expectations to students; incorporate higher-level thinking skills; develop empathy, rapport, and personal interactions with students; and integrate instruction with other subject areas.

Effective teachers are effective planners. Lessons are well-planned and organized. New learnings are related to previous learning, and instruction proceeds from simple and concrete to more complex and abstract. Instruction is enhanced by teacher illustrations, analogies, examples and nonexamples, demonstrations, and explanations and, most important, by modeling the behavior that teachers expect students to exhibit.

The development of the Lesson Cycle in Texas was a direct result of the education reform movement that occurred in Texas in the 1980s. The Lesson Cycle consists of two phases: planning and teaching/learning (see Appendix B for a diagram and explanations). In the planning phase the teacher uses task analysis after careful consideration of the appropriate Texas Essential Knowledge and Skills (TEKS) (available at www.tea.state.tx.us/teks/) to decide what the students need to know and how to teach it to them. In the teaching/learning phase the teacher implements what he or she has planned using the following components: focus, explanation, check for understanding, reteaching, guided practice, check for mastery, independent practice, enrichment, and closure. These components do not necessarily all occur in a single lesson, nor is there a particular sequential order that must be followed. The Lesson Cycle model encourages high engagement levels of all students and makes the teacher an active, dynamic instructor who continually questions, monitors, and checks. Further, the Lesson Cycle model is a flexible model that can be adjusted to fit either a teacher-directed approach (for instance, direct instruction) or a student-centered approach (for example, discovery learning). (See Appendix B for sample lesson formats.)

Constructivist teachers have developed the "Five-E" lesson plan model, which accentuates the constructivist ideal of student-centered learning. The "Five Es" are:

1. *Engage.* The teacher identifies the instructional task and helps students relate the content to their lives and experiences. Interest and excitement are created as the teacher uses this as a means to focus students' attention on the learning activity.

2. *Explore.* Students work together in teams to get directly involved with the phenomena and materials. The teacher becomes a facilitator, providing materials as the students engage in active inquiry.

3. *Explain.* Working in groups, the students support each other's understandings as they discuss their ideas, observations, questions, and predictions. Correct terminology is introduced only *after* students have had hands-on experiences. Depth of understanding and possible misconceptions can be determined by students' creative works, such as drawings, videos, models, and writings.

4. *Elaborate.* Students expand on the concepts learned, make connections to other related concepts, and apply their understandings to real-world settings.

5. *Evaluate.* In Texas, the last "E" is more directly about *assessment* than evaluation. The teacher assesses student understanding. Evidence of students' progress may be obtained through informal assessment (such as observation, listening, and taking notes while students discuss their findings) and/or formal assessment (such as portfolios and projects).

The "Five-E" model is not incompatible with the Lesson Cycle model. On the contrary, the two models overlap (for instance, engage = focus) and both are designed to accomplish learning objectives.

Students at all levels need to be engaged in the identification of problems, higher-level thinking, decision making, and problem solving. Research on learning and motivation suggests that learning is greatest when the learning environment is structured to engage active participation by students. When designing instruction, teachers should carefully consider the desired learner outcomes, input from students, learners' backgrounds, the content of instruction, appropriate teaching strategies, available materials and resources, time and space constraints, and assessment issues.

Competency 007

The teacher uses effective verbal, nonverbal, and media communication techniques to shape the classroom into a community of learners engaged in active inquiry, collaborative exploration, and supportive interactions.

Effective teachers are effective communicators. Teachers constantly send messages to students and also receive messages from them. They should emphasize to students that the critical elements of verbal communication are accuracy of language, accuracy of information, standardization of language, and clearly defined expectations. Since communication is critical to the learning process, teachers need to be effective speakers. Not only are the words spoken important, but also the way they are said. Changes in voice loudness, rate, tone, inflection, and pitch can change the meaning of words and the emphasis of the message. Projection of the voice so it can be heard by all students is also necessary.

Asking good questions is another method of verbal communication. Questions should be determined by the lesson objectives. Questions should be clear and should yield student responses, even though the answers are not always correct. Effective teachers provide supportive feedback to incorrect responses by students. Around 75 percent (70 percent for high-ability students; 80 percent for low-ability students) of teachers' questions should yield correct responses. Questions can be categorized as narrow (convergent) or broad (divergent) depending on whether or not the teacher is seeking knowledge of information or is trying to generate ideas and stimulate thinking. If a teacher wants to determine the level of student learning, a focusing question is appropriate. To increase student interaction, a teacher will ask a prompting question. In order to clarify or justify an answer, a probing question is used. Teachers who ask questions first and wait three to five seconds before calling on students to answer will find that more students respond and that their answers are more complete as well as correct. Similarly, increased *wait time*, the amount of time a teacher waits for a student to respond to a question before moving on to another student or answering the question, increases the probability of student participation and affects achievement positively. (See Appendix B for guidelines.)

The importance of nonverbal communication such as facial expressions (for instance, smiling), gestures (for instance, pointing), and body language (for instance, turning away) should not be underestimated. Many times, nonverbal communication speaks louder than words. Students as well as teachers communicate nonverbally. Teachers need to "hear" the message students are sending them by nonverbal behavior. Using these clues, instruction can be adjusted as needed.

Media/technology communication is communication through the use of overhead projectors, computers, videos, laser videodiscs, CD-ROM disks, movies, and television. (See Competency 009.) Advanced technology adds new dimensions to teaching and learning. Instead of writing with pen and paper, students can use word processors with spell checkers, thesauruses, and grammar checks to create written documents such as letters, themes, essays, and research papers. The advantage of word processing is that corrections and revisions can be made without retyping the entire document. Students can access resource material like *Compton's Multimedia Encyclopedia* from CD-ROM disks or use a videodisc lesson package like *Adventures in Mathland*. They can also link up to other resources and to students at other schools in the state, country, and in the world through the Internet. Advanced technology can help schools create a learning environment that changes and interacts with students' needs. Teachers must learn to use this powerful tool effectively. They should be knowledgeable and selective in choosing the appropriate media/technology for instructional purposes.

Competency 008

The teacher uses a variety of instructional strategies and roles to facilitate learning and to help students become independent thinkers and problem solvers who use higher-order thinking in the classroom and the real world.

Not only must teachers know what they are teaching, they also must know how to teach. This means using a wide range of instructional strategies and resources based on knowledge of content pedagogy and characteristics of the learners. The teacher's philosophy and experience will determine which strategies the teacher will use. The maturity and experience of the students should also be considered.

Some of the instructional strategies teachers may select when teaching are *direct instruction, lecture, discovery learning, inquiry, simulations/games/role play, individualized instruction, cooperative learning,* and *interdisciplinary instruction.*

Direct instruction is a teaching approach that is teacher directed and helps students master basic skills. (See Competency 004.) It emphasizes teacher control of all classroom events and the presentation of highly structured lessons. The teacher arranges the lesson sequentially into small steps and moves from the simple to the more complex. The lesson begins with the teacher securing the attention of the students. Then the teacher lets the students know what they are going to learn. The teacher then explains and models what the students will be doing, secures feedback as to their understanding of the lesson, then gives them opportunities to practice under teacher supervision, giving assistance when needed. The students will then be ready to work independently.

In the *lecture* method, the teacher tries to convey knowledge to the learner orally. The recommended length for teacher lectures is 10 to 15 minutes. Although the lecture method is not recommended in elementary schools, it is a very common method of teaching in secondary schools; however, it is one of the least effective as measured by enduring effect. Lecture encourages superficial learning, low-level simple recall, or no learning at all. It promotes passive rather than active learning, and is the least effective instructional method in most classes in middle school, junior high, and high school. Most skills and processes can be learned better by demonstration and hands-on practice than by having someone talk about them.

Nevertheless, teachers continue to use the lecture method, most likely because it has the advantage that the teacher can organize facts and ideas and present them in an orderly way with a minimum amount of time and effort. If learning from a lecture is to be effective, several factors are of primary importance, such as motivation of the learner, relevance to the learner, and the extent to which the activity is a two-way process. Most students have become good at "tuning out" a speaker; thus, if any learning is to happen their attention must be engaged. Is the learning a two-way activity, where the mind of the learner is "tuned in" to the words and ideas of the lecturer? This sometimes happens without any outward signs except, perhaps, gestures or facial expressions. It is much more likely to happen if the learners are given opportunities to respond, to ask questions, and to react to the speaker's point of view, whether it is to express agreement or disagreement.

Discovery learning is designed to encourage students to be active learners while exploring new concepts, developing new skills, and figuring things out for themselves. It promotes and capitalizes on the natural curiosity of the learner. The theory behind discovery learning is that active manipulation, thinking, and reasoning will increase the students' understanding and increase the likelihood that they will develop appropriate generalizations and concepts.

Inquiry is a process students engage in when they have identified a problem to be solved. The process involves the awareness of a problem, generating possible solutions, developing a hypothesis, gathering data, and testing the hypothesis. Inquiry requires students to use higher-level thinking skills, reasoning ability, and decision-making skills.

Simulations, games, and role playing are instructional strategies designed to allow students to learn through their experiences in a learning activity. *Simulation* is a learning activity designed to reflect reality. Students might set up a mock business, "play the stock market," and so on. *Games* are learning activities that have rules and involve students in competitive situations, having winners and losers. In *role playing*, students act out characters or situations based on real-world models. Role playing is a necessary part of simulations. Students must act out the roles they assume in the simulation. In addition to classroom-based simulations and games, teachers have available a wide array of commercially produced computer simulations and games for the various subject areas. Advantages associated with simulations and games are:

- They are an experiential form of learning (that is, students learn from what they are doing).
- They provide for authentic (realistic) learning.
- They engage students' interest and motivation.
- They provide for participation by everyone.
- They are student-centered.
- They allow for risk taking in a safe atmosphere.
- They promote critical thinking and problem solving.
- They allow students to practice social and communication skills.

Individualized instruction is characterized by a shift in responsibility for learning from the teacher to the student. Effective individualized programs are tailored to meet the interests, needs, and abilities of the student with consideration given to the appropriateness of the subject matter. Individualized instruction can take various forms, such as independent study or peer tutoring. It can be as simple as allowing a student to complete the same lessons as the rest of the students but at a different pace, or modifying the objective requirements for a particular student. Three well-known, more structured strategies for individualizing instruction are programmed instruction, tutorials, and computer assisted instruction (CAI).

Cooperative learning is an instructional strategy in which students are placed in small groups where they work together on a collective task that has been clearly defined and explained. (See Appendix B for guidelines.) The students are expected to complete the assigned task without direct and immediate teacher supervision. The use of cooperative learning methods provides students with opportunities to develop interpersonal and small-group social skills through a variety of structured team-building activities. These are lifelong survival skills that are vital for the democratic decisions of citizenship and the teamwork required in the work place. Cooperative learning groups enable learners to further develop their critical thinking, reasoning, and problem-solving skills. The students are able to examine their own values, attitudes, and forms of social behavior and to consider alternative points of view.

Planning for cooperative learning activities requires the teacher to focus on teacher-student interaction, student-teacher interaction, task specification and materials, roles, and expectations. Although there are variations in the application of the cooperative learning concept, the four critical attributes of cooperative learning are positive interdependence, individual accountability, group processing of social skills, and face-to-face interaction. Three generic team-oriented cooperative learning methods in widespread use are:

Student Teams-Achievement Division (STAD): This framework for cooperative learning uses teaching, team study, testing, and team recognition.

Teams Games Tournaments (TGT): This framework for using cooperative learning uses teaching, team study, tournaments, and team recognition.

Jigsaw and Jigsaw II: This framework for cooperative learning uses teaching, reading, expert group discussion, team reporting, testing, and team recognition.

These methods are applicable to a broad range of grade levels and subjects. Two methods that combine the use of cooperative learning with strategies designed specifically for teaching content are:

Team-Assisted Individualization (TAI): This combines some of the characteristics of individualized and cooperative learning, teaching, and team averages. TAI is specifically designed to teach mathematics to young students or older remedial students.

Cooperative Integrated Reading and Composition (CIRC): This uses teaching, team study, independent practice, peer preassessment, and testing. Special elements are direct instruction in reading comprehension and the integration of language arts and writing. CIRC is specifically designed to enhance the reading and writing skills of intermediate-grade students.

The basic purpose underlying all cooperative learning models is to motivate individuals to help each other learn. Group members take responsibility for their own learning and for the learning of each other. The positive interdependence that is an essential component of cooperative learning is a strong motivational incentive for the students. Students perceive that it is to their advantage if other students in their group learn and to their disadvantage if others in their group do poorly. Also, a group-incentive structure allows all students, even those who usually perform poorly, an opportunity to succeed that can be highly motivating for these students. Group membership is usually long term to allow for intergroup responsibility and collaboration to build, although group membership should not be permanent for the entire year. The activities are learner-centered, with the teacher functioning as both an academic expert and a classroom manager to promote effective group functioning.

Cooperative learning groups can be used across the full range of student populations regardless of age, ethnicity, or ability level. (See Appendix B for guidelines.) Research indicates that when cooperative learning strategies are used, students benefit academically, as well as personally and socially. In addition to such benefits as increased time-on-task, cooperative learning has been found to have positive effects on student achievement and retention of information, self-esteem, self-direction, human relations skills, trust among students, acceptance of others, and emotional involvement in and commitment to learning. Research indicates that, in particular, minority, at-risk, and physically or mentally handicapped children benefit from involvement in cooperative learning instruction.

Critics have challenged the use of cooperative learning strategies with gifted students, arguing that high-achieving students are penalized by working in mixed-ability cooperative learning groups. They complain that high achievers feel used and frustrated by low achievers who are not motivated to perform well.

This view is supported by the Council for Exceptional Children, which reported research findings that indicate:

- Gifted students often become tutors and learn less academic content when mixed-ability cooperative learning is used.
- Gifted students waste a lot of time in a mixed-ability classroom, developing bad habits, such as constant daydreaming.
- Many gifted students think and learn differently from their chronological age-mates.
- Gifted children should be placed with similar students in their areas of strength.
- Gifted students are more likely to socialize "normally" when they are with students of similar intellectual ability.

Nevertheless, there is ample research that disagrees with these findings, maintaining instead that high-achieving students learn as much in cooperatively structured classes as they do in traditional classes; and, futhermore, that they benefit socially from the opportunity to work collaboratively with and help others who are not their intellectual age-mates. Even so, high achievers should also be given opportunities to work cooperatively with other high achievers or on independent projects.

Most research supports the positive outcomes for all students when cooperative learning is used; however, it is important to realize that teachers and students require adequate training in order for cooperative learning to be implemented successfully. Because the behaviors called for in cooperative learning groups are radically different from those required in traditional classroom settings, prior to engaging students in cooperative learning, teachers need to use team-building activities designed to develop the social behaviors students need for cooperating and working successfully with each other. These behaviors include sharing ideas and information, keeping the group on task, making sure no one person takes over the group, making sure everyone has an opportunity to participate, praising and encouraging the contributions of others, and checking to make sure everyone in the group understands what is being taught. As students work in their groups, teachers should monitor and give feedback on students' cooperative behavior, as well as encouraging the students to take time as they work to discuss how well they are functioning as a group.

Teachers need to be familiar with different types of grouping and know when to use them. Whole-group instruction is very effective when basic skills are being taught or when the teacher needs to demonstrate or model a concept for all the students. Small-group work provides a low-risk environment for students to practice new or difficult skills. Using too many small groups, however, can create management problems, so teachers should experiment to determine how many groups work best in their classroom. Students should also be provided the opportunity to demonstrate knowledge and skills in an individual setting; however, teachers need to be aware that solitary tasks can foster competition since students often compete to see who does the best. Although competition can increase scholarship, excessive competition can reduce motivation, communication, and higher-level thinking. Teachers who evaluate students on a competitive basis find that students succeed only if others with whom they compete fail. Students who are not at the "top" of the class often become discouraged and give up. Cooperative learning minimizes competition in the classroom while at the same time increasing critical thinking without sacrificing academic achievement. Cooperative learning is an effective strategy, yet if teachers use it exclusively as the only means for interaction in the classroom, their students may never have the opportunity for independent learning or the experience of competition. A combination of all three types of learning structures—whole-group, small-group, and individual—should be practiced so that learning is realistic and meaningful for the student.

Research findings regarding ability grouping are mixed. Few dispute that grouping based on readiness and achievement for specific subjects like math or reading for part of the day can be beneficial, particularly if regrouping as students gain skills takes place frequently. Furthermore, grouping gifted students in special classes for the purpose of instructional acceleration has resulted in academic benefits for those students. Small-group work is an effective way to increase students' verbal interactions with each other and can provide better use of instructional time through more efficient student management. Some findings indicate that in ability groups, higher-ability students seem to learn better, moderate-ability students appear to learn neither more nor less, and low-ability students seem to learn less. The harmful effects of ability grouping are most pronounced for low-ability students, including low expectations for their achievement and behavior, less instruction time resulting in less learning, and lowered self-esteem, all of which has a stigmatizing effect on these students. In short, ability groups are beneficial for student achievement when students remain in heterogeneous classes most of the day and are regrouped by performance level only in instances when reducing heterogeneity is particularly important, such as in teaching specific math or reading skills. Competent teachers know there are multiple ways to group students. They select the appropriate grouping arrangement for a given instructional goal and student characteristics.

Interdisciplinary instruction is the result when a teacher combines several disciplines into one lesson or unit. At the elementary level, it is very common for teachers to identify the primary discipline, such as reading or social studies, and then incorporate other subject areas into the lesson. At the middle and secondary levels, it is common for teachers from different disciplines to form interdisciplinary teams that collaboratively plan integrated learning activities. (See Competency 012.) Information and activities from other disciplines are used to illustrate, elaborate, and enrich the learning. The information should be practical and relevant to real life and should not neglect the affective domain. Interdisciplinary instruction is supported by:

- the constructivist movement
- the knowledge explosion
- flexible use of both space and time
- relevance of the instruction
- public approval
- opportunities for individualization
- the abundant assessment and evaluation opportunities it affords

The premise behind this approach is that the world is not divided into neat subject-area compartments, so schools should design instructional material that reflects the complexity of the real world in order to prepare students for life.

Some school programs choose to approach instruction by maintaining the separate identity of each subject. This is the *intradisciplinary* approach.

Teachers who structure the learning environment to promote higher-level thinking of students usually use a classification system of thinking developed by Benjamin Bloom. *Bloom's taxonomy* consists of six levels of cognitive thought in hierarchical order, from lowest to highest. These are *knowledge, comprehension, application, analysis, synthesis,* and *evaluation.* Teachers need to remember that the development of higher-order, critical, and creative thinking skills depends on a solid foundation of factual knowledge.

In summary, effective teachers develop a repertoire of instructional methodologies to help students learn. To decide which strategy to use, each teacher should keep in mind the lesson objective, the maturity level and experience of the students, classroom space, time of day, weather, and the teacher's own abilities. Teaching models use two basic instructional approaches: teacher-directed and student-centered. The teacher-directed strategies are the more traditional ones like lecture and direct instruction. The student-centered strategies involve students in directing their learning and include cooperative learning, inquiry, discovery, and so forth.

Competency 009

The teacher uses a variety of instructional materials and resources (including human and technological resources) to support individual and group learning.

Teaching today is an involved process. In addition to knowing content and using appropriate teaching strategies, teachers usually have access to many teaching materials, resources, and technology. In order to use these effectively, teachers must be knowledgeable and informed consumers.

Most teachers are familiar with a variety of teaching materials that are readily available through teacher supply companies and catalogs. They have access to a variety of materials and resources in their school libraries and media centers and some have extensive collections of their own. Many teachers use community resources, guest speakers, parents, and field trips. In addition, there are manipulatives, visuals, audio equipment, audiovisuals, and computers. The technological trend has great potential for classroom use. In the near future, all teachers will be using VCRs, laser disks, CD-ROMs, interactive videos, scanners, and telecommunications. The number of computers in schools continues to grow. Teachers have access to CAI teaching materials, e-mail, and the Internet, which allows teachers and their students to obtain information from all over the world.

All Texas teachers should join and become knowledgeable and proficient in the use of TENET, the Texas Education Network. Its purpose is to advance and promote education in Texas. It is a rich source of information and resources that all teachers and students can use.

To use appropriate technology and resources, teachers need to know their students well enough to be able to determine if they are auditory, visual, or kinesthetic learners. (See Competency 004 and Appendix B.) Some will be a combination of these. The needs of students as well as their interests should always be considered when selecting appropriate resources for a lesson.

Competency 010

The teacher uses processes of informal and formal assessment to understand individual learners, monitor instructional effectiveness, and shape instruction.

Assessment is a process in which data about students' performance is collected. *Evaluation* is the process of making a *judgment* (for instance, regarding effectiveness of a program) after critically examining assessment data and other relevant information. Assessment should be ongoing in the classroom in both formal and informal ways. Teachers need continuous feedback if they are to plan, monitor, and evaluate instruction. There are two main types of assessment: *formative* and *summative*.

Formative assessment occurs before and during instruction. Before instruction begins, a teacher may want to determine students' level of skills and knowledge of a subject. For example, a teacher of reading may want to determine each student's reading ability, comprehension, and skills level. Formative assessment in the form of a *diagnostic* test can provide the desired information. Diagnostic tests are administered before instruction. Pretest results should be used in tailoring instruction to fit the needs of particular students. Formative assessment during instruction involves teacher observation, classroom questioning, student activities, seat work, homework, quizzes, and tests. The information obtained can be used to reteach, adjust instruction, vary the pace of instruction, or adjust the curriculum.

Summative assessment is most often used to determine student achievement for the purpose of grades. It occurs after instruction has taken place. Assessment types include standardized tests; student projects; unit, chapter, and weekly tests; daily grades; and sometimes homework.

Some methods of assessment, such as a quiz, can be used in both categories depending on the purpose of the teacher. The teacher may use a quiz to help in diagnosis or feedback or for a grade.

If a method of assessment is to be valuable to the teacher in making important decisions about children, it must have *reliability* and *validity*. *Reliability* refers to the consistency of a measurement over time and repeated measurements. If teachers give alternate forms of the same test periodically over several months and the students' performance scores remain relatively the same, the test has reliability.

Validity has to do with whether or not the assessment instrument measures what it is supposed to measure. Validity can be determined by comparing a test score against some separate or independent observation of whatever is being measured. If a teacher wants to measure math skills, the test must measure math skills, not reading skills. The teacher can also compare the daily or weekly grades of students to their test scores. If they are similar, then the test probably has validity.

All teachers need to be familiar with the terms *mean, median,* and *mode,* known as *measures* of *central tendency*. These are used frequently for determining certain information in assessment. *Mean* is the (arithmetic) average score and is determined by adding up all the scores and dividing this sum by the total number of scores that were added. The *median* is the midpoint in a distribution of scores from highest to lowest. The *mode* is the score in a distribution that appears most frequently. In a distribution of 95, 90, 88, 86, and 86, the mean is 89, the median is 88, and the mode is 86.

All three of these measures provide a way to describe the score of a "typical" or "average" student. The mean is usually the best indicator of the average; however, when there are a few scores that are either very high or very low compared to the rest of the scores, the median is a better choice to use for the average. The mode is not used as often as the mean or median, but it is appropriate when a large number of the scores are the same.

Although measures of central tendency are important for summarizing sets of student scores, their usefulness often hinges on how spread out the scores are. Two sets of scores may have the same mean, but one set of scores may be extremely consistent with scores clustered close together, while the other set of scores may be very erratic with a lot of spread. Measures of *variability* are used to describe the amount of spread. Two important measures of variability are the *range* and the *standard deviation.*

The *range* is the simplest measure of variability. It is the largest score minus the smallest score in a set of scores. In the set of scores above, the range is 95–86, or 9.

The range gives some indication of the spread of the scores, but its value is determined by only two scores. A measure of variability that takes into account all the scores is the *standard deviation*. The standard deviation tells how spread out the scores are around the mean. If there is no variability in a set of scores, each score would be the same as the mean, giving a standard deviation of zero; the more the scores vary from the mean, the larger the standard deviation. The standard deviation is used extensively in education, particularly with the normal curve and standardized tests.

A *standardized test* is one that has been carefully constructed and field-tested so that (ideally) it has a high degree of reliability and validity. Directions for taking the test and conditions for administering and scoring it are uniform and rigorously monitored. A *norm-referenced test* (such as SAT) is one that assesses students by comparing their performance to that of a norm group in the content area. Usually, the norm group is representative of students of the same age or grade level as the test takers. A *criterion-referenced* test assesses students by comparing their performance to a predetermined level of mastery. The Texas Assessment of Academic Skills (TAAS) test is a criterion-referenced test. An advantage of criterion-referenced tests over norm-referenced tests is their diagnostic, placement, and remediation use. To that end, teachers in Texas are expected to analyze TAAS performance data to address remediation needs of individual students. *Disaggregation* of the data (that is, separating it) by subject, gender, and ethnicity must be used by schools and teachers to identify groups of students needing remediation.

Teacher-made tests (see Appendix B for guidelines) can provide valuable information about what students have learned. The key to preparing good teacher-made tests is ensuring that they accurately reflect what has been taught. Teachers should try to make sure that content that was given more emphasis in class is given more weight on the test. Planned reviews before testing are also important. Moreover, weekly or monthly reviews of previously learned material will help students' retention. Research on the effectiveness of testing has consistently found that tests promote learning. This is especially true if what is to be learned is first tested soon after it was introduced. The most effective tests are those given frequently and at consistent intervals. Finally, frequent cumulative tests result in more learning than do infrequent tests or tests given only on content covered since the last test.

Another way for teachers to find out what students have learned is through homework assignments. When homework is given as independent practice, it should be

- appropriate for the ability and maturity level of the students;
- closely tied to what was taught in class;
- worthwhile (not meaningless worksheets);
- coordinated with what the students' other teachers are requiring them to do;
- given immediately after presentation of the subject matter;

- given frequently as a means of extending guided practice with new material;
- clearly understood by the students before they leave class;
- frequently checked orally in class;
- quickly checked and returned to students, when collected;
- graded and commented on;
- successfully completed by most of the students; and
- *never* given as punishment.

In the elementary and middle-school grades, students should be given homework to help them develop good study habits, develop positive attitudes toward school, and realize that learning is something that happens not only at school but at home, also. For elementary school students, homework assignments should be short and should require only materials commonly found in the students' homes. For middle-school students, homework assignments can be longer, taking from one to two hours per night. These students may also be assigned voluntary homework. These assignments should involve tasks that students of middle-school age are intrinsically motivated to do.

In high school, teachers should assign homework on a regular basis. It is not unreasonable to expect homework assignments in high school to require materials not commonly found in the students' homes and to take several hours to complete.

Regardless of grade level, teachers should provide parents with information on homework policies and assignments and try to elicit support from parents to help with homework and to monitor their child's study time. Research shows that students whose parents are involved in their schooling have greater academic achievement than other students.

Teachers today are moving toward multiple and more authentic (that is, realistic) assessments of students, such as checklists, performance observations (in person, by video and/or audiotapes), work samples (tests, papers, projects), process observations and products, interviews, and portfolios. Authentic assessment enables the examiner to directly assess meaningful and complex educational performances. Assessment is integrated into everyday classroom practice and real contexts. Performance assessments have long been used in the assessment of music, art, drama, and physical education. Process and product assessment are usually more evident in science, math, social studies, and language arts. Student portfolio assessment is currently standard practice in most classrooms.

A *portfolio* is a meaningful collection of student work. It provides various and comprehensive summaries of student performance in particular contexts. Portfolio assessment requires students to collect and reflect on examples of their work and provide documentation of what they can do.

Student *self-assessment* is also important. There are many ways students can assess themselves, such as grading their own papers, group participation, and portfolio assessment.

In summary, teachers assess their students for a number of reasons: to gain understanding of their skills and knowledge, to assign grades, to make decisions about what to teach, to find out which students need extra help and which students need to be challenged more, and so forth.

Effective teachers keep track of their students' progress, hold students accountable for their work, and use interventions to improve student learning.

Competency 011

The teacher structures and manages the learning environment to maintain a classroom climate that promotes the lifelong pursuit of learning and encourages cooperation, leadership, and mutual respect.

The key to being a successful classroom manager is planning and preplanning. Planning means being prepared each day with lesson plans and everything needed to implement those plans. Preplanning means going through each lesson mentally from the student's point of view and anticipating explanations, information, and directions they will need in order to carry out the lesson successfully.

Effective managers are able to secure the cooperation of students, maintain their involvement in instructional tasks, and attend to the clerical or business duties of the classroom quickly and smoothly. They are courteous and respectful, they maximize academic learning time, and, in discipline situations, they use the least intrusive interventions necessary to stop or redirect inappropriate behavior, ensuring at all times that the dignity of the student, even the seriously disruptive student, is preserved. For instance, to keep the flow of the lesson going, effective classroom managers first deal with students who are off-task or behaving inappropriately by using nonverbal interventions (for instance, eye contact, moving in the direction of the student). If the inappropriate behavior continues, the teacher may use verbal interventions (for instance, say the student's name and ask a question related to the lesson, say the student's name and shake head disapprovingly). Stronger measures are used only when essential. (See Appendix B for guidelines.) They establish, teach, and reteach classroom routines and procedures. They post classroom rules that are fair and appropriate for the grade level. For the rules to be effective, the students must know the rules and their consequences, and the teacher must enforce the rules consistently and impartially. In general, rules should be positively stated and should number between three and five.

Kounin believed it is important that teachers display *withitness*. By this he meant that they are aware of what is happening in the classroom at all times. He also advocated they develop the skill of *overlapping* and the use of the *ripple effect*. *Overlapping* means being able to do more than one thing at a time, such as moving to stand beside a student who is off-task, answering a question from another student, and monitoring cooperative learning groups, all simultaneously. The *ripple effect* occurs when a teacher reminds an off-task student to get back to work and all the other off-task students also return to their assignment.

A critical time for establishing classroom order occurs in the first few days of school. Slavin's examination of the research indicated that to start the year off right, effective classroom managers should:

1. have a clear, specific plan for introducing students to classroom rules and procedures and spend as many days as necessary carrying out the plan until students know how to line up, ask for help, and so on.

2. work with the whole class initially (even if they plan to group students later).

3. spend much of the first days of school introducing procedures, discussing class rules (often encouraging students to suggest rules themselves), and reminding students of class rules every day for at least the first week of school.

4. teach students specific procedures (like how to move into learning groups quickly and quietly).

5. use simple, enjoyable tasks as activities for the first lessons; give out instructions and procedures gradually to avoid overloading the students with too many instructions before asking them to get to work; and use materials that are well-prepared, clearly presented, and varied.

6. respond immediately to stop or redirect any misbehavior.

Effective managers are also effective leaders. Effective leaders are able to build positive relationships with students and communicate effectively with them. They strive to build a positive physical, social, and intellectual environment that is conducive to learning and motivating for students. Successful classroom managers are skilled both in prevention of behavior problems and in dealing appropriately with them. They arrange the physical layout of the room so that they can see the students from anywhere in the classroom. Being proactive is far better than having to deal with a problem after it occurs.

Effective managers know that the physical arrangement of the classroom influences the way teachers and students feel, think, and behave. The arrangement of desks can determine the kind and extent of interaction that will take place. Clusters of three to five desks or students seated at small tables promote social contact and interaction. Students can easily share materials, have group discussions, and work together on assignments. This arrangement is particularly appropriate when teachers want to use cooperative learning activities. Teachers who want their students to exchange ideas know that the more the students see each other, the more they will be involved in discussions. Thus for whole-group settings, circles and U-shaped designs promote discussion. Teachers who use these arrangements usually place their own desks in an out-of-the-way place or in a corner.

Arranging desks in rows is particularly appropriate for teacher-centered instruction. Rows tend to reduce the interaction among students and make it easier for them to work individually. Rows also direct the students' attention toward the teacher. Teachers who use this type of physical arrangement typically place their desks in front of the room where they are easily visible.

Where students are seated in the classroom can also influence participation patterns. Planned seating is better than random seating.

When desks are arranged in rows, students who are seated in the front and center are in the "action zone." These students interact most frequently with the teacher. Students who are seated in the back and corners participate less. Some evidence indicates that teachers may communicate differently with students, depending on where the students are seated. Students in the action zone receive a more permissive and interactive style of communication, while students in the back and corners receive more lecturing and one-way communication.

Effective teachers arrange and change the environment as needed to encourage learning. They make sure that movement in the classroom and acquisition of materials can occur with little disruption; that students can see and be seen by the teacher; and that students can see the blackboard, overhead projector, VCR, and so forth, when necessary.

Successful classroom management also involves managing time, establishing routines, establishing classroom rules with student input, and using pacing and smooth transitions. Good managers maximize academic learning time—the time students are actively engaged and experiencing success; minimize the time students spend waiting for activities to get started, making transitions between activities, sitting with nothing to do, or engaging in misbehavior; and teach and model appropriate behavior. Brophy recommended that, in the early elementary grades, teachers need to spend a large amount of time formally teaching students rules, procedures, and routines of the classroom. In the middle elementary grades, teachers need to reinforce the expected classroom rules and procedures. In grades 5 through 10, disciplinary aspects of classroom management become more pronounced. In grades 11 and 12, teachers can spend more time on instruction since most students have passed through the rebellious stages of adolescence, although the teacher still will need to reinforce expected appropriate behavior.

When teachers are working with groups, they need to be clear about directions and expectations. Additionally, they need to spend a lot of time moving through the room and checking on the groups so that they can offer reinforcement and feedback to students about their academic work as well as their group process skills.

Teachers need to use appropriate management strategies for students with special needs. For instance, mainstreamed hyperactive students need classrooms structured with well-defined rules, definite consequences for breaking them, and consistency in enforcing them. These students need planned opportunities for physical movement (for example, passing out materials, erasing the chalkboard, running errands) and low levels of classroom noise.

In general, when dealing with discipline problems teachers should be quick to stop or redirect off-task or inappropriate behavior using the least intrusive means; for instance, dealing with potentially serious disruptions early by using eye contact, moving around the room, or providing short, quiet comments to the disruptive student; and talking privately with students who misbehave to avoid power struggles and face-saving gestures. When talking with a student who has misbehaved, teachers need to make sure the student knows he or she has done something that is unacceptable and they should ask for an explanation from the student. It is important that the student understand why the behavior is unacceptable and cannot be tolerated. Teachers should be careful to talk about the behavior, not the student. Effective teachers will describe what they saw, how they feel about it, and what needs to be done. They try to get the student to accept responsibility for the misbehavior and to agree not to commit the offense again. In some cases, the teacher may need to help the student develop a plan for changing his or her behavior so that it becomes acceptable.

Students want structure and need limits. They also expect teachers to treat them with dignity and be consistent and fair in enforcing classroom rules. Teachers who create the proper classroom atmosphere will be encouraging students to develop control of their own behavior.

Practice Questions on Domain II

Ms. Jones likes to involve her eighth-grade students actively in the learning process. During a follow-up discussion after groups experimented with magnets, she asks, "Why did the magnet attract some things and not others?" Sam and Mary have their hands waving in the air before she is finished. Ms. Jones then says, "I'll give everyone a few minutes to think about the question." Then she repeats it. After a few minutes of watching the students' faces, she asks different ones if they have an answer. By posing the question to the whole class before calling on individual students, Ms. Jones is most likely attempting to promote learning by:

    A. encouraging students to be creative problem solvers.
    B. providing students with clear learning expectations.
    C. ignoring overanxious students so that they do not monopolize class discussion time.
    D. encouraging more students to respond.

The question is asking about Ms. Jones' purpose in using a particular questioning strategy, so it deals with **communication.** Thus, the primary focus of this question is Competency 007: *The teacher uses effective verbal, nonverbal and media communication techniques to shape the classroom into a community of learners engaged in active inquiry, collaborative exploration, and supportive instruction.* Eliminate A because it doesn't fit with the stimulus—the students will be making conjectures, not problem solving. Eliminate B because it doesn't fit with the stimulus—Ms. Jones is not providing information. Eliminate C because it is inconsistent with treating students courteously and respectfully (Competency 011, **classroom management**). The stimulus provides the information that Ms. Jones wants to involve her students actively in the learning process. Choice D is consistent with educational principles and concepts. Asking a question *first* and *then* calling a student's name is an effective method teachers can use to keep all students mentally involved in the learning process. When the question comes before a student's name, all students are given the opportunity to think and process their answers because the teacher has not yet identified the student who will be asked to respond. Research shows that asking the question first increases the number of responses as well as eliciting more correct and longer responses. Choice D is the correct response.

Mr. Green is a fourth-grade teacher in his first year of teaching. He is trying to put into practice what he learned at the university. Several times he has tried letting the students work in small groups, but things have not gone well. Today he is trying group work again, but he is still experiencing difficulty. He begins class by instructing the students to move their desks and get into their assigned groups. They are very noisy when doing this, and by the time he has them quiet, several students are hollering out, "What do we do now?" Mr. Green manages to explain the group task, but as soon as he finishes, several students in different groups speak up to say, "We don't understand." At this point Mr. Green is ready to call it quits on group work. The *first* step Mr. Green should take to make small-group work more effective is:

    A. help the students understand they need to work together.

    B. teach students specific procedures on how to move into learning groups.

    C. break tasks down so that each group member has a specific part.

    D. present the learning task in writing to each group.

Mr. Green is having a problem with **classroom management.** Thus, the primary focus of this question is Competency 011: *The teacher structures and manages the learning environment to maintain a classroom climate that promotes the lifelong pursuit of learning and encourages cooperation, leadership, and mutual respect.* This question is a priority-setting question—you have to decide what Mr. Green should do *first.* Choices A, C, and D are measures Mr. Green might take to promote effective group work (although Choice D—presenting the task in writing—is not a requirement for effective group work, so long as the task is clearly defined and explained). The problem is that these measures come too late—after the disruption caused by students moving into groups has occurred. At the beginning of the school year, successful classroom managers establish and teach classroom routines to create a smoothly functioning learning community. To make small-group work more effective, Mr. Green *first* should teach his fourth-graders specific procedures on how to move into learning groups. Choice B is the correct response.

Ms. Liebermann enjoys teaching her economics students. They are especially excited about anything having to do with the stock market. During today's lesson, however, she sees a number of confused looks on the faces of the students, and when she asks several questions, the students are unable to respond correctly. Ms. Liebermann decides to reteach this lesson tomorrow in a different way. This decision *best* illustrates:

    A. effective use of formative assessment.

    B. failure to plan appropriate activities.

    C. effective use of student interest in planning lessons.

    D. effective use of teacher reinforcement.

This question deals with both **planning** (Ms. Liebermann decides to reteach the lesson in a different way) and **assessment** (Ms. Liebermann is monitoring instructional effectiveness). Thus, the primary focus of this question is either Competency 006 or Competency 010. Let's see if we can determine an answer choice without deciding for sure which of these two best applies. Eliminate D because reinforcement relates to **motivation** (Competency 005) or **classroom management** (Competency 011), not **planning** (Competency 006) or **assessment** (Competency 010). Eliminate B because deciding to reteach is not failure to plan appropriate activities. On the contrary, reteaching when students are confused is totally appropriate. Eliminate C, as from the stimulus we know that Ms. Liebermann made her decision because she was concerned that the students did not appear to understand, not because of their interest in the stock market. This situation illustrates how a teacher uses ongoing observational techniques of formative assessment to determine the needs of her students. Choice A is the correct response.

Since Choice A deals with **assessment,** you now know that the primary focus of this question is Competency 010: *The teacher uses processes of informal and formal assessment to understand individual learners, monitor instructional effectiveness, and shape instruction.*

CHAPTER 9

DOMAIN III—UNDERSTANDING THE TEACHING ENVIRONMENT

Competency 012

The teacher is a reflective practioner who knows how to promote his or her own professional growth and can work cooperatively with other professionals in the system to create a school culture that enhances learning and encourages positive change.

Research studies have identified certain characteristics that are essential for effective teaching. They found that effective teachers are clear about instructional goals and accept responsibility for student learning; choose, adapt, and use materials effectively; have a firm command of subject matter and teaching strategies; motivate students by communicating expectations to students; incorporate higher-level thinking skills; develop empathy, rapport, and personal interactions with students; and integrate instruction with other subject areas. Furthermore, effective teachers possess personality characteristics which include enthusiasm, warmth, supportiveness of students, sensitivity, interest in people, flexibility, and self-confidence.

Effective teachers constantly reflect about their teaching. Before, during, and after a lesson they are observing whether or not students are learning, and they adjust the lesson accordingly. They are always making decisions based on the "readiness" of their students. They ask themselves: "What is the best teaching strategy to use for this lesson? What available materials and resources are the most appropriate for today's activities?" This process is sometimes referred to as *reflective teaching*.

Other ways that teachers assess themselves are by videotaping lessons for later viewing and critiquing of their instructional performance. In recent years, peer coaching has become popular with teachers. It involves two or more teachers sharing ideas and then providing feedback on one another's teaching. All teachers need to engage in self-assessment in order to continually improve their complex craft. Some teachers keep a daily or weekly journal of their thoughts and feelings to encourage self-reflection and evaluation.

Teachers should also recognize the importance of working collegially with their colleagues. To strengthen the effectiveness and quality of instruction, teachers should engage actively in an exchange of ideas with other teachers. Teachers should see themselves as part of a learning community that works together to solve problems, deal with stress, explore innovative ideas, and assess the effectiveness of instruction.

At the middle- and secondary-school levels, it is common for teachers from different disciplines to form interdisciplinary teams that collaboratively plan integrated learning activities. (See Competency 008.) The team consists of four or five teachers from different subject areas. Very often, this set of teachers comes from the core subjects of English, mathematics, science, and social studies. Usually, these teachers instruct the same group of about 125 students, share a common planning period, and meet frequently on a regular basis to plan curriculum and discuss the progress and needs of their students. The advantages of interdisciplinary teams are the following:

- members provide an expanded pool of ideas and solutions to problems;
- members collaboratively can plan and coordinate instructional activities;
- members provide support and guidance for each other;
- beginning teachers have the benefit of experienced teachers' advice and help;
- members tend to work harder on improving instructional quality;
- members help substitute teachers when a team member is absent;
- members can collaborate in dealing with individual students.

Since 1995 staying up-to-date and acquiring new professional skills are no longer an option for Texas teachers. Since then, the Texas Education Code (TEC) has mandated that educators in Texas must engage in professional development and use the skills thus acquired to improve student learning. Also in 1995, the State Board for Educator Certification (SBEC) was established to recognize public school teachers as professionals and, along with other duties related to teacher education, to oversee the continuing education of public school educators. The TEC further mandated that the commissioner of education adopt an appraisal system for teachers based on observable, job-related behavior, including (a) teachers' implementation of discipline management procedures and (b) the performance of teachers' students. As a result, the Professional Development and Appraisal System (PDAS) was developed. Performance on the PDAS is based on eight domains:

Domain I: Active, successful student participation in the learning process

Domain II: Learner-centered instruction

Domain III: Evaluation and feedback on student progress

Domain IV: Management of student discipline, instructional strategies, time, and materials

Domain V: Professional communication

Domain VI: Professional development

Domain VII: Compliance with policies, operating procedures, and requirements

Domain VIII: Improvement of academic performance for all students on the campus (based on indicators included in the Academic Excellence Indicator System).

Although a school district may adopt a state-approved alternative instrument for teacher appraisal, the majority of districts in Texas have elected to use the state-created instrument. Teachers may satisfy the professional development component of the PDAS in a number of ways; however, it is imperative that professional development activities consistently result in improved learning of students in the teachers' respective classrooms. Teachers should select activities that are directly related to their teaching assignment and to the needs and characteristics of their students. The TEC requires that inservice training provided by school districts be predominantly campus-based, related to campus and/or district goals, and include training in technology, conflict resolution, and discipline strategies. The campus professional development activities may be collaboratively planned by the campus staff and may be offered in the form of workshops, seminars, or conferences or conducted using study teams, individual research, peer coaching, or other deliveries that have potential to improve student performance. Teachers are not limited to campus-based self-improvement; they may also choose to participate in appropriate professional opportunities offered by colleges, universities, or regional education service centers or to engage in individually guided self-study.

Teachers may wish to become members of professional organizations associated with their fields of interest, such as:

National Association for the Education of Young Children (NAEYC)
www.naeyc.org

International Reading Association (IRA)
www.ira.org

National Council of Teachers of English (NCTE)
www.ncte.org

National Council of Teachers of Mathematics (NCTM)
www.nctm.org

National Science Teachers Association (NSTA)
www.ncta.org

National Council of Social Studies (NCSS)
www.socialstudies.org

National Council for Agriculture Education (The Council)
www.agriculture.com

National Academy of Sciences (NAS)
www.nas.edu

**Texas Association of Health, Physical Education,
Recreation and Dance**
www.tahperd.org

The National Education Association (at www.nea.org) is the largest of the national teachers' organizations. A teacher who joins the NEA also becomes a member of the Texas State Teachers Association (TSTA) (at www.tsta.org). Other noteworthy groups are:

American Federation of Teachers (AFT)
www.aft.org

Association of Texas Professional Educators (ATPE)
www.atpe.org

Texas Classroom Teachers Association (TCTA)
www.tcta.org

Association for Supervision and Curriculum Development (ASCD)
www.ascd.org

Texas Association of School Boards (TASB)
www.tasb.org

Texas Association of Secondary School Principals (TASSP)
www.tassp.org

Texas Elementary Principals and Supervisors Association (TEPSA)
www.tepsa.org

Professional development will become a greater concern for teachers beginning September 1, 1999. On that date and thereafter, those who successfully complete the requirements for teacher certification will be issued a Standard Certificate, which must be renewed every five years contingent upon the educator completing a specified number of continuing education clock hours. The continuing education activities must be correlated with the campus and/or district learning priorities as well as with the educator's own personal improvement plan. All provisional and professional lifetime certificates issued prior to September 1, 1999, will be exempted from the renewal requirement; however, educators may voluntarily choose to opt into the renewable certificate. For more information, you can call the SBEC Information and Support Center toll free at (888) 863-5880 or e-mail your request to sbec@esc20.net.

Competency 013

The teacher knows how to foster strong school-home relationships that support student achievement of desired learning outcomes.

When school faculties and administrations share the responsibility of the total school program with parents or guardians by involving them in all aspects of schooling, everyone benefits, especially the students. The person with the most opportunities to build a positive parent-school relationship is the classroom teacher. The art of communicating with parents is an integral part of being an effective teacher. The first communication with parents should come from the child's early childhood teacher, and this should continue throughout the child's school career. Before the first day of school, you will receive a list of the names of the students in your class. This is the time to start building a positive relationship with the parents of your students by writing a letter to them. You can introduce yourself, tell them some activities the class will be doing during the upcoming year, and let them know that you are looking forward to having their son or daughter in your classroom. You should also invite them to visit the school anytime and include a telephone number and the time it will be convenient for them to contact you. Arrange to have the letters translated into the parents' primary language for those whose home language is other than English. Most parents are protective of their children; positive first contact from the teacher is very reassuring for them. During the year, continue the communication in the form of weekly or monthly telephone calls. A positive phone call will be appreciated by a parent who has received only negative reports in the past. The campus policy handbook will usually contain suggestions for communicating with parents or guardians. The handbook should also inform you of what kinds of records of contact to keep.

Communication between the school and the home should be purposeful and ongoing. Teachers and parents share responsibility for creating a working partnership that fosters student learning. When parents participate and are involved in their child's learning, the child has a greater chance of success. This is true for students from kindergarten to high school. Teachers can be effective public relations agents by building a solid partnership with the parents of their students. Positive telephone calls, notes, and letters throughout the year to all parents telling of class happenings and their children's achievements will be most welcome and appreciated.

Parents can be invited to attend student performances and to become involved in school activities. Parent-teacher organizations are another way schools can reach out to parents. They will care about the school when they feel ownership in it. This can be further enhanced when schools invite parents to be on-site volunteers or at-home volunteers. Among other things, parents can serve as tutors; share a specific skill, talent, interest, or hobby; read to students or listen to them read; make bulletin boards; set up centers or labs; perform clerical tasks; help with special activities; or serve as aides and room mothers/fathers. The nature of parent-teacher conferences may differ depending upon the age and grade level of the student. Parents are usually more involved in their child's education during the early grades than at the middle or high school levels, where students assume more responsibility for their educational development. Regardless of the age or grade level, the basic principles for *successful* parent-teacher conferences remain the same (see Appendix B for guidelines). Conferences should always be scheduled. Traditionally, conferences take place at the school where the parents and teacher can meet face to face. Nowadays, conferences can be through telephone conference calls and via computer. For busy parents whose schedules make it difficult to set up a mutually convenient time for a conference, this may be the best way to "meet." When scheduling a conference time, the teacher should use a written form, giving the parents some time options as well as alternative days if possible. Allow ample time for the parents to complete the form and return it. Prepare for the conference beforehand by gathering appropriate records and samples of the student's work. Make a written agenda so that you will stay on task. When it's time for the parents to arrive, if they have not visited before meet them at the school office or entrance to the building. Parents are on foreign turf, and they may be tense, fearful, or anxious. They will appreciate your friendly gesture. Next, proceed to the conference room or the classroom. Make sure the environment for the conference is friendly and conducive to open communication. Introduce yourself using your first and last name and offer them some refreshments. Have the area already set up, so that everyone can see and hear in a quiet, relaxed setting. Do *not* sit behind your desk. This gives the impression of a barrier between you and the parents and, thus, will limit communication. Begin and end the conference on a positive note. It is important to recognize that parents need their share of "talk time." Although you are conducting the conference, parents should have the opportunity to initiate conversation and ask questions. During the conference it is important to stay tuned to what the parents are communicating. Should parents ask questions that you feel you shouldn't answer, direct their questions to the school counselor or principal. Anytime you expect to have a difficult conference, ask one of these individuals to be present and participate. During the conference, use your interpersonal skills effectively. Successful parent-teacher conferences can be the key that enhances the student's growth and promotes learning. You must always exhibit self-control and never become defensive. Remember, it is normal for the parent to take the side of the child. Parents and teachers share the same goal—obtaining what is best for the child. Immediately following the conference or soon after, document and date what was discussed and proposed. These should be kept and filed for future reference or need. If further action should be taken, it should be noted and a time-frame developed. The principal should be kept informed of all conferences and should receive a brief, written report after each. You should write a personal note to the parents thanking them for their time and informing them of when you will contact them with an update. You should make positive comments to the student as soon as possible to dispel any fears and to reassure him or her.

In the past, the child was included in the parent-teacher conference only under special circumstances. Nowadays, it is becoming more common to include them, especially the older student, and to let them be actively involved.

Competency 014

The teacher understands how the school relates to the larger community and knows strategies for making interactions between school and community mutually supportive and beneficial.

Teachers can foster positive interactions between the school and the community and, at the same time, take advantage of community resources to foster student growth by inviting a variety of members of the community to serve as guest speakers, local experts, and volunteers. This should raise students' awareness and understanding of resources in the local community, as well as encourage their appreciation of the diverse characteristics of the community population. Teachers should be mindful to not impose upon invited guests who are donating their time and expertise in the teachers' classrooms. For example, invited guests should not be asked to assume responsibilities (like grading papers, designing lessons) that are time-consuming or for which they feel they lack the expertise to do properly. To enhance students' understanding of the local community, students can go on field trips to local sites and businesses. To heighten students' awareness of the benefits of positive school-community relationships, teachers can invite the local media to cover school events and solicit members of the community to sponsor student events.

The school should recognize that the businesses that serve its community have a vested interest in the quality of educational programs and services that the school offers the students. By helping the school, they are ultimately helping themselves and the whole community. School-business partnerships can be established whereby businesses sponsor apprenticeships, internships, or work/study programs. Such mutually beneficial programs serve as vehicles for establishing ongoing communication links with the business community through which the school and community can learn more about each other.

Students should be encouraged to make positive contributions to the community (such as volunteering for community projects), thus promoting their sense of social responsibility. Teachers should publicize the accomplishments of their students, so that local businesses will be more willing to underwrite awards dinners, parent receptions, and scholarships and to donate to fund-raisers. Also, teachers should make sure that the students acknowledge the generosity of the community by having them write thank-you notes to the guest speaker, volunteer, local business, sponsor, or other supporter.

Competency 015

The teacher understands requirements, expectations, and constraints associated with teaching in Texas and can apply this understanding in a variety of contexts.

Under the United States Constitution, education is a state function. In Texas, the state's public school law is set forth in the Texas Education Code (TEC). In 1995, Senate Bill 1—the recodification of the TEC—was passed and signed into law. The TEC provides that governance of public education will be under the direction of the Texas Education Agency (TEA), composed of the commissioner of education and the agency staff, and the State Board of Education (SBOE). Also in 1995, Senate Bill 1 established the State Board for Educator Certification (SBEC) to recognize public school teachers as professionals and, along with other duties related to teacher education, to oversee the continuing education of public school educators. At the local level are the independent school districts. School districts have the power to perform all educational functions not specifically delegated to the TEA or the SBOE. Each school district has a board of trustees (school board), which oversees the management of the public schools in the district, and a superintendent, who is the educational leader and chief executive officer of the district responsible for managing the day-to-day operation of the district. The principals are the instructional leaders of the schools in the district, responsible for the day-to-day operations of their schools. In addition, the principals assign, evaluate, and promote teachers assigned to their campuses. Before 1995, all decision making in school districts was done by the school boards and administrators, usually without input from teachers, parents, or the community. Senate Bill 1 mandated *site-based decision making*, which moved some decisions traditionally made by the central office to the campus level. It requires involvement from the teachers, parents, and community in the decision-making process for the district as members of state-mandated district- and campus-level planning and decision-making committees. With involvement of the district-level committee, school boards determine the respective roles and responsibilities of the superintendent, central office staff, principals, teachers, district-level committee members, and campus-level committee members. The degree of authority granted the campus-level, site-based, decision-making committees varies from district to district. Most districts in Texas have made restructuring efforts to shift authority from the central office to the local campus committee and principal.

Teachers in Texas are hired under a *probationary contract* of not more than one year, renewable for two additional one-year periods. After the probationary period, the district grants either a *term contract* or a *continuing contract*, depending on factors such as position of employment or length of service. Term contracts are for a fixed term, not to exceed five years. Districts must list reasons for nonrenewal of term contracts. The teacher may request a hearing on a nonrenewal before the school board, and, if the decision is unfavorable, may appeal to the commission for a review of the case. A *continuing contract* does not have a preset time limit. A teacher suspended or discharged "for good cause" at any time during a continuing contract can request a hearing before a commissioner-appointed hearing examiner. The school board has the option of rejecting or changing the hearing examiner's conclusions or proposals. The teacher may appeal to the commissioner and, thereafter, to a local or Austin district clerk for review of the case.

To ensure compliance with statutory law, teachers should take time to carefully read the sections of the TEC (available at www.capitol.state.tx.us/statutes/edtoc.html) that apply to them and their normal duties at school (see Appendix C for a summary). Some new provisions included in Senate Bill 1 that teachers should be aware of are:

- Teachers are entitled to 450 minutes of planning and preparation time for each two-week period. The time is to be allotted in increments of not less than 45 minutes during the instructional day.
- Teachers are entitled to at least five days of personal leave each year, with no limits on the accumulation of personal leave, which is transferable among districts.
- In addition to all other leave, a teacher who is physically assaulted during the performance of his or her regular duties is entitled to the number of days necessary to recuperate from all physical injuries sustained during the assault.
- School districts may provide for a period of silence at the beginning of the school day for students to reflect or meditate.
- Parents have the right to review their child's records, teaching materials, and state assessment instruments.
- Parents have the right to temporarily remove their child from a class or activity that conflicts with their religious or moral beliefs; however, the parent must notify the teacher in writing before removing the child.
- Under no-pass, no-play, a student who fails a course will be suspended from participating in any UIL- or district-sponsored

activity for three weeks; however, the student may continue to practice or rehearse.

- Teachers have the right to remove a disruptive student from class if the student's behavior is so unruly, disruptive, or abusive as to seriously interfere with the ability of the student's classmates to learn or the teacher to teach. Upon such removal, the principal may not return the student to the teacher's class without the teacher's permission, unless the Placement Review Committee—two teachers selected by the faculty and one member chosen by the principal—determines that such placement is the best or only alternative available.
- School districts must provide a separate alternative education setting to which students removed from class may be sent.

To promote professional ethical governing of the education profession, Texas adopted a Code of Ethics and Standard Practices for Texas Educators, revised in 1998. (See Appendix D.) This code addresses professional ethical conduct, professional practices and performance, ethical conduct toward students, and ethical conduct toward parents and community. Any teacher who is charged with and found guilty of violating any part of this code is subject to having his or her teaching certificate permanently revoked.

The 14th Amendment provides that no state shall deprive a person of life, liberty, or property without due process of law. The core element of due process is fairness. Most states have laws describing in detail a teacher's rights and the applicable time limitations regarding due process proceedings within that state. Although due process requirements vary from state to state, certain basic elements generally are recognized:

1. The teacher must be given timely detailed written notice of the charges.

2. The teacher must be accorded a hearing and sufficient time to prepare a defense.

3. The teacher has a right to be represented by legal counsel.

4. The teacher may present written and oral evidence including witnesses.

5. The teacher may cross-examine witnesses and challenge evidence.

6. The hearing is to be conducted before an impartial body.

7. The teacher is entitled to a written transcript of the proceedings.

8. The teacher has the right to appeal an adverse ruling to a higher legal authority, usually the state court system.

School districts in Texas have considerable authority to hire, assign, reassign, not renew, and dismiss employees as long as employees' due process and equal protection rights are observed. Collective bargaining and strikes, used by teachers in other states as leverage to gain favorable contracts, are expressly prohibited in Texas. Section 1 of Texas Civil Statute 5154C declares it to be against the public policy of the state for any public employer to enter into a collective bargaining contract with a labor organization with respect to the wages, hours, or conditions of employment of public employees. It specifies that any such contracts are to be null and void.

In recent years, it has become increasingly important that teachers be knowledgeable regarding federal and state laws that protect the rights of students with disabilities and guarantee, as eloquently expressed by the National Information Center for Children and Youth with Disabilities (NICHCY) (address: www.nichcy.org), "that children with disabilities can go to school every day, learn what other children learn, except perhaps in different ways, and have their individual needs addressed and identified." Two of the most important laws for students with disabilities are the Individuals with Disabilities Education Act and the Rehabilitation Act of 1973, especially Section 504.

In 1975, Congress passed the Education for All Handicapped Children Act (Public Law 94-142), sometimes referred to as the "mainstreaming" law. It was revised and renamed as the Individuals with Disabilities Education Act (IDEA) in 1990. The current law is called the Individuals with Disabilities Education Act Amendments of 1997 (PL 105-17). Its purpose is to provide a free and appropriate public education for all children with disabilities from age 3 to 21. The law requires every local education agency to have a continuum of services, ranging from mainstream to residential placement, available to meet individual student needs. According to IDEA, a "child with a disability" in general is a child who has one (or more) of the following disabilities and who, because of that disability, needs special education and related services:

- mental retardation
- hearing impairments (including deafness)
- speech or language impairments
- visual impairments (including blindness)
- emotional disturbance
- orthopedic impairments
- autism
- traumatic brain injury
- other health impairments
- specific learning disabilities

In addition, for a child ages 3 through 9, the term *child with a disability* may be, at the discretion of the state and the local educational agency and as measured by appropriate diagnostic instruments and procedures, a child who is experiencing developmental delays in one or more of the following areas: physical development, cognitive development, communication development, social or emotional development, or adaptive development, and who, for that reason, needs special education and related services. Under IDEA 97, if a child has a lack of instruction in math or reading or has limited English proficiency, he or she must not be identified as being a "child with a disability," if any one of these is the reason for determining the child has a disability.

The term *special education* means specially designed instruction at no cost to parents, to meet the unique needs of the child with a disability. But what are "related services"? The regulations for Public Law 94-142 list thirteen related services that students with disabilities may require to benefit from their special education programs. These are:

- audiology
- occupational therapy
- physical therapy
- psychological services
- medical services for diagnostic or evaluation purposes only
- school health services
- transportation services
- counseling services
- speech-language pathology
- social work services
- parent counseling and training
- recreation therapy
- early identification and assessment of disabilities in children (34 Code of Federal Regulations [CFR] Section 300.13 [b][1]-[13], 1988)

Plainly, the regulations define a wide variety of services that must be provided to children with disabilities. However, the law also states that this long list of services is not exhaustive and may include other developmental, corrective, or support services "as may be required to assist a child with a disability to benefit from special education" (The Individuals with Disabilities Education Act, 20 U.S.C. Chapter 33, Section 1401[17]). The NICHCY points out that although related services can be quite expensive, school districts may not charge families of students with disabilities for the cost of the services. Just as special and regular education must be provided to a student with a disability at no cost to the parent or guardian, so, too, must related services. As a result of federal law, it is the state's responsibility to provide a free, appropriate public education to all students with disabilities, and that includes any related services necessary to ensure they benefit from their education.

Sec. 29.001 of the Texas Education Code provides that the Texas Education Agency "develop, and modify as necessary, a statewide design, consistent with federal law, for the delivery of services to children with disabilities." Accordingly, the statewide plan includes the following six principles identified by the NICHCY that "rise up out of the spirit" of IDEA:

- **Free appropriate public education (FAPE)**—All specially designed instruction, including appropriate supplementary aids and services, is provided without charge, but does not preclude incidental fees that are normally charged to nondisabled students or their parents as part of the regular education program, and the education that a child with disabilities receives needs to address (that is, be appropriate for) his or her special education needs; has to meet standards of the TEA and include an appropriate Texas preschool, elementary, or secondary school education; and must be provided in conformity with the student's individualized education program (IEP).
- **Appropriate evaluation**—For a student to be considered for special education services, a referral is needed. The referral may be made by school personnel, the student's parent or legal guardian, a physician, a community agency, or any other appropriate person. A written report

of a comprehensive individual assessment of a student for purposes of special education services shall be completed not later than the 60th calendar day following the date on which the referral for assessment was initiated. The law requires that the school district establish an admission, review, and dismissal (ARD) committee that must include the parents of the child, at least one regular education teacher of the child (provided the child is participating in a regular education classroom), at least one special education teacher of the child, a representative of the school who is qualified to provide or supervise the provision of special services, someone who can interpret evaluation results, and other individuals who may be of help in designing an Individualized Education Program (IEP), including at least one teacher or specialist knowledgeable about the area of the child's suspected disability. Evaluation must be individualized and in all areas of suspected disability; nondiscriminatory (that is, not racially or culturally biased against the child), multifactor (that is, use more than one procedure to determine the child's educational program), and with assessment in the primary language or most proficient mode of communication of the child. When tests and other evaluations are completed, the determination of whether the child is eligible for special education must be made by the ARD committee and <u>cannot</u> be based on a lack of instruction in reading or math or limited English proficiency. Reevaluation with informed parental consent is required every 3 years.

- **Individualized education program (IEP)**—The IEP is developed by the ARD committee and must include the following: a statement of the child's present levels of educational performance; a statement of annual goals, including short-term instructional objectives; a statement of how the child's progress toward the annual goals will be measured and the parents will be kept regularly informed of that progress; a statement of the specific special education and supplementary aids and services to be provided to the child and the extent, if any, that the child will not participate with nondisabled peers in the regular class and in extracurricular and nonacademic activities; a statement as to how the IEP will be evaluated (at least once a year) to determine if the child's needs are being met; beginning at age 14, a statement of needed transition services that the student will need to prepare for life after high school; a statement of how the administration of state or district-wide assessments will be modified for the child so that he or she can participate or an explanation why the assessment is not appropriate and how the child will be alternatively assessed; and a recommendation for an appropriate placement in the educational setting that provides the child with the least restrictive environment.

- **Least restrictive environment (LRE)**—A child's LRE is the environment where the child can receive an appropriate education designed to meet his or her special education needs, while still being educated with nondisabled peers to the maximum extent possible. It is based on the presumption that children with disabilities are most appropriately educated with their nondisabled peers and that special classes, separate schooling, or other removal of children with disabilities from the regular education environment occur only when the nature or severity of the disability of the child is such that education in regular classes with the use of supplementary aids and services cannot be achieved satisfactorily. Depending on the child's individual needs, the LRE could be the regular classroom, with or without supplementary aids and services; a pull-out program for part of the day, with the remainder of the day being spent in the regular classroom or in activities with students who do not have disabilities; a special education class within the child's neighborhood school; or even a separate school specializing in a certain type of disability. Thus, one child's LRE may be very different from that of another child's. Each student's LRE is determined based upon that child's individual needs; however, a student's placement in the general education classroom is the first option the ARD committee must consider.

- **Parent and student participation in decision-making**—The law expects and requires that schools actively involve parents in steps along the way in the education of their child with disabilities, from identification of their child as potentially having a disability, through the evaluation and eligibility process, through planning the IEP and determining their child's placement, and in participating in any meetings necessary to address problems or concerns with respect to their child's education. In their turn, parents must be responsive to the school as their partner in decision making, including notifying the school about their concerns and intentions. IDEA 97 strengthened the parents' role in meeting the needs of a special education child. The document *An Explanation of Rights and Procedural Safeguards of a Parent with a Child with Disabilities in School*, produced by the TEA and available at www.tea.state.tx.us/special.ed/explansaf/ html/esp-txt.txt, contains a comprehensive summary of the law governing a parent's rights. You should become knowledgeable of the rights of parents to ensure that you do not unknowingly violate their rights or misinform them concerning their rights. Informed parental consent for both initial evaluation and reevaluation of a child is required. The school must send written notice to the parents of scheduled ARD committee meetings at least five school days before the meeting and the notice must state the purpose, time, and place for the meeting and list the people who will attend. Parents are full members of the ARD committee; their input must be solicited during the evaluation process; and they are entitled to participate in making the decision regarding their child's educational placement. A parent may be accompanied to the ARD meeting by anyone the parent desires, including an attorney. If the parents are hearing impaired or have a primary language other than English, the school must provide an interpreter at the meeting. Parents may audiotape-record any ARD committee meeting as long as they inform all members present that they are doing so. They have the right to sign the IEP and to indicate on the IEP whether they agree or disagree with the decisions made by the ARD committee; and they have the right to challenge or appeal any decision related to the identification, evaluation, or educational placement of their child. Parents have the right to inspect and review any education records relating to their child that the school collects, maintains, or uses. In addition, they have the right to inspect and review all educational records with respect to identification, evaluation, and educational placement of the child. Parents have the right to obtain an independent educational evaluation of their child at public expense if the parent disagrees with an evaluation obtained by the school. Parents are entitled to be notified of their child's progress at least as often as parents are notified of their nondisabled children's progress. Students must be invited to participate in their own IEP meeting beginning no later than age 16. Parents and teachers can involve students at younger ages, of course, and it makes good sense to do so.

- **Procedural safeguards**—*An Explanation of Rights and Procedural Safeguards of a Parent with a Child with Disabilities in School* is to be given to parents upon initial referral for evaluation of their child, upon each notification of an ARD meeting concerning their child, upon each reevaluation of their child, and upon a school district's request for a "due process hearing" about the child.

The Rehabilitation Act of 1973, which includes Section 504, was developed and passed in the 1970s. This law prohibits schools (and other institutions receiving federal funds) from discriminating against students who have disabilities. Relatively recent interpretations and applications of Section 504 of the Rehabilitation Act of 1973 have expanded the IDEA disabilities that qualify students for special services. Section 504 refers broadly to "any person who (i) has a physical or mental impairment which substantially limits one or more . . . major life activities, (ii) a record of such impairment, or (iii) is regarded has having such impairment." The broader definition means that some students who may not qualify for special services under IDEA may be eligible under Section 504. For example, some students, such as those with drug or alcohol addiction, heart disease, dyslexia, AIDS, or chronic asthma, may have a Section 504 disability. Needless to say, special education has become far more complicated as a result of the expanded interpretation of Section 504.

In 1991, Texas began to focus on student achievement, excellence, and equity in education for all students, including students with disabilities. A Leadership Initiative for Improving Special Education Services in Texas was developed in 1992 to help move toward this goal by increasing the achievement of students with disabilities. This plan will provide directions to the agency and the state for the next five to ten years.

The major focus of the initiative is on providing educational services to students with disabilities in the regular classroom. The words "full inclusion for all students" are used to mean the provision of all educational and related services in the regular classroom. Full inclusion occurs when children with disabilities learn in a regular classroom, with all the necessary supports, alongside their nondisabled peers. These supports are provided with extensive teamwork and, always, with consideration for the best interests of all concerned.

Many types of accommodations can be provided under IDEA and Section 504, including preferential seating, alternative or reduced assignments, extended time for test taking, oral test taking, sign-language assistance, tutoring, instruction and assistance in organizational skills, homework monitoring, enlarged reading material, taping of content material, calculator or computer access, and Braille writer or other assistive technology device access. Although "full inclusion" will be possible for many students with disabilities, there will still be those who will be unable to function in the regular classroom. The intent of "full inclusion" is to move the state toward a unified, integrated, and supported educational system for students with disabilities at the prekindergarten, early childhood, elementary, middle, and high school levels.

Other federal and state legislation directly affecting the public schools are the following:

Chapter I (formerly Title I) of the Elementary and Secondary Education Act (ESEA) was passed in 1965. Since 1965, the program has provided extra educational services in reading, writing, and mathematics to low-achieving children who live in low-income neighborhoods. The program has shown positive gains in the achievement of educationally disadvantaged children. In 1988, Congress reauthorized Chapter I with the mandate to the nation's schools to close the gap between low- and high-achieving students, stressing accountability for performance, program improvement, and flexibility to produce results.

Funds were first provided for the development and evaluation of effective models of bilingual programs in 1968 with the passage of *Title VII of the Elementary and Secondary Education Act (ESEA)*. Today, this is often referred to as the *Bilingual Education Act*. This legislation made funds available, but development of such programs is voluntary. In 1981, the Texas legislature mandated districts to provide bilingual education from kindergarten through grade three and to fund programs through grade five. The State Board of Education also prescribed instruction in English as a second language (ESL) for all limited-English-proficiency (LEP) students not enrolled in a bilingual program.

The 1978 *Gifted and Talented Act* indicated that the gifted and talented are children identified as possessing "demonstrated or potential abilities in areas such as intellectual, creative, specific academic, or leadership, or in the performing or visual arts." It is reasonable to expect that somewhere between three and five percent of all students are truly gifted or talented. Districts provide for the gifted and talented in a variety of ways. Some of these are acceleration, enrichment, and special schools for certain subject areas like the sciences and the arts. Acceleration is rapid promotion through advanced studies, and enrichment involves activities that are designed to broaden or deepen the knowledge of students who master information quickly.

The Family Rights and Privacy Act of 1974, better known as the Buckley Amendment, gives students and their parents access to student records and restricts disclosure of record content.

Title IX prohibits sex discrimination in any public school.

Texas Family Code 261.101 requires any persons having cause to believe that a child's physical or mental health or welfare has been or may be adversely affected by abuse or neglect to report the case to any local or state law enforcement agency or to the Department of Protective and Regulatory Services. Educators and other state-certified professionals are mandated to report within forty-eight hours from the moment the abuse is discovered or suspected. Conscious failure to do so is a Class B misdemeanor, punishable by imprisonment of up to 180 days and a fine of up to $1,000. The law says they may not "delegate to or rely on another person to make the report" (for instance, report to the principal or counselor of the school and rely on that person to make the official report). The identity of a person making a report is kept confidential, and he or she is immune from liability unless the report is knowingly or intentionally false.

Under TEC Sec. 26.004, a parent is entitled to access to all written records of a school district concerning the parent's child, including:

1. attendance records

2. test scores

3. grades

4. disciplinary records

5. counseling records

6. psychological records

7. applications for admission

8. health and immunization information

9. teacher and counselor evaluations

10. reports of behavioral patterns

(See Appendix C for a legislative summary.)

Practice Questions on Domain III

Mr. Travis, a high school English teacher, is new to the district and anxious to fit in and be accepted by his coworkers and his students. He feels things are going fairly well until the basketball coach confronts him one morning about one of the basketball players who is failing English. The coach proceeds to explain, in no uncertain terms, that it is up to Mr. Travis to see that this young man receives a passing grade at the end of the six weeks. Mr. Travis responds that he will be happy to tutor the student outside of class, but that the student's grade depends on the student's performance. Mr. Travis' response to the confrontation *best* illustrates which of the following principles?

    A. Teachers should respect their colleagues, but not be intimidated by them.

    B. Teachers should uphold their professional ethics and standards.

    C. Teachers should manifest positive working relationships with colleagues.

    D. Teachers should make a reasonable effort to uphold instructional integrity.

Possibly, two competencies apply to this question, since it deals with **professionalism** (Mr. Travis and the coach, a colleague, are interacting concerning a student) and **ethical, legal, and professional standards** (the coach is suggesting that Mr. Travis change the failing student's grade to passing, even if the student does not earn a passing grade). Thus, the primary focus of this question is either Competency 012 or Competency 015. Eliminate Competency 012 as the primary focus of the question because Mr. Travis and the coach are not working together, but, rather, are at odds with each other. Thus, the primary focus of this question is Competency 015: *The teacher understands requirements, expectations, and constraints associated with teaching in Texas and can apply this understanding in a variety of contexts.* Eliminate A and C because they deal with working with colleagues, which is associated with **professionalism** (Competency 012). Eliminate D because teachers should do more than make a reasonable effort to uphold instructional integrity. Undoubtedly, Mr. Travis is familiar with the ethical responsibilities placed on members of the teaching profession. By telling the coach that the student's performance will determine the grade, Mr. Travis is upholding the Code of Ethics and Standard Practices for Texas Educators, Principle I, Standard 6: "The educator shall not falsify records, or direct or coerce others to do so." Choice B is the correct response.

Mr. Smith is very frustrated because his third graders do not seem to listen to instructions. He tries to explain carefully what to do and then writes the assignment on the board. He also asks students if they have questions. The class barely gets started on their work before several hands go up signaling they have questions. Other students begin talking to neighbors, asking them questions. After answering the same question several times, he instructs the students to stop what they are doing and to listen as he goes over the instructions again. This sometimes happens several times each day. Finally, Mr. Smith decides to videotape himself while teaching a lesson. He believes the video will provide him with information as to what is really happening in his classroom. Mr. Smith's decision to videotape a lesson for personal critiquing *best* demonstrates that he:

A. probably was not adequately prepared to teach.
B. understands the importance of reflection and self-evaluation.
C. values and respects his colleagues.
D. realizes he must become more assertive and "take charge" of his class.

Viewing the videotape of the lesson will allow Mr. Smith to reflect on his performance in the classroom and modify his classroom practices accordingly. This activity is related to being a reflective practitioner—a component of **professionalism.** Thus, the primary focus of this question is Competency 012: *The teacher is a reflective practioner who knows how to promote his or her own professional growth and can work cooperatively with other professionals in the system to create a school culture that enhances learning and encourages positive change.* Eliminate A because it relates to **planning** (Competency 006). You can eliminate C for two reasons: (a) in the stimulus, no colleagues are mentioned and (b) Choice C relates to **professionalism** (Competency 012). You can eliminate D for two reasons: (a) in the stimulus, Mr. Smith did not express a desire to "become more assertive and 'take charge'" (don't read too much into a question) and (b) D relates to **classroom management** (Competency 011). This teacher understands how to engage in reflective teaching and self-evaluation. He also knows how to use technology to enhance his teaching ability. Choice B is the correct response.

Ms. Rodriguez and her first graders have decided to collect toys and clothes for the children in the recent earthquake in Nicaragua who are now homeless. As the students begin to make plans for their project, one of the students suggests they could collect a lot more if some of the stores in town would donate toys and clothes. Ms. Rodriguez and the other children agree this is a good idea. Ms. Rodriguez suggests the students write letters to a list of businesses explaining their project and inviting them to participate. Many of the students say their parents could help collect the items, so the class decides they should also write letters to the parents, asking them to become a part of the effort. The students are delighted when they get telephone calls and letters from community members and parents saying they are eager to help.

Ms. Rodriguez's class project is *most* likely to result in:

A. the children's scoring high on achievement tests.
B. strengthening school-community relationships.
C. students' developing their leadership skills.
D. parents and the community's working together for school improvement.

Ms. Rodriguez's class is involved in a joint effort with the community, which relates to **school-community relationships.** Thus, the primary focus of this question is Competency 014: *The teacher understands how the school relates to the larger community and knows strategies for making interactions between school and community mutually supportive and beneficial.* Eliminate A because expecting the class project to directly cause achievement test performance to increase is unrealistic. Eliminate C because, other than making suggestions in the stimulus, the children are not assuming leadership roles in the project. Eliminate D because school improvement is not the goal of the children's project. This teacher is aware of and understands the value of working with local citizens to establish strong and positive ties between the school and the community. Choice B is the correct response.

PART FOUR

Test Yourself

CHAPTER 10

A PRACTICE ELEMENTARY PROFESSIONAL DEVELOPMENT TEST

Practice Test Directions

The test consists of 90 multiple-choice questions with four answer choices. Read each question carefully and choose the ONE best answer. Mark your answer on the answer sheet (see page 425) beside the number that matches the question number. Completely fill in the space that has the same letter as the answer you have selected.

Sample Question

1. Austin is the capital of what state?

   A. Arkansas
   B. California
   C. Tennessee
   D. Texas

Austin is the capital of Texas. Choice D is the correct response. You would mark your answer beside question number 1 on the answer sheet and you would fill in the space corresponding to the letter D as follows:

1. Ⓐ Ⓑ Ⓒ ●

Mark only one answer for each question. If you change an answer, completely erase the old answer before marking the new one. You should answer all the questions since *you are not penalized for a wrong answer*.

You will have approximately five hours to complete the test. You may go back and forth through the test as you desire. When you have completed the test, turn to the answer key and answer explanations at the end of the test to check your answers.

SET 1 BEGINS HERE

Ms. Blackwell has been hired as a second-grade teacher at Oakdale Elementary School. At the beginning of the year, Mr. Neal, the principal, tells Ms. Blackwell that 10 of her 22 students are "at-risk" students. Mr. Neal explains, "These children are slower learners who have done poorly since kindergarten. You will have to work extra hard with these low achievers if you want them to catch up with their age-peers." Ms. Blackwell assures Mr. Neal that she strongly believes that all students, including slower learners, are capable of academic success and she plans to do her best for all her students.

1. Ms. Blackwell's attitude about success for all students is *most* in accord with which of the following principles?

    A. The teacher should select materials that are developmentally appropriate.
    B. The teacher should view differences as opportunities for learning.
    C. The teacher should recognize factors that influence students' perceptions of their own worth.
    D. The teacher should recognize the social implications of diversity.

2. Ms. Blackwell's expression of confidence in the ability of the slower learners is an example of:

    A. positive reinforcement.
    B. positive achievement motivation.
    C. positive teacher expectations.
    D. positive contingencies.

3. All of the following describe at-risk students *except:*

    A. usually identified as learning disabled
    B. usually have low self-esteem
    C. usually are concrete thinkers
    D. usually need structured environments

4. Research indicates that teachers vary in their behavior toward students they perceive to be high or low achievers by:

    A. seating high achievers far from the teacher.
    B. using longer wait time for low achievers.
    C. demanding less work and effort from low achievers.
    D. giving high achievers fewer nonverbal cues.

Ms. Blackwell decides she should consult the curriculum supervisor for professional advice on working with at-risk students. Ms. Blackwell tells the curriculum supervisor, "I want to help these children learn, but I am not sure that I know how best to make that happen. Wouldn't it help them more if they were placed in a class where all the children are below level?" The curriculum supervisor tells Ms. Blackwell, "The campus committee at Oakdale Elementary is opposed to between-class ability grouping. Most of these children already have feelings of inferiority. Tracking them into lower-level classes would do them more harm than good."

5. Ms. Blackwell's decision to consult the curriculum supervisor is *most* in accord with which of the following principles?

   A. Teachers should understand that different students learn in different ways and can apply this understanding to promote learning.
   B. Teachers should know how to design outcome-oriented learning experiences that enhance academic achievement for all students.
   C. Teachers should be reflective practitioners who know how to work within a learning community to enhance students' academic performance.
   D. Teachers should use effective communication to shape the classroom into a community of learners.

6. Research indicates that when students are placed in between-class ability groups:

   A. higher-ability students usually learn less than when in mixed-ability classes.
   B. lower-ability students often experience a less challenging curriculum.
   C. moderate-ability students usually learn more than when in mixed-ability classes.
   D. higher-ability students usually experience lowered self-esteem.

7. The curriculum supervisor's comment ("Most of these children already have feelings of inferiority") is likely to be based on her awareness that children at this age develop a sense of inferiority if they:

   A. are unable to form close relationships with peers of the opposite sex.
   B. gain a considerable degree of autonomy in a relatively short time.
   C. fail to experience satisfaction or success with the completion of tasks they are assigned.
   D. are unable to develop a sense of identity.

8. Which of the following instructional strategies would be an appropriate recommendation for the curriculum supervisor to make to Ms. Blackwell?

   A. Use a competitive reward structure in the classroom.
   B. Assign the at-risk students independent study projects.
   C. Assign the at-risk students intensive drill-and-practice seatwork.
   D. Use direct instruction when teaching at-risk students basic skills.

9. The curriculum supervisor suggests that Ms. Blackwell invite grandparents to serve as volunteer tutors in her classroom. Besides helping the students academically, the *most* probable benefit of this will be which of the following?

   A. It will foster positive ties between the school and the community.
   B. It will create community awareness of teachers' problems.
   C. It will allow the students, while at school, the opportunity to discuss their problems with a family member.
   D. It will improve student behavior in the community.

10. Ms. Blackwell is concerned about the low self-esteem of the at-risk students. Which of the following would be *most* effective for Ms. Blackwell to do?

    A. Provide a caring environment in which these students are urged to try harder.
    B. Plan activities in which these students achieve success and know how they contributed to it.
    C. Allow these students to be more involved in making decisions about class activities.
    D. Plan activities in which the class discusses the importance of feeling good about oneself.

Ms. Blackwell's class of 22 students is composed of 12 girls and 10 boys. The class consists of 9 Anglo-American children, 6 African-American children, 5 Hispanic-American children, and 2 Native-American children. Ms. Blackwell is excited about the opportunities afforded by the diversity in her classroom. She wants to promote multicultural education, including gender equity, in her school.

11. Which of the following activities would be *most* developmentally appropriate in promoting students' multicultural awareness and appreciation?

    A. Have students learn about geographic and environmental characteristics of the countries represented by the different cultural groups in the class.
    B. Have a class discussion in which students are led to discover common elements in their various cultural backgrounds, as well as unique features of their own culture.
    C. Have students read about cultural traditions of several countries and discuss them in class, followed by a short quiz over the reading material.
    D. Have each student memorize a song from a different country and sing it to the class, followed by a question-and-answer period during which classmates can ask questions about the song's meaning.

12. Regarding gender equity, the 1992 American Association of University Women report *How Schools Shortchange Girls* confirmed what other researchers have found, which is that:

    A. there is no differential treatment of girls and boys in today's schools.
    B. boys and girls are equally encouraged to excel in mathematics and in the sciences.
    C. boys see themselves reflected less in the curriculum than girls do.
    D. girls receive less attention in class than boys do.

13. Recently during a math lesson, Paul tells Ms. Blackwell, "My mom loves math and she is really good at it." Immediately, Joey remarks, "Girls aren't supposed to like math—that's weird. Anyway, guys are better at math than girls." Others in the class nod their heads in agreement. Which of the following would be the *best* way for Ms. Blackwell to dispel stereotypical impressions about women and mathematics?

A. Discuss with the students that Joey's remark is a form of prejudice against women and the class should avoid such statements.

B. Have the students research and write reports on famous women mathematicians.

C. Plan a week in which the class celebrates the contributions of women in mathematics.

D. Arrange for men and women in the community to visit the class throughout the school year to talk about how they use math in their work and everyday lives.

SET 1 ENDS HERE

SET 2 BEGINS HERE

Mr. Payne is a sixth-grade teacher at Southside Middle School. He has his social studies class involved in doing research on the Vietnam War. The class plans to interview local men and women who lived during that time and write about what these individuals personally experienced during the war. Class members anticipate collecting an abundance of information and plan to compile it into a book they will publish themselves. Mr. Payne assigns the students to cooperative learning groups, each of which will be responsible for interviewing one individual and writing a "chapter" for the class book based on the interview.

14. Mr. Payne's research project on the Vietnam War *best* demonstrates the principle that learning is enhanced when:

   A. cross-cultural experiences are an integral part of the learning experience.
   B. instruction is designed to facilitate learning in different situations.
   C. instruction is made relevant to students' own needs and purposes.
   D. students assume a measure of responsibility for their own learning.

15. The *most* efficient way for the students to compile the information they collect from the interviews would be to use:

   A. a computer.
   B. CAI.
   C. a graphics calculator.
   D. a spiral notebook.

16. Mr. Payne can *best* assess the students' prior knowledge about the Vietnam War by:

   A. using an advance organizer.
   B. giving students time to do some reading on the topic.
   C. having small-group discussions.
   D. having a guest speaker.

17. To comply with the principles of cooperative learning, how should Mr. Payne assign students to groups?

   A. Allow students to self-select their groups.
   B. Assign students of high, middle, and low ability in social studies to each group.
   C. Assign students with similar academic ability in social studies to the same groups.
   D. Use the previously established mathematics groups in his class.

18. For the interviews, Mr. Payne decides to assign a specific role to each cooperative group member—organizer, recorder, data manager, and interviewer. What explanation for how the roles are assigned is Mr. Payne *most* likely to give?

   A. Group members need to be given roles in line with their academic ability; the more capable students should get the "harder" roles.
   B. Only one group member should assume a leadership role; having more than one leader is likely to lead to conflict.
   C. Everyone is capable of learning leadership skills; leadership responsibilities should be given to all group members over time.
   D. Some students are natural leaders, and others not; students should be assigned roles in accordance with their leadership capabilities.

Prior to starting the project on the Vietnam War, Mr. Payne has, except for math, used whole-group instruction with this class. He enjoys telling the students about historical events and occasionally finds that he has lectured for as long as 30 minutes without stopping. Upon seeing his students' excitement and enthusiasm as they are collaborating on the social studies project, Mr. Payne decides to do less whole-group instruction in the future.

19. Mr. Payne sometimes lectures for as long as 30 minutes to his sixth-grade class. Most authorities agree that lecturing:

    A. is the least effective instructional strategy for elementary school, but is very effective in middle school.
    B. should be used occasionally in elementary school to prepare students for its use in the upper-level grades.
    C. should be used in elementary school when a lot of content needs to be covered in a short time.
    D. should be avoided in elementary school.

20. Mr. Payne's decision to consider using less whole-group instruction *best* demonstrates which of the following?

    A. Effective decision making about instructional content and method takes into account individual students' level of development.
    B. Effective teachers take advantage of positive environmental factors that affect learning.
    C. Effective teachers are reflective practitioners who deliberate on the quality of their teaching and are responsive to what they determine.
    D. Effective teachers know strategies for making interactions between the school and the community mutually beneficial.

21. When planning for cooperative learning, Mr. Payne needs to consider that using cooperative learning groups will require him to:

    I. have a system for rewarding individual students who assume leadership roles.
    II. assess and guide individual and group collaborative skills.
    III. become less visible and involved, since he is needed less.
    IV. make sure group tasks are well planned and well organized.

    A. I and II only
    B. I, II, and III only
    C. II, III, and IV only
    D. II and IV only

22. Which of the following seating arrangements would be *best* for promoting student interaction during cooperative group work?

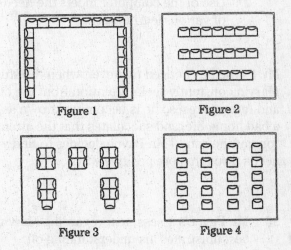

Figure 1   Figure 2

Figure 3   Figure 4

    A. Figure 1
    B. Figure 2
    C. Figure 3
    D. Figure 4

Southside Middle School has a computer lab that is available to Mr. Payne's students. Mr. Payne enlists the help of the computer lab coordinator, who will assist the students with the computer skills necessary for desktop publishing. In addition, Mr. Payne confers with the language arts teacher, who agrees to work with the students on critiquing, editing, and rewriting their chapters as part of their language arts instruction.

23. Having students engage in a project such as this, which involves students using skills from various disciplines, *best* illustrates which of the following?

   A. The teacher is giving control of learning to students.
   B. The teacher is using an interdisciplinary approach in teaching.
   C. The teacher is using an intradisciplinary approach in teaching.
   D. The teacher is giving direction to the students' learning task.

24. Mr. Payne's *primary* instructional reason for his students to use computers is probably which of the following?

   A. The students' keyboarding skills will improve.
   B. Use of the computer eliminates gender bias.
   C. Use of the computer is a form of positive reinforcement.
   D. Use of the computer meets the needs of various learning styles.

25. Which of the following is *most* in accord with current principles of professional development of Texas teachers?

   A. Teachers should have expertise in computer program development.
   B. Teachers should acquire and practice computer maintenance skills.
   C. Teachers should be literate in the use of computers.
   D. Teachers should have basic skills in computer hardware repair.

Mr. Payne has noticed that even when the students are working in their groups on the class project, Marvin constantly seeks attention from the other students. Marvin likes to make distracting noises and funny faces, so he is becoming known as "the class clown." Mr. Payne is aware that Marvin has a bad home life, and speculates that the attention Marvin gets from the class makes him feel like "one of the gang." Mr. Payne decides to find ways he can allow Marvin to gain the attention he needs through more positive ways.

26. Mr. Payne's assessment regarding Marvin *best* illustrates his understanding of:

   A. behavioral modification techniques.
   B. psychomotor developmental processes.
   C. appropriate discipline procedures.
   D. students' need for belonging and acceptance.

27. Mr. Payne is aware that Marvin wants attention, which is a reasonable explanation for Marvin's misbehavior in class; however, Mr. Payne decides there may also be other, less obvious, reasons why Marvin is misbehaving. The best *first* step for Mr. Payne to take to pursue this speculation would be to:

    A. have a conference with Marvin's parents.
    B. examine Marvin's school records.
    C. discuss the problem with the school counselor.
    D. have Marvin tested for a learning disability.

28. Marvin's behavior in Mr. Payne's class is probably associated with fears related to:

    A. being rejected by peers.
    B. displeasing authority figures.
    C. failing to achieve academically.
    D. failing to learn cultural norms.

José and Mary, students in Mr. Payne's class, are extremely active, talkative, and inattentive. It is difficult for either of them to stay seated for more than a few minutes.

29. If the behavior exhibited by José and Mary were to continue over an extended period, which of the following is *most* likely to happen?

    A. José is more likely to be evaluated as having ADHD.
    B. Mary is more likely to be evaluated as having ADHD.
    C. José and Mary are equally likely to be evaluated as having ADHD.
    D. Both José and Mary are too young to be accurately evaluated as having ADHD.

SET 2 ENDS HERE

SET 3 BEGINS HERE

> Mr. Paul is a new fifth-grade teacher at Wildwood Intermediate School. He is feeling very nervous about his new job and wonders if the activity he has planned for his first day is appropriate. Mr. Paul hopes to create a problem-solving environment in his classroom wherein the students are consistently eager and excited about learning.

30. Which of the following would be an *inappropriate* first activity for Mr. Paul to use?

    A. Make the first lesson fairly difficult, to ensure that students understand how hard they will need to work in his class.
    B. Spend most of the time introducing procedures and discussing classroom rules.
    C. Show the students a highly motivating video.
    D. Make the first lesson fairly simple and enjoyable.

31. To create a problem-solving climate in math, Mr. Paul should choose mathematical tasks that:

    I.   focus on recall of correct answers.
    II. require students to go through a sequence of steps to reach a given solution.
    III. are open-ended and allow for a number of solutions.
    IV. actively engage students in trying to persuade other members of the class of the correctness of their solutions.

    A. I, II, and III only
    B. II, III, and IV only
    C. II and IV only
    D. III and IV only

32. Mr. Paul wants to have sufficient time for brainstorming when students are generating ideas for problem solving. Which of the following strategies would be *most* effective for this purpose?

    A. Increase the length of time he lectures each period by five minutes.
    B. Have classroom rules clearly posted.
    C. Post a DO NOT DISTURB sign on the classroom door during class discussion time.
    D. Require students to chorally respond to his questions during class discussions.

33. Which of the following cognitive abilities should Mr. Paul expect that most of his students are likely to be in the process of developing?

    A. relating numbers to the numerals that represent them
    B. thinking hypothetically
    C. thinking in concrete terms
    D. learning to reverse operations

Since Mr. Paul is a new teacher, he feels it would benefit him to have Ms. Keenan, the principal, come in and do an informal classroom observation of his teaching. Before the classroom observation, Ms. Keenan tells Mr. Paul that the observation will focus on observable behaviors only. After the observation is completed, Mr. Paul is pleased to hear from Ms. Keenan that he has done well. Ms. Keenan comments that, during the lesson, Mr. Paul displayed many of the attributes of effective teachers.

34. Which of the following describe effective teachers?

  I.   Effective teachers provide for active participation by students.
  II. Effective teachers use inquiry techniques to challenge students.
  III. Effective teachers align instruction with work and life application.
  IV. Effective teachers use instruction that allows more than one pathway or approach for new learning.

  A. I and II only
  B. I, II, and III only
  C. II and IV only
  D. I, II, III, and IV

35. Which of the following does *not* describe an effective teacher?

  A. Effective teachers provide for active participation by students.
  B. Effective teachers extend students' responses and contributions.
  C. Effective teachers do not cite the specific offender when disruptive behavior occurs.
  D. Effective teachers do not allow delay of initial class activities.

36. Which of the following is an example of an observable behavior Mr. Paul might have demonstrated during Ms. Keenan's observation of him?

  A. Mr. Paul remained confident throughout the lesson.
  B. Mr. Paul walked over to Patricia, who was daydreaming.
  C. Mr. Paul was pleased with Shawn's good behavior.
  D. Mr. Paul liked the way Joe Don responded to a question.

At the end of his first language arts unit, Mr. Paul is concerned about constructing the first unit test. He wants to use items that test students at both the higher and the lower levels of Bloom's taxonomy. He makes the following list of tentative items:

1. A direct object is always in the
   _____ case.

2. Mark Twain was the pen name for Samuel Coleridge. True or False?

3. How is the word *town* used in the sentence below?
   Eastside Middle School is a block off one of the corners of the town square.

   A. as a verb
   B. as an adverb
   C. as a noun
   D. as an adjective

4. Suppose you wake up one morning and look in the mirror to discover that you are completely bald—you do not have one hair on your head! Write a paragraph explaining what could have happened to cause this horrendous event.

37. On which item does guessing have the most effect?

   A. Item 1
   B. Item 2
   C. Item 3
   D. Item 4

38. Subjectivity in grading is the major problem with which type of item?

   A. Item 1
   B. Item 2
   C. Item 3
   D. Item 4

39. Which item requires a knowledge-level open response for the students to make?

   A. Item 1
   B. Item 2
   C. Item 3
   D. Item 4

40. Which item needs revision in the formatting?

   A. Item 1
   B. Item 2
   C. Item 3
   D. Item 4

41. Which of the following types of assessment is *most* likely to yield valid information about what students have learned?

   A. a matching test
   B. a multiple-choice exam
   C. a performance observation
   D. a true-false test

Julio, one of Mr. Paul's students, will be unable to participate in UIL art competition because Julio failed social studies for the six-week term. Julio's parents are upset with this situation and ask to examine Julio's grades and also the grades of his classmates.

42. Which of the following would be the *most* appropriate action for Mr. Paul to take in response to Julio's parents' request?

   A. Mr. Paul should tell Julio's parents that he cannot show them other students' grades.
   B. Mr. Paul should show Julio's parents the other students' grades, but caution that they must keep them confidential.
   C. Mr. Paul should tell Julio's parents that teachers have the sole right to determine grades.
   D. Mr. Paul should tell Julio's parents that their request must go through the principal's office first.

43. According to the Family Educational Rights and Privacy Act, Julio's parents have the right to:

   A. select the classes that Julio will take in the next six weeks.
   B. inspect and review Julio's grades.
   C. attend class with Julio to monitor his progress.
   D. request a hearing with the principal.

Mr. Paul is concerned about what to do with Mario, a student in his class. Mario seldom turns in his work, and when he does, it may be only half-complete. His grades reflect his poor work habits, and he is becoming a discipline problem. Mario is quite puzzling to Mr. Paul. Mario reads scientific magazines, and in science lab he has built a small engine, yet he neglects his regular class work.

44. Mario's behavior is *most* closely associated with that of:

   A a child who has a learning disability.
   B. a child who has ADHD.
   C. a child who has limited English proficiency.
   D. a child who is academically gifted.

45. Which of the following would be *most* appropriate to use with Mario?

   I.   Give him more advanced work.
   II. Give him more of the same work.
   III. Give him work to broaden and deepen understanding.
   IV. Give him work that is less challenging.

   A. I and II only
   B. II and IV only
   C. I and III only
   D. III and IV only

SET 3 ENDS HERE

Ms. Brazil has been teaching third grade for several years. Her class of 23 students is made up of 14 boys and 9 girls. They are a diverse group, ethnically and academically. Ms. Brazil believes in creating an environment that respects and confirms the dignity of students as human beings. When assigning roles and responsibilities, she is careful to deal ethically and fairly with all students. Her philosophy is, "Every child can be successful." She expects this, and her students know it. Parents like Ms. Brazil and want their children in her room because their children do well in her class.

46. Ms. Brazil's philosophy is *most* in accord with the concept of:

    A. the self-fulfilling prophecy.
    B. engaging students in challenging activities.
    C. encouraging students to use their utmost abilities.
    D. allowing all students to participate regardless of disabilities.

47. Graciela is an LEP student who has been placed in Ms. Brazil's class because Graciela's parents successfully appealed Graciela's placement in an ESL classroom. How can Ms. Brazil *best* address Graciela's academic needs?

    A. using visuals, manipulatives, graphic organizers, media, and other sources to explain concepts
    B. encouraging Graciela to speak her primary language at home only
    C. having a conference with Graciela's parents to convince them that Graciela would be better served in an ESL classroom
    D. explaining to the class that Graciela is an LEP student and enlisting their help in making sure Graciela understands what to do in class

48. During question-and-answer activities, Ms. Brazil should:

    A. call only on other students until Graciela feels more comfortable in class.
    B. call on Graciela only when she volunteers, to avoid embarrassing her.
    C. address questions to Graciela using body language and gestures to enhance meaning.
    D. try to address only yes-or-no questions to Graciela.

49. Which of the following beliefs are essential in meeting the needs of diverse learners?

    I. Multiculturalism is for minorities only.
    II. There is a positive correlation between self-esteem and academic achievement.
    III. There is a positive correlation between teacher expectations and academic performance.
    IV. Teachers should hold high expectations for all students, regardless of ethnicity, gender, or exceptionality.

    A. I and III only
    B. I, II, and III only
    C. II and III only
    D. II, III, and IV only

Ms. Brazil has planned a thematic unit on studying the environment. On an outside tour of the school, the students work in pairs collecting trash and dump it all together in one large bag. "Look at all the trash," says James. "Yes," says Robin, "and it makes our school look ugly." Graciela wants to know if everyone has that much trash. Students begin to voice dismay about how much people throw away. "Is there going to be room for us with all this trash in the world?" asks Jay. Ms. Brazil responds to the whole class, "What do you think about Jay's concern?" A lively discussion ensues. James suggests, "I know what we can do to help get rid of the trash." "What?" Latoya asks. "We can recycle," says James. Robin asks, "Do you mean at school?" Several students chorus, "Yes, that's a great idea!" Ms. Brazil asks, "What will you recycle?" After further discussion, the class decides they want to collect newspapers and aluminum cans for recycling. Nadia proposes that they should involve the entire school, and the rest of the class agrees. Ms. Brazil comments, "You have done some good thinking today. This will be a fine project for our class."

50. Ms. Brazil's question to the whole class ("What do you think about Jay's concern?") in response to Jay's question is an example of:

    A. using a student's contribution to make a point.
    B. modifying a student's contribution by putting it into different words to make it more understandable to the rest of the class.
    C. using a student's contribution as an example.
    D. acknowledging a student's contribution by using it to stimulate additional discussion.

51. The discourse orchestrated by Ms. Brazil among the students and with herself *best* illustrates which of the following?

    A. Student assessment is aligned with real-life applications.
    B. Students demonstrate a connection of their learning to other disciplines.
    C. Students consistently take reasonable risks in responding to the teacher or peers.
    D. Students are consistently engaged in appropriate self-management.

52. By accepting the students' idea about the recycling project, Ms. Brazil demonstrates her understanding of learners by:

    I. promoting a sense of responsibility for one's own learning.
    II. recognizing and respecting differences in her classroom.
    III. creating an environment in which students feel competent and productive.
    IV. fostering a view of learning as a purposeful pursuit.

    A. I and IV only
    B. II and III only
    C. I, II, and III only
    D. I, III, and IV only

53. Ms. Brazil realizes that she needs to know what the students understand about recycling. To obtain this information, all of the following would be appropriate *except*:

    A. evaluation questions.
    B. semantic mapping.
    C. webbing.
    D. whole-class discussion.

54. Which of the following instructional strategies would be *most* appropriate for the recycling project?

    A. individualized instruction
    B. cooperative groups
    C. whole-class demonstration
    D. Jigsaw I and II

55. Given the diverse nature of Ms. Brazil's class, which of the following are *most* probable as a result of the students' involvement in the recycling project?

  I. The project will improve students' research skills.
  II. The project will enhance students' interpersonal skills.
  III. The project will foster class cooperation and unity.
  IV. The project will reinforce stereotyping of students.

  A. I and II only
  B. I, II, and III only
  C. II and III only
  D. II and IV only

56. To help students gain additional information about recycling, Ms. Brazil invites a representative from the sanitation department, along with several parents who have said they recycle at home, to speak with the class about recycling. This decision indicates that Ms. Brazil:

  A. recognizes how the school relates to the larger community.
  B. provides a supportive classroom that promotes self-esteem.
  C. is aware of the expectations of the community.
  D. nurtures a sense of community within the classroom.

57. If Ms. Brazil decides to put the students into groups for this project, which grouping method should she use?

  A. homogeneous grouping
  B. achievement grouping
  C. ability grouping
  D. heterogeneous grouping

When the speaker from the sanitation department informs Ms. Brazil about a recycling workshop being held in a nearby city, she decides to attend. She is eager to gain information she can put to use for the students' recycling project. Ms. Brazil is not disappointed when she attends the workshop. She obtains many useful materials and resources that her students can use. The workshop presenter also suggests that the Internet is another useful resource.

58. Ms. Brazil's decision to attend the workshop *best* illustrates:

  A. establishing a strong community relationship.
  B. fostering a strong school-home relationship.
  C. being a reflective practitioner.
  D. motivating student interest.

59. The *first* thing Ms. Brazil should do in order to attend the workshop is:

  A. request that the principal hire a substitute for that day.
  B. request permission from the principal to attend the workshop.
  C. complete and mail the necessary registration papers.
  D. request permission from the school board to attend the workshop.

60. Taking the advice of the workshop presenter, Ms. Brazil locates several Internet Web sites where her students can obtain facts and information about recycling. This behavior demonstrates that Ms. Brazil understands how to do which of the following?

  I. structure and manage the learning environment
  II. select appropriate materials and resources
  III. use technology as a learning tool
  IV. encourage students to become independent thinkers and problem solvers

  A. I and II only
  B. II and III only
  C. II and IV only
  D. I and III only

The day after the students begin gathering information from the Web sites, Leaia tells Ms. Brazil, "My mom doesn't want me doing this. She says there are bad things on the Internet." Ms. Brazil is aware that the school computers are equipped with Internet child-safety filtering software, but she has not mentioned this to the students. During her planning period, Ms. Brazil calls Ms. Selder, Leaia's mother.

61. Ms. Brazil can *best* deal with Ms. Selder's concerns by:

    A. sending Ms. Selder a copy of the school's rules for online safety.
    B. explaining to Ms. Selder that the benefits of the Internet far outweigh any dangers.
    C. inviting Ms. Selder to visit the school, so that Ms. Brazil can demonstrate the child-safety Internet software to Ms. Selder.
    D. Assure Ms. Selder that Ms. Brazil will personally see to it that Leaia does not access any inappropriate or disturbing material.

62. For young children Leaia's age, attitudes toward an issue, such as child safety on the Internet, tend to be most influenced by their:

    A. personal experiences related to the issue.
    B. peers' attitudes.
    C. cognitive abilities.
    D. families' attitudes toward the issue.

63. Ms. Brazil can *best* guard against a future incident like the one she experienced with Leaia's mother by:

    A. warning students not to tell their parents that they are using the Internet.
    B. providing parents with regular updates about class activities.
    C. contacting students' families to solicit parent volunteers to help with the recycling project.
    D. administering a survey to the parents to determine their interest in helping with class activities.

From the Educational Service Center in the area, Ms. Brazil obtains a video on recycling that she shows to the students. As the students view the video, Ms. Brazil periodically stops the tape and poses questions about the ideas presented. During the showing of the video, Ms. Brazil notices that several students seated at a table across the room from Ms. Brazil are not paying close attention. Wilma and Jane are whispering to each other, Kamia is drawing a picture, and Consuela is writing a note. Unobtrusively, Ms. Brazil walks over to stand near the table where the off-task girls are seated. When the off-task behavior continues, Ms. Brazil quietly calls Wilma and Janet by name and gives them a stern look. Immediately, all of the off-task behavior ceases, and the girls direct their attention back to the video.

64. When dealing with the off-task behavior in her classroom, Ms. Brazil displays effective classroom management skills. Which of the following is *not* a classroom management skill?

    A. overlapping
    B. halting time
    C. ripple effect
    D. withitness

65. As the students view the video, Ms. Brazil periodically stops the tape and poses questions about the ideas presented. This strategy is *most* probably motivated by Ms. Brazil's awareness of which of the following?

    A. Effective teachers do not allow delays to occur due to disruptive behavior.
    B. Students stay on task when they are aware that they are being monitored.
    C. Teachers' efforts to maintain and reinforce student involvement correlates with students' cognitive engagement.
    D. Effective teachers use a variety of verbal and nonverbal signals to stop misbehavior.

66. After the video, Ms. Brazil engages the students in a discussion. She wants them to think about the recycling project and how they can move forward with it. To encourage students to think and engage in problem solving, what types of questions should she ask?

    A. convergent questions
    B. divergent questions
    C. who, what, where, and when questions
    D. affective domain questions

SET 4 ENDS HERE

SET 5 BEGINS HERE

Ms. Kawasaki, a first-year fourth-grade teacher, discovers that her principal's philosophy of a conducive learning climate is different from her own. The principal, Ms. Oliver, believes that, to maximize learning, a classroom should be completely orderly at all times, and that direct instruction to students who are sitting quietly should be the primary teaching strategy. Although Ms. Kawasaki concurs that orderliness is important, she believes that classroom discourse is a powerful way students clarify, change, or reinforce conceptions. Her classroom interactions are often lively exchanges, with Ms. Kawasaki and the students thinking, talking, conjecturing, and agreeing and disagreeing among themselves. Consequently, the noise level in her classroom often becomes elevated. She believes her role as a teacher is to facilitate students' pursuit of new understandings, not through the traditional teacher-telling model of direct instruction but through creating an environment in which the students are constructing their own knowledge through inquiry and experience. She has discussed her difference in philosophy with Ms. Oliver on several occasions.

67. Ms. Kawasaki's approach to teaching is *most* consistent with:

   A. assertive discipline.
   B. constructivism.
   C. teacher-centered instruction.
   D. expository teaching.

68. What other action would be *most* appropriate for Ms. Kawasaki to take toward building a positive working relationship with Ms. Oliver?

   A. teach differently when Ms. Oliver visits the classroom
   B. send examples of her students' work to Ms. Oliver's office
   C. invite Ms. Oliver to frequently drop by to observe Ms. Kawasaki's methods and their effects
   D. organize parents to send a petition to Ms. Oliver supporting Ms. Kawasaki's methods

69. Ms. Kawasaki uses questioning as an integral component of her instructional strategy. She is likely to be aware that when asking questions, effective teachers:

   A. ask more questions of students sitting in the back of the room.
   B. ask more convergent questions.
   C. provide supportive feedback to responses.
   D. provide the right answer if no one responds immediately.

70. Ms. Kawasaki is skillful in allowing sufficient wait time after posing questions to her students. However, many teachers find it difficult to apply the recommended three-second wait time for students' responses to questions. Which of the following is probably the *main* reason for this?

    A. The teacher fears that silence might disturb the momentum of the lesson.
    B. There is a strong norm in American culture against silence.
    C. The teacher fears that silence might lead to student misbehavior.
    D. The teacher fears that student achievement will suffer.

71. When writing lesson plans, Ms. Kawasaki uses the 5E-model—*engage, explore, explain, elaborate,* and *evaluate. Evaluate* corresponds to which of the following components of the traditional lesson cycle?

    A. focus
    B. guided practice
    C. check for mastery
    D. closure

72. Ms. Kawasaki knows that critical thinking is essential for constructing meaning from content. Which of the following should Ms. Kawasaki do to promote the development of critical-thinking skills?

    I. She should teach for deeper understanding of content.
    II. She should have students memorize rules for critically analyzing content material.
    III. She should require students to justify the reasoning behind their conclusions.
    IV. She should help students develop metacognitive strategies.

    A. I, II, and IV only
    B. II and III only
    C. I, III, and IV only
    D. I, II, III, and IV

73. When Ms. Kawasaki's students work in groups, she allows them to adjust the time frame for activities based on their own needs and preferences. This decision is *most* likely meant to:

    A. promote the students' ability to monitor and clarify their own understandings.
    B. help students link new learning to prior knowledge and experience.
    C. promote student ownership in a smoothly functioning learning community.
    D. help students develop the motivation to achieve.

Ms. Kawasaki and Ms. Harrison, a second-grade teacher, have worked out an arrangement whereby Ms. Kawasaki's students serve as tutors for Ms. Harrison's students. The student tutors have expressed to Ms. Kawasaki how much they enjoy helping the younger children.

74. Research regarding cross-age tutoring indicates that in general:

    A. academic achievement of the tutee increases, but not that of the tutor.
    B. achievement of both the tutors and the tutees increases.
    C. the results are much the same regardless of the expertise of the tutor.
    D. achievement motivation increases, but neither tutor nor tutee benefits significantly.

75. Ms. Kawasaki believes that tutors should be informed about the importance of praise when working with children. Which of the following describe effective praise?

    I. Praise should be nonspecific and given freely to all.
    II. Praise should reward participation rather than accomplishment.
    III. Praise should specify the behavior or accomplishment.
    IV. Praise should give students feedback on the quality of their work.

    A. I and II only
    B. III and IV only
    C. I and III only
    D. II and IV only

In the faculty lounge one day, a group of teachers are discussing the 1998 revisions to the *Code of Ethics and Standard Practices for Texas Educators*. One teacher remarks that the wording of some of the standards has been changed slightly. Having just recently completed her teacher-preparation program, Ms. Kawasaki is familiar with the *Code of Ethics and Standard Practices for Texas Educators*.

76. Which of the following is *not* a standard in the *Code of Ethics and Standard Practices for Texas Educators*?

    A. The educator shall continue professional growth.
    B. The educator shall maintain a classroom climate that promotes the lifelong pursuit of learning.
    C. The educator shall not use institutional or professional privileges for personal or partisan advantage.
    D. The educator shall not offer any favor, service, or thing of value to obtain special advantage.

77. Ms. Kawasaki regularly makes connections between a lesson's content and familiar stories and information from the home and community. This practice complies *most* closely with which of the following standards of the *Code of Ethics and Standard Practices for Texas Educators*?

    A. The educator shall organize instruction that seeks to accomplish objectives related to learning.
    B. The educator shall endeavor to present facts without distortion.
    C. The educator shall endeavor to understand community cultures and relate the home environment of students to the school.
    D. The educator shall continue professional growth.

The administrators in Ms. Kawasaki's school district want to find out how well the district is achieving the academic goals set by the district strategic planning committee, composed of community members, teachers, and administrators. The strategic planning committee recommends to the administration that the district should give local tests to find out how students are progressing.

78. What type of tests would be *best* for this purpose?

   A. norm-referenced
   B. teacher-made
   C. criterion-referenced
   D. psychomotor

79. After the district testing, several members of the strategic planning committee suggest that the district should adopt a policy that grades will be based on mastery. The *first* step when grading based on mastery is to:

   A. decide the cut-off scores for each letter grade.
   B. determine prior knowledge using a standardized test.
   C. compute the mean score of the students on an initial assessment.
   D. define the content and skill objectives to be learned.

80. One committee member recommends that teachers begin "grading on the curve." Grading on a curve often creates which of the following dilemmas?

   A. Should the more able students be required to perform more work than the less able?
   B. Should a descriptive report card be sent home?
   C. Should all students receive a passing grade?
   D. Should a given percentage of a class of intellectually gifted students receive failing marks?

81. The implementation of standardized tests, such as the Texas Assessment of Academic Skills test, has resulted in a movement for teacher accountability. In Texas, *accountability* as it relates to teachers means which of the following?

   I. Teachers are responsible for the progress of their students.
   II. Teachers are responsible for school dropouts.
   III. Teachers are responsible for "teaching to the test."
   IV. Teachers are responsible for the discipline in their classrooms.

   A. I, II, and III only
   B. I and IV only
   C. II and III only
   D. III and IV only

SET 5 ENDS HERE

SET 6 BEGINS HERE

Ms. Cantu, a first-grade teacher, has planned a science unit concerning the ocean. The first day of the unit, the children enter the classroom to see "seaweed" hanging from the ceiling, displays of seashells on tables, and pictures of ocean life on the wall. Ocean sounds are playing in the background, as Ms. Cantu begins the day's lesson by asking, "Can you guess where we are pretending to be?" Several children chorus, "The ocean!" "Tell me everything you know about the ocean," says Ms. Cantu. As the children excitedly respond, Ms. Cantu writes on a flipchart everything the children say. The contributions on the flipchart are then taped to the chalkboard. Then, making no judgments about the children's contributions, Ms. Cantu encourages the children to discuss their contributions and question each other.

82. What was Ms. Cantu's *probable* purpose for transforming her classroom into an "ocean"?

    A. to provide a concrete experience for the children
    B. to allow the children to have choices in their learning
    C. to promote student ownership in a smoothly functioning learning community
    D. to give students control over their learning experiences

83. What is the probable reason Ms. Cantu makes no judgments when the children discuss their contributions about the ocean?

    A. She wants to find out about the children's understandings of the ocean before sharing her own understandings.
    B. She wants to encourage student inquiry by asking thoughtful, open-ended questions.
    C. She wants to provide supportive feedback for the students' contributions to the discussion.
    D. She wants to nurture the children's curiosity about what she knows about the ocean.

84. Ms. Cantu writes the children's contributions on the flipchart, then displays them on the chalkboard. This behavior *best* demonstrates her understanding of which of the following?

    A. Effective teachers lead their students to pursue problems that are meaningful to them.
    B. Effective teachers design instruction to help students learn how to learn.
    C. Effective teachers help students make connections between their current skills and understandings and those that are new to them.
    D. Effective teachers understand factors that influence students' perceptions of their own worth and potential.

Ms. Cantu recognizes the importance of establishing and maintaining strong school-home relationships. She believes communication between the school and the home should be purposeful and ongoing. Before the opening of school every year, she tries to contact by telephone the children's parents/guardians.

85. During the school year, what other methods would be *most* appropriate for communicating with the children's parents/guardians?

   I. Send e-mail to parents/guardians at their work.
   II. Write personal notes in report cards.
   III. Schedule parent-teacher conferences.
   IV. Send a letter to each parent/guardian.

   A. I, III, and IV only
   B. I, II, and III only
   C. II, III, and IV only
   D. I, II, III, and IV

86. When preparing for a parent-teacher conference, which of the following are appropriate?

   I. have a written agenda
   II. collect samples of several students' work to show the parents
   III. review current daily grades and test results
   IV. keep anecdotal records

   A. I, II, and III only
   B. II, III, and IV only
   C. I, III, and IV only
   D. II and III only

Tabatha, a new student in Ms. Cantu's class, has been showing signs of stress at not being able to do things that the other children in the class can already do. Ms. Cantu is concerned about this situation and wants to help Tabatha.

87. Which of the following would be *most* appropriate for Ms. Cantu to do?

   A. Pair Tabatha with a more capable child during activities that Ms. Cantu suspects Tabatha will find difficult.
   B. Assign Tabatha to work at the art center when the children are participating in more difficult activities.
   C. Reassure Tabatha that she will be able to do just as well as the other children after she's been in the class awhile.
   D. Ensure that activities are available that will appeal to Tabatha and that she will be likely to perform successfully.

88. Ms. Cantu would like Tabatha's parents to come to the school for a parent-teacher conference. Without stating her concerns about Tabatha, Ms. Cantu has called the parents several times to arrange a conference; however, the parents are reluctant to come to the school. In dealing with this situation, which of the following should Ms. Cantu do *first*?

   A. Ask Tabatha if she knows why her parents are reluctant to come for the conference.
   B. In the next phone call, tell Tabatha's parents her reasons for wanting to have a parent-teacher conference.
   C. In the next phone call, explain to Tabatha's parents that all parents are expected to come for at least one parent-teacher conference during the school year.
   D. In the next phone call, tell Tabatha's parents that no other parents have refused to come for a parent-teacher conference.

To keep the noise level down in her classroom, Ms. Cantu constructs the device below to allow students to indicate agreement or disagreement without shouting out their positions.

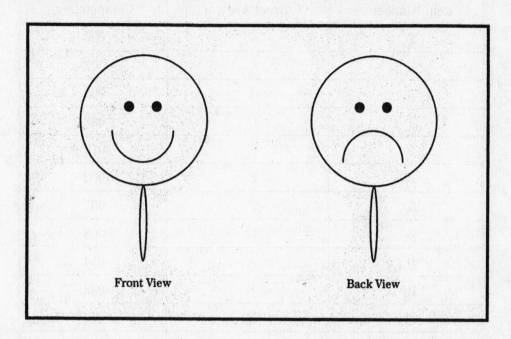

Front View   Back View

89. She teaches according to the 5E model. In which components of the lesson will the smiley-sad-face device be useful?

I.   Engage
II. Explore
III. Explain
IV. Evaluate

A. I and III only
B. II and III only
C. II and IV only
D. I, II, III, and IV

90. Which of the following types of learners will *least* benefit from using the smiley-sad-face device?

A. left-brain dominant learners
B. visual learners
C. tactile/kinesthetic learners
D. right-brain-dominant learners

SET 6 ENDS HERE

Answer Key

Item Number	Correct Answer	Competency
1	C	002
2	C	002
3	A	003
4	C	002
5	C	012
6	B	002
7	C	001
8	D	008
9	A	014
10	B	002
11	B	001
12	D	003
13	D	003
14	D	004
15	A	009
16	A	010
17	B	008
18	C	002
19	D	001
20	C	012
21	D	006
22	C	011
23	B	008
24	D	009
25	C	012
26	D	011
27	B	015
28	A	001
29	A	003

30	A	011
31	D	008
32	C	011
33	B	001
34	D	012
35	C	012
36	B	012
37	B	010
38	D	010
39	A	010
40	C	010
41	C	010
42	A	015
43	B	015
44	D	003
45	C	003
46	A	002
47	A	003
48	C	007
49	D	003
50	D	007
51	C	007
52	D	004
53	A	010
54	B	008
55	C	006
56	A	014
57	D	008
58	C	012
59	B	015
60	B	009

61	C	013
62	D	001
63	B	013
64	B	011
65	C	007
66	B	007
67	B	004
68	C	012
69	C	007
70	B	007
71	C	006
72	C	008
73	D	005
74	B	008
75	B	005
76	B	012
77	C	012
78	C	010
79	D	010
80	D	010
81	B	012
82	A	006
83	A	004
84	D	002
85	C	013
86	C	013
87	D	002
88	B	013
89	D	006
90	A	004

Answer Explanations

1. **C** This question deals with teacher expectations, which relates to **students' self-esteem.** Thus, its primary focus is Competency 002: *The teacher considers environmental factors that may affect learning in designing a supportive and responsive classroom community that promotes all students' learning and self-esteem.* Eliminate A because it deals with **developmentally appropriate instruction** (Competency 001). Eliminate B and D because they deal with **diversity** (Competency 003). By holding expectations of success for all her students, Ms. Blackwell is recognizing factors (that is, teacher expectations) that influence students' perceptions of their own worth. Choice C is the correct response.

2. **C** This question deals with teacher expectations, which relates to **students' self-esteem.** Thus, its primary focus is Competency 002: *The teacher considers environmental factors that may affect learning in designing a supportive and responsive classroom community that promotes all students' learning and self-esteem.* Eliminate A, B, and D because they relate to **motivation** (Competency 005). A teacher's opinions of students' abilities to be successful are called *teacher expectations.* Choice C is the correct response.

3. **A** This question deals with **diversity.** Thus, its primary focus is Competency 003: *The teacher appreciates human diversity, recognizing how diversity in the classroom and the community may affect learning and creating a classroom environment in which both the diversity of groups and the uniqueness of individuals are recognized and celebrated.* Low achievers, or "at-risk" students, are most often found among students who test just below average in intelligence. In general, these students have low self-esteem (B), are concrete thinkers (C), and need structured environments (D). These slower learners are the students who "fall through the cracks" between special education and regular education. Seldom would they be identified as "learning disabled." Choice A is the correct response.

4. **C** This question deals with **students' self-esteem.** Thus, its primary focus is Competency 002: *The teacher considers environmental factors that may affect learning in designing a supportive and responsive classroom community that promotes all students' learning and self-esteem.* Good and Brophy described ways teachers vary in their behavior toward students they perceive to be high or low achievers. They seat low achievers far from the teacher (eliminate A), allow longer wait time for responses from high achievers (eliminate B), give low achievers fewer nonverbal cues (eliminate D), and demand less work and effort from low achievers (C). Choice C is the correct response.

5. **C** This question deals with **professionalism.** Thus, its primary focus is Competency 012: *The teacher is a reflective practitioner who knows how to promote his or her own professional growth and can work cooperatively with other professionals in the system to create a school culture that enhances learning and encourages positive change.* Eliminate A because it relates to **how learning occurs** (Competency 004). Eliminate B because it relates to **planning** (Competency 006). Eliminate D because it relates to **communication** (Competency 007). Ms. Blackwell understands the importance of self-reflection and self-evaluation. She recognizes that she is a member of a learning community and knows how to work effectively with all members of that community to promote student learning. Choice C is the correct response.

6. **B** This question deals with **students' self-esteem.** Thus, its primary focus is Competency 002: *The teacher considers environmental factors that may affect learning in designing a supportive and responsive classroom community that promotes all students' learning and self-esteem.* Grouping practices can affect students' perceptions of themselves and their own worth. Some research findings indicate that in ability groups, higher-ability students seem to learn better (eliminate A), moderate-ability students appear to learn neither more nor less (eliminate C), and low-ability students seem to learn less. Eliminate D because it is not supported by research results. The harmful effects of ability grouping are most pronounced for low-ability students, including low expectations for their achievement and behavior; less instruction time, resulting in less learning; lowered self-esteem; and less opportunity to experience higher-level topics (B). Choice B is the correct response.

7. **C** This question deals with **developmentally appropriate instruction.** Thus, its primary focus is Competency 001: *The teacher uses an understanding of human developmental processes to nurture student growth through developmentally appropriate instruction.* According to Erikson, children go through stages of personality development as they mature. At each stage, there are major social-emotional tasks. Eliminate A and D because these are social-emotional tasks of early adolescence. Eliminate B because gaining a considerable degree of autonomy in a relatively short time does not generally foster a sense of inferiority. During the middle and later childhood years, if youngsters fail to experience satisfaction and success with the completion of tasks they are assigned or initiate, they will not feel good about themselves and thus will develop a sense of inferiority. Choice C is the correct response.

8. **D** This question deals with **instructional strategies.** Thus, its primary focus is Competency 008: *The teacher uses a variety of instructional strategies and roles to facilitate learning and to help students become independent thinkers and problem solvers who use higher-order thinking in the classroom and the real world.*

Eliminate A because it relates to **motivation** (Competency 005). Eliminate B because at-risk students may not be adequately prepared to assume the major responsibility for their own learning that independent study requires. Eliminate C because it reflects a "poor" teaching practice. Ms. Blackwell might consider using direct instruction when teaching basic skills to the at-risk students. Research indicates that this instructional model is particularly appropriate when teaching a well-defined body of subject matter or skills to slower learners. Choice D is the correct response.

9. **A** This question deals with **school-community relationships.** Thus, its primary focus is Competency 014: *The teacher understands how the school relates to the larger community and knows strategies for making interactions between school and community mutually supportive and beneficial.* This is a priority-setting question—you must select the *most* probable answer choice. Eliminate C because it would be inappropriate for volunteer tutors to assume such a role. Eliminate B and D because these may occur inadvertently but would not be *most* likely. Since community members, especially grandparents, have a vested interest in the schools, they are a valuable resource to teachers. By using grandparent volunteers, Ms. Blackwell is cultivating strong community-school partnerships, thus fostering positive ties between the school and the community. Choice A is the correct response.

10. **B** This question deals with **students' self-esteem.** Thus, its primary focus is Competency 002: *The teacher considers environmental factors that may affect learning in designing a supportive and responsive classroom community that promotes all students' learning and self-esteem.* This is a priority-setting question—you must select the *most* effective answer choice. Eliminate A because this may negatively affect students' self-esteem if they are not successful after being urged to try harder. Eliminate C and D because these are measures Ms. Blackwell might take to enhance self-esteem, but they would not be as effective as Choice B. Students who have a pattern of failure may be victims of *learned helplessness.* They may feel doomed to failure because they believe their abilities are fixed; and thus, they are incapable of success. They may not attribute success to their own efforts unless the teacher helps them make this link. By planning activities in which the students achieve success and know how they contributed to it, Ms. Blackwell can help them make the critical connection, which in turn will enhance their feelings of self-sufficiency and self-worth. Choice B is the correct response.

11. **B** This question deals with **developmentally appropriate instruction.** Thus, its primary focus is Competency 001: *The teacher uses an understanding of human developmental processes to nurture student growth through developmentally appropriate instruction.* This is a priority-setting question—you must select the activity that is *most* developmentally appropriate. Fostering an

appreciation of another's culture in a child of this age can best be approached by showing similarities and differences with the child's familiar cultural forms. Eliminate A because this would be limited to physical characteristics, and besides, it focuses on differences. Eliminate C because the countries selected may not represent any of the cultural groups in the class. Eliminate D because third-graders would have difficulty with this activity. Having students participate in a class discussion about cultural similarities and differences in their own classroom could readily be expanded into a discussion about the diversity of American culture. Also, this would be the most developmentally appropriate and meaningful of all the described activities. By seeing that they have things in common, the students will be less suspicious of each other's cultures; and by identifying features that are unique, they will still be able to retain their cultural identities. Choice B is the correct response.

12. **D** This question deals with **diversity.** Thus, its primary focus is Competency 003: *The teacher appreciates human diversity, recognizing how diversity in the classroom and the community may affect learning and creating a classroom environment in which both the diversity of groups and the uniqueness of individuals are recognized and celebrated.* The 1992 American Association of University Women report *How Schools Shortchange Girls* confirmed what other researchers have found: that boys and girls are treated differently in today's schools (eliminate A). Particularly, boys are encouraged to excel in mathematics and in the sciences more often than girls are (eliminate B), see themselves reflected more often in the curriculum than girls do (eliminate C), and receive more attention in class than girls do (D). Choice D is the correct response.

13. **D** This question deals with **diversity.** Thus, its primary focus is Competency 003: *The teacher appreciates human diversity, recognizing how diversity in the classroom and the community may affect learning and creating a classroom environment in which both the diversity of groups and the uniqueness of individuals are recognized and celebrated.* This is a priority-setting question—you must select the *best* answer choice. Eliminate A, even though this is the first action Ms. Blackwell should take—that is, take issue with Joey and deal directly with his statement. You have to select the choice that would be *best* for changing students' opinions. Research about learning and prejudice suggests that telling students they shouldn't make prejudicial statements about women (A) is likely to result in few, if any, students (who agreed with Joey) changing their stereotypical opinions. Eliminate B because it is developmentally inappropriate. Eliminate C because it may send the message that recognizing and celebrating women mathematicians need receive attention only during that period. Indeed, research findings indicate that such measures may be too brief or superficial and, as a result, are unlikely to change attitudes. From what research tells us about prejudice and learning, long-term

interventions work best. By bringing in both men and women to talk about how they use math, Ms. Blackwell will provide positive role models for all her students. Choice D is the correct response.

14. **D** This question deals with **how learning occurs.** Thus, its primary focus is Competency 004: *The teacher understands how learning occurs and can apply this understanding to design and implement effective instruction.* This is a priority-setting question—you must select the *best* answer choice. Eliminate A because it relates to **diversity** (Competency 003). Eliminate C because it relates to **instructional strategies** (Competency 008) and, further, is not supported by the stimulus. Eliminate B because Mr. Payne is not helping students learn how to learn. Mr. Payne is aware that students' learning is enhanced when instructional strategies promote a sense of responsibility for one's own learning. Choice D is the correct response.

15. **A** This question deals with technology, which comes under **materials and resources.** Thus, its primary focus is Competency 009: *The teacher uses a variety of instructional materials and resources (including human and technological resources) to support individual and group learning.* This is a priority-setting question— you must select the answer choice that is *most* efficient. Eliminate B because computer-aided instruction (CAI) is a program of instruction. Eliminate C because a graphics calculator would be limited for storing qualitative data. Eliminate D because it would be too time-consuming. Using the computer is the best way to compile the information for use at a later time. A computer will allow students to efficiently complete all the necessary steps in producing and publishing their book. Choice A is the correct response.

16. **A** This question deals with **assessment.** Thus, its primary focus is Competency 010: *The teacher uses processes of informal and formal assessment to understand individual learners, monitor instructional effectiveness, and shape instruction.* This is a priority-setting question—you must select the *best* answer choice. Eliminate B because this would not assess the students' prior knowledge. Eliminate D because the students would be expected to listen to the guest speaker, not tell what they know about the topic. Mr. Payne recognizes that teachers should be proactive in ensuring that prior learning for new learning is in place. He is likely to understand that this can be accomplished through using informal assessments. Eliminate C because Mr. Payne might have small-group discussions to assess prior knowledge; but using an advance organizer (for example, a structured overview) would be a better strategy because it will help students see the structure of key concepts and topics, which might not occur in the small-group discussions. Choice A is the correct response.

17. **B** This question deals with **instructional strategies.** Thus, its primary focus is Competency 008: *The teacher uses a variety of instructional strategies and roles to facilitate learning and to help students become independent thinkers and problem solvers who use higher-order thinking in the classroom and the real world.* Eliminate A and D because if students self-select for group membership or are assigned based on their mathematics group, they may not be mixed in ability in social studies. Eliminate C because it is contrary to cooperative learning principles of which heterogeneous grouping is an essential component. Although critics have challenged the use of cooperative learning strategies with gifted students, most authorities agree that heterogeneous grouping (B) benefits all students. However, this does not mean that high-ability students will have to learn and work at the same pace as lower-ability students, nor does it mean that they will not be given opportunities to work alone or cooperatively with other high achievers. Mr. Payne should assign students of high, middle, and low ability in social studies to each group. Choice B is the correct response.

18. **C** This question deals both with **students' self-esteem** (Mr. Payne will be assigning roles to students, which may affect how they perceive themselves) and **instructional strategies** (How are roles assigned for cooperative learning?). Glancing at the answer choices, you can see they all relate to **students' self-esteem.** Thus, although you also may use your knowledge of effective practices for cooperative learning, the primary focus of this question is Competency 002: *The teacher considers environmental factors that may affect learning in designing a supportive and responsive classroom community that promotes all students' learning and self-esteem.* The roles used in cooperative learning are designed to promote responsibility and leadership for all students. Mr. Payne should model respect for all learners and encourage them to feel capable of taking on leadership roles. Eliminate A, B, and D because they conflict with the principle that teachers should provide a supportive classroom climate in which all students feel valued and capable. Over time, each student should have the opportunity to experience a variety of leadership roles—some easy and some more demanding. Choice C is the correct response.

19. **D** This question deals with both **developmentally appropriate instruction** (Is lecturing appropriate for a sixth-grade class?) and **instructional strategies** (What does the research say about lecturing?). Glancing at the answer choices, you can see that they are mainly focused on the appropriateness of lecturing at various grade levels. Thus, the primary focus of this question is Competency 001: *The teacher uses an understanding of human developmental processes to nurture student growth through developmentally appropriate instruction.* Eliminate A, because most authorities agree that lecturing is the least effective instructional strategy for all prekindergarten-through-grade-twelve

classrooms; further, it is an inappropriate instructional strategy for use with elementary school students. Eliminate B and C. Choice D is the correct response.

20. **C** This question deals with **professionalism.** Thus, its primary focus is Competency 012: *The teacher is a reflective practitioner who knows how to promote his or her own professional growth and can work cooperatively with other professionals in the system to create a school culture that enhances learning and encourages positive change.* Eliminate A because it deals with **developmentally appropriate instruction** (Competency 001). Eliminate B because it relates to **students' self-esteem** (Competency 002). Eliminate D because it relates to **school-community relationships** (Competency 014). Mr. Payne understands that effective teachers continuously monitor and adjust their classroom practices. He recognized that the students' motivation and interest appeared to increase in the collaborative setting, so he decided that whole-group instruction should be de-emphasized. This decision demonstrates that he is a reflective practitioner who strives to strengthen the quality of his teaching. Choice C is the correct response.

21. **D** This question deals with **planning.** Thus, its primary focus is Competency 006: *The teacher uses planning processes to design outcome-oriented learning experiences that foster understanding and encourage self-directed thinking and learning in both individual and collaborative settings.* Eliminate Roman I because it would probably create resentment among the students. Eliminate A and B. The remaining Choices C and D both contain II and IV, so you need only decide whether Roman III should be included. Mr. Payne needs to be aware of the important role the teacher must assume when using a collaborative setting. He should monitor each group, assessing and guiding individual and group collaborative skills (Roman II). Eliminate Roman III. Eliminate C. Mr. Payne should understand the relationship between careful planning and student success in the classroom. For cooperative group activities, it is essential that group tasks be well prepared and well organized (Roman IV). Choice D is the correct response.

22. **C** This question deals with **classroom management.** Thus, its primary focus is Competency 011: *The teacher structures and manages the learning environment to maintain a classroom climate that promotes the lifelong pursuit of learning and encourages cooperation, leadership, and mutual respect.* Mr. Payne should know how to promote student membership in a smoothly functioning learning community and to facilitate a positive social and emotional atmosphere in the classroom that encourages class participation. This is a priority-setting question—you must select the *best* seating arrangement. Seating the students in a U-shape as in Figure 1 is a useful arrangement for whole-group discussion, because it facilitates student interaction with each other

and the teacher; but it would not be the *best* arrangement for small-group activities. Eliminate A. Seating students in rows as in Figures 2 and 4 will limit student participation. When students are seated in rows, students sitting near the front and center of the room are likely to speak more freely than students seated elsewhere; further, with these arrangements, students seated in the back of the row may lose interest. Eliminate B and D. Seating students in clusters as in Figure 3 promotes more group interaction and participation when students are working in cooperative learning groups. Choice C is the correct response.

23. **B** This question deals with **instructional strategies.** Thus, its primary focus is Competency 008: *The teacher uses a variety of instructional strategies and roles to facilitate learning and to help students become independent thinkers and problem solvers who use higher-order thinking in the classroom and the real world.* This is a priority-setting question—you must select the *best* answer choice. Eliminate A because it relates to **motivation** (Competency 005). Eliminate C because *intradisciplinary* means within the same discipline. Eliminate D because it is unrelated to the question, which is about students using skills from various disciplines, not about the students' learning task. The use of an interdisciplinary approach requires teachers to integrate other disciplines into their curriculum. Choice B is the correct response.

24. **D** This question deals with **technology.** Thus, its primary focus is Competency 009: *The teacher uses a variety of instructional materials and resources (including human and technological resources) to support individual and group learning.* This is a priority-setting question—you must select the *primary* instructional reason. Eliminate A, since this would not be Mr. Payne's primary instructional reason for his students to use computers, because Mr. Payne is teaching social studies, not computer literacy, even though some students might, with repeated computer use, improve their keyboarding skills. Eliminate B because it relates to **diversity,** and besides, it is not supported by research. Eliminate C because it relates to **motivation,** and besides, teachers should make use of available technology as a part of the instructional process, not for rewards. Mr. Payne understands the value of using computers to meet the needs of various learning styles (for instance, tactile/kinesthetic) of students. Choice D is the correct response.

25. **C** This deals with **professional development.** Thus, its primary focus is Competency 012: *The teacher is a reflective practitioner who knows how to promote his or her own professional growth and can work cooperatively with other professionals in the system to create a school culture that enhances learning and encourages positive change.* This is a priority-setting question—you must select the answer choice that is *most* in accord with current principles of professional development of Texas teachers. The use of technology

adds a new dimension to teaching and learning. It can be used to create a learning environment that changes and interacts with students' needs. Today in Texas, it is vital that teachers know how to enhance learning for students through the appropriate use of technological resources like computers. Eliminate A because teachers can use computers effectively in their classrooms without knowing computer programming. Eliminate B and D because teachers should not be expected to have computer maintenance skills or know how to repair computer hardware. All Texas teachers need to be computer literate in order to use this technology effectively in the classroom. Choice C is the correct response.

26. **D** The question asks about Mr. Payne's assessment of Marvin, not about what he plans to do to change Marvin's behavior; so the question is not about **classroom management** (Competency 011). Mr. Payne recognizes that Marvin needs attention, which relates to **students' self-esteem.** Thus, its primary focus is Competency 002: *The teacher considers environmental factors that may affect learning in designing a supportive and responsive classroom community that promotes all students' learning and self-esteem.* Eliminate A because *behavioral modification* is a structured technique for changing behavior and thus relates to **classroom management.** Eliminate B because it pertains to **developmentally appropriate instruction.** Eliminate C because it relates to **classroom management.** Mr. Payne understands Maslow's Hierarchy of Human Needs and recognizes the importance of establishing a positive classroom environment. Students who seek attention by misbehavior are often wanting to belong and feel accepted. Choice D is the correct response.

27. **B** This question deals with **ethical, legal, and professional standards.** Thus, its primary focus is Competency 015: *The teacher understands requirements, expectations, and constraints associated with teaching in Texas, and can apply this understanding in a variety of contexts.* This is a priority-setting question—you must decide what Mr. Payne should do *first.* Teachers should know how to work within the system to address problems and make decisions appropriately. To make a decision about Marvin, Mr. Payne needs accurate and reliable information, which he can obtain from examining Marvin's school records. Eliminate A and C because these measures may occur later but would not be Mr. Payne's *first* step, because he needs information before he can make an intelligent decision about whether meeting with parents or the counselor is necessary. Eliminate D because Mr. Payne cannot legally do this without the permission of Marvin's parents. Mr. Payne should check Marvin's records to see whether there is an indication of a prior problem. For instance, Marvin might be developmentally delayed in maturity, which can affect behavior. Choice B is the correct response.

28. **A** This questions deals with **developmentally appropriate instruction.** Thus, its primary focus is Competency 001: *The teacher uses an understanding of human developmental processes to nurture student growth through developmentally appropriate instruction.* Mr. Payne's students are sixth-graders, so most of them are between twelve and thirteen years old. A major source of anxiety for adolescents this age is fear of rejection by peers, because peer relations are so important. By comparison, failing to achieve academically, learn cultural norms, and please authority figures are less important sources of anxiety for most adolescents. Choice A is the correct response.

29. **A** This question deals with **diversity.** Thus, its primary focus is Competency 003: *The teacher appreciates human diversity, recognizing how diversity in the classroom and the community may affect learning and creating a classroom environment in which both the diversity of groups and the uniqueness of individuals are recognized and celebrated.* Eliminate B, C, and D because they conflict with expert opinion regarding diagnosis of Attention Deficit Hyperactivity Disorder (ADHD) in children. ADHD is the psychiatric term used to describe a set of symptoms reflecting excessive inattention, overactivity, and impulsive responding. Experts agree that ADHD is a disorder that is far more prevalently diagnosed in male children than in female children. Choice A is the correct response.

30. **A** This question deals with **classroom management.** Thus, its primary focus is Competency 011: *The teacher structures and manages the learning environment to maintain a classroom climate that promotes the lifelong pursuit of learning and encourages cooperation, leadership, and mutual respect.* A critical time for establishing classroom order occurs in the first few days of school. Slavin's examination of the research indicated that to start the year out right, effective classroom managers should spend most of the time introducing procedures and discussing classroom rules (eliminate B) and use simple, enjoyable tasks (eliminate D), such as watching a highly motivating video (eliminate C), as activities for the first lessons. Mr. Paul should avoid starting on the first day with a fairly difficult lesson because that might focus the students' attention away from instructions and procedures that need to be learned. Choice A is the correct response.

31. **D** This question deals with **instructional strategies.** Thus, its primary focus is Competency 008: *The teacher uses a variety of instructional strategies and roles to facilitate learning and to help students become independent thinkers and problem solvers who use higher-order thinking in the classroom and the real world.* Eliminate Roman I because focusing on recall of correct answers requires only lower-level thinking skills. Eliminate A. Eliminate Roman II because going through a step-by-step procedure to reach a given solution does not challenge students to think at high levels.

Eliminate B and C. Open-ended questions (Roman III) allow students to use divergent thinking, which develops problem-solving ability. Further, the students will clarify their own thinking when justifying answers (Roman IV). Mr. Paul should use problems that are open-ended and allow for a number of solutions, and he should require students to convince others their solutions are correct. Choice D is the correct response.

32. **C** This question deals with **classroom management.** Thus its primary focus is Competency 011: *The teacher structures and manages the learning environment to maintain a classroom climate that promotes the lifelong pursuit of learning and encourages cooperation, leadership, and mutual respect.* This is a priority-setting question—you must select the answer choice that is *most* effective. It is important for Mr. Paul to maximize the amount of class time spent in learning. Eliminate A, B, and D because their effectiveness is diminished when class is interrupted. Mr. Paul should be aware that one important source of lost instructional time is interruptions. Interruptions not only cut into instructional time; they also break momentum. Mr. Paul should post a DO NOT DISTURB sign on the classroom door when students are brainstorming ideas for problem solving, to avoid unnecessary interruptions. Choice C is the correct response.

33. **B** This question deals with **developmentally appropriate instruction.** Thus, its primary focus is Competency 001: *The teacher uses an understanding of human developmental processes to nurture student growth through developmentally appropriate instruction.* Mr. Paul's students are fifth-graders, so most of them are between 11 and 12 years old. Eliminate A, C, and D because these cognitive abilities are normally acquired during earlier stages of cognitive development. Most fifth-graders are in the process of developing the ability to think hypothetically. They are able to handle contrary-to-fact propositions and can develop and test hypotheses. Choice B is the correct response.

34. **D** This question deals with **professionalism.** Thus, its primary focus is Competency 012: *The teacher is a reflective practitioner who knows how to promote his or her own professional growth and can work cooperatively with other professionals in the system to create a school culture that enhances learning and encourages positive change.* The Professional Development and Appraisal System (PDAS) specifies appropriate teacher behaviors for Texas teachers. Among these appropriate teacher behaviors from the PDAS are the following: provides for active participation by students (Roman I), uses inquiry techniques to challenge students (Roman II), aligns instruction with work and life application (Roman III), and uses instruction that allows more than one pathway or approach for new learning (IV). Choice D is the correct response.

35. **C** This question deals with **professionalism.** Thus, its primary focus is Competency 012: *The teacher is a reflective practitioner who knows how to promote his or her own professional growth and can work cooperatively with other professionals in the system to create a school culture that enhances learning and encourages positive change.* Mr. Paul should know that effective teachers provide for active participation by students (eliminate A), extend students' responses and contributions (eliminate B), and do not allow delay of initial class activities (eliminate D); further, they cite the specific offender when disruptive behavior occurs (C). Choice C is the correct response.

36. **B** This question deals with **professionalism.** Thus, its primary focus is Competency 012: *The teacher is a reflective practitioner who knows how to promote his or her own professional growth and can work cooperatively with other professionals in the system to create a school culture that enhances learning and encourages positive change.* Observable behaviors are overt actions by an individual. Remaining confident (eliminate A), being pleased (eliminate C), or liking the way a student responds (eliminate D) takes place within the individual, so is not an overt action. Walking over to a student (B) is an overt action by the teacher; therefore, it is an observable behavior. Choice B is the correct response.

37. **B** This question deals with **assessment.** Thus, its primary focus is Competency 010: *The teacher uses processes of informal and formal assessment to understand individual learners, monitor instructional effectiveness, and shape instruction.* Teacher-made tests can provide valuable information about what students have learned. When designing tests, teachers should be aware that guessing by students can compromise the validity of results. Although guessing can be a factor on any type of test, it has the most effect on true-false items. Choice B is the correct response.

38. **D** This question deals with **assessment.** Thus, its primary focus is Competency 010: *The teacher uses processes of informal and formal assessment to understand individual learners, monitor instructional effectiveness, and shape instruction.* Teacher-made tests can provide valuable information about what students have learned. In designing tests, a key decision to be made is the form that test items should take. As a general rule, true-false, matching, and multiple-choice questions are considered objective, and short-answer and essay questions are considered subjective. In fact, subjectivity in grading is the major problem with essay items. Choice D is the correct response.

39. **A** This question deals with **assessment.** Thus, its primary focus is Competency 010: *The teacher uses processes of informal and formal assessment to understand individual learners, monitor instructional effectiveness, and shape instruction.* Teacher-made tests can provide valuable information about what students have

learned. When selecting a test item, the teacher should be aware of the level of thinking that will be tested by the item. Most fill-in-the-blank items require an open response at the knowledge level of thinking, but students are restricted by the format in the type of response they can make. Choice A is the correct response.

40. **C** This question deals with **assessment.** Thus, its primary focus is Competency 010: *The teacher uses processes of informal and formal assessment to understand individual learners, monitor instructional effectiveness, and shape instruction.* As a general rule, the response choices in a multiple-choice item should be listed in some logical or sequential order (for instance, alphabetically). Item 3 would be improved if the responses were listed alphabetically. Choice C is the correct response.

41. **C** This question deals with **assessment.** Thus, its primary focus is Competency 010: *The teacher uses processes of informal and formal assessment to understand individual learners, monitor instructional effectiveness, and shape instruction.* Teachers today are moving toward multiple and more authentic assessment of students, including performance observation. Seeing a student actually perform behavior to demonstrate knowledge is more likely to yield valid assessment of learning than written tests like matching (eliminate A), multiple-choice (eliminate B), and true-false (eliminate D). Choice C is the correct response.

42. **A** This question deals with **ethical, legal, and professional standards.** Thus, its primary focus is Competency 015: *The teacher understands requirements, expectations, and constraints associated with teaching in Texas, and can apply this understanding in a variety of contexts.* Eliminate B because it conflicts with the law. Eliminate C because it works against developing effective parent-teacher partnerships. Eliminate D because the principal cannot legally grant Julio's parents' request to see other students' grades. Mr. Paul should be aware that his legal responsibility is to deny Julio's parents' request to see other students' grades. According to the Family Educational Rights and Privacy Act (also known as the Buckley Amendment), Mr. Paul would violate the right to privacy of the other students in the class if he doesn't deny Julio's parents' request to see other students' grades. Choice A is the correct response.

43. **B** This question deals with **ethical, legal, and professional standards.** Thus, its primary focus is Competency 015: *The teacher understands requirements, expectations, and constraints associated with teaching in Texas, and can apply this understanding in a variety of contexts.* Eliminate A, C, and D because the Buckley Amendment does not contain these provisions. According to the Buckley Amendment, parents have the right to inspect and review their children's educational records. Choice B is the correct response.

44. **D** This question deals with **diversity.** Thus, its primary focus is Competency 003: *The teacher appreciates human diversity, recognizing how diversity in the classroom and the community may affect learning and creating a classroom environment in which both the diversity of groups and the uniqueness of individuals are recognized and celebrated.* Eliminate A, B, and C because Mario's behavior does not reflect that of a child with a learning disability or limited English proficiency (he reads scientific magazines and has built a small engine). Research on children who are academically gifted reveals that many do poorly in school, mainly because they go unidentified and thus their needs are not met. Choice D is the correct response.

45. **C** This question deals with **diversity.** Thus, its primary focus is Competency 003: *The teacher appreciates human diversity, recognizing how diversity in the classroom and the community may affect learning and creating a classroom environment in which both the diversity of groups and the uniqueness of individuals are recognized and celebrated.* Eliminate Roman II because giving Mario more of the same work would leave matters as they are, which is not a good situation for Mr. Paul or Mario. Eliminate A and B. The remaining answer choices, C and D, both contain Roman III, so you need to decide between Roman I and IV. Eliminate Roman IV because giving Mario less challenging work would probably result in Mario's giving less attention to his school work. Eliminate D. Given that Mario has been reading scientific magazines, it is reasonable to expect that giving him more advanced work (Roman I) and work that will broaden and deepen his understanding (Roman III) would stimulate his interest. Choice C is the correct response.

46. **A** Ms. Brazil's philosophy is about having high expectations for all her students, which, according to research, affects **students' self-esteem.** Thus, the primary focus of this question is Competency 002: *The teacher considers environmental factors that may affect learning in designing a supportive and responsive classroom community that promotes all students' learning and self-esteem.* Eliminate B, C, and D because these are teacher behaviors, not concepts. Further, you can eliminate B because it deals with **instructional strategies** (Competency 008), eliminate C because it deals with **motivation** (Competency 005), and eliminate D because it deals with **diversity** (Competency 003). Choices B, C, and D are likely to occur in Ms. Brazil's class as she puts into practice her positive philosophy regarding students' abilities. This philosophical attitude is in accord with the concept of the self-fulfilling prophecy. The *self-fulfilling prophecy* is the phenomenon that occurs when teachers expect students to be successful and the teachers get what they expect. Choice A is the correct response.

47. **A**   This question deals with **diversity.** Thus, its primary focus is
Competency 003: *The teacher appreciates human diversity,*
recognizing how diversity in the classroom and the community
may affect learning and creating a classroom environment in
which both the diversity of groups and the uniqueness of
individuals are recognized and celebrated. A student of limited
English proficiency (LEP) is one "whose primary language is other
than English and whose English language skills are such that the
student has difficulty performing ordinary classwork in English"
(TEC 29.052). Usually these students are placed in a bilingual or
ESL (English as a second language) program after evaluation by the
LPAC (language proficiency assessment committee); however, a
student's parent must approve the placement and may appeal the
decision under TEC 29.064. Eliminate B because this would send a
negative message to Graciela about her primary language. Eliminate
C because Ms. Brazil should respect the parents' wishes and not
second-guess their decision. Eliminate D because this would single
out Graciela in front of the class, which would be likely to
embarrass Graciela. Ms. Brazil can best meet Graciela's academic
needs by using visuals, manipulatives, graphic organizers, media,
and other less language-dependent means to explain concepts.
Choice A is the correct response.

48. **C**   This question concerns both **diversity** (How should Ms. Brazil deal
with Graciela, an LEP student?) and **communication** (How should
Ms. Brazil communicate with Graciela during question-and-answer
activities?). Glancing at the answer choices, you can see that they
center on questioning strategies, so the primary focus of this
question is Competency 007: *The teacher uses effective verbal,*
nonverbal, and media communication techniques to shape the
classroom into a community of learners engaged in active
inquiry, collaborative exploration, and supportive interactions.
Notwithstanding, you will probably have to use your understanding
of both competencies to select the appropriate answer choice.
Eliminate A, B, and D because these measures would exclude
Graciela from full participation in class activities and would
probably not go unnoticed by her classmates. Graciela's classmates
might resent that she is not being challenged as much as they are in
the class. Teachers should know how to foster effective,
constructive, and purposeful communication by and among all
students in the class. By addressing questions to Graciela using
body language and gestures to enhance meaning, Ms. Brazil will be
not only involving Graciela more fully, but also modeling to the
other students how to communicate more effectively with Graciela.
Choice C is the correct response.

49. **D**   This question deals with **diversity.** Thus, its primary focus is
Competency 003: *The teacher appreciates human diversity,*
recognizing how diversity in the classroom and the community
may affect learning and creating a classroom environment in
which both the diversity of groups and the uniqueness of

individuals are recognized and celebrated. Eliminate Roman I because multiculturalism means understanding, accepting, and constructing relations among people of all cultures, including both dominant and minority cultures. Eliminate A and B. The remaining Choices C and D both contain Roman II and III, so you need only decide whether Roman IV should be included. Multiculturalism is facilitated when teachers hold high expectations for all students, regardless of ethnicity, gender, or exceptionality (Roman IV) and believe that self-esteem (Roman II) and teacher expectations (Roman III) go hand-in-hand with academic achievement. Choice D is the correct response.

50. **D**   This question deals with **communication.** Thus, its primary focus is Competency 007: *The teacher uses effective verbal, nonverbal, and media communication techniques to shape the classroom into a community of learners engaged in active inquiry, collaborative exploration, and supportive interactions.* Eliminate A and C because Ms. Brazil is not making a point with Jay's concern or using it as an example, she is merely calling attention to it. Eliminate B because Ms. Brazil did not modify Jay's contribution. Ms. Brazil uses Jay's contribution as a springboard for further class discussion. Choice D is the correct response.

51. **C**   This question deals with **communication.** Thus, its primary focus is Competency 007: *The teacher uses effective verbal, nonverbal, and media communication techniques to shape the classroom into a community of learners engaged in active inquiry, collaborative exploration, and supportive interactions.* This is a priority-setting question—you must select the *best* answer choice. Eliminate A because it deals with **assessment** (Competency 010). Eliminate B because it is not supported by the stimulus—other disciplines were not mentioned. Eliminate D because it relates to **classroom management** (Competency 011). The discourse in a classroom is an integral part of active learning. Effective teachers know how to create a climate of trust, respect, support, and inquiry in which students consistently take reasonable risks in responding to the teacher or peers. Choice C is the correct response.

52. **D**   This question deals with Domain I, Understanding Learners (How is Ms. Brazil demonstrating her understanding of learners?). Thus, it potentially deals with the five competencies under that domain: **developmentally appropriate instruction** (Competency 001), **students' self-esteem** (Competency 002), **diversity** (Competency 003), **how learning occurs** (Competency 004), and **motivation** (Competency 005). Eliminate Roman II because diversity was not a factor in Ms. Brazil's accepting the students' idea about the recycling project. Eliminate B and C. The remaining Choices A and D both contain Roman I and IV, so you need only decide whether to include Roman III. Since Roman I and IV both relate to **how learning occurs,** you could say that the primary focus of this question is Competency 004: *The teacher understands how*

learning occurs and can apply this understanding to design and implement effective instruction. By accepting the students' idea about the recycling project, Ms. Brazil is promoting a sense of responsibility for one's own learning (Roman I), creating an environment in which students feel competent and productive (Roman III), and fostering a view of learning as a purposeful pursuit (Roman IV). Choice D is the correct response.

53. **A**   This question deals with **assessment.** Thus, its primary focus is Competency 010: *The teacher uses processes of informal and formal assessment to understand individual learners, monitor instructional effectiveness, and shape instruction.* Ms. Brazil recognizes that teachers should be proactive in ensuring that prior learning for new learning is in place. She is likely to understand that this can be accomplished through informal assessments. She might use an advance organizer such as semantic mapping (eliminate B) or webbing (eliminate C) that helps students see the structure of key concepts and topics, or she might choose to have a whole-class discussion (eliminate D). Evaluation questions (A) involve students judging or valuing, so would be inappropriate as a means to determine prior knowledge. Choice A is the correct response.

54. **B**   This question deals with **instructional strategies.** Thus, its primary focus is Competency 008: *The teacher uses a variety of instructional strategies and roles to facilitate learning and to help students become independent thinkers and problem solvers who use higher-order thinking in the classroom and the real world.* Eliminate A because *individualized instruction* is guided by individual students' needs and abilities, not common purposes. Eliminate C and D because these strategies are used on a temporary or one-time basis. Ms. Brazil knows that cooperative learning groups allow the students to work together for an extended period to achieve a common goal. Choice B is the correct response.

55. **C**   This question deals with **planning.** Thus, its primary focus is Competency 006: *The teacher uses planning processes to design outcome-oriented learning experiences that foster understanding and encourage self-directed thinking and learning in both individual and collaborative settings.* Eliminate Roman I because it is not supported by the stimulus; you do not know that the project will require the students to do research. Eliminate A and B. The remaining Choices C and D both contain Roman II, so you must decide between Roman III and IV. Eliminate Roman IV because experiences in which students work together toward a common purpose usually promote a sense of community among the students and fosters positive interactions and feelings. Eliminate D. The class project is likely to enhance students' interpersonal skills and foster class cooperation and unity. Choice C is the correct response.

56. **A**   Upon first reading, this question appears to deal both with **school-community relationships** (Ms. Brazil invites a community member to speak with the class) and **school-home relationships** (Ms. Brazil invites parents to speak with the class). Glancing at the answer choices, you can see that none deal with the parents or the home; thus, the primary focus of this question is Competency 014: *The teacher understands how the school relates to the larger community and knows strategies for making interactions between school and community mutually supportive and beneficial.* Eliminate B because it relates to **students' self-esteem** (Competency 002). Eliminate D because it relates to **diversity** (Competency 003). Eliminate C because it is off-topic—inviting guest speakers has nothing to do with community expectations. Ms. Brazil recognizes the importance of school-community relationships. By inviting guest speakers from the community to come visit with her class, she is fostering positive ties between the school and the community. Choice A is the correct response.

57. **D**   This question deals with **instructional strategies.** Thus, its primary focus is Competency 008: *The teacher uses a variety of instructional strategies and roles to facilitate learning and to help students become independent thinkers and problem solvers who use higher-order thinking in the classroom and the real world.* Eliminate A because it has to do with grouping similar students together, usually according to academic ability. Eliminate B and C because they involve (academic) ability grouping. According to research, ability grouping should be avoided except for skill subjects such as reading and math, and then only when the groups will stay intact on a short-term basis (that is, as skills are learned, group membership changes). For the recycling project, Ms. Brazil should recognize that heterogeneous grouping will be the most beneficial to all students, regardless of ability or achievement, and will facilitate the class goal of implementing a successful recycling project. Choice D is the correct response.

58. **C**   This question deals with **professionalism.** Thus, its primary focus is Competency 012: *The teacher is a reflective practitioner who knows how to promote his or her own professional growth and can work cooperatively with other professionals in the system to create a school culture that enhances learning and encourages positive change.* Eliminate A because it relates to **school-community relationships.** Eliminate B because it relates to **school-home relationships.** Eliminate D because it relates to **motivation.** As a professional practitioner, Ms. Brazil understands the importance of reflection and self-evaluation, and in doing so, she realizes her limited knowledge of recycling. The workshop gives her an opportunity to enhance her knowledge and skills about this topic. Choice C is the correct response.

59. **B** This question deals with **ethical, legal, and professional standards.** Thus, its primary focus is Competency 015: *The teacher understands requirements, expectations, and constraints associated with teaching in Texas, and can apply this understanding in a variety of contexts.* This is a priority-setting question—you must decide what Ms. Brazil should do *first.* Eliminate A and C because they will be unnecessary if Ms. Brazil does not attend the workshop. Eliminate D because Ms. Brazil knows that the role of the school board is to set district policy, not micromanage local schools in the district. As a professional, Ms. Brazil knows the importance of following the "chain of command." She is aware that teachers should never bypass the school principal on important matters such as being away from school. Choice B is the correct response.

60. **B** This question deals with **technology.** Thus, its primary focus is Competency 009: *The teacher uses a variety of instructional materials and resources (including human and technological resources) to support individual and group learning.* Eliminate Roman I because it deals with **classroom management.** Eliminate A and D. The remaining answer Choices B and C both contain Roman II, so you need to decide between Roman III and IV. Eliminate Roman IV because the students will be obtaining facts and information, not using higher-order thinking skills. Eliminate C. Choice B is the correct response.

61. **C** This question deals with **school-home relationships.** Thus, its primary focus is Competency 013: *The teacher knows how to foster strong school-home relationships that support student achievement of desired learning outcomes.* This is a priority-setting question—you must select the *best* answer choice. Eliminate B because this is unlikely to be successful, especially with parents who are protective of their children. Eliminate D because this is unlikely to satisfy Leaia's mother, since she is probably concerned about the other children in Leaia's class, too. Eliminate A because Ms. Brazil or the school should have provided all parents, including Ms. Selder, with these rules already. If this has not occurred, providing a copy to Ms. Selder at this point would not be as effective as inviting Ms. Selder to visit the school for a demonstration of the child-safety Internet software. Seeing firsthand that Leaia, or any other child, will be unable to access inappropriate or disturbing material should greatly assuage this parent's concerns. Choice C is the correct response.

62. **D** This question deals with **developmentally appropriate instruction.** Thus, its primary focus is Competency 001: *The teacher uses an understanding of human developmental processes to nurture student growth through developmentally appropriate instruction.* Eliminate A and C because children Leaia's age are too young to have the experiences or cognitive abilities to form strong opinions on issues, such as child safety on the Internet. They rely

more on the opinions of their family members (D), such as older siblings, in forming their own attitudes. As they mature into young adolescents, the attitudes of their peers will begin to exert more influence, but not at this stage of their development (eliminate B). Choice D is the correct response.

63. **B** This question deals with **school-home relationships.** Thus, its primary focus is Competency 013: *The teacher knows how to foster strong school-home relationships that support student achievement of desired learning outcomes.* This is a priority-setting question—you must select the *best* answer choice. Eliminate A because it violates TEC 26.008, which states, "An attempt by any school district employee to encourage or coerce a child to withhold information from the child's parent is grounds for discipline." Eliminate C and D because they deal only with volunteers and thereby leave out parents who, for whatever reason, do not volunteer. The *best* guard against upsetting parents about what their child is doing in school is to be proactive in keeping them informed about class activities. Ms. Brazil should provide parents/guardians with regular updates about class activities, so that they are given timely and accurate information (which might not happen if they learn about the activities secondhand from their child). Choice B is the correct response.

64. **B** This question deals with **classroom management.** Thus, its primary focus is Competency 011: *The teacher structures and manages the learning environment to maintain a classroom climate that promotes the lifelong pursuit of learning and encourages cooperation, leadership, and mutual respect.* Jacob Kounin believed that teachers should display certain management skills, including *overlapping*, use of the *ripple effect*, and *withitness.* Eliminate A because *overlapping* is the classroom management skill of being able to do more than one thing at a time, such as moving to stand beside students who are off-task, monitoring the rest of the class, and staying tuned to the instructional task, all simultaneously. Eliminate C because the *ripple effect* is the classroom management skill that occurs when a teacher reminds an off-task student to get back to work and all the other off-task students also return to their assignment. Eliminate D because *withitness* is the classroom management skill that means a teacher is aware of what is happening in the classroom at all times—the teacher has "eyes in the back of the head," so to speak. *Halting time* is <u>not</u> a classroom management skill. Choice B is the correct response.

65. **C** This question deals with **communication.** Thus, its primary focus is Competency 007: *The teacher uses effective verbal, nonverbal, and media communication techniques to shape the classroom into a community of learners engaged in active inquiry, collaborative exploration, and supportive interactions.* This is a priority-setting question—you must select the *most* probable

answer choice. Eliminate A, B, and D because they deal with keeping students on task, which relates to **classroom management** (Competency 011). Ms. Brazil's questioning strategy may result in better classroom behavior, but this probably is not Ms. Brazil's *primary* reason for stopping the video and prompting the students to consider the ideas presented. Classroom management is an important teacher function; however, teachers' primary concerns should be with helping students construct meaning from their classroom experiences. Ms. Brazil is *most* probably motivated by her awareness that teachers' efforts to maintain and reinforce student involvement correlates with students' cognitive engagement. Giving students opportunities to think about and discuss the ideas in the video will help them create new understandings and reflect on old ones. By posing key questions, Ms. Brazil is likely to keep the students focused, involved, and engaged in learning. Choice C is the correct response.

66. **B**   This question deals with **communication.** Thus, its primary focus is Competency 007: *The teacher uses effective verbal, nonverbal, and media communication techniques to shape the classroom into a community of learners engaged in active inquiry, collaborative exploration, and supportive interactions.* Eliminate A and C because these types of questions elicit closed responses at lower levels of thinking. Eliminate D because *affective* refers to feelings and emotions, not problem solving. Divergent questions are open-ended and thus would elicit a variety of ideas for problem solving. Choice B is the correct response.

67. **B**   This question deals with **how learning occurs.** Thus, its primary focus is Competency 004: *The teacher understands how learning occurs and can apply this understanding to design and implement effective instruction.* This is a priority-setting question—you must select the *most* consistent answer choice. Eliminate A because it relates to **classroom management** (Competency 011). Ms. Kawasaki's classroom interactions reflect a learner-centered approach. Eliminate C and D because they are teacher-centered approaches. Ms. Kawasaki's approach to teaching is consistent with constructivism. *Constructivism* is a learner-centered approach to teaching that emphasizes teaching for understanding predicated on the concept that students construct knowledge for themselves based on what they already know and by interactions with their environment. Choice B is the correct response.

68. **C**   This question deals with **professionalism.** Thus, its primary focus is Competency 012: *The teacher is a reflective practitioner who knows how to promote his or her own professional growth and can work cooperatively with other professionals in the system to create a school culture that enhances learning and encourages positive change.* Eliminate A and D because these measures are unprofessional and inappropriate. Eliminate B because it involves a

one-way communication (Ms. Kawasaki to the principal), which is less likely to build a positive relationship between Ms. Kawasaki and the principal than Choice C. Currently, principals are accustomed to "walk-throughs" (unannounced visits). So, Ms. Kawasaki should invite Ms. Oliver to frequently stop by to observe Ms. Kawasaki's methods and their effects. Choice C is the correct response.

69. **C**   This question deals with **communication.** Thus, its primary focus is Competency 007: *The teacher uses effective verbal, nonverbal, and media communication techniques to shape the classroom into a community of learners engaged in active inquiry, collaborative exploration, and supportive interactions.* Eliminate A because effective teachers ask questions of all students, regardless of where they are seated. Eliminate B because convergent questions elicit lower-level thinking. Eliminate D because effective teachers provide sufficient wait time, rephrase the question, and/or provide supportive feedback (For example, "Why don't you pursue that thought, Ricardo?") to increase the number and quality of student responses. Choice C is the correct response.

70. **B**   This question deals with **communication.** Thus, its primary focus is Competency 007: *The teacher uses effective verbal, nonverbal, and media communication techniques to shape the classroom into a community of learners engaged in active inquiry, collaborative exploration, and supportive interactions.* This is a priority-setting question—you must select the *main* reason. Research regarding wait time indicates that the desire to avoid silence, a cultural norm in our society, can cause a teacher to become very uncomfortable and unable to wait three seconds or more for students' responses (B), even though waiting for students to respond communicates positive expectations for them and results in more thoughtful responses, thereby enhancing achievement. Choices A, C, and D are possible reasons teachers may find the three-second wait time difficult to implement, but research indicates that the cultural norm against silence is the strongest factor working against sufficient wait time. Choice B is the correct response.

71. **C**   This question deals with **planning.** Thus, its primary focus is Competency 006: *The teacher uses planning processes to design outcome-oriented learning experiences that foster understanding and encourage self-directed thinking and learning in both individual and collaborative settings.* Eliminate A because *focus* in the traditional lesson cycle would correspond to *Engage* in the 5E model. Eliminate B because *guided practice* in the traditional lesson cycle generally would occur during the *Explain* component of the 5E model. Eliminate D because *closure* would occur during the *Elaborate* component of the 5E model. In Texas, the last *E* in the 5E model is more directly about *assessment*, rather than about

evaluation. During *Evaluate*, the teacher assesses the students' understanding of concepts. This component would correspond to the *check for mastery* component of the traditional lesson cycle. Choice C is the correct response.

72. **C** This question deals with **instructional strategies.** Thus, its primary focus is Competency 008: *The teacher uses a variety of instructional strategies and roles to facilitate learning and to help students become independent thinkers and problem solvers who use higher-order thinking in the classroom and the real world.* Critical thinking is the mental process of acquiring information, then evaluating it to reach a logical conclusion. Eliminate Roman II because memorizing rules does not promote critical thinking. Eliminate A, B, and D. To promote critical thinking in her classroom, Ms. Kawasaki should teach for deeper understanding of content, because deeper understanding of content and thinking critically are inseparable (Roman I); require students to justify the reasoning behind their conclusions, because this will force students to critically analyze their and others' thinking (Roman III); and help students develop metacognitive strategies (Roman IV), because when students receive instruction and guidance in how to become aware of their own thinking processes (metacognition), they become better critical thinkers. Choice C is the correct response.

73. **D** This question deals with **motivation.** Thus, its primary focus is Competency 005: *The teacher understands how motivation affects group and individual behavior and learning and can apply this understanding to promote student learning.* Eliminate A and B because they relate to **how learning occurs** (Competency 004). Eliminate C because it pertains to **classroom management** (Competency 011). Ms. Kawasaki is likely to be aware that giving students control over their learning experiences motivates students to achieve. Choice D is the correct response.

74. **B** This question deals with **instructional strategies.** Thus, its primary focus is Competency 008: *The teacher uses a variety of instructional strategies and roles to facilitate learning and to help students become independent thinkers and problem solvers who use higher-order thinking in the classroom and the real world.* Eliminate A, C, and D because they disagree with research findings. Ms. Kawasaki and Ms. Harrison are likely to be aware that most often it is recommended that tutors and tutees be separated by two to three grade levels. Slavin suggests that this is partly because students may look up to an older student and accept the person as a tutor, but might resent a same-age classmate appointed to tutor them. Research investigating the effects of cross-age tutoring on student achievement has found that, in general, the achievement of both tutors and tutees increases. Choice B is the correct choice.

75. **B** This question deals with **motivation.** Thus, its primary focus is Competency 005: *The teacher understands how motivation affects group and individual behavior and learning and can apply this understanding to promote student learning.* Eliminate Roman I because praise should be specific and given contingent on appropriate behaviors or accomplishments. Eliminate A and C. The remaining Choices B and D both contain Roman IV, so you need to decide between Roman II and III. Eliminate Roman II because praise that is given for participation may be viewed as superficial by the student. Eliminate D. Teachers should be discriminate in their use of praise. It should specify the behavior or accomplishment (Roman III) and give students feedback on the quality of their work (Roman IV). Choice B is the correct response.

76. **B** This question deals with **professionalism.** Thus, its primary focus is Competency 012: *The teacher is a reflective practitioner who knows how to promote his or her own professional growth and can work cooperatively with other professionals in the system to create a school culture that enhances learning and encourages positive change.* Teachers in Texas are expected to exhibit the highest standards of professionalism and ethical conduct. They should become familiar with the *Code of Ethics and Standard Practices for Texas Educators.* Eliminate A, C, and D because these are standards in the *Code of Ethics and Standard Practices for Texas Educators.* Choice B is the correct response.

77. **C** This question deals with **professionalism.** Thus, its primary focus is Competency 012: *The teacher is a reflective practitioner who knows how to promote his or her own professional growth and can work cooperatively with other professionals in the system to create a school culture that enhances learning and encourages positive change.* Eliminate A and D because the question is about how Ms. Kawasaki teaches, not about how she organizes her instruction or about how she enhances her own skills and knowledge (professional growth). Eliminate B because it is off-topic. Principle V of the *Code of Ethics and Standard Practices for Texas Educators* requires ethical conduct toward parents and communities. By making connections between a lesson's content and familiar stories and information from the home and community, Ms. Kawasaki is endeavoring to understand community cultures and relate the home environment of students to the school (Standard 2 of Principle V). Choice C is the correct response.

78. **C** This question deals with **assessment.** Thus, its primary focus is Competency 010: *The teacher uses processes of informal and formal assessment to understand individual learners, monitor instructional effectiveness, and shape instruction.* There are advantages and disadvantages associated with different assessment tools. Eliminate A because *norm-referenced* assessment refers to the use of standardized tests that focus on a comparison of students' score to those of a "norm" group of students, so would not

necessarily show achievement of district academic goals. Eliminate B because teacher-made tests may lack validity and/or reliability. Eliminate D because *psychomotor* tests assess physical, not academic, skills. Teachers should know that *criterion-referenced* tests are used to compare scores against a predetermined minimum standard of competency. These types of tests would be the *best* indicators to help the district assess student progress toward the academic goals set by the strategic planning committee. Choice C is the correct response.

79. **D** This question deals with **assessment.** Thus, its primary focus is Competency 010. *The teacher uses processes of information and formal assessment to understand individual learners, monitor instructional effectiveness, and shape instruction.* This is a priority-setting question—you must select the *first* step. Eliminate A and B because mastery grading is based on the number of units completed or skills mastered, not on cut-off scores or improvement based on prior knowledge. Eliminate C because means are immaterial—students' individual mastery of skills determines their scores. To implement grading based on mastery, the *first* step is to define the content and skill objectives to be learned. Choice D is the correct response.

80. **D** This question deals with **assessment.** Thus, its primary focus is Competency 010: *The teacher uses the processes of informal and formal assessment to understand individual learners, monitor instructional effectiveness, and shape instruction.* Educators should be aware of the ramifications of various grading practices and their effects on students. The phrase "grading on a curve" means that the grades A, B, C, D, and F are distributed among the students according to percentages consistent with a normal curve distribution. Students' scores are determined relative to the mean of all the scores—with scores near the mean receiving grades of C, scores specified distances below the mean receiving grades of D or F, and scores specified distances above the mean receiving grades of B or A. Thus, the more able students need only do better than their classmates to earn a high grade, which may or may not mean they have to do more work. Eliminate A. Eliminate B because it is unrelated to the idea of "grading on a curve." Eliminate C because if a teacher truly grades on a curve, then a certain percentage of the students must make Fs. The strategic planning committee should be made aware that "grading on a curve" means at least some of the students, no matter how bright, should receive failing marks. Choice D is the correct response.

81. **B** This question deals with **professionalism.** Thus, its primary focus is Competency 012: *The teacher is a reflective practitioner who knows how to promote his or her own professional growth and can work cooperatively with other professionals in the system to create a school culture that enhances learning and encourages positive change.* Teachers should be aware that accountability

refers to professionalism and effective teaching practices. According to TEC 21.351, teachers are to be appraised based on observable, job-related behavior, including (a) teachers' implementation of discipline management procedures (Roman IV) and (b) the performance of teachers' students (Roman I). Eliminate A, C, and D. Choice B is the correct response.

82. **A** This question deals with **planning.** Thus, its primary focus is Competency 006: *The teacher uses planning processes to design outcome-oriented learning experiences that foster understanding and encourage self-directed thinking and learning in both individual and collaborative settings.* Eliminate B and D because they relate to **motivation** (Competency 005); besides, Ms. Cantu did not involve the students when she transformed the classroom into an "ocean." Eliminate C because it relates to **classroom management.** When planning how to begin her lesson, Ms. Cantu was likely to have been aware that providing the children with a concrete experience would make their study of the ocean more meaningful. Choice A is the correct response.

83. **A** This question deals with **how learning occurs.** Thus, its primary focus is Competency 004: *The teacher understands how learning occurs and can apply this understanding to design and implement effective instruction.* Eliminate B and C because they relate to **communication** (Competency 007); besides, they are not supported by the stimulus—you are not told that Ms. Cantu is asking questions or providing feedback during the discussion. Ms. Cantu is aware that when teachers share their understandings before the children have an opportunity to express their understandings, the children often quit thinking and simply accept whatever the teacher has to say as "correct." Eliminate D. By not judging the contributions, Ms. Cantu does not prematurely shut off the children's thinking. Choice A is the correct response.

84. **D** This question deals with **students' self-esteem.** Thus, its primary focus is Competency 002: *The teacher considers environmental factors that may affect learning in designing a supportive and responsive classroom community that promotes all students' learning and self-esteem.* Eliminate A because it relates to **motivation** (Competency 005). Eliminate B because it relates to **how learning occurs** (Competency 004). Eliminate C because it relates to **developmentally appropriate instruction** (Competency 001). By displaying students' ideas, Ms. Cantu sends them the positive message that she values what they have to say, which enhances their feelings of self-worth. This behavior demonstrates that Ms. Cantu understands factors that influence students' perceptions of their own worth and potential. Choice D is the correct response.

85. **C** This question deals with **school-home relationships.** Thus, its primary focus is Competency 013: *The teacher knows how to foster strong school-home relationships that support student achievement of desired learning outcomes.* Eliminate Roman I because this probably is inappropriate—some employers would prefer that employees not receive personal e-mail at work. Eliminate A, B, and D. Teachers need to recognize the importance of ongoing and positive relationships with parents/guardians. Writing personal notes in report cards (Roman II), scheduling parent-teacher conferences (Roman III), and sending letters to parents/guardians (Roman IV) would all be appropriate ways to communicate with parents/guardians during the school year. Choice C is the correct response.

86. **C** This question deals with **school-home relationships.** Thus, its primary focus is Competency 013: *The teacher knows how to foster strong school-home relationships that support student achievement of desired learning outcomes.* Eliminate Roman II because it would violate the Family Educational Rights and Privacy Act (also known as the Buckley Amendment) to show a student's work to parents other than the parents of the student whose work it is. Eliminate A, B, and D. Successful parent-teacher conferences can be the key that enhances the student's growth and promotes learning. When preparing for a parent-teacher conference, have a written agenda (Roman I), review current daily grades and tests results (Roman III), and keep anecdotal records (Roman IV). Choice C is the correct response.

87. **D** This question deals with **students' self-esteem.** Thus, its primary focus is Competency 002: *The teacher considers environmental factors that may affect learning in designing a supportive and responsive classroom community that promotes all students' learning and self-esteem.* Eliminate A and B because these measures may heighten Tabatha's stress level by making her more aware of her limitations in comparison to the rest of the class. Eliminate C because a "pep talk" is unlikely to convince Tabatha that she is capable. Students who have a pattern of failure may be victims of *learned helplessness.* They may feel doomed to failure because they believe their abilities are fixed and thus they are incapable of success. By planning activities in which Tabatha achieves success, Ms. Cantu will help Tabatha feel capable and competent. Choice D is the correct response.

88. **B** This question deals with **school-home relationships.** Thus, its primary focus is Competency 013: *The teacher knows how to foster strong school-home relationships that support student achievement of desired learning outcomes.* Eliminate A because this would be inappropriate and unprofessional. Eliminate C and D because these measures are coercive. Ms. Cantu recognizes the importance of establishing and maintaining strong school-home relationships. In the future, when setting up parent conferences she

should make it a practice to inform parents the reason for the conference when she first contacts them. Tabatha's parents may be reluctant because they fear Ms. Cantu is upset with Tabatha about something. Ms. Cantu can *best* deal with these parents by explaining, in the next phone call, her reasons for the parent-teacher conference. This step should alleviate any concerns that the parents may be having. Choice B is the correct response.

89. **D** This question deals with **planning.** Thus, its primary focus is Competency 006: *The teacher uses planning processes to design outcome-oriented learning experiences that foster understanding and encourage self-directed thinking and learning in both individual and collaborative settings.* The 5E model for lessons encourages student discourse and interaction during all the components. Classroom interactions are often lively exchanges, with the teacher and the students thinking, talking, conjecturing, and agreeing and disagreeing among themselves during the various components of the lesson, even *evaluation.* The smiley-sad-face device could be used throughout the lesson. Choice D is the correct response.

90. **A** This question deals with **how learning occurs.** Thus, its primary focus is Competency 004: *The teacher understands how learning occurs and can apply this understanding to design and implement effective instruction.* The smiley-sad-face device is something the children can touch and see, but not hear. Eliminate B and D because visual and right-brain-dominant children prefer to learn by seeing or reading something. Eliminate C because tactile/kinesthetic children prefer to learn by using physical objects or being physically involved. Left-brain-dominant learners respond to verbal instruction. Therefore, they would *least* benefit from using the smiley-sad-face device. Choice A is the correct response.

CHAPTER 11

A PRACTICE SECONDARY PROFESSIONAL DEVELOPMENT TEST

Practice Test Directions

The test consists of 90 multiple-choice questions with four answer choices. Read each question carefully and choose the ONE best answer. Mark your answer on the answer sheet (see page 427) beside the number that matches the question number. Completely fill in the space that has the same letter as the answer you have selected.

Sample Question

1. Austin is the capital of what state?

    A. Arkansas
    B. California
    C. Tennessee
    D. Texas

Austin is the capital of Texas. Choice D is the correct response. You would mark your answer beside question number 1 on the answer sheet and you would fill in the space corresponding to the letter D as follows:

1.  Ⓐ Ⓑ Ⓒ ●

Mark only one answer for each question. If you change an answer, completely erase the old answer before marking the new one. You should answer all the questions since *you are not penalized for a wrong answer.*

You will have approximately five hours to complete the test. You may go back and forth through the test as you desire. When you have completed the test, turn to the answer key and answer explanations at the end of the test to check your answers.

Ms. Smith, a new tenth-grade English language arts teacher, is having a frustrating year. She assigns a writing assignment on "What Is the Value of an Education?" to her class and is disappointed when most of the papers she receives from the students are boring and uninteresting. She discusses her dismay with her colleague, Mr. Christopher, who has also given his tenth-grade English class a writing assignment. She tells him, "The students are very nice and well-behaved, but they seem either overwhelmed or uninterested in the writing assignments." When Mr. Christopher shows Ms. Smith the papers he has collected from his class, she is impressed that they are neatly typed, contain few technical errors, and, most important, the majority of the papers are imaginative and creative. She asks Mr. Christopher how he motivates his students to write such good papers. He tells her that he begins by brainstorming with the whole class to obtain a list of possible topics that students can write on. Then he allows the students to select the topics they want to write on from the class-generated list. He assigns the students to cooperative learning groups in which they help each other plan their essays, critique each other's drafts, and help each other with editing. Each group works at a computer station to create the written drafts and final versions to be turned in.

1. Ms. Smith's decision to consult Mr. Christopher *best* illustrates which of the following principles?

    A. Teachers should be reflective practitioners who know how to work within a learning community to promote professional growth.
    B. Teachers should understand how motivation affects individual behavior and can apply this understanding to promote learning.
    C. Teachers should know how to design outcome-oriented learning experiences that encourage self-directed thinking in a collaborative setting.
    D. Teachers should know how to use effective verbal communication techniques to shape the classroom into a community of learners.

2. When talking to Ms. Smith, Mr. Christopher describes classroom strategies that he uses. Which of the following is Mr. Christopher likely using to motivate students?

    I.   extrinsic motivation
    II. intrinsic motivation
    III. group dynamics
    IV. self-fulfilling prophecy

    A. I and II only
    B. I, II, and III only
    C. II and III only
    D. II and IV only

3. Which of the following is probably Mr. Christopher's purpose for allowing the students in the cooperative learning groups to critique each other's papers?

A. Grading the papers after they are turned in will be easier for Mr. Christopher because the brighter students can correct the other students' mistakes before he sees the papers.

B. Students who write poorly will have an opportunity to compare their writing ability to that of more capable students and, as a result, be inspired to try harder.

C. Students will have the opportunity to help and encourage each other, and, as a result, enhance each other's learning.

D. Students will have the opportunity to critically assess their own strengths and weaknesses regarding their ability to write.

4. Which of the following computer applications did Mr. Christopher's students most likely use for creating drafts and finished versions of their papers?

A. database
B. graphing
C. spreadsheet
D. word processing

5. Which of the following is most in accord with current principles of professional development of Texas teachers?

A. Teachers should have expertise in computer program development.
B. Teachers should acquire and practice computer maintenance skills.
C. Teachers should be literate in the use of computers.
D. Teachers should have basic skills in computer hardware repair.

Prior to her discussion with Mr. Christopher, Ms. Smith had been using whole-group instruction in the form of lecturing to her class. She usually lectured most of the fifty-five-minute class period because she could present many facts and ideas to her students without using a lot of equipment and materials. Furthermore, the students seldom interrupted, so she was able to cover a lot of the subject matter each class period. After visiting with Mr. Christopher, she recognizes that she may be limited in her instructional strategies and decides to experiment with other ways of teaching students. One of the first "new" instructional strategies Ms. Smith wants to try is letting her students work in cooperative learning groups. From Mr. Christopher, she has obtained an authoritive book that offers some helpful guidelines on using cooperative learning.

6. Ms. Smith usually lectured most of the class period; however, most authorities agree that classroom lectures should be no longer than:

A. 15 minutes.
B. 20 minutes.
C. 25 minutes.
D. 30 minutes.

7. Ms. Smith will need to learn that changing from whole-class instruction to students working in small groups likely will require her to:

I. eliminate the need for teacher presentations to convey information and skills.

II. have a system for appointing the highest achieving students as group leaders.

III. prepare students for working in small groups.

IV. organize and structure group tasks.

A. I and II only
B. I, II, and III only
C. II, III, and IV only
D. III and IV only

8. While Ms. Smith's students are working in their groups, it is important that she actively monitor the groups at all times in order to:

   A. prevent errors and illogical thinking on the part of students.
   B. assign students to tell the other students what to do if a group takes too much time.
   C. assess and guide individual and group collaborative skills.
   D. direct student plans for displaying completed papers.

As the year progresses, Ms. Smith and Mr. Christopher find many opportunities to visit and exchange teaching ideas. One afternoon, Ms. Smith asks Mr. Christopher for suggestions about how to improve her communication skills. Mr. Christopher recommends that she monitor her classroom interactions with students. A few days afterward, the following episode occurs in Ms. Smith's class.

Ms. Smith: Class, today your daily ten-minute writing activity is on the subject of school uniforms. Please begin writing in your journals and stop when I give the signal.

[Ms. Smith, noticing that Sarah is frowning, walks over to Sarah's desk.]

Sarah: What do you want us to write? I don't understand.

Ms. Smith: Just tell what you think about school uniforms. Do you think adopting school uniforms is a good idea or a bad idea?

Sarah: It's a dumb idea, and I think writing for ten minutes every day is also a dumb idea.

Ms. Smith: You sound upset, Sarah. Would you like to talk to me about what's bothering you?

Sarah: Well, you know I haven't been going to this school very long. I'm afraid you'll make me read what I write and the other kids will make fun of it.

Ms. Smith: Your journal is your personal writing. You will not have to read aloud what you write unless you want to. I think you probably have some good ideas about school uniforms. What don't you try jotting down a few thoughts? You may even want to read your journal entry aloud to the class when you're finished.

9. Which of the following tenets would be *most* helpful for Ms. Smith to consider when beginning the next ten-minute writing assignment?

   A. Effective teachers communicate instructional tasks clearly to students.
   B. Effective teachers know how to shape the classroom into a community of learners engaged in active inquiry.
   C. Effective teachers use a variety of modes and tools of communication.
   D. Effective teachers appreciate the cultural dimensions of communication.

10. In her interactions with Sarah, which of the following elements of effective communication did Ms. Smith exhibit?

    I. simplifying and restating
    II. being sensitive to nonverbal cues
    III. being a thoughtful questioner
    IV. being a reflective listener

    A. I, II, and III only
    B. I, II, and IV only
    C. II and III only
    D. III only

11. Cooperative learning would be *most* useful when:

   A. the teacher wants an ongoing support system for students.
   B. the teacher wants to engage the students in guided practice.
   C. students are younger or less mature.
   D. the topic has simple concepts to which students will react in similar ways.

12. Ms. Smith is aware that some parents are opposed to the use of cooperative learning groups in schools. When she discusses this with Mr. Christopher, he tells her he has not had any complaints from parents; however, he might go on to explain to Ms. Smith that a major justification for the use of cooperative learning groups in the classroom is:

   A. the prevalence of group and human interaction in everyday life, especially in the workplace.
   B. the need for students to develop an understanding of the society in which they will live.
   C. the failure of parents to accept responsibility for teaching their children collaborative skills.
   D. the necessary respite that group work provides from the more mentally challenging activities of other instructional strategies.

SET 1 ENDS HERE

SET 2 BEGINS HERE

> Mr. Hennington teaches economics at Springfield High School. His first instructional unit each semester is on the stock market. As an introduction, he shows the students a video that includes real footage of the New York Stock Exchange. He then tells the students they are going to "play the market" this semester as members of an investment team. Using transparency copies from the *Wall Street Journal*, he shows the students how stock prices are listed on a daily basis and goes on to present additional information on how the stock market functions. After his presentation, he assigns students to teams of five students each. Each team is allowed $10,000 with which they may "purchase" stock. The team must decide among themselves which stocks and how much of each they wish to invest in. This will become their stock market "portfolio."

13. Mr. Hennington began his first lesson on the stock market by showing the students a videotape on the topic. This *best* demonstrates application of which of the following principles?

    A. The teacher knows how to enhance learning for all students through the appropriate use of instructional materials and resources.
    B. The teacher knows how to make instruction relevant to students' own needs and purposes.
    C. The teacher knows how to help students acquire strategies and skills that will be useful to them in the real world.
    D. The teacher is aware of the value of technology in promoting efficient time use and professional growth.

14. Before he showed the videotape to his class, Mr. Hennington previewed it. Which of the following would be the *least* important reason for Mr. Hennington to preview the video?

    A. He wants to judge the quality of the video material.
    B. He wants to make sure the material is appropriate for the grade level of his students.
    C. He wants to make sure the content matches the instructional objectives.
    D. He wants to make sure the video is entertaining.

15. Mr. Hennington has set aside thirty-five minutes for the students to work in their teams. This time set aside for the activity is *best* described as:

    A. academic learning time.
    B. allocated time.
    C. wait time.
    D. time-on-task.

16. The actual time Mr. Hennington's students appear to be working in their teams is *best* described as:

    A. academic learning time.
    B. allocated time.
    C. wait time.
    D. time-on-task.

17. The amount of time an individual student spends learning successfully while working in a team is *best* described as:

    A. academic learning time.
    B. allocated time.
    C. wait time.
    D. time-on-task.

Two years ago, Mr. Hennington attended a summer staff-development training program on learning styles. He now has a reputation for being able to teach even the lowest-ability students. Students enjoy learning in his class because he makes them feel special and successful. He believes that teachers can enhance their effectiveness by providing instructional activities that accommodate various learning styles.

18. Mr. Hennington's attention to learning style *best* illustrates which of the following principles?

    A. Effective teachers should use outcome-oriented learning experiences that foster self-directed thinking.
    B. Effective teachers hold students accountable for reasonable standards of performance.
    C. Effective teachers group students appropriately for the activity and the environment.
    D. Effective teachers are aware of factors that affect learning and design instruction accordingly.

19. Which of the following types of learners will *least* likely benefit from Mr. Hennington's video and transparency presentation?

    A. auditory learners
    B. visual learners
    C. tactile/kinesthetic learners
    D. left-brain dominant learners

20. Educators refer to the way a student takes in information through the five primary senses as:

    A. sensory aptitude strength.
    B. sensory dependency strength.
    C. sensory modality strength.
    D. sensory motor strength.

21. Maria, a student in Mr. Hennington's class, has a field-dependent learning style. Mr. Hennington might expect Maria to experience particular difficulty:

    A. in social situations.
    B. with unstructured learning activities.
    C. using intuition.
    D. working in groups.

22. Ryan, another of Mr. Hennington's students, has the ability to find hidden patterns which suggests that Ryan:

    A. is likely to prefer studying in nonscientific areas.
    B. tends to be influenced by suggestion.
    C. may have difficulty collaborating when working in groups.
    D. may require more frequent feedback.

23. Mr. Hennington regularly makes connections between a lesson's content and familiar stories and information from the home and community. This practice complies *most* closely with which of the following standards of the *Code of Ethics and Standard Practices for Texas Educators*?

    A. The educator shall organize instruction that seeks to accomplish objectives related to learning.
    B. The educator shall endeavor to present facts without distortion.
    C. The educator shall endeavor to understand community cultures and relate the home environment of students to the school.
    D. The educator shall continue professional growth.

Ms. Allen, who has the room across the hall from Mr. Hennington, is a veteran teacher with twenty years' experience. After school one day, she walks into Mr. Hennington's classroom and asks, "Are you sure this stock market game your students are doing is educational? It sounds to me like they are just playing around." Although Mr. Hennington feels confident about the educational merits of the stock market simulation activity, he has been apprehensive that teachers like Ms. Allen, who use more traditional types of instructional strategies, might see it as "playing around." He does not want to be argumentative with Ms. Allen, so he explains calmly and politely why he feels the activity is worthwhile.

24. Which of the following is a *major* value of a simulation activity?

    A. It will enhance students' community awareness.
    B. It will enhance the students' role-playing skills.
    C. It will encourage students to seek out knowledge actively.
    D. It will require less time than expository teaching methods.

25. A *major* limitation of using simulation activities is that:

    A. they focus too much on basic skills.
    B. they often require a considerable amount of time.
    C. students usually do not find them interesting or fun.
    D. students find the realism too threatening.

26. By involving his students in a stock market simulation, Mr. Hennington is most likely attempting to do which of the following?

    I.   He wants to give students an opportunity to plan and try out strategies for attacking problems.
    II. He wants to deepen the students' insights and understandings of economics.
    III. He wants to lead students to recognize that most problems in the real world have one right answer.
    IV. He wants to give students an opportunity to engage in a real-life situation, but with harmful factors removed.

    A. I, II, and III only
    B. I, II, and IV only
    C. II, III, and IV only
    D. II and IV only

27. To ensure the success of the simulation, Mr. Hennington should avoid:

    A. becoming directly involved in the make-believe situation.
    B. permitting the students freedom to make mistakes.
    C. giving the students assistance when they ask for it.
    D. assigning roles to the students.

28. Mr. Hennington chose *not* to be argumentative with Ms. Allen. This decision is *most* in accord with which of the following?

    A. The teacher is a reflective practitioner who knows how to promote his or her professional growth.
    B. The teacher appreciates the cultural dimensions of communication.
    C. The teacher knows how to work within the system to address issues and make decisions appropriately.
    D. The teacher knows how to work effectively as a member of a learning community.

29. Later that afternoon, the principal tells Mr. Hennington that Ms. Allen has complained to the principal that Mr. Hennington was rude and unprofessional toward Ms. Allen during their earlier conversation. Ms. Allen's behavior violates which of the standards regarding ethical conduct toward professional colleagues?

   A. The educator shall not reveal confidential information concerning colleagues unless disclosure serves professional purposes or is required by law.
   B. The educator shall not intentionally deny or impede a colleague in the exercise or enjoyment of any professional right or responsibility.
   C. The educator shall not use coercive means or promise special treatment in order to influence professional decisions or colleagues.
   D. The educator shall not willfully make false statements about a colleague of the school system.

Each week the investment teams must draw graphs depicting the daily activities for each of the various stocks in their portfolios. They also have to determine their overall profit or loss status on a weekly basis. At the end of the semester, they must summarize their activities and present a report to the entire class.

30. Mr. Hennington's purpose for having students work in investment teams most likely is:

   A. to provide peer support for academic performance.
   B. to add a measure of individual inquiry to whole-group instruction.
   C. to provide opportunities for the teacher to direct team decisions.
   D. to provide a highly sequenced structure for instruction.

31. During the simulation activity, Mr. Hennington's primary role should be as:

   A. a judge.
   B. a supervisor.
   C. an arbitrator.
   D. a facilitator.

32. Mr. Hennington arranges for his students to go to the school computer lab and use a computerized presentation package to create their final reports. He *most* likely is attempting to:

   A. encourage students to develop multiple perspectives.
   B. relate lessons to students' personal interests.
   C. encourage students to use technology to enhance communication.
   D. use a variety of techniques to influence students' perceptions of technology.

At midsemester, Mr. Hennington has the students complete the following questionnaire:

Please respond to the following questions. You do not have to sign your name.
There are no right or wrong answers. Just be honest about how you feel. Use the back of the page if more room is needed.

1. What do you like *best* about this course?

2. What do you like *least* about this course?

3. What improvements would you suggest for this course?

---

33. This type of assessment is called a:

    A. criterion-referenced assessment.
    B. formative assessment.
    C. norm-referenced assessment.
    D. summative assessment.

34. By involving the students in this way, Mr. Hennington is *most* likely promoting learning by:

    A. increasing the students' desire for teacher-directed activities.
    B. enhancing students' inferential skills.
    C. enhancing students' self-esteem.
    D. increasing students' self-evaluation skills.

At the end of the semester, Mr. Hennington asked the students to assess the effectiveness of their investment team's stock market strategies as they participated in the simulation activity.

35. This type of assessment is called a:

    A. criterion-referenced assessment.
    B. formative assessment.
    C. norm-referenced assessment.
    D. summative assessment.

36. Which of the following is a *major* benefit of having the students reflect on the effectiveness of their investment team's decision making?

    A. It will promote a healthy competitive spirit among the students.
    B. It will allow Mr. Hennington to identify those students who exhibited leadership skills.
    C. It will allow Mr. Hennington to evaluate the students' mastery of the objectives for the economics unit.
    D. It will promote self-assessment on the part of the student.

37. As part of his ongoing effort to encourage his students to use higher-order thinking, which of the following would Mr. Hennington *most* likely use to promote evaluation-level thinking?

    A. Give a comprehensive multiple-choice exam over stock market terminology.
    B. Give a comprehensive true-false exam over stock market principles.
    C. Have students write a paragraph explaining the procedure for purchasing stocks.
    D. Hold a class discussion on the merits of the stock market simulation activity.

SET 2 ENDS HERE

> Ms. Mendoza, an eighth-grade history teacher, is the team leader of an interdisciplinary team at Cullen Middle School. The members of Ms. Mendoza's team are Mr. Simmons, the new language arts teacher, Ms. Stewart, the mathematics teacher, and Mr. Zhong, the science teacher. Together this group of teachers instructs the same group of 102 students. They share a common planning period so that they can meet on a weekly basis to plan the curriculum and discuss the progress and needs of their students.

38. Establishing interdisciplinary teams is *most* in accord with which of the following principles?

    A. Teachers should vary their roles in the instructional process in relation to the level of need of their students.
    B. Teachers should know how to work cooperatively with colleagues to create a school culture that enhances learning.
    C. Teachers should know how to foster effective, constructive, and purposeful communication with others.
    D. Teachers should know how to promote student ownership of and membership in a smoothly functioning learning community.

39. Which of the following is *not* an advantage of using interdisciplinary instruction?

    A. The public views it as what schools should be doing.
    B. Students can carry out realistic problem-solving.
    C. Scheduling of students can be implemented with ease.
    D. Opportunities to individualize instruction are optimized.

40. Which of the following should be heeded when planning interdisciplinary instruction?

    I. Include affective objectives.
    II. Use a variety of teaching strategies.
    III. Focus evaluation on peer comparison.
    IV. Make the information practical.

    A. I, II, and III only
    B. I, II, and IV only
    C. I and II only
    D. III and IV only

Mr. Simmons, the new teacher on the interdisciplinary team, has been having a discipline problem in his third-period class. Becky, who frequently completes her work before everyone else does, usually spends the rest of the class period entertaining her classmates. Other class members laugh out loud when Becky makes comic faces or funny comments. Clearly, Becky enjoys the attention she is getting with her antics. Mr. Simmons is unsure of what he should do to discourage Becky's misbehavior, but he is reluctant to discuss his problem at the weekly meeting of his interdisciplinary team.

41. What is the most likely basis for Mr. Simmons' reluctance to ask his fellow team members for assistance?

    A. Mr. Simmons believes he will be perceived as ill-prepared or incompetent.
    B. Mr. Simmons believes that the best way to learn is to work through problems by yourself.
    C. Ms. Simmons believes that experienced teachers just don't have time to give beginning teachers assistance once school starts.
    D. Mr. Simmons believes that most strategies used by experienced teachers are too difficult for a beginning teacher to use.

42. Finally, Mr. Simmons decides to tell the other team members about the problem he is having with Becky. Of the following suggestions, which is *best* for them to recommend?

    A. He should reprimand Becky every time she causes a disruption.
    B. He should warn Becky that he is going to call her parents the next time she causes a disruption.
    C. He should tell the class that Becky's behavior is inappropriate and that they should ignore it.
    D. He should isolate Becky from the rest of the class when she misbehaves.

43. Another approach that would be particularly effective in dealing with a situation like Mr. Simmons' problem with Becky is to use:

    A. punishment.
    B. praising other students.
    C. group contingencies.
    D. nonverbal cues.

Later in the meeting, Ms. Mendoza tells the team about the phone call she received earlier from Becky's mother, Ms. Turner. She tells them that Ms. Turner wants to meet with the interdisciplinary team to discuss placing Becky in a gifted/talented program. She goes on to say, "Ms. Turner feels Becky is not being challenged by the work she is given at school. She believes Becky is intellectually gifted, and that she needs to be in a challenging and enriching program." The interdisciplinary team spends some time telling one another about Becky's performance in their classes. They determine, that except for mathematics, Becky's grades are not very good. They all agree that, usually, when Becky is working on an assignment or test, she concentrates more on speed than on accuracy. They then go on to discuss how they should handle this situation.

44. When the interdisciplinary team meets with Ms. Turner, it is *most* appropriate that they:

A. begin immediately to tell Ms. Turner about the problems they have had with Becky.
B. tell Ms. Turner that most of the time when parents get involved in their child's schooling, it only hurts the child.
C. make sure that all of the team members have an opportunity to tell Ms. Turner about their experiences with Becky.
D. end the conference by sharing information about Becky's achievements.

45. Which of the following would be the *most* appropriate way for the interdisciplinary team to respond to Ms. Turner's belief that Becky should be in the gifted/talented program?

A. Suggest that Ms. Turner needs to discuss her concerns with the gifted/talented teacher first.
B. Discuss Becky's grades with Ms. Turner and explain that Becky's performance indicates her level of ability is below that of a gifted student.
C. Tell Ms. Turner that Becky's misbehavior in Mr. Simmons' class indicates that she is most likely not intellectually gifted.
D. Explain the gifted/talented program to Ms. Turner and agree to initiate procedures to evaluate Becky.

46. The teacher's description of how Becky works indicates that Becky is *most* likely:

A. a field-independent learner.
B. a field-dependent learner.
C. a reflective learner.
D. an impulsive learner.

47. Becky has shown low performance in most of her classes. Research indicates that many gifted students perform:

A. below their ability level.
B. at their ability level.
C. slightly above their ability level.
D. far above their ability level.

48. If Becky is placed in a gifted/talented
     program, she may be allowed to progress
     more rapidly through the standard
     curriculum through a process *best* known
     as:

     A. higher-order learning.
     B. student-centered inquiry.
     C. adjusted curriculum.
     D. acceleration.

49. Another approach used with
     gifted/talented students is to provide
     special learning experiences that broaden
     or deepen their knowledge of the
     standard curriculum. This is *best* known
     as:

     A. extension.
     B. broadening.
     C. enrichment.
     D. discovery learning.

50. When working with intellectually gifted
     students in a heterogeneous classroom,
     the research on grouping suggests that:

     A. gifted students should work on
         independent projects and not be
         involved in whole-class learning.
     B. a mix of homogeneous and hetero-
         geneous grouping should be used.
     C. cooperative learning groups should
         not be used.
     D. the types of group structure used have
         little consequence.

When Ms. Mendoza's team meets the week before Thanksgiving break, they decide they will begin the next semester with a two-week thematic unit entitled "I Don't Have Anything to Wear!" Mr. Zhong volunteers to create a form they can use for listing an activity for each subject area. Ms. Stewart suggests that after they complete the form, they distribute it to the students as an overview when they begin the unit. Ms. Mendoza says she will be responsible for giving the students the overview and telling them about the unit.

51. The discussion among the team members *best* illustrates that in interdisciplinary teams:

    A. members can provide an expanded pool of ideas.
    B. members can provide support and guidance for each other.
    C. members tend to work harder on improving instructional quality.
    D. members can collaborate in dealing with individual students.

After much discussion and revision, the team reaches consensus on the following overview:

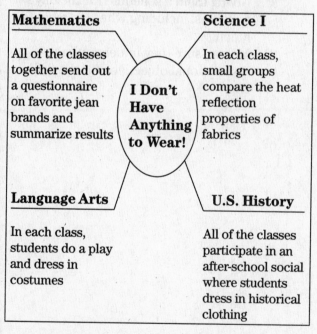

Mathematics	Science I
All of the classes together send out a questionnaire on favorite jean brands and summarize results	In each class, small groups compare the heat reflection properties of fabrics
Language Arts	U.S. History
In each class, students do a play and dress in costumes	All of the classes participate in an after-school social where students dress in historical clothing

(Center: I Don't Have Anything to Wear!)

52. This graphic overview will likely be *most* beneficial for students whose learning style is primarily

    A. analytic.
    B. inductive.
    C. right-brain dominant.
    D. left-brain dominant.

53. In which class is the activity *least* consistent with a tactile/kinesthetic learning style?

    A. language arts
    B. mathematics
    C. Science I
    D. U. S. history

54. Which of the following is most likely to occur when the U.S. history activity takes place?

    A. Both field-independent learners and field-dependent learners will be actively involved.
    B. Field-independent learners will tend to be more passive than field-dependent learners.
    C. Field-dependent learners will tend to be more passive than field-independent learners.
    D. Both field-independent learners and field-dependent learners will be passive.

After the two-week thematic unit on "I Don't Have Anything to Wear!" the team begins a unit organized around the stars and galaxies. Mr. Zhong, the science teacher, invites an astronomer from NASA, which is not far from the school, to visit his class to show and discuss slides taken by the Hubble Space Telescope. After the presentation, the students are very excited and tell Mr. Zhong that they want to learn more about the stars and galaxies. Mr. Zhong tells them that the interdisciplinary team has planned a field trip for the following week to the planetarium at a local university to a show entitled "Mars: The Red Planet."

55. Prior to the astronomer's visit, Mr. Zhong can *best* promote the success of the slide show presentation by:

    A. Visiting the astronomer beforehand to preview and critique the presentation.
    B. Providing the astronomer with the chapter on stars and galaxies from the students' textbook to read beforehand.
    C. Asking the astronomer to recommend some hands-on activities that Mr. Zhong can use with the students after the presentation.
    D. Telling the astronomer what the students already know about the Hubble Space Telescope.

56. Mr. Zhong can best prepare the students for the field trip by:

    I. Reviewing the prior knowledge or concepts needed to understand the planetarium show.
    II. Having the students generate questions about Mars they would like to have answered.
    III. Reviewing conduct rules immediately before leaving for the field trip.
    IV. Giving them a handout that provides suggestions on how to write about their experiences at the planetarium.

    A. I and II only
    B. III and IV only
    C. I, II, and III only
    D. I, II, III, and IV

57. The interdisciplinary team will have ten parent-volunteers to accompany them with the students on the planetarium field trip. The members of the team can *best* prepare the parent-volunteers by:

    A. Telling them beforehand which students in the class are likely to be discipline problems on the field trip.
    B. Asking two parents to volunteer to stay behind and show a video to students who are disciplinary problems.
    C. Giving them a schedule for the day's activities, including where to meet for lunch.
    D. Making sure they understand the instructional objectives for the field trip.

SET 3 ENDS HERE

SET 4 BEGINS HERE

Johnson High School, in which Mr. Harrison teaches ninth-grade health and physical education, has implemented full inclusion. Mr. Harrison recently served on the ARD committee that developed an IEP for Cody, a student who has cerebral palsy and is confined to a wheelchair. The IEP specifies that Cody be mainstreamed into regular health and physical education classes. Although Cody has a serious disability, the committee determined that the "least restrictive environment" for Cody is a regular classroom and physical education class.

58. In planning for instruction, which of the following teaching methods is *most* in accord with the philosophy underlying full inclusion?

   A. programmed instruction
   B. individualized instruction
   C. computer-assisted instruction
   D. cooperative learning

59. According to PL 94-142, placing disabled students in the "least restrictive environment" is *best* in accord with which of the following?

   A. Disabled students are placed in a setting that enables them to function to their fullest capability.
   B. Disabled students are placed in a regular classroom but receive instruction solely from a resource teacher who is also in the room.
   C. Disabled students participate in all regular school activities, regardless of their disabilities.
   D. Disabled students can choose to have instruction in a resource room or in a regular classroom.

60. Mr. Harrison decides to review legislation related to inclusion. When he looks at PL 94-142, he is reminded that this law obligates each state to:

   A. ensure that mildly disabled children are mainstreamed into regular classrooms.
   B. give federal support to arrangements made by local jurisdictions for disabled children.
   C. provide a free and appropriate public education for all disabled children.
   D. integrate all disabled children into regular classrooms.

61. Which of the following are true of the IEP?

   I. The IEP is mandated by the Individuals with Disabilities Education Act.
   II. The IEP is developed after the child has been identified as eligible for special services.
   III. The IEP is developed by a committee.
   IV. The classroom teacher must comply with the IEP.

   A. I, II, and III only
   B. II and IV only
   C. II, III, and IV only
   D. I, II, III, and IV

62. "Due process" under IDEA gives parents the right to:

    A. participate in the decision-making process regarding the educational placements for their children.

    B. select the public schools their children will attend.

    C. interpret the instructional implications of evaluation results.

    D. determine the most appropriate interventions for their children.

Mr. Harrison requests a meeting with Ms. Gauss, the principal, because he is concerned about the inclusion of Cody in his physical education class. He tells Ms. Gauss, "I do not have training in special education. I know that Cody is emotionally and intellectually capable, so I am sure he will do fine in health. I am just not sure that I will be able to meet his needs in physical education class appropriately."

63. Ms. Gauss should inform Mr. Harrison that as Cody's physical education teacher, he can *best* meet his legal and ethical responsibilities by:

    A. updating the IEP for Cody on a regular basis.

    B. providing physical exercise for Cody in a special class composed of students who are similarly physically disabled.

    C. focusing on Cody's progress relative to the specifications of the IEP.

    D. giving Cody physical fitness tests designed especially for disabled students.

64. The *first* thing Mr. Harrison should do in working with Cody in physical education class is:

    A. pair Cody with a sympathetic classmate who can help him maneuver around.

    B. talk with Cody about what kinds of activities he feels capable of doing.

    C. ask the special education teacher to visit the class regularly to observe and evaluate Cody's performance of activities.

    D. ask the special education teacher to provide additional information about how to meet Cody's unique individual needs.

65. Which of the following accommodations for Cody should Mr. Harrison make in the health classroom?

    I. Provide preferential seating for Cody, if needed.

    II. Minimize distractions, such as colorful bulletin boards, in work areas.

    III. Arrange the physical layout to minimize obstructions.

    IV. Arrange the desks so Cody will be able to have privacy.

    A. I and III only

    B. II and IV only

    C. III and IV only

    D. III only

Mr. Harrison has been deliberating on the effectiveness of his classroom management strategies. He has been particularly concerned about how to deal with Larry, a student in his second-period health class. For several months, Mr. Harrison has noticed that Larry often has difficulty paying attention, listening when talked to, following directions, and staying on task. Also, he has observed that Larry often fidgets, talks excessively, interrupts others, and gets up and down out of his seat.

66. Larry's behavior is *most* characteristic of a student who:

    A. has attention deficit hyperactivity disorder.
    B. is severely emotionally disturbed.
    C. is learning disabled.
    D. is educable mentally retarded.

67. The *most* appropriate strategy for Mr. Harrison to use with Larry in health class would be to:

    A. ignore Larry's inappropriate behavior.
    B. provide planned opportunities for physical movement.
    C. send Larry to a time-out room.
    D. use a group-contingencies program.

68. When Mr. Harrison is considering the effectiveness of his classroom management strategies, he should remember that effective classroom managers:

    I. teach and model appropriate behavior.
    II. expect that students should be able to endure lulls in classroom routines or lessons without misbehaving.
    III. organize the classroom and instruction to eliminate conditions conducive to misbehavior.
    IV. help students understand the reasons why inappropriate behavior is unacceptable and cannot be tolerated.

    A. I, II, and III only
    B. I, III, and IV only
    C. II, III, and IV only
    D. I, II, and IV only

69. Which of the following is *least* important for effective classroom management?

    A. communicating clear expectations for student behavior
    B. maintaining accurate and detailed grading procedures
    C. building a positive relationship with students
    D. limiting the amount of time allocated to seatwork

70. For ninth graders, which of the following would be the *most* essential strategy for Mr. Harrison to use for maintaining good classroom order?

    A. Formally teach classroom rules for appropriate behavior.
    B. Have a whole-class discussion on appropriate classroom behavior.
    C. Consistently enforce classroom rules and consequences.
    D. Post a list of classroom rules.

71. Mr. Harrison's students often tell him, "You must have eyes in the back of your head," because he is aware of what they are doing, even when he's not looking directly at them. Mr. Harrison is displaying:

    A. overlapping.
    B. ripple effect.
    C. withitness.
    D. overseeing.

SET 4 ENDS HERE

SET 5 BEGINS HERE

Ms. Reagan has just gotten her first teaching job as an Algebra II teacher at North High School. She has been excited, but also very nervous, about beginning her new job. During the inservice days prior to the first day of classes, the principal tells Ms. Reagan, "I've asked Ms. Flores, who also teaches Algebra II, to be your mentor teacher this year. She should be able to help you with questions or problems that might come up as you get started this year." At the first opportunity, Ms Reagan meets with Ms. Flores to get advice about how she should start off the year. She tells Ms. Flores that before she starts planning instruction, she would like to use some type of assessment to find out how well-prepared the students are for Algebra II in terms of their strengths and weaknesses.

72. Ms. Flores should tell her that the *most* appropriate assessment tool for Ms. Reagan to use to determine the strengths and weakness of her Algebra II students is:

    A. a standardized achievement test.
    B. the final grade in Algebra I.
    C. a diagnostic test.
    D. a norm-referenced test.

73. Ms. Reagan describes a group activity she is considering using as her lesson for the first day of class to Ms. Flores. She tells Ms. Flores, "I think this will allow the students to get acquainted with each other on the first day. What do you think?" Which of the following recommendations should Ms. Flores make to Ms. Reagan?

    A. The group activity should be replaced with an activity that involves the whole class.
    B. Ms. Reagan should complete the activity with a group processing skills assessment.
    C. She should monitor the social interactions of the students while they are working in their groups.
    D. She should sit at her desk while the students are working in their groups so the students will be more relaxed.

Ms. Reagan tells Ms. Flores that one of her goals this year is to foster higher-order thinking and enhance problem-solving skills in her students; therefore, she has decided to use inquiry, discovery learning, and cooperative learning groups in her classroom. Ms. Reagan asks Ms. Flores for advice on grouping students for the variety of instructional approaches in her classroom. Ms. Flores says, "When I use cooperative learning activities, I group heterogeneously. For most other instruction, I group students on the basis of ability level and assign independent activities to the high-achieving students."

74. Ms. Flores's grouping practices *best* illlustrate

   A. using effective classroom management.
   B. adapting instruction to the characteristics of the learner.
   C. matching teaching strategies to the type of learning task.
   D. matching student characteristics to the learning objective.

75. The teaching strategies that Ms. Reagan has decided to use will likely:

   A. foster self-directed learning.
   B. establish a competitive goal structure.
   C. provide more structured learning.
   D. sequence instruction.

76. In keeping with her desire to foster higher-order thinking and enhance problem-solving skills, which of the following strategies would be *least* desirable for Ms. Reagan to use in algebra?

   A. She should establish a teacher-controlled structured classroom climate.
   B. She should encourage students to wait before deciding on a solution when they are initially given a word problem.
   C. She should allow more opportunity for problems requiring analytical skills than for basic computation problems.
   D. She should help students to rely more on themselves to determine whether something is mathematically correct.

77. Which of the following would *best* prepare Ms. Reagan's students to understand a lesson on finding the areas of different geometric figures?

   A. The day before the lesson, give the students a handout that shows the different geometric shapes and the formulas for the areas of each and tell them to review the formulas before they come to class the next day.
   B. The day before the lesson, ask the students to review a worksheet that they will have to complete after she goes over the formulas the next day in class.
   C. The day before the lesson, have the students write down and discuss in small groups all the things they already know about geometric figures and their areas.
   D. The day of the lesson, begin by drawing large diagrams of the geometric figures on the chalkboard, then writing the formula and an example of its application underneath each figure.

In keeping with her plan to foster higher-order thinking and enhance problem-solving skills, Ms. Reagan gives the following homework assignment:

---

1. What comes next?

2. All singers wear red. All participants are singers. Therefore, _____

3. Write a least two word problems that can be solved using the following equations:
$$5x - 2(40 - x) = 160.$$

4. Use what you know about adding two fractions in arithmetic to write out a plan for adding two algebraic fractions.

---

78. In giving students problem 1, where they must draw a general conclusion based on several examples, Ms. Reagan is *most* likely attempting to promote students' use of:

    A. deductive reasoning.
    B. differential reasoning.
    C. evaluative reasoning.
    D. inductive reasoning.

79. In giving students problem 2, where they must reason from basic assumptions to a logical conclusion, Ms. Reagan is most likely attempting to promote students' use of:

    A. deductive reasoning.
    B. differential reasoning.
    C. evaluative reasoning.
    D. inductive reasoning.

80. Which of the following was *most* likely Ms. Reagan's primary purpose for giving problem 3?

    A. It will reinforce the students' basic addition and subtraction skills.
    B. It will help students learn that most math problems have one right answer.
    C. It will enhance students' appreciation of the application of equations to real-world problem solving.
    D. It will improve the students' understanding of mathematical principles.

81. In giving students problem 4, Ms. Reagan is *most* likely attempting to promote students' use of:

    A. generalization.
    B. overlearning.
    C. discrimination.
    D. creativity.

After school has been under way for several weeks, Ms. Reagan takes time to reflect on some of her instructional procedures. She feels very strongly that giving homework is important in mathematics; however, she is unsure of how to use it most effectively. She decides to consult Ms. Flores, who, as an experienced teacher of Algebra II, may have some established guidelines that she has found effective when using homework. When Ms. Reagan approaches Ms. Flores for assistance, Ms. Flores immediately offers information and guidance.

82. Ms. Flores's response to Ms. Reagan's request *best* illustrates which of the following principles?

   A. Teachers should know the value of cultivating positive interpersonal relationships with colleagues.
   B. Teachers should know how to work effectively with their colleagues to accomplish educational goals.
   C. Teachers should know how to use different sources of information and guidance to enhance student achievement.
   D. Teachers should recognize personal factors that affect their roles as professionals.

83. Ms. Flores should advise Ms. Reagan that for high school students, homework assignments should be used *primarily* to:

   I.   improve academic achievement.
   II. help students develop good study habits.
   III. foster positive attitudes toward school.
   IV. enhance student's self-discipline.

   A. I only
   B. I and II only
   C. I, II, and III only
   D. I, II, III, and IV

84. One suggestion Ms. Flores will likely *not* make with regard to homework for Ms. Reagan's students is:

   A. frequently check homework orally in class.
   B. keep homework assignments short.
   C. coordinate homework assignments with what the students' other teachers are requiring them to do.
   D. give homework assignments that can be successfully completed by most of the students.

85. Ms. Reagan tells Ms. Flores about Arty, who seldom does his homework. Ms. Flores suggests that Ms. Reagan initially praise Arty every time he does homework, then switch to praising him every second time, and then every third time, and so on. If Ms. Reagan implements Ms. Flores's suggestion, she can expect:

   A. that Arty will stop doing his homework unless she praises him every time he does it.
   B. that the frequency with which Arty does homework will increase, but its quality will decrease.
   C. that the frequency with which Arty does homework will increase and will be highly resistant to extinction.
   D. that Arty will continue to do little homework.

SET 5 ENDS HERE

SET 6 BEGINS HERE

Mr. McGruder teaches seventh-grade language arts at Eastside Middle School. He and some of the other teachers are having a discussion about their grading policies. Ms. Evertson tells him, "I grade based on mastery in my science class." Mr. Luna says, "Even though some teachers criticize it, I prefer grading on the curve myself. It works very well in my mathematics class." Mr. McGruder says, "I think students are not as concerned with what type of evaluation procedures we use as they are with whether or not our grading procedures are fair and consistent. Personally, I think it is vitally important that we design learning experiences that will likely result in success for all our students."

86. Mr. McGruder's attitude about success for all students *best* illustrates which of the following principles?

   A. The teacher should select materials that are developmentally appropriate.
   B. The teacher should recognize factors that influence students' perceptions of their own worth.
   C. The teacher should view differences as opportunities for learning.
   D. The teacher should recognize the social implications of diversity.

87. The *first* thing Ms. Evertson should do when grading on mastery is:

   A. decide the cut-off scores for each letter grade.
   B. determine prior knowledge with a standardized test.
   C. compute the class's mean score on the test.
   D. define the content and skill objectives to be learned.

88. Mr. Luna commented that "some teachers criticize" grading on the curve. Which of the following dilemmas does this grading method create?

   A. Should the more able students be required to perform more work than the less able?
   B. Should a descriptive report card be sent home?
   C. Should all students receive a passing grade?
   D. Should a given percentage of a class of gifted students receive failing marks?

After grading his first unit test, Mr. McGruder is very concerned about the poor performance of some of his slower learners. He remembers that at the beginning of the year, Mr. Weiner, the principal, had told him that about one-third of his heterogeneously mixed class were "at-risk" students. "These students are slower learners who generally fall between the cracks. They typically function below grade level and have a pattern of academic failure, but often do not meet eligibility requirements for special education services. You will need to work very hard if you want these students to be successful on the TAAS," explained Mr. Weiner.

89. Mr. McGruder has observed that his at-risk students exhibit low self-worth. Which of the following would be most effective for him to use in order to enhance the self-worth of these students?

A. Provide a caring environment in which these students are urged to try harder.
B. Allow these students to be more involved in making decisions about class activities.
C. Plan activities in which these students achieve success and know how they contributed to it.
D. Plan activities in which the class discusses the importance of feeling good about oneself.

90. Mr. McGruder arranges for grandparents to serve as volunteer tutors for his at-risk students. A likely benefit of this arrangement will be which of the following?

A. It will establish a sense of community ownership of the school.
B. It will create community awareness of problems of teachers.
C. It will allow the students, while at school, the opportunity to discuss their problems with a family member.
D. It will improve student behavior in the community.

SET 6 ENDS HERE

Answer Key

Item Number	Correct Answer	Competency
1	A	012
2	B	005
3	C	006
4	D	009
5	C	012
6	A	008
7	D	008
8	C	011
9	A	007
10	B	007
11	A	008
12	A	013
13	A	009
14	D	009
15	B	011
16	D	011
17	A	011
18	D	004
19	C	004
20	C	004
21	B	004
22	C	004
23	C	012
24	C	008
25	B	008
26	B	008
27	A	008
28	D	012
29	D	012

30	A	006
31	D	008
32	C	009
33	B	010
34	C	002
35	D	010
36	D	010
37	D	008
38	B	012
39	C	008
40	B	006
41	A	012
42	D	011
43	C	011
44	D	013
45	D	013
46	D	004
47	A	003
48	D	015
49	C	015
50	B	008
51	A	012
52	C	004
53	B	004
54	B	003
55	D	014
56	C	004
57	C	013
58	D	006
59	A	015
60	C	015

61	D	015
62	A	015
63	C	015
64	D	012
65	A	011
66	A	003
67	B	011
68	B	011
69	B	011
70	C	001
71	C	011
72	C	010
73	A	011
74	B	008
75	A	008
76	A	008
77	C	004
78	D	006
79	A	006
80	D	006
81	A	006
82	B	012
83	A	001
84	B	001
85	C	005
86	B	002
87	D	010
88	D	010
89	C	002
90	A	014

Answer Explanations

1. **A** This question deals with **professional development**. Thus, its primary focus is Competency 012: *The teacher is a reflective practitioner who knows how to promote his or her own professional growth and can work cooperatively with other professionals in the system to create a school culture that enhances learning and encourages positive change.* Eliminate B because it deals with **motivation** (Competency 005). Eliminate C because it deals with **planning** (Competency 006). Eliminate D because it deals with **communication** (Competency 007). By consulting Mr. Christopher, Ms. Smith demonstrates that she has reflected on her own teaching and recognizes that her teaching colleagues can serve as resources for accomplishing educational goals in her own classroom. She knows that she is a member of a learning community and actively seeks out opportunities to enhance her professional skills and knowledge. Choice A is the correct response.

2. **B** This question deals with **motivation**. Thus, its primary focus is Competency 005: *The teacher understands how motivation affects group and individual behavior and learning and can apply this understanding to promote learning.* Eliminate Roman IV because it relates to **students' self-esteem** (Competency 002). Eliminate D. Mr. Christopher is aware that allowing students control over their learning (generating the writing topics list themselves, directing the activities in their groups) enhances intrinsic motivation (Roman II). Both extrinsic (Roman I) and intrinsic (Roman II) motivation can be enhanced when students are allowed to use technology in the classroom. Being allowed to use a computer can serve as a tangible reward (extrinsic motivation) and at the same time tap students' innate curiosity and positive attitudes (intrinsic motivation) toward technology. In addition, Mr. Christopher understands that when students work together in groups, they are likely to encourage and help each other (Roman III—group dynamics), which again enhances motivation. Choice B is the correct response.

3. **C** This question deals with **planning**. Thus, its primary focus is Competency 006: *The teacher uses planning processes to design outcome-oriented learning experiences that foster understanding and encourage self-directed thinking and learning in both individual and collaborative settings.* Eliminate A because it is likely to have a negative impact on the lower-ability students. Eliminate B because it fosters competition. Eliminate D because it is not supported by the stimulus—there is no indication the students will be doing this. When planning writing activities, Mr. Christopher understands the value of collaborative learning. He knows that when students work together, they experience positive interdependence; enhance each other's learning by helping, sharing, and encouraging one another; and explain, discuss, and teach each other. Choice C is the correct response.

4. **D** The question deals with **materials and resources.** Thus, its primary focus is Competency 009: *The teacher uses a variety of instructional materials and resources (including human and technological resources) to support individual and group learning.* The assignment is a written paper. Eliminate A because a database is used to collect information such as a list of birthdays and addresses for a set of individuals. Eliminate B because a graph is a pictorial representation of data. Eliminate C because a spreadsheet is used to arrange information and formulas into rows and columns, such as a ledger or worksheet for a business. Instead of writing with pen and paper, students can use word processors with spell checkers, thesauruses, and grammar checks to create written documents such as letters, themes, essays, and research papers. The advantage of word processing is that corrections and revisions can be made without retyping the entire document. Since the assignment is a written paper, Choice D is the correct response.

5. **C** This question deals with **professional development.** Thus, its primary focus is Competency 012: *The teacher is a reflective practitioner who knows how to promote his or her own professional growth and can work cooperatively with other professionals in the system to create a school culture that enhances learning and encourages positive change.* The use of technology adds a new dimension to teaching and learning. It can be used to create a learning environment that changes and interacts with students' needs. Today in Texas, it is vital that teachers know how to enhance learning for students through the appropriate use of technological resources like computers. Eliminate A because teachers can use computers effectively in their classrooms without knowing computer programming. Eliminate B and D because teachers should not be expected to have computer maintenance skills or know how to repair computer hardware. All Texas teachers need to be computer literate in order to use this technology effectively in the classroom. Choice C is the correct response.

6. **A** This question deals with **instructional strategies.** Thus, its primary focus is Competency 008: *The teacher uses a variety of instructional strategies and roles to facilitate learning and to help students become independent thinkers and problem solvers who use higher-order thinking in the classroom and the real world.* Lectures are usually teacher-centered presentations. Most authorities agree that lectures should not be overused in secondary school classes because they can fail to involve students sufficiently. They can be boring and frustrating for students whose attention spans are short, who have poor listening skills, and/or who lack note-taking skills. For many students, attention declines after the first 15 minutes of a lecture. After 30 or 40 minutes, little knowledge is being absorbed. Consequently, when lectures are used they should be limited to 10 to 15 minutes. Choice A is the correct response.

7. **D** This question deals with **planning.** Thus, its primary focus is Competency 006: *The teacher uses planning processes to design outcome-oriented learning experiences that foster understanding and encourage self-directed thinking and learning in both individual and collaborative settings.* Eliminate Roman I because some topics may require Ms. Smith to present new information or teach skills before students work in groups. Eliminate A and B. Eliminate Roman II because it sends a negative message to average- and low-ability students. Eliminate C. It is important that Ms. Smith understand the relationship between careful planning and student success in the classroom. Research indicates that small-group activities can increase student achievement more than traditional lessons if students are well prepared to work in small groups and the group task is well organized. Choice D is the correct response.

8. **C** This question deals with **classroom management.** Thus, its primary focus is Competency 011: *The teacher structures and manages the learning environment to maintain a classroom climate that promotes the lifelong pursuit of learning and encourages cooperation, leadership, and mutual respect.* Eliminate A because students can learn from their mistakes, so Ms. Smith should not control the activities to the extent that she does not allow the students to make errors or think illogically. Eliminate B because it is likely to create resentment among students; and, besides, groups should be given sufficient time to complete tasks without being pressured. Eliminate D because it is teacher-directed rather than student-centered. Ms. Smith needs to be aware of the important role the teacher must assume when using a collaborative setting. She should monitor each group, assessing and guiding individual and group collaborative skills. Choice C is the correct response.

9. **A** This question deals with **communication.** Thus, its primary focus is Competency 007: *The teacher uses effective verbal, nonverbal, and media communication techniques to shape the classroom into a community of learners engaged in active inquiry, collaborative exploration, and supportive interactions.* Eliminate B because it is not supported by the stimulus—Ms. Smith wants the students to write on a topic, not analyze and solve a problem as in active inquiry. Eliminate D because it is not supported by the stimulus—you are not told the cultural makeup of Ms. Smith's class. Eliminate C because Ms. Smith's problem is not with her means of communication but, rather, with her message. Ms. Smith should have explained the ten-minute writing assignment more precisely, so that the instructional task would have been clearer to the students. Instead of telling the students to write on the subject of school uniforms, which is rather vague, she might have clarified the assignment by saying, "Write why you would or would not be in favor of having school uniforms." Effective teachers communicate instructional tasks clearly to students. Choice A is the correct response.

10. **B** This question deals with **communication.** Thus, its primary focus is Competency 007: *The teacher uses effective verbal, nonverbal, and media communication techniques to shape the classroom into a community of learners engaged in active inquiry, collaborative exploration, and supportive interactions.* Eliminate Roman III because a *thoughtful questioner* is one who asks questions that elicit different levels of thinking (that is, as in Bloom's taxonomy). Ms. Smith is trying to determine why Sarah is upset about the writing assignment; she is not trying to elicit different levels of thinking from Sarah. Eliminate A, C, and D. In her interactions with Sarah, Ms. Smith notices Sarah's frown and responds to this nonverbal cue (Roman II); she simplifies and restates the writing prompt (Roman I) and listens reflectively to Sarah's concerns (Roman IV). Choice B is the correct response.

11. **A** This question deals with **instructional strategies.** Thus, its primary focus is Competency 008: *The teacher uses a variety of instructional strategies and roles to facilitate learning and to help students become independent thinkers and problem solvers who use higher-order thinking in the classroom and the real world.* This is a priority-setting question. You must select the answer choice that is *most* useful. Cooperative learning can be used across the full range of student populations, regardless of age or maturity level (eliminate C) and is appropriate for simple or complex tasks (eliminate D). Eliminate B because guided practice is a teacher-directed component of the lesson cycle. In effective cooperative learning groups, students encourage and help each other, thus providing an ongoing support system for members. Choice A is the correct response.

12. **A** This question deals with **parent-school relationships** (Some parents are opposed to the use of cooperative learning groups) but also requires knowledge of **instructional strategies** (Ms. Smith may need to justify her use of cooperative learning groups to parents). Thus, its primary focus is Competency 013: *The teacher knows how to foster strong school-home relationships that support student achievement of desired learning outcomes.* Teachers should know the importance of communicating with parents, respecting their opinions, and providing rationales for classroom decisions. Eliminate B because it is not an expected outcome of using cooperative learning. Eliminate C because schools should not expect parents to do this. Eliminate D because it conflicts with research on cooperative learning indicating that students are usually involved in challenging and meaningful learning. Mr. Christopher is likely to know that the use of cooperative learning methods provides students with opportunities to develop interpersonal and small-group social skills. These lifelong survival skills are vital for making the democratic decisions for citizenship and teamwork required in the workplace. Choice A is the correct response.

13. **A** This question deals with technology, which comes under **materials and resources.** Thus, its primary focus is Competency 009: *The teacher uses a variety of instructional materials and resources (including human and technological resources) to support individual and group learning.* This is a priority-setting question—you must select the *best* response. Eliminate B and C because they contain key ideas related to **instructional strategies** (Competency 008). Eliminate D because it relates to **professionalism** (Competency 012). Teachers should know how to enhance learning of all students through the appropriate use of instructional materials and resources. Mr. Hennington uses the videotape to get students' attention and focus that attention on the lesson topic that is to follow. Choice A is the correct response.

14. **D** This question deals with technology, which comes under **materials and resources.** Thus, its primary focus is Competency 009: *The teacher uses a variety of instructional materials and resources (including human and technological resources) to support individual and group learning.* Mr. Hennington knows that learning can be enhanced through the appropriate use of multiple resources in instruction. He previews the material so that he can judge its quality (A) and to make sure that the content is appropriate for his students' level of understanding (B) and matches the instructional objectives (C) for the lesson. Entertainment is also an important function of media, but it is not as important as the quality and appropriateness of the content. Choice D is the correct response.

15. **B** This question deals with class time spent in learning, which comes under **classroom management.** Thus, its primary focus is Competency 011: *The teacher structures and manages the learning environment to maintain a classroom climate that promotes the lifelong pursuit of learning and encourages cooperation, leadership, and mutual respect.* Eliminate A because *academic learning time* is when students are actually on-task and engaged successfully in learning. Eliminate C because *wait time* is the amount of time a teacher waits for a student to respond to a question. Eliminate D because *time-on-task* is the time when students are actively engaged in academic tasks. *Allocated time* is the time appropriated to each activity. Choice B is the correct response.

16. **D** This question deals with class time in learning, which comes under **classroom management.** Thus, its primary focus is Competency 011: *The teacher structures and manages the learning environment to maintain a classroom climate that promotes the lifelong pursuit of learning and encourages cooperation, leadership, and mutual respect.* Eliminate A because *academic learning time* is when students are actually on task and engaged *successfully* in learning. Eliminate B because *allocated time* is the time appropriated to each activity. Eliminate C because *wait time*

is the amount of time a teacher waits for a student to respond to a question. The actual time a student spends engaged in an academic task, whether or not successfully, is called *time-on-task*, or engaged time. Choice D is the correct response.

17. **A** This question deals with class time in learning, which comes under **classroom management.** Thus, its primary focus is Competency 011: *The teacher structures and manages the learning environment to maintain a classroom climate that promotes the lifelong pursuit of learning and encourages cooperation, leadership, and mutual respect.* Eliminate B because *allocated time* is the time appropriated to each activity. Eliminate C because *wait time* is the amount of time a teacher waits for a student to respond to a question. Eliminate D because *time-on-task* is the actual time a student spends engaged in an academic task, whether or not successfully. The actual time a student spends in successful learning is called *academic learning time.* Choice A is the correct response.

18. **D** This question deals with **how learning occurs.** Thus, its primary focus is Competency 004: *The teacher understands how learning occurs and can apply this understanding to design and implement effective instruction.* Eliminate A because it deals with **planning** (Competency 006). Eliminate B because it deals with **assessment** (Competency 010). Eliminate C because it deals with grouping decisions based on the activity and environment, not on learning styles. Mr. Hennington is aware of factors that affect learning (such as, learning style) and designs instruction to facilitate learning for all his students. Choice D is the correct response.

19. **C** This question deals with **how learning occurs.** Thus, its primary focus is Competency 004: *The teacher understands how learning occurs and can apply this understanding to design and implement effective instruction.* Students who learn best by listening are auditory learners (A); students who prefer to learn by seeing or reading something are visual learners (B); students who need to touch and experience in a hands-on fashion while learning are tactile/kinesthetic learners (C); and left-brain dominant learners respond to verbal instruction (D). Therefore, instruction given in the manner described is likely to *least* benefit a tactile/kinesthetic learner, since it provides no planned opportunity for the learner to be physically involved in the instruction. Choice C is the correct response.

20. **C** This question deals with **how learning occurs.** Thus, its primary focus is Competency 004: *The teacher understands how learning occurs and can apply this understanding to design and implement effective instruction.* Eliminate A, B, and D because they do not refer to the five primary senses. Educators refer to the way a student takes in information through the five primary

senses (see, hear, smell, taste, touch) as sensory modality strength. Choice C is the correct response.

21. **B**   This question deals with **how learning occurs.** Thus, its primary focus is Competency 004: *The teacher understands how learning occurs and can apply this understanding to design and implement effective instruction.* Field-dependent learners have the ability to perceive objects as a whole rather than as individual parts, tending to have difficulty separating out specific parts from a situation or pattern; tend to see relational and inferential concepts; tend to be active in social situations (eliminate A); tend to be more influenced by suggestion; tend to reach consensus in discussion groups more readily; and tend to study in programs requiring interpersonal, nonscientific orientation, such as history, literature, and the helping professions. In learning situations, field-dependents prefer more externally imposed structure (B), direction, and feedback; and learn best when content is organized into smaller units. They have difficulty when problem solving involves analysis, doing better at applying rules and using intuition (eliminate C). They tend to work well in groups (eliminate D) and to be comfortable with learning and problem solving through collaboration. Mr. Hennington might expect Maria to experience particular difficulty with unstructured learning activities. Choice B is the correct response.

22. **C**   This question deals with **how learning occurs.** Thus, its primary focus is Competency 004: *The teacher understands how learning occurs and can apply this understanding to design and implement effective instruction.* Ryan's ability to find hidden patterns suggests that he is a field-independent learner. Field-independent learners are passive in social situations; tend to be less influenced by their peers (eliminate B); and tend to study in programs requiring analytical, abstract, impersonal spheres, such as electronics, engineering, and mathematics (eliminate A). In learning situations, field-independents require less frequent feedback (eliminate D), are able to provide their own structure when it is lacking, and are able to handle larger units of content. They tend to be better at analytical problem solving, accommodate well to abstraction, and have a high need for achievement. They may have difficulty collaborating when working in groups (C), tending to prefer independent or individual study. Choice C is the correct response.

23. **C**   This question deals with **professionalism.** Thus, its primary focus is Competency 012: *The teacher is a reflective practitioner who knows how to promote his or her own professional growth and can work cooperatively with other professionals in the system to create a school culture that enhances learning and encourages positive change.* Eliminate A and D because the question is about how Mr. Hennington teaches, not about how he organizes his instruction or about how he enhances his own skills and knowledge

(professional growth). Eliminate B because it is off-topic. Principle V of the *Code of Ethics and Standard Practices for Texas Educators* requires ethical conduct toward parents and communities. By making connections between a lesson's content and familiar stories and information from the home and community, Mr. Hennington is endeavoring to understand community cultures and relate the home environment of students to the school (Standard 2 of Principle V). Choice C is the correct response.

24. **C** This question deals with **instructional strategies.** Thus, its primary focus is Competency 008: *The teacher uses a variety of instructional strategies and roles to facilitate learning and to help students become independent thinkers and problem solvers who use higher-order thinking in the classroom and the real world.* This is a priority-setting question—you must select the response that is a *major* value. Teachers should use an array of instructional strategies to actively engage students in learning. Eliminate A because the stock market is not necessarily part of the community where students live. Eliminate B because this is likely to happen when simulations are used, but it would not be considered a *major* value of the activity. Eliminate D because simulations usually take more time than expository teaching methods. Mr. Hennington knows that, during the simulation, the students will need to actively seek out knowledge so they can plan and try out strategies for making investment decisions in the stock market simulation activity. Choice C is the correct response.

25. **B** This question deals with **instructional strategies.** Thus, its primary focus is Competency 008: *The teacher uses a variety of instructional strategies and roles to facilitate learning and to help students become independent thinkers and problem solvers who use higher-order thinking in the classroom and the real world.* This is a priority-setting question—you have to select the answer choice that is a *major* limitation. Eliminate A because simulations usually require higher-order thinking skills. Eliminate C because students usually enjoy participating in simulations and find them fun and interesting. Eliminate D because, for a few students the realism may be too threatening; but it is not a *major* limitation, since most simulations are artificial situations with the risks encountered in real life removed. Teachers should use an array of instructional strategies to actively engage students in learning. A major limitation of simulations that Mr. Hennington is likely to know is that they often require a considerable block of time. Choice B is the correct response.

26. **B** This question deals with **instructional strategies.** Thus, its primary focus is Competency 008: *The teacher uses a variety of instructional strategies and roles to facilitate learning and to help students become independent thinkers and problem solvers who use higher-order thinking in the classroom and the real world.* Eliminate Roman III because most real-world problems have many

solutions. Eliminate A and C. Mr. Hennington knows that simulations provide an artificial situation with the risks encountered in real life removed (Roman IV); nevertheless, the students will act, react, and make decisions, as well as plan and try out strategies for attacking problems (Roman I) as they would have to do in real life. These experiences are likely to deepen their insights and understandings of economics (Roman II). Choice B is the correct response.

27. **A** This question deals with **instructional strategies.** Thus, its primary focus is Competency 008: *The teacher uses a variety of instructional strategies and roles to facilitate learning and to help students become independent thinkers and problem solvers who use higher-order thinking in the classroom and the real world.* Mr. Hennington should know that simulations work best when the teacher avoids becoming actively involved in the make-believe situation (A). However, this does not mean that he relinquishes his responsibility to facilitate the process by assigning students roles (eliminate D) and providing assistance, as needed (eliminate C). In order to obtain maximum benefit from the activity, students should be permitted to make mistakes, just as they would be allowed to do in a real-life situation (eliminate B). Choice A is the correct response.

28. **D** This question deals with **professionalism.** Thus, its primary focus is Competency 012: *The teacher is a reflective practitioner who knows how to promote his or her own professional growth and can work cooperatively with other professionals in the system to create a school culture that enhances learning and encourages positive change.* This is a priority-setting question—you must select the answer choice with which Mr. Hennington's decision is *most* in accord. Eliminate A and C because it is not supported by the stimulus—Mr. Hennington is not enhancing his professional knowledge and skills, nor is he working within the system to address an issue when he refuses to be argumentative. Eliminate B because the stimulus does not provide you with sufficient information about the school culture for you to know whether Mr. Hennington's decision is influenced by it. By choosing *not* to be argumentative with Ms. Allen, Mr. Hennington demonstrates that he recognizes the importance of maintaining professional harmony in the school. He recognizes that he is a member of a learning community and knows how to work with his colleagues to create a positive school culture. Choice D is the correct response.

29. **D** This question deals with **professionalism.** Thus, its primary focus is Competency 012: *The teacher is a reflective practitioner who knows how to promote his or her own professional growth and can work cooperatively with other professionals in the system to create a school culture that enhances learning and encourages positive change.* Eliminate A, B, and C because they are not supported by the stimulus. Ms. Allen did not reveal confidential

information about Mr. Hennington (A), deny or impede Mr. Hennington in the exercise or enjoyment of his professional rights or responsibilities (B), or use coercive means to influence professional decisions (C). Ms. Allen made false statements to the principal about Mr. Hennington. Choice D is the correct response.

30. **A** This question deals with **planning.** Thus, its primary focus is Competency 006: *The teacher uses planning processes to design outcome-oriented learning experiences that foster understanding and encourage self-directed thinking and learning in both individual and collaborative settings.* Eliminate B because it is not supported by the stimulus—the students will be working together in groups, not as individuals in a whole-group setting. Eliminate C and D because they are teacher-directed, not student-centered. Mr. Hennington is likely to know that when students work together as a team to achieve a common goal, they perceive that it is to their advantage if others students on their team learn and to their disadvantage if others on their team do poorly. They take responsibility for their own academic performance and provide peer support for the academic performance of their teammates. Choice A is the correct response.

31. **D** This question deals with **instructional strategies.** Thus, its primary focus is Competency 008: *The teacher uses a variety of instructional strategies and roles to facilitate learning and to help students become independent thinkers and problem solvers who use higher-order thinking in the classroom and the real world.* In a simulation, the students are primarily in control, so eliminate A, B, and C because Mr. Bentley's acting as judge, supervisor, or arbitrator—dominant roles—would act against student control. Mr. Hennington knows when to vary his role in the instructional process in relation to the content and purposes of instruction and the levels of need and independence of the students. He wants the students to assume responsibility for and direct their own learning. Therefore, his primary function should be to facilitate learning in the instructional process. Choice D is the correct response.

32. **C** This question deals with technology, which comes under **materials and resources.** Thus, its primary focus is Competency 009: *The teacher uses a variety of instructional materials and resources (including human and technological resources) to support individual and group learning.* This is a priority-setting question—you must select the *most* likely answer choice. Eliminate A because it is off-topic—multiple perspectives has to do with looking at issues from various viewpoints. Eliminate B because it relates to **motivation** (Competency 005). Eliminate D because although showing a video (as Mr. Hennington did at the beginning of the unit) and having the students use a computerized presentation package to prepare their reports at the end of the unit may influence students' perceptions of technology, Mr. Hennington *most* likely knows that technology is a powerful communication tool and wants

to encourage students to experience the advantages of using technology to produce their reports. A computerized presentation package will allow the students to produce informative, artistic, and professional-looking presentations. Choice C is the correct response.

33. **B** This question deals with **assessment.** Thus, its primary focus is Competency 010: *The teacher uses processes of informal and formal assessment to understand individual learners, monitor instructional effectiveness, and shape instruction.* Teachers should be knowledgeable of the uses and limitations of different types of assessments. Eliminate A because *criterion-referenced* assessment refers to the use of tests designed to measure mastery of specific skills. Eliminate C because *norm-reference* assessment refers to the use of standardized tests focused on a comparison of a student's score with those of other students. Eliminate D because *summative* assessment is assessment that follows instruction and occurs at the end of a unit, semester, and so forth. *Formative* assessment is designed to acquire feedback before the end of a unit, semester, and so forth. It is used to guide the content and pace of lessons and may take various forms (for example, informal survey, diagnostic instrument, pretest, ungraded skills checklist). Mr. Hennington is using a questionnaire to acquire information before the end of the semester. Choice B is the correct response.

34. **C** This question deals with **students' self-esteem.** Thus, its primary focus is Competency 002: *The teacher considers environmental factors that may affect learning in designing a supportive and responsive classroom that promotes all students' learning and self-esteem.* Eliminate A because this would not be expected when students are asked to be involved in making suggestions about the course. Eliminate B and D because they are not supported by the stimulus—students are not drawing inductive conclusions, nor are they self-evaluating. Mr. Hennington understands Maslow's Hierarchy of Human Needs and recognizes the importance of establishing a positive classroom environment. He knows that soliciting students' ideas will help them feel recognized and accepted, thereby enhancing their self-esteem. Choice C is the correct response.

35. **D** This question deals with **assessment.** Thus, its primary focus is Competency 010: *The teacher uses processes of informal and formal assessment to understand individual learners, monitor instructional effectiveness, and shape instruction.* Teachers should be knowledgeable of the uses and limitations of different types of assessments. Eliminate A because *criterion-referenced* assessment refers to the use of tests designed to measure mastery of specific skills. Eliminate B because *formative* assessment aims to acquire feedback before the end of a unit, semester, and so forth. Eliminate C because *norm-referenced* assessment refers to the use of standardized tests focused on a comparison of a student's score

with those of other students. *Summative* assessment is assessment that follows instruction and occurs at the end of a unit, semester, and so forth. Mr. Hennington is using a questionnaire to acquire feedback at the end of the semester. Choice D is the correct response.

36. **D** This question deals with **assessment.** Thus, its primary focus is Competency 010: *The teacher uses processes of informal and formal assessment to understand individual learners, monitor instructional effectiveness, and shape instruction.* Eliminate A because when the students are self-reflecting, they would not be in competition with others. Eliminate B because it is off-topic. Eliminate C because Mr. Hennington is likely to assess mastery of objectives using a different type of assessment. When students reflect on and evaluate their own behaviors, they are participating in self-assessment. They are using critical, higher-order thinking skills, engaging in the highest level of Bloom's taxonomy of educational objectives. Choice D is the correct response.

37. **D** This question deals with **instructional strategies.** Thus, its primary focus is Competency 008: *The teacher uses a variety of instructional strategies and roles to facilitate learning and to help students become independent thinkers and problem solvers who use higher-order thinking in the classroom and the real world.* Evaluation-level thinking requires students to use criteria or standards to form judgments or opinions about the value of the topic or phenomenon being considered. Eliminate A, B, and C because each of these require lower-level thinking in which students are not asked to form judgments or opinions. A class discussion in which students evaluate the merits of the simulation activity would work best for engaging students in evaluation-level thinking. Choice D is the correct response.

38. **B** This question deals with **professionalism.** Thus, its primary focus is Competency 012: *The teacher is a reflective practitioner who knows how to promote his or her own professional growth and can work cooperatively with other professionals in the system to create a school culture that enhances learning and encourages positive change.* Eliminate A because it deals with **instructional strategies** (Competency 008). Eliminate C because it deals with **communication** (Competency 007). Eliminate D because it deals with **classroom management** (Competency 011). Interdisciplinary teams require teachers to work together to solve problems, deal with stress, explore innovative ideas, and assess the effectiveness of instruction. These teachers work together to create a school culture that enhances learning. Choice B is the correct response.

39. **C** This question deals with **instructional strategies.** Thus, its primary focus is Competency 008: *The teacher uses a variety of instructional strategies and roles to facilitate learning and to help students become independent thinkers and problem solvers who*

use higher-order thinking in the classroom and the real world. Reasons supporting the use of interdisciplinary instruction include the following: the knowledge explosion, flexible use of both space and time, relevance of the instruction, public approval (eliminate A), opportunities for individualization and realistic problem solving (eliminate B and D), and abundant assessment and evaluation opportunities; however, scheduling students can be difficult. Choice C is the correct response.

40. **B** This question deals with **planning.** Thus, its primary focus is Competency 006: *The teacher uses planning processes to design outcome-oriented learning experiences that foster understanding and encourage self-directed thinking and learning in both individual and collaborative settings.* Interdisciplinary teams collaboratively plan instruction to meet the needs of their students. Eliminate Roman III because it fosters competition. Eliminate A and D. Since B and C both contain Roman I and II, you need only to decide whether or not Roman IV should be included. Affective objectives (Roman I) are important and can be reached by making the instructional information relevant and practical (Roman IV). Eliminate C. Additionally, teachers should use an array of instructional strategies to actively engage students in learning (Roman II). Choice B is the correct response.

41. **A** The question deals with **professionalism.** Thus, its primary focus is Competency 012: *The teacher is a reflective practitioner who knows how to promote his or her own professional growth and can work cooperatively with other professionals in the system to create a school culture that enhances learning and encourages positive change.* This is a priority-setting question—you must select the *most* likely answer choice. Eliminate B, C, and D because these may be beliefs that prevent Mr. Simmons from asking for assistance, but the *most* likely reason is that Mr. Simmons is fearful that he will be perceived as ill-prepared or incompetent to teach. Like many new teachers, Mr. Simmons is too embarrassed to ask for help, because he doesn't want the other teachers to know he is having a problem. Rather than being reluctant to seek assistance from his fellow team members, he should view them as a rich source of support and guidance. Choice A is the correct response.

42. **D** This question deals with **classroom management.** Thus, its primary focus is Competency 011: *The teacher structures and manages the learning environment to maintain a classroom climate that promotes the lifelong pursuit of learning and encourages cooperation, leadership, and mutual respect.* This is a priority-setting question—you must select the *best* answer choice. It appears that Becky is motivated to misbehave in order to receive attention from her classmates. As experienced teachers, Mr. Simmons' fellow team members undoubtedly know that to reprimand Becky every time she misbehaves (eliminate A) or to draw the attention of the class to her (eliminate C) would most

likely reinforce her disruptive behavior. They undoubtedly also know that threatening students (eliminate B) is an ineffective practice. Therefore, of the suggestions listed, the one Mr. Simmons' fellow team members should recommend is that he isolate Becky from the rest of the class when she misbehaves (D). This action would remove the reinforcement Becky has been receiving for her disruptive behavior. Choice D is the correct response.

43. **C** This question deals with **classroom management.** Thus, its primary focus is Competency 011: *The teacher structures and manages the learning environment to maintain a classroom climate that promotes the lifelong pursuit of learning and encourages cooperation, leadership, and mutual respect.* It appears that Becky is motivated to misbehave in order to get attention and approval from her classmates. She is performing for their amusement. Strategies for reducing peer-supported misbehavior must involve reducing the reinforcement received from peers. There are two primary strategies for discouraging peer-supported behavior. One is to use time-out (that is, isolate the student from the rest of the class). Another is to use group contingencies (C), strategies in which the entire class is rewarded on the basis of everyone's behavior. Under group contingencies, peer support for the disruptive behavior diminishes or disappears. Choice C is the correct response.

44. **D** The question deals with **school-home relationships.** Thus, its primary focus is Competency 013: *The teacher knows how to foster strong school-home relationships that support student achievement of desired learning outcomes.* This is a priority-setting question—you must select the *most* appropriate answer choice. The interdisciplinary team should understand basic principles of conducting parent-teacher conferences. The conference should begin and end on a positive note. Eliminate A because it begins the conference on a negative note. Eliminate B because it conflicts with research findings indicating that students do better in school when their parents are involved in their schooling. Eliminate C because it is not paramount that each team member do this; in some situations it would be better to have a spokesperson summarize the team's concerns. The most appropriate option would be to end the conference on a positive note by sharing information about Becky's achievements. Choice D is the correct response.

45. **D** The question assesses Competency 013: *The teacher knows how to foster strong school-home relationships that support student achievement of desired learning outcomes.* This is a priority-setting question—you must select the *most* appropriate answer choice. According to TEC 29.121, "a 'gifted and talented student' means a child or youth who performs at or shows the potential for performing at a remarkably high level of accomplishment when compared to others of the same age, experience, or environment and who: (1) exhibits high performance capability in an intellectual,

creative, or artistic area; (2) possesses an unusual capacity for leadership; or (3) excels in a specific academic field." Eliminate A because this would be dodging the issue and putting Ms. Turner off on the gifted/talented teacher. Eliminate B and C because, until a proper evaluation of Becky has been administered, the teachers should avoid telling Ms. Turner that Becky is not a candidate for the gifted/talented program. The interdisciplinary team should recognize the importance of maintaining ongoing parent-teacher communication and understand strategies for promoting effective communication. Listening to Ms. Turner's concerns and showing they take them seriously by acting on them in an appropriate manner will foster positive school-home relationships. Choice D is the correct response.

46. **D** This question deals with learning styles, which come under **how learning occurs.** Thus, its primary focus is Competency 004: *The teacher understands how learning occurs and can apply this understanding to design and implement effective instruction.* This is a priority-setting question—you must select the *most* likely answer choice. Eliminate A and B because information is insufficient to determine Becky's field-independence or -dependence. Eliminate C because a reflective learner thinks before acting. Becky is most likely an impulsive learner. Impulsive students tend to work and make decisions quickly. They respond to situations with the first thought that occurs to them, often finishing assignments and tests before everyone else. They tend to concentrate on speed more than on accuracy. Choice D is the correct response.

47. **A** This question deals with **diversity.** Thus, its primary focus is Competency 003: *The teacher appreciates human diversity, recognizing how diversity in the classroom and the community may effect learning and creating a classroom environment in which both the diversity of groups and the uniqueness of individuals are recognized and celebrated.* According to Gallagher, teacher identification of high-ability, or intellectually gifted, students has been flawed. Their identification is determined by how well the child fits the "perfect" student model (performs well in school, behaves well, turns in work on time, and so on). They often overlook large numbers of intellectually superior children because these children may not be performing well in school. In reality, the percentage of gifted students who perform below their ability level is high. Choice A is the correct response.

48. **D** This question deals with **ethical, legal, and professional standards.** Thus, its primary focus is Competency 015: *The teacher understands requirements, expectations, and constraints associated with teaching in Texas, and can apply this understanding in a variety of contexts.* This is a priority-setting question—you must select the *best* answer choice. Eliminate A because *higher-order learning* is a general term applied to learning

that engages students at the higher levels of cognition: analysis, synthesis, and evaluation. Eliminate B because it relates to **instructional strategies** (Competency 008). Eliminate C because it is not an educational term. TEC 29.122 mandates that "each school district shall adopt a process for identifying and serving gifted and talented students in the district and shall establish a program for those students in each grade level." Districts provide for the gifted/talented in varied ways. Some of these are acceleration, enrichment, and special schools for certain subject areas, such as the sciences and the arts. *Acceleration* is rapid promotion through the use of advanced studies, which enables students to progress more rapidly through the standard curriculum. Choice D is the correct answer.

49. **C** This question deals with **ethical, legal, and professional standards.** Thus, its primary focus is Competency 015: *The teacher understands requirements, expectations, and constraints associated with teaching in Texas, and can apply this understanding in a variety of contexts.* This is a priority-setting question—you must select the *best* answer choice. Eliminate A because *extension* is an instructional technique in which additional information to a student's response contribution is obtained or given. Eliminate B because it is not an educational term. Eliminate D because it relates to **instructional strategies** (Competency 008). TEC 29.122 mandates that "each school district shall adopt a process for identifying and serving gifted and talented students in the district and shall establish a program for those students in each grade level." Districts provide for the gifted/talented in varied ways. Some of these are acceleration, enrichment, and special schools for certain subject areas, such as the sciences and the arts. *Enrichment* is the process of providing richer and more varied content that supplement the standard curriculum. It involves using assignments or activities designed to broaden or deepen students' knowledge. Choice C is the correct answer.

50. **B** This question deals with **instructional strategies.** Thus, its primary focus is Competency 008: *The teacher uses a variety of instructional strategies and roles to facilitate learning and to help students become independent thinkers and problem-solvers who use higher-order thinking in the classroom and the real world.* Competent teachers know that there are multiple ways to group students. They select the appropriate grouping arrangement for a given instructional goal and group of students. Eliminate D because it disagrees with research suggesting that grouping practices affect learning. Critics have challenged the use of cooperative learning strategies with gifted students, arguing that high-achieving students are penalized by working in heterogeneous cooperative learning groups. They complain that high achievers feel used and frustrated by low achievers, who are not motivated to perform well. Nevertheless, ample research indicates that high-achieving students learn as much in cooperatively structured classes as they do in

traditional classes and, further, that they benefit socially from the opportunity to work collaboratively and help others. Considering all these factors, high achievers should be involved in whole-class learning (eliminate A) and be given opportunities to work cooperatively with other high achievers (eliminate C) or on independent projects. This would indicate that a mix of homogeneous and heterogeneous grouping should be used. Choice B is the correct response.

51. **A** This question deals with **professionalism.** Thus, its primary focus is Competency 012: *The teacher is a reflective practitioner who knows how to promote his or her own professional growth and can work cooperatively with other professionals in the system to create a school culture that enhances learning and encourages positive change.* This is a priority-setting question—you must select the *best* answer choice. Eliminate B and D because these do occur in interdisciplinary teams, but the stimulus does not support that they are taking place in the discussion among the team members. The team is planning a unit together and deciding responsibility for various aspects of the unit, not supporting and guiding one another or dealing with an individual student. Eliminate C because it is an incomplete answer choice; you are not told to whom the team is being compared—members tend to work harder than whom? The discussion best illustrates that in interdisciplinary teams, the member can provide an expanded pool of ideas for solving problems and creating a school culture that enhances learning. Choice A is the correct response.

52. **C** This question deals with **how learning occurs.** Thus, its primary focus is Competency 004: *The teacher understands how learning occurs and can apply this understanding to design and implement effective instruction.* The concept of *brain hemisphericity* is closely linked to the work on student learning modality. Each hemisphere of the brain is associated with certain thinking traits and therefore certain learning styles. Considerable research supports the notion that people who are left-brain-dominant learn in different ways than do right-brain-dominant people. The terms *left/right, analytic/global,* and *inductive/deductive* are often used interchangeably to describe learners. *Left/analytic/inductive* learners respond to verbal instruction; process thought logically; think from part to whole; depend on words and language for meaning; prefer lessons that proceed in a step-by-step logical order, where details build on one another; and prefer well-structured assignments. The graphic overview would not be as critical for this type of learner. Eliminate A, B, and D. *Right/global/deductive* learners respond to visual and kinesthetic instruction; process thought holistically, seeing patterns and relationships; think from whole to part, preferring to see the "big picture" before exploring the small details; depend on images and pictures for meaning; and can work on several parts of a task at the same time. Each of us is a whole-brain person, but usually with

a preference for receiving information through either the left or the right hemisphere. Neither preference is in any way superior to the other, although instruction in most public schools in America typically favors the left-brain-dominant student. Right-brain-dominant learners respond to visual and kinesthetic instruction; they depend on images and pictures for meaning and prefer to see the "big picture" first. The graphical overview is likely to be most beneficial for students who are right-brain-dominant learners. Choice C is the correct response.

53. **B** This question deals with **how learning occurs.** Thus, its primary focus is Competency 004: *The teacher understands how learning occurs and can apply this understanding to design and implement effective instruction.* This is a priority-setting question—you must select the answer choice that is *least* consistent with a tactile/kinesthetic learning style. Tactile/kinesthetic learners prefer to learn by touching objects, by feeling shapes and textures, and by moving things around. Eliminate A because the students will be acting out a play, which is tactile/kinesthetic. Eliminate C because the students will be involved in a hands-on activity, which is tactile/kinesthetic. Eliminate D because the students will be dressing up in costumes and participating in an after-school social, which is tactile/kinesthetic. The mathematics activity affords the least opportunity for the learner to be physically involved, so it is least consistent with a tactile/kinesthetic learning style. Choice B is the correct response.

54. **B** This question deals with **diversity.** Competency 003: *The teacher is a reflective practitioner who knows how to promote his or her own professional growth and can work cooperatively with other professionals in the system to create a school culture that enhances learning and encourages positive change.* According to Witkin, field-independent learners tend to be passive in social situations. Eliminate A. In contrast, field-dependent learners tend to be active in social situations. Eliminate C and D. Choice B is the correct response.

55. **D** This question deals with **school-community relationships.** Thus, its primary focus is Competency 014: *The teacher understands how the school relates to the larger community and knows strategies for making interactions between school and community mutually supportive and beneficial.* This is a priority-setting question—you must select the *best* answer choice. Mr. Zhong knows that teachers can foster positive interactions between the school and the community and at the same time take advantage of community resources to foster student growth by inviting varied community members to serve as guest speakers. Eliminate A because it would be presumptuous for Mr. Zhong to do this. Eliminate B and C because these would be time-consuming tasks for the guest speaker. By telling the astronomer what the students already know

about the Hubble Space Telescope, Mr. Zhong is providing information that will help the astronomer make the presentation more meaningful to the students. Choice D is the correct response.

56. **C** Upon first reading, it is not apparent which competency is addressed by this question. This may happen occasionally. Don't waste time trying to figure it out; just start reading the answer choices. This is a priority-setting question—you must select the *best* answer choice. Eliminate IV because it is teacher-directed, not student-centered. Eliminate B and D. Since the remaining answer choices contain Roman I and Roman II, you now know that this question deals with **how learning occurs.** Thus, it assesses Competency 004: *The teacher understands how learning occurs and can apply this understanding to design and implement effective instruction.* Instructionally, Mr. Zhong understands that learning is enhanced when students are able to connect new material to prior knowledge (Roman I). When they generate questions (beforehand) about what they would personally like to learn on the field trip (Roman II), they are more likely to view learning as a purposeful pursuit and thus learn better. However, this question also deals with **classroom management** (Competency 011) because, managerially, reviewing conduct rules immediately before leaving on the field trip (Roman III) will remind students that appropriate behavior is as important on field trips as it is in the classroom. Choice C is the correct response.

57. **C** The question deals with **school-home relationships.** Thus, its primary focus is Competency 013: *The teacher knows how to foster strong school-home relationships that support student achievement of desired learning outcomes.* Eliminate A and B because these measures would conflict with treating students with dignity. Eliminate D because this may be of interest to some parents but it will not be as important as providing them with a schedule for the day's activities and telling them where to meet for lunch. Choice C is the correct response.

58. **D** This question deals with **planning.** Thus, its primary focus is Competency 006: *The teacher uses planning processes to design outcome-oriented learning experiences that foster understanding and encourage self-directed thinking and learning in both individual and collaborative settings.* This is a priority-setting question—you must select the answer choice that is *most* in accord with the philosophy underlying inclusion. The philosophy underlying inclusion is that children who have special needs should be accepted and valued among their nondisabled peers. The teaching method that is most in accord with the philosophy of inclusion is cooperative learning. It can be used across the full range of student populations. Research indicates that, in particular, physically or mentally disabled children benefit from involvement in cooperative learning instruction. Eliminate A, B, and C because these methods tend to isolate students from each other and so are

not as supportive of the inclusion philosophy as cooperative learning. Choice D is the correct response.

59. **A** This question deals with **ethical, legal, and professional standards.** Thus, its primary focus is Competency 015: *The teacher understands requirements, expectations, and constraints associated with teaching in Texas, and can apply this understanding in a variety of contexts.* This is a priority-setting question—you must select the *best* answer choice. According to PL 94-142, placement in the "least restrictive environment" means placement of the student in the regular classroom to the maximum extent appropriate. By law, the ARD committee must place the student in a classroom with his or her peers, unless the student's disability is so severe that education in a regular classroom setting cannot be achieved satisfactorily. Eliminate D because placement of a student is determined by the ARD committee, not by the student alone (although, if appropriate, the student may serve on the ARD committee). Eliminate B and C because these placements may or may not occur under "least restrictive environment." Placing disabled students in a setting that enables them to function to their fullest capacity best reflects the concept of "least restrictive environment." Choice A is the correct response.

60. **C** This question deals with **ethical, legal, and professional standards.** Thus, its primary focus is Competency 015: *The teacher understands requirements, expectations, and constraints associated with teaching in Texas, and can apply this understanding in a variety of contexts.* It is appropriate for Mr. Harrison to make sure he has a clear understanding of the laws applying to the students with special needs who come to his classroom. Eliminate A, B, and D because these measures are not mandated in PL 94-142. PL 94-142, the Education for All Handicapped Children Act of 1975, subsequently revised and now known as the Individuals with Disabilities Education Act (IDEA), obligates each state to provide free and appropriate public education for all children. Choice C is the correct response.

61. **D** This question deals with **ethical, legal, and professional standards.** Thus, its primary focus is Competency 015: *The teacher understands requirements, expectations, and constraints associated with teaching in Texas, and can apply this understanding in a variety of contexts.* The Individuals with Disabilities Education Act (IDEA) mandates that the individualized education program (IEP) be developed (Roman I) by the admissions, review, and dismissal (ARD) committee (Roman II) after the child has been identified as eligible for special services (Roman III), and it requires the teacher to follow the IEP (Roman IV). Choice D is the correct response.

62. **A** This question deals with **ethical, legal, and professional standards.** Thus, its primary focus is Competency 015: *The teacher*

understands requirements, expectations, and constraints associated with teaching in Texas, and can apply this understanding in a variety of contexts. Eliminate B because this is not a parental right specified under IDEA. Eliminate C and D because, generally, parents do not have the professional training necessary to interpret evaluation data or determine appropriate interventions. Due process under IDEA gives parents the right to participate in the evaluative and decision-making process regarding the educational placement of their disabled child. Choice A is the correct response.

63. **C** This question deals with **ethical, legal, and professional standards.** Thus, its primary focus is Competency 015: *The teacher understands requirements, expectations, and constraints associated with teaching in Texas, and can apply this understanding in a variety of contexts.* This is a priority-setting question—you must select the *best* answer choice. Eliminate A because only the ARD committee can update the IEP of a student. Eliminate B because the ARD committee determined that the physical education class was the LRE, so Mr. Harrison cannot place Cody in a different setting, like a special class. Eliminate D because although this may be a modification consistent with Cody's IEP, this response is not the *best* answer choice. Ms. Gauss should inform Mr. Harrison that, according to federal and state law, he can *best* meet his legal and ethical responsibilities as Cody's teacher by ensuring that instruction for Cody is consistent with the goals and specifications of the IEP. Choice C is the correct response.

64. **D** Upon first reading, this question appears to deal with **diversity** (What does Mr. Harrison do *first* when working with a special education student?). Go with that for the moment. This is a priority-setting question—you must decide what Mr. Harrison should do *first.* In order to plan appropriate physical activities for Cody, Mr. Harrison must first know more about Cody's condition and degree of physical impairment. Eliminate A because this may be a measure Mr. Harrison might take later, but it is not the *first* thing he should do. Eliminate B because Mr. Harrison needs accurate, reliable information regarding Cody's condition that Cody may or may not know. Now that A and B have been eliminated, a quick glance reveals that the remaining answer choices deal with **professionalism.** Thus, the primary focus of this question is Competency 012: *The teacher is a reflective practitioner who knows how to promote his or her own professional growth and can work cooperatively with other professionals in the system to create a school culture that enhances learning and encourages positive change.* Eliminate C because this may impose on the special education teacher's time; however, it would be appropriate for Mr. Harrison to ask the special education teacher to provide additional information about how to meet Cody's unique individual needs. Choice D is the correct response.

65. **A** This question deals with **classroom management.** Thus, its primary focus is Competency 011: *The teacher structures and manages the learning environment to maintain a classroom climate that promotes the lifelong pursuit of learning and encourages cooperation, leadership, and mutual respect.* Eliminate Roman II because Mr. Harrison has no reason to believe that Cody may be easily distracted, so minimizing distractions would not be necessary in Cody's case. Eliminate B. Eliminate Roman IV because this would isolate Cody from the rest of the class, which would be inconsistent with Cody's IEP. Eliminate B and C. The accommodations Mr. Harrison should make are to provide preferential seating (Roman I), if needed, and to arrange the physical layout to facilitate Cody's movement around the room by minimizing obstructions (Roman III). Choice A is the correct response.

66. **A** This question deals with **diversity.** Thus, its primary focus is Competency 003: *The teacher appreciates human diversity, recognizing how diversity in the classroom and the community may affect learning, and creating a classroom environment in which both the diversity of groups and the uniqueness of individuals are recognized and celebrated.* Eliminate B because *severely emotionally disturbed* refers to a psychotic disorder such as schizophrenia or autism. Eliminate C because *learning disabled* refers to children whose achievement does not match their IQ potential—from the information provided in the stimulus, you have no reason to conclude this is the case with Larry. Eliminate D because *educable mentally retarded* children are usually not instructed in the regular education classroom. Larry exhibits the symptoms associated with attention deficit hyperactivity disorder (ADHD). The primary symptoms of ADHD are inattention, impulsiveness, and overactivity. Since frequently, over months, Larry has exhibited behaviors in each of these categories, it is likely that he has ADHD. Choice A is the correct response.

67. **B** This question deal with **classroom management.** Competency 011: *The teacher structures and manages the learning environment to maintain a classroom climate that promotes the lifelong pursuit of learning and encourages cooperation, leadership, and mutual respect.* Eliminate A because effective classroom managers are quick to respond to inappropriate behavior even when it is exhibited by students with special needs. Teachers need to use appropriate management strategies for students with special needs. For instance, hyperactive students need classrooms structured with well-defined rules, definite consequences for breaking them, and consistency in enforcing them. These students need planned opportunities for physical movement (for instance, passing out materials, erasing the chalkboard, or running errands). Eliminate C and D because these could be inappropriate for a student with ADHD. Choice B is the correct response.

68. **B** This question deals with **classroom management.** Thus, its primary focus is Competency 011: *The teacher structures and manages the learning environment to maintain a classroom climate that promotes the lifelong pursuit of learning and encourages cooperation, leadership, and mutual respect.* Eliminate Roman II because successful classroom managers minimize the time students spend waiting for activities to get started, making transitions between activities, sitting with nothing to do, or engaging in misbehavior. Eliminate A, C, and D. Effective classroom managers teach and model appropriate behavior (Roman I), and they organize the classroom and instruction to eliminate conditions conducive to misbehavior (Roman III). Further, when talking to a student who has behaved inappropriately, effective classroom managers help the student understand the reasons why inappropriate behavior is unacceptable and cannot be tolerated (Roman IV). Choice B is the correct response.

69. **B** This question deals with **classroom management.** Thus, its primary focus is Competency 011: *The teacher structures and manages the learning environment to maintain a classroom climate that promotes the lifelong pursuit of learning and encourages cooperation, leadership, and mutual respect.* Effective classroom managers build a positive relationship with students (eliminate C) and communicate clear expectations for appropriate student behavior (eliminate A). They maximize the time students are actively engaged in worthwhile academic tasks while minimizing the amount of time allocated to seatwork (eliminate D). Maintaining accurate and detailed grading procedures is important but is not a classroom management function. Choice B is the correct response.

70. **C** This question deals both with **developmentally appropriate instruction** (Which strategy is essential for ninth-graders?) and with **classroom management** (Mr. Harrison wants to maintain classroom order). Glancing at the answer choices, you can see that the four answer choices express appropriate classroom management strategies, so you will have to make your decision based on the developmental level of the students. Therefore, the primary focus of this question is Competency 001: *The teacher uses an understanding of human developmental processes to nurture student growth through developmentally appropriate instruction.* This is a priority-setting question—you must select the *most* essential answer choice. In grade nine, disciplinary aspects of classroom management become more pronounced. Eliminate A because formally teaching classroom rules is not as essential for high school students as it is for elementary school children. Ninth-graders function at the conventional level of Kohlberg's stages of moral development. At this stage, judgments are based on obeying the laws and rules of society. Eliminate B and D because these are appropriate measures Mr. Harrison may take, but it is *most* essential that Mr. Harrison consistently enforce the classroom rules

and their consequences so as to be consistent with the students' moral stage of development. Choice C is the correct response.

71. **C** This question deals with **classroom management.** Competency 011: *The teacher structures and manages the learning environment to maintain a classroom climate that promotes the lifelong pursuit of learning and encourages cooperation, leadership, and mutual respect.* Kounin believed that teachers should display certain management skills, including *overlapping*, use of the *ripple effect*, and *withitness*. Eliminate A because *overlapping* is the skill of being able to do more than one thing at a time, such as moving to stand beside a student who is off-task, answering a question from another student, and monitoring cooperative learning groups, all simultaneously. Eliminate B because the *ripple effect* occurs when a teacher reminds an off-task student to get back to work and all the other off-task students also return to their assignment. Eliminate D because *overseeing* is not an educational term. By *withitness*, Kounin means that teachers are aware of what is happening in the classroom at all times—they have "eyes in the back of their heads," so to speak. Mr. Harrison is displaying withitness in his classroom. Choice C is the correct response.

72. **C** This question deals with **assessment.** Thus, its primary focus is Competency 010: *The teacher uses processes of informal and formal assessment to understand individual learners, monitor instructional effectiveness, and shape instruction.* Eliminate A because it would be impractical for Ms. Reagan to arrange for her students to be tested using a standardized achievement test. Eliminate B because the final grade in Algebra I would provide information about overall performance, not about specific algebraic skills. Eliminate D because a norm-referenced test focuses on a comparison of a student's score to those of other students and may not provide information about specific algebraic skills. Diagnostic tests provide teachers with specific information about students' abilities relative to subject matter subskills. They are effective tools for assessing students' strengths and weaknesses. Choice C is the correct response.

73. **A** This question deals with **classroom management.** Thus, its primary focus is Competency 011: *The teacher structures and manages the learning environment to maintain a classroom climate that promotes the lifelong pursuit of learning and encourages cooperation, leadership, and mutual respect.* The first days of school are critical in establishing classroom order. Research indicates that during the first days of school, effective classroom managers initially are involved with the whole class. Ms. Reagan should not break students into groups on the first day. Eliminate B and C because Ms. Reagan should not be doing small-group activities on the first day. Eliminate D because this is an inappropriate teacher behavior. Choice A is the correct response.

74. **B** This question deals with grouping practices, which come under **instructional strategies.** Thus, the primary focus of this question is Competency 008: *The teacher uses a variety of instructional strategies and roles to facilitate learning and to help students become independent thinkers and problem solvers who use higher-order thinking in the classroom and the real world.* This is a priority-setting question—you must select the *best* strategy. Eliminate A because it relates to **classroom management** (Competency 011). Eliminate C and D because they focus on the learning task and not the learner—they are not learner-centered. Ms. Flores takes account of factors relevant to instructional planning, such as the varied characteristics of the learners in her classroom. She recognizes the importance of adapting instruction to meet the needs of the more able learners, as well as the needs of the less able learners. Choice B is the correct response.

75. **A** This question deals with **instructional strategies.** Thus, its primary focus is Competency 008: *The teacher uses a variety of instructional strategies and roles to facilitate learning and to help students become independent thinkers and problem solvers who use higher-order thinking in the classroom and the real world.* This is a priority-setting question—you must select the *most* likely answer choice. Eliminate C and D because these may occur but would not necessarily result from inquiry, discovery, and cooperative learning. Eliminate B because this is an unlikely outcome of these teaching strategies. Ms. Reagan's plans are likely to foster self-directed learning, since the teaching strategies she has decided to use will give the students more responsibility for their own and each other's learning. Choice A is the correct response.

76. **A** This question deals with **instructional strategies.** Thus, its primary focus is Competency 008: *The teacher uses a variety of instructional strategies and roles to facilitate learning and to help students become independent thinkers and problem solvers who use higher-order thinking in the classroom and the real world.* This is a priority-setting question—you must select the *least* desirable answer choice. Eliminate B because when students are encouraged to wait before deciding on a solution to a problem, they spend more time thinking about and analyzing the problem. Eliminate C because more problems requiring analytical skills than basic computation problems would be more conducive to higher-order thinking and problem solving. Eliminate D because when students rely more on themselves to determine whether something is mathematically correct, they engage in critical thinking in order to clarify their mathematical thinking. Ms. Reagan should be aware that establishing a teacher-controlled, structured classroom climate is likely to discourage higher-order thinking and problem solving. Choice A is the correct response.

77. **C** This question deals with **how learning occurs.** Thus, its primary focus is Competency 004: *The teacher understands how learning*

occurs and can apply this understanding to design and implement effective instruction. Eliminate A, B, and D because they focus on learning formulas, which do not promote student understanding. Ms. Reagan should recognize the importance of prior knowledge in the learning process. By writing down and discussing in small groups what they already know about the lesson topic, the students will review their prior knowledge on the topic. This will make it easier for them to link new knowledge encountered to their prior understandings. Choice C is the correct response.

78. **D** This question deals with **planning.** Thus, its primary focus is Competency 006: *The teacher uses planning processes to design outcome-oriented learning experiences that foster understanding and encourage self-directed thinking and learning in both individual and collaborative settings.* This is a priority-setting question—you must select the *most* likely answer choice. Eliminate B because differential reasoning would be used to decide only how items are different. Eliminate C because evaluative reasoning would involve some kind of value judgment. Eliminate A because *deductive reasoning* starts with basic assumptions or facts and proceeds step by step to a logical conclusion. *Inductive reasoning* involves looking at specific examples and trying to identify a pattern or trend that fits the given examples in order to determine a general rule. Since the students are to draw a general conclusion based on several examples, Ms. Reagan is most likely attempting to promote their use of inductive reasoning. Choice D is the correct response.

79. **A** This question deals with **planning.** Thus, its primary focus is Competency 006: *The teacher uses planning processes to design outcome-oriented learning experiences that foster understanding and encourage self-directed thinking and learning in both individual and collaborative settings.* This is a priority-setting question—you must select the *most* likely answer choice. Eliminate B because differential reasoning would be used to decide only how items are different. Eliminate C because evaluative reasoning would involve some kind of value judgment. Eliminate D because *inductive reasoning* involves looking at several specific examples and trying to identify a pattern or trend that fits the given examples in order to determine a general rule. *Deductive reasoning* starts with basic assumptions or facts and proceeds step by step to a logical conclusion. Since the students are to reach a conclusion based on two assumptions, Ms. Reagan is most likely attempting to promote their use of deductive reasoning. Choice A is the correct response.

80. **D** This question deals with **planning.** Thus, its primary focus is Competency 006: *The teacher uses planning processes to design outcome-oriented learning experiences that foster understanding and encourage self-directed thinking and learning in both*

individual and collaborative settings. This is a priority-setting question—you must select the *most* likely answer choice. Eliminate B because the problem given does not have just one right answer. Eliminate C because it is not supported by the stimulus—the students are not required to make up a "real-world" problem for the equation. The stimulus tells us that Ms. Reagan wants to foster higher-order thinking and enhance problem-solving skills. Posing open-ended problems that have many correct solutions requires students to use their reasoning powers in addition to their knowledge of basic skills. Eliminate A because this is likely to occur but is not the *most* likely reason for Ms. Reagan to give problem 3. Ms. Reagan is likely to know that allowing the students to figure out for themselves what will work for this problem will help them to develop a deeper understanding of the mathematical principles involved. Choice D is the correct response.

81. **A** This question deals with **planning.** Thus, its primary focus is Competency 006: *The teacher uses planning processes to design outcome-oriented learning experiences that foster understanding and encourage self-directed thinking and learning in both individual and collaborative settings.* This is a priority-setting question—you must select the *most* likely answer choice. Eliminate B because *overlearning* is practicing beyond the point of mastery to improve retention. Eliminate C because *discrimination* would involve recognizing differences. Eliminate D because *creativity* involves putting together information to come up with new ideas or understandings. Ms. Reagan wants the students to take a skill they have learned in one setting and use it in a new setting. The ability to carry over learning from one setting to a different setting is known as *generalization.* Choice A is the correct response.

82. **B** This question deals with **professionalism.** Thus, its primary focus is Competency 012: *The teacher is a reflective practitioner who knows how to promote his or her own professional growth and can work cooperatively with other professionals in the system to create a school culture that enhances learning and encourages positive change.* This is a priority-setting question—you must select the *best* answer choice. Eliminate C because Ms. Flores is acting as a resource, not using a resource. Eliminate D because Ms. Flores is not examining her role as a professional. Eliminate A because by helping Ms. Reagan, Ms. Flores may be cultivating a positive relationship with Ms. Reagan, but Ms. Flores's actions *best* illustrate that she recognizes she is a member of a learning community and knows how to work with all members of that community (for instance, by mentoring) to accomplish educational goals. Choice B is the correct response.

83. **A** This question deals both with **developmentally appropriate instruction** (For high school students, why use homework?) and with **assessment** (Homework is a type of assessment). Glancing at the answer choices, you can see that Roman I through IV express

appropriate reasons for giving homework, so you will have to make your decision based on the developmental level of the students. Therefore, the primary focus of this question is Competency 001: *The teacher uses an understanding of human developmental processes to nurture student growth through developmentally appropriate instruction.* This is a priority-setting question—you must select the *primary* reason(s) for using homework in high school. Teachers should understand the importance of ongoing assessment as an instructional tool. One important method for teachers to find out what students have learned and to increase academic achievement is through assigning homework. In the elementary and middle school grades, students should be given homework to help them develop good study habits (eliminate Roman II), develop positive attitudes toward school (eliminate Roman III), and realize that learning is something to do not only at school but also at home. Eliminate B, C, and D. In high school, teachers should assign homework on a regular basis. For students at this developmental stage, homework is *primarily* used as a means to increase academic achievement. Choice A is the correct response.

84. **B** This question deals both with **developmentally appropriate instruction** (For her high school students, what guidelines for homework should Ms. Reagan use?) and with **assessment** (Homework is a type of assessment). Glancing at the answer choices, you can see that the four answer choices express appropriate guidelines for homework, so you will have to make your decision based on which are appropriate for high school students. Therefore, the primary focus of this question is Competency 001: *The teacher uses an understanding of human developmental processes to nurture student growth through developmentally appropriate instruction.* Among recommendations for the use of homework at all grade levels are that it should be frequently orally checked in class (eliminate A), coordinated with what the students' other teachers are requiring them to do (eliminate C), and successfully completed by most of the students (eliminate D); also, it is not unreasonable to expect homework assignments in high school to take several hours to complete. Choice B is the correct response.

85. **C** This question deals with reinforcement, which comes under **motivation.** Thus, its primary focus is Competency 005: *The teacher understands how motivation affects group and individual behavior and learning and can apply this understanding to promote learning.* The appropriate use of reinforcement, the recognition and rewarding of students' good behavior, is a long-recognized and essential skill for classroom teachers. The basic principle of reinforcement is that students will continue good behaviors that are reinforced and discontinue undesirable behaviors when they are not reinforced. The effects of reinforcement depend on many factors, including the frequency

with which reinforcement is given. Eliminate A because this would result if Arty were on a continuous reinforcement schedule (that is, a desirable behavior is reinforced every time it occurs). Eliminate B and D because they contradict the basic principle of reinforcement. When a desirable behavior initially is reinforced every time it occurs, then reinforcement switches to every second time, then every third time, and so on, the frequency of the behavior increases and the behavior becomes highly resistant to extinction. Choice C is the correct response.

86. **B** This question deals with teacher expectations, which relate to **students' self-esteem.** Thus, its primary focus is Competency 002: *The teacher considers environmental factors that may affect learning in designing a supportive and responsive classroom community that promotes all students' learning and self-esteem.* This is a priority-setting question—you must select the *best* answer choice. Eliminate A because it deals with **materials and resources** (Competency 009). Eliminate C and D because they deal with **diversity** (Competency 003). By holding expectations of success for all his students, Mr. McGruder is recognizing factors (that is, teacher expectations) that influence students' perceptions of their own worth. Choice B is the correct response.

87. **D** This question deals with **assessment.** Thus, its primary focus is Competency 010: *The teacher uses processes of information and formal assessment to understand individual learners, monitor instructional effectiveness, and shape instruction.* This is a priority-setting question—you must decide what Ms. Evertson should do *first. Mastery learning* proposes that all children can learn when provided with the appropriate learning conditions in the classroom. Students must demonstrate mastery of well-defined, appropriately sequenced units as they progress through the content of the course. The teacher provides frequent and specific feedback. Mastery grading is based on the number of units completed or skills mastered. Assessment is through criterion-referenced tests, rather than norm-referenced tests, and students are allowed ample time to relearn material that is not mastered. Eliminate A because mastery learning allows students ample time to master the material, so cut-off scores would be inappropriate. Eliminate C because this measure would not be helpful to a teacher who is assessing students on their individual attainment of specific skills. Eliminate B because Ms. Evertson is likely to do this, but not before she defines the content and skill objectives to be learned. Choice D is the correct response.

88. **D** This question deals with **assessment.** Thus, its primary focus is Competency 010: *The teacher uses the processes of informal and formal assessment to understand individual learners, monitor instructional effectiveness, and shape instruction.* Mr. Luna should be aware of the ramifications involved for various grading practices and their impact on students and the class, in general. The

phrase "grading on a curve" means that the grades A, B, C, D, and F are distributed among the students according to percentages consistent with a normal curve distribution. Students' scores are determined relative to the mean of all the scores—with scores near the mean receiving grades of C, scores a specified distance below the mean receiving grades of D or F, and scores a specified distance above the mean receiving grades of B or A. Thus, the more able students need only do better than their classmates to earn a high grade, which may or may not mean they have to do more work. Eliminate A. Eliminate B because it is unrelated to the idea of "grading on a curve." Eliminate C because if a teacher truly grades on a curve, then a certain percentage of the students must make F's. Mr. Luna should know that "grading on a curve" means that at least some of the students, no matter how bright, will receive failing marks. Choice D is the correct response.

89. **C** This question deals with **students' self-esteem.** Thus, its primary focus is Competency 002: *The teacher considers environmental factors that may affect learning in designing a supportive and responsive classroom that promotes all students' learning and self-esteem.* This is a priority-setting question—you must select the *most* effective answer choice. Eliminate A because this may negatively affect self-worth if the students are not successful after having been urged to try harder. Eliminate B and D because these are measures Mr. McGruder might take to enhance self-worth, but they would not be as effective as choice C. Students who have a pattern of failure may be victims of *learned helplessness.* They may feel doomed to failure because they believe their abilities are fixed and thus they are incapable of success. They may not attribute success to their own efforts unless the teacher helps them make this link. By planning activities in which the students achieve success and know how they contributed to it, Mr. McGruder can help them make this link, which in turn will enhance their feelings of self-sufficiency and self-worth. Choice C is the correct response.

90. **A** This question deals with **school-community relationships.** Thus, its primary focus is Competency 014: *The teacher understands how the school relates to the larger community and knows strategies for making interactions between school and community mutually supportive and beneficial.* This is a priority-setting question—you must select the *most* likely answer choice. Eliminate C because it would be inappropriate for volunteer tutors to assume such a role. Eliminate B and D because these may occur inadvertently but would not be *most* likely. Since community members, especially grandparents, have a vested interest in the schools, they are a valuable resource to teachers. By using grandparent-volunteers, Mr. McGruder is cultivating strong community-school partnerships and thus fostering positive ties between the school and the community and establishing a sense of community ownership of the school. Choice A is the correct response.

APPENDIX A

APPENDIX

Supplemental Materials

GLOSSARY OF IMPORTANT TERMS

ability   The degree of competence present in a student to perform a given physical or mental act.

ability grouping   The grouping of students for instruction by ability or achievement for the purpose of reducing heterogeneity.

abstract concepts   Those concepts that can be acquired only indirectly through the senses or that cannot be perceived directly through the senses.

academic learning time   The time a student is actually on-task and engaged successfully in learning.

acceleration   Rapid promotion through advanced studies; enables students to progress more rapidly through the standard curriculum.

accommodation   The modification of an existing way of doing something to fit a new experience.

accountability   A concept in which the school system, and especially teachers, are held responsible for the quality of instruction and the progress of their students.

achievement   Level of attainment or proficiency.

achievement motivation   The generalized tendency to strive for success without extrinsic reward.

achievement test   A standardized test designed to measure levels of knowledge, understanding, abilities, or skills acquired in a particular subject already learned.

active listening   Being in tune with the words and thoughts of the speaker.

ADD (attention deficit disorder)   A condition characterized by an inability to concentrate.

ADHD (attention deficit hyperactivity disorder)   A label applied to individuals who are extremely active, impulsive, distractible, and excitable and have great difficulty concentrating on what they are doing.

advance organizers   Preview questions and comments that provide structure for new information to be presented to increase learners' comprehension.

AEIS (Academic Excellence Indicator System)   The State Board of Education accountability system for Texas public schools based on performance on a set of indicators of the quality of learning on a campus (TEC 39.051).

AEP (alternative education program)   An educational program, provided in a setting other than a student's regular classroom, that provides for disruptive students to be separated from other students (TEC 37.008).

affective domain   The realm of feelings, emotions, and attitudes in people.

affective objectives   Behavioral objectives that emphasize changes in interest, attitudes, and values, or a degree of adjustment, acceptance, or rejection.

affiliation motive   The intrinsic desire to be with others.

AFT (American Federation of Teachers)   One of two national educators' unions.

alignment   Matching learning activities with desired outcomes; or matching what is taught to what is tested.

algorithm   A set of rules or procedures for performing a task.

allocated time   The time set aside for specific school activities, such as teaching or lunch.

alternative assessment   assessment that is different from conventional test formats (for instance, see authentic assessment).

analysis   Learning that involves the subdividing of knowledge to show how it fits together.

anxiety   A feeling of uneasiness associated with the fear of failure.

application   Learning that requires applying knowledge to produce a result; problem solving.

aptitude test   A standardized test designed to predict future performance in a subject area.

ARD (admission, review, and dismissal) committee   Under IDEA, a committee formed by the school to identify a child as requiring special education or related services and to develop, review, or revise a child's individualized education program (IEP); must meet at least once a year (TEC 5.001).

ASEP (Accountability System for Educator Preparation)   The State Board for Educator Certification accountability system, under which educator preparation programs are held accountable for the readiness for certification of educators completing the programs (TEC 21.045).

ASL (American Sign Language)   A widely used language system employed by the hearing impaired.

assertive discipline   A classroom management approach that stresses the need for teachers to communicate classroom rules firmly, but without hostility.

assessment   A measure of what students know and are able to do; a measure of the degree to which instructional objectives have been attained.

assimilation   The process of fitting a new experience into existing ways of doing things.

assistive technology device   Any item, piece of equipment, or product system... that is used to increase, maintain, or improve functional capabilities of individuals with disabilities (20 U.S.C. Chapter 33, § 1401[25]). Example, Braille writers, speech synthesizers.

at risk   Describing a student with socioeconomic challenges, such as poverty or teen pregnancy, that may place him or her at a disadvantage in achieving academic, social, or career goals (TEC 29.081). Also used to describe a student who is a low-achieving, slower learner who falls between regular and special education, but who may have a problem (physical, mental, educational, etc.) requiring further evaluation and/or intervention.

attending behavior   Use of verbal and nonverbal cues by listeners that demonstrate they are listening with attention to what is being said.

attitude   A predisposition to act in a positive or negative way toward persons, ideas, or events.

attraction   Friendship patterns in the classroom area.

authentic assessment   Assessment of students' performances in real-world, knowledge application tasks; includes but is not limited to the use of projects, presentations, hands-on science demonstrations, oral interviews, portfolios, reflective journals, and so forth.

basal reader   A reading book that incorporates simple stories and practice exercises.

base-line score   A score calculated as a point of comparison with later test scores; relatively stable indicator of typical performance in a content area.

basic skills   The foundational knowledge and skills students are expected to acquire in elementary and middle school, in such areas as reading and mathematics.

behavior   What someone does.

behavior disorder   A form of behavior that is socially unacceptable.

behavior modification   The use of learning theory to reduce or eliminate undesirable behavior or to teach new responses.

behavioral learning theory   Explanations of learning that emphasize observable changes in behavior.

behavioral (instructional) objectives   Aims of instruction (or any learning activity) stated in terms of observable behavior.

behaviorism   School of psychological thought that seeks to explain learning through observable changes in behavior.

benchmark   A baseline of data.

between-class ability grouping   A system of grouping in which students are assigned to classes according to achievement and abilities.

bilingual   Capable of using two languages, but usually with differing levels of skills.

bilingual education program   A full-time program of dual-language instruction that provides for learning basic skills in the primary language of the students enrolled in the program and for carefully structured and sequenced mastery of English language skills; must be designed to consider the students' learning experiences and must incorporate the cultural aspects of the students' backgrounds (TEC 29.055).

Bloom's taxonomy   A system that describes six levels of learning: knowledge, comprehension, application, analysis, synthesis, and evaluation.

brain-based learning   Using "brain-compatible" strategies for learning based on how the brain works.

brain hemisphericity   Refers to a person's preference for receiving information through either the left or right hemisphere of the brain.

brainstorming   A teaching strategy in which students generate ideas, judgments of the ideas of others is forbidden, and ideas are used to create a flow of new ideas.

burnout   The condition of losing interest and motivation in teaching.

CAI (computer assisted instruction)   Instruction in which a computer is used to present instructional material.

campus leadership   Refers to the principal, the assistant principal, or the campus leadership team.

campus-level committee   A state-mandated committee of representative professional staff, parents of students enrolled in the district, and community members that makes decisions affecting the campus (TEC 11.251).

campus plan   A plan developed each school year, by the principal of the school campus with the assistance of the campus-level committee, for the purpose of improving student performance for all student populations with respect to the academic excellence indicators adopted under TEC 39.051 and any other appropriate performance measures for special-needs populations (TEC 11.253).

Carnegie unit   A credit representing the completion of a core of high school courses.

centration   Focusing attention on only one aspect of an object or situation.

CD-ROM   An acronym for "compact disk–read only memory," used to describe a device for storing information.

Chapter I   A federal program that gives money for education to districts that have a high number of disadvantaged students; currently called Title I.

character education   Deliberate instruction in basic virtues or morals.

charter schools   Schools run independently of the traditional public school but receiving public funding; authorized in Texas under TEC 12.001.

checking for mastery   A component in the lesson cycle in which the teacher determines whether the students have mastered the concepts.

checking for understanding   A component in the lesson cycle in which the teacher determines whether students have knowledge and comprehension of new material.

child abuse or child neglect   See Texas Family Code 261.001 (available at http://www.capitol.state.tx.us/statutes/codes/FA000070.html).

choral response   Response to a question made by the whole class in unison; useful when there is only one correct answer.

chronological age   Age in calendar years.

classical conditioning   A form of conditioning in which a neutral stimulus (such as the bell in Pavlov's experiment) comes to elicit a response (such as salivation) after it is repeatedly paired with reinforcement (such as food).

classroom climate   The atmosphere or mood surrounding classroom interactions.

classroom control   The process of influencing student behavior in the classroom.

classroom management   The teacher's system of establishing a climate for learning, including techniques for preventing and redirecting or stopping student misbehavior.

closure   A component in the lesson cycle in which the teacher summarizes and brings the lesson to an appropriate conclusion.

coaching   Teaching by an "expert" who gives feedback on performance; can be as effective as athletic coaching; results in about 83 percent retention of learning.

Code of Ethics and Standard Practices   Standards of ethical conduct of teachers, violation of which may subject educators to disciplinary action (TEC 21.041).

cognition   The mental operations involved in thinking.

cognitive development   Increasing complexity of thought and reasoning.

cognitive dissonance   Mental confusion that occurs when new information received conflicts with existing understandings.

cognitive domain   The psychological field of mental activity.

cognitive objectives   Behavioral objectives that emphasize remembering or reproducing something that has presumably been learned, or that involves the solving of some intellectual task.

cognitive sciences   The area of study that focuses on how people think and learn.

cohesiveness   The collective feeling that the class members have about the classroom group; the sum of the individual members' feelings about the group.

compensatory education   Federally funded education for disadvantaged students.

competency test   Test of performance of certain functions, especially basic skills, usually at a level required by the state or school district.

comprehension   Learning that involves making interpretations of previously learned materials.

compulsory education   Legally mandated school attendance for every child (unless specifically exempted under state law) who is at least six years of age and who has not yet reached his or her 19th birthday (TEC 25.085).

concept   An abstract idea common to a set of objects, conditions, events, or processes.

concept map   A procedure for organizing and graphically displaying relationships among ideas relevant to a given topic.

concrete concepts   Concepts that can be perceived directly through one of the five senses.

conditioned reinforcers   Reinforcers that are learned.

consequence   A condition that follows a behavior, designed to weaken or strengthen the behavior.

conservation   The logical thinking ability to recognize an invariant property under different conditions.

constructivism   a learner-centered approach to teaching that emphasizes teaching for understanding predicated on the concept that students construct knowledge for themselves based on what they already know and by interactions with their environment.

content validity   The degree to which the content covered by a measurement device matches the instruction that preceded it.

continuous reinforcement schedule   A reinforcement schedule in which every occurrence of the desired behavior is reinforced.

convergent question   A question that has only one correct response.

convergent thinking   Thinking that occurs when the task, or question, is so structured that the number of possible appropriate conclusions is limited (usually one conclusion).

cooperative learning   A teaching strategy in which students work together on assigned tasks and are rewarded on the basis of the success of the group.

core curriculum   The curriculum required for all students.

correlation   The amount of relationship between two variables; usually expressed numerically as a number between –1 and +1; positive correlation occurs when, generally, high values on one variable correspond to high values on another; and negative correlation occurs when, generally, high values on one variable correspond to low values on another.

CPDT (Center for Professional Development of Teachers)   A center for professional development at an institution of higher education for the purpose of integrating technology and innovative teaching practices in the preservice and staff development training of public school teachers and administrators; usually established through a collaborative process involving public schools, regional education service centers, and other entities or businesses (TEC 21.047).

creation   Cognitive learning that entails combining elements and parts in order to form a new whole or to produce an evaluation based on specified criteria.

creative thinking   Putting together information to come up with new ideas or understandings.

criterion-referenced test   A standardized test that assesses the level of mastery of specific knowledge and skills that are anchored to curriculum objectives.

critical thinking   Complex thinking skills that include the ability to evaluate information, generate insights, and reach objective conclusions by logically examining the problem and the evidence.

cross-age tutoring   Peer tutoring in which an older student teaches a younger student.

cues   Signals that indicate which behaviors will be reinforced or punished.

cultural pluralism   The condition in which all cultural groups are valued components of the society, and the language and traditions of each group are maintained.

culturally fair test   A test designed to reduce cultural bias.

dangle   A lesson transition during which the teacher leaves a lesson hanging while tending to something else in the classroom.

decentralization   A term that refers to decision making being done at the lowest possible level rather than, traditionally, at the highest level.

decision making   The making of choices from among several alternatives.

deductive learning   Learning that proceeds from the general to the specific.

deductive reasoning   Reasoning that proceeds from general principles to a logical conclusion.

deficiency needs   Maslow's term for the lower-level needs in his hierarchy: survival, safety, belongingness, and self-esteem.

delayed reinforcement   Reinforcement of desired action that took place at an earlier time.

descriptive data   Data that have been organized, categorized, or quantified by an observer but do not involve a value judgment.

development   Growth, adaptation, or change over the course of a lifetime.

diagnostic procedure   Procedures to determine what pupils are capable of doing with respect to given learning tasks.

diagnostic test   An assessment that provides information that can be used to identify specific areas of strength and weakness.

direct instruction   A deductive model of instructional delivery that encourages high engagement of learners and requires structured, accomplishable tasks.

disability   Any hindrance or difficulty imposed by a physical, mental, or emotional problem.

disabled   The condition of an individual who has lost physical, social, or psychological functioning that significantly interferes with normal growth and development.

discipline   In teaching, the process of controlling student behavior in the classroom.

discourse   The interactive exchanges including talking, sharing, explaining, justifying, defending, agreeing, and disagreeing among the students and the teacher in the classroom.

discovery learning   Learning that proceeds in the following sequence: identification of a problem, development of hypotheses, testing of hypotheses, arrival at conclusion; also, instructional approach in which students learn through their own active explorations of concepts and principles.

disjunctive concepts   Concepts that have two or more sets of alternative conditions under which the concept appears.

distance education   The use of telecommunications to deliver live instruction by content experts to remote geographic settings.

distributed practice   Practice repeated at intervals over time.

divergent thinking   The type of thinking whereby an individual arrives at a new or unique answer that has not been completely determined by earlier information.

diversity   The condition of having a variety of groups in the same setting.

drill and practice   Learning through repeated performance.

due process   Procedural safeguards afforded students, parents, and teachers that protects individual rights.

dyscalculia   A math-related learning disability characterized by an inability to grasp and remember math concepts, rules, and formulas, despite conventional instruction, adequate intelligence, and sociocultural opportunity.

dyslexia   A disorder manifested by a difficulty in learning to read, write, or spell, despite conventional instruction, adequate intelligence, and sociocultural opportunity (TEC 38.003)

early childhood (preschool years)   The period from the end of infancy to about 5 or 6 years of age.

eclectic   Using a variety of sources.

educational goal   A desired instructional outcome that is broad in scope.

educational placement   The setting in which a student receives educational services.

effective school correlates   A body of research identifying the characteristics of effective and ineffective schools. They are: (a) safe and orderly environment, (b) climate of high expectations for success, (c) instructional leadership, (d) clear and focused mission, (e) opportunity to learn and student time on task, (f) frequent monitoring of student progress, and (g) home/school relations.

effective schools research   Educational research focused on identifying unusually effective schools, studying the underlying attributes of their programs and personnel, and designing techniques to operationalize these attributes in less effective schools.

effective teacher   One who is able to bring about intended learning outcomes.

egocentric   Believing that everyone sees the world as you do.

egocentrism Piaget's term for the preoperational child's inability to distinguish between his or her own and another's perceptions.

e-mail   Electronic mail, usually delivered by interconnecting computers.

empathy   The ability to understand the feelings of another person.

empirical questions   Questions that require that a judgment be made or a value be put on something.

emotional disability   A disorder in which the capacity to manage individual or interactive behaviors is limited, impaired, or delayed and is exhibited by difficulty that persists over time and in more than one setting in one or more of the following areas: the ability to understand, build, or maintain interpersonal relationships; the ability to react/respond within established norms; the ability to keep normal fears, concerns, and/or anxieties in perspective; the ability to control aggressive and/or angry impulses or behavior.

engaged time (time on-task)   The actual time individual students spend as active participants in the learning process.

enrichment The process of providing richer and more varied content through strategies that supplement the standard curriculum; involves assignments or activities designed to broaden or deepen the knowledge of students who master classroom lessons quickly.

epistemology   The study of how knowledge is acquired.

equal opportunities for success   In cooperative learning, calculations of team achievement designed to ensure that equal individual improvement results in equal individual contribution to the team score, despite differences among teammates in absolute achievement.

equilibration   The process of restoring balance between what is understood and what is experienced.

ESEA (Elementary and Secondary Education Act)   A sweeping law that provides federal funding for elementary and secondary compensatory education programs.

ESL (English as a second language) program   A program of intensive instruction in English from teachers trained in recognizing and dealing with language differences; must be designed to consider students' learning experiences and must incorporate the cultural aspects of students' backgrounds (TEC 20.055).

essentialism   Educational philosophy that holds that a common core of knowledge and ideals should be the focus of the curriculum.

ethnicity   The ethnic identity (Caucasian, African-American, Hispanic-American, Native American, Asian-American, and so on) of an individual or group.

ethnocentrism   The belief that one's culture is better than any other culture.

Eurocentrism The belief that European culture is superior to others.

evaluation The cognitive process of establishing and applying standards in judging materials and methods.

evaluation questions   Questions that require that a judgment be made or a value be put on something.

exceptional child   A child who deviates from the average child in any of the following ways: mental characteristics, sensory ability, neuromotor or physical characteristics, social behavior, communication ability, or multiple handicaps.

ExCET (Examination for the Certification of Educators in Texas)   State-mandated test for educator certification (TEC 21.048).

explaining behavior   Planned teacher talk designed to clarify any idea, procedure, or process not understood by a student.

explanation   A component in the lesson cycle that contains what the teacher does to move learning to the student and the way in which the teacher accomplishes this transfer.

extension   A component in the lesson cycle that involves enlarging or expanding the original objective; also, a process by which a teacher asks a student to give additional information based on a student response contribution or by which the teacher provides such information.

extinction   The gradual disappearance of a behavior through the removal or the withholding of reinforcement.

extrinsic motivation   Motivation created by events or rewards outside the individual.

facilitative teaching   See indirect teaching.

facts   Well-grounded, clearly established pieces of information.

factual questions   Questions that require the recall of information through recognition or rote memory.

FAPE (free appropriate public education)   Provision of IDEA (formerly PL 94-142) that guarantees special education and related services to children with disabilities, at public cost.

feedback   Information from the teacher to the student, or vice versa, that provides disclosure about the reception of the intended message.

field-dependent   Learning style in which patterns are perceived as wholes.

field-independent   Learning style in which separate parts of a pattern are apparent.

fine-tuning   Making small adjustments in the planned procedures for a lesson during its teaching.

fixed-interval reinforcement schedule   A pattern in which reinforcement is given after a desired observable behavior has occurred only at certain periodic times; often results in a great deal of work (cramming) at the last minute, just before the reinforcement is given. *Example:* Final exams are fixed-interval reinforcements.

fixed-ratio reinforcement schedule   A pattern in which reinforcement is given after a desired observable behavior has occurred a fixed number (1, 5, 10, or so on) of times; effective in motivating students to do a great deal of work, but runs the risk of losing its value if the reinforcing is done too frequently. *Example:* Giving students stars after they read ten books is fixed-ratio reinforcement.

flip-flop   A lesson transition in which the teacher changes back and forth from one subject or activity to another.

focus   Component in the lesson cycle in which the teacher secures the attention of the students and communicates the lesson objectives.

focusing question   A question used to focus students' attention on a lesson or on the content of a lesson.

formative assessment   Assessment that takes place both before and during the learning process; used to guide the content and pace of lessons.

frequency measurement   A measure of the number of times specified, observable behaviors are exhibited in a constant time interval.

gender bias   Conscious or unconscious favorable treatment of females or males based on their sex.

generalization   The carryover of learning from one setting to a different setting.

gifted   A label applied to students who are exceptionally intelligent, creative, or talented.

goals   Extremely broad statements of school or instructional purposes.

Goals 2000   A federal program that codifies national educational goals. (See Goals 2000: Educate America Act, available at http://inet.ed.gov/legislation/GOALS2000/TheAct/index.html.)

goal structure   The degree to which students have to cooperate or compete for classroom rewards.

graphic organizers   Visual, hierarchical overviews designed to show relationships among the important concepts of a lesson; types include semantic mapping, webbing, clustering, and structured overviews.

group contingencies   Strategies in which the entire class is rewarded on the basis of everyone's behavior; removes peer support for misbehavior.

group discussion   Verbal interaction with other learners.

group-focus behaviors   Behaviors teachers use to maintain a focus on the group, rather than on an individual student, during individual recitations.

group investigation   A cooperative learning strategy in which students brainstorm a set of questions on a subject, form learning teams to find answers to questions, and make presentations to the whole class.

grouping, heterogeneous   A method of grouping in which students with a broad range of abilities, interests, achievement levels, and backgrounds are grouped together.

grouping, homogeneous   A method of grouping in which students with a relatively high degree of abilities, interests, achievement levels, and backgrounds are grouped together.

growth needs   Maslow's term for the three higher-level needs in his hierarchy: intellectual achievement, aesthetic appreciation, and self-actualization.

guided practice   A component in the lesson cycle in which the student practices the learning under the direct guidance of the teacher.

halting time   A teacher's pause in talking, used to give students time to think about presented materials or directions.

handicap Any hindrance or difficulty imposed by a physical, mental, or emotional problem.

hands-on Describing work by students with tools, processes, procedures, and so forth.

Head Start A federal program that provides economically deprived preschoolers with education, nutrition, health, and social services.

hidden curriculum The unintended and nonacademic learning that occurs in schools.

holistic evaluation Determination of the overall quality of a piece of work or an endeavor.

home schooling The practice of parents teaching their children at home rather than sending them to public school.

humanistic education Educational system designed to achieve affective outcomes or psychological growth; oriented toward improving self-awareness and mutual understanding among people.

hypermedia A nonlinear presentation of information that allows users to access related materials or images from a single computer screen.

hypothesize To make an educated guess to explain a phenomenon.

IDEA (Individuals with Disabilities Education Act) Far-reaching legislation that provides special education and services for children with disabilities.

Idealism The educational philosophy that embraces a belief in unchanging principles and eternal truths.

identity diffusion Inability of an adolescent to develop a clear sense of self.

identity foreclosure An adolescent's premature choice of a role.

IEP (individualized education program) Program or plan developed to meet the educational needs of a special education student.

illiterate The condition of being unable to read or write or perform everyday tasks (for example, understanding a bus schedule).

imagery Use of mental imagery to improve retention.

I-messages Clear teacher messages that tell students how the teacher feels about problem situations and implicitly ask for corrected behaviors.

imitation Carrying out the basic rudiments of a skill when given directions and supervision.

improvement scores Scores calculated by comparing the entering achievement levels with the performance after instruction.

impulsivity The tendency to respond quickly, but often without regard to accuracy.

inclusion Refers to the commitment to educate each child, to the maximum extent appropriate; it involves bringing the support services to the child and requires only that the child will benefit from being in class (rather than having to keep up with other students).

independent practice A component in the lesson cycle in which the student practices the learning on his or her own.

independent study An instructional strategy in which students are allowed to pursue a topic in depth on their own over an extended period.

indirect teaching Learner-centered teaching using discovery and inquiry instructional strategies.

individual accountability   In cooperative learning, making sure all individuals are responsible for their own learning.

individualized instruction   An instructional strategy characterized by a shift in responsibility for learning from the teacher to the student.

inductive reasoning   The process of drawing a general conclusion based on several examples.

inference A conclusion derived from and bearing some relation to assumed premises.

information superhighway   The developing network of digital communications, including satellite systems, the Internet, cable television, and telephone networks.

informational objectives   Abbreviated instructional objectives in which only the student performance and the product are specified.

inquiry Obtaining information by asking.

inquiry/discovery model   An inductive teaching model focusing on student investigation and explanation of a situation and designed to promote problem-solving skills and critical thinking skills; steps involved are defining the problem, developing hypotheses, data gathering, organizing and formulating explanations, and analyzing the process.

inquiry learning   Like discovery learning, except that the learner designs the processes to be used in resolving a problem; requires higher levels of mental operation than does discovery learning.

inservice training   The professional development workshops, lectures, and so forth provided by a district to keep teachers current in their fields.

instructional event   Any activity or set of activities in which students are engaged (with or without the teacher) for the purpose of learning.

instructional grouping   Dividing a class into small subunits for purposes of teaching.

instructional strategy   The plan for teaching a lesson, unit, or course; has two components: the methodology and the procedure.

instructional teams   A group of teachers that share responsibility for planning, instructing, and evaluating a common group of students.

instructional time   Blocks of class time used for productive learning activities.

integrated language arts   Teaching reading, writing, and spelling, not as separate subjects, but as an unsegregated whole.

intelligence General ability to learn and understand.

interdisciplinary instruction   Teaching by themes or activities that cross subject area boundaries; most frequently, involves bringing ideas, concepts, and/or facts from one subject area to bear on issues or problems raised in another (also called multidisciplinary approach).

interference A process that occurs when information to be recalled gets mixed up with other information.

intermediate grades   Usually, grades four though six.

intermittent reinforcement schedule   A pattern in which correct responses are reinforced often but not following each occurrence of the desirable behavior.

internalization The extent to which an attitude or value becomes a part of the learner.

Internet   A widely used, worldwide public computer network, initially developed by the U.S. military, that links smaller computer networks and allows users to communicate with one another on a global scale.

interval reinforcement schedule   A pattern in which reinforcement is dispensed after desired observable behavior has occurred for a specified length of time.

intrinsic motivation   An internal source of motivation associated with activities that are rewarding in themselves.

intuition Knowing without conscious reasoning.

invented spelling   Spelling based on how a word sounds; used when the writer does not know the conventional spelling of the word.

inventory questions   Questions asking individuals to describe their thoughts, feelings, and manifested actions.

IQ (Intelligence Quotient)   A measure of intelligence for which 100 is the score assigned to those of average intelligence.

judgment   Estimate of present conditions or prediction of future conditions; involves comparing information to some referent.

knowledge learning   Cognitive learning that entails the simple recall of learned materials.

knowledge questions   Questions requiring the student to recognize or recall information.

labeling   Assigning a category (especially a special education category) to an individual.

laboratory learning model   An instructional model focusing on "hands-on" manipulation and firsthand experience.

language experience approach   An approach to teaching reading and language arts that uses words and stories from the student's own language and experiences.

large muscle activity   Physical movement involving the limbs and large muscles.

leadership   Those behaviors that help the group move toward the accomplishment of its objectives.

learned helplessness   The learned belief, based on experience, that one is doomed to failure.

learning   A relatively permanent change in an individual's capacity for performance as a result of experience.

learning center   A defined space where materials are organized in such a way that children learn without the teacher's constant presence and direction.

learning disability   In general, a discrepancy between a child's intelligence and his or her academic ability.

learning environment   The surrounding conditions in which instruction takes place.

learning style   Orientation for approaching learning tasks and processing information.

lecture   Planned teacher talk designed to convey important information in an effective and efficient manner.

LEP (limited English proficiency)   Used to describe a student whose primary language is other than English and whose English language skills are such that the student has difficulty performing ordinary classwork (TEC 29.052).

lesson cycle   An instructional approach recommended by the Texas Education Agency that includes the following components: focus, explanation, check for understanding, reteach, guided practice, check for mastery, independent practice, enrichment, and closure. The components of the lesson cycle do not necessarily all occur in a single lesson, nor must a particular sequential order be followed.

Likert scale   Usually, a five-point attitude scale with linked options: strongly agree, agree, undecided, disagree, and strongly disagree.

long-term memory   Component of the memory system that can hold a large amount of information for a long time.

LRE (least restrictive environment)   Required setting in which disabled students must be placed to enable them to function to their fullest capabilities; one of the principles outlined in the Individuals with Disabilities Education Act (IDEA).

magnet school   A school that focuses on special themes (science, mathematics, language arts, and so on).

mainstreaming   Including students with special needs in regular education classrooms for part or all of the school day.

maintenance   The continuation of a behavior.

mandated time   The set amount of time, established by the state, during which school is in session.

manipulation   Independent performance of a skill.

massed practice   Repeated practice over and over in a concentrated period.

mastery learning   A teaching strategy designed to permit as many students as possible to achieve objectives to a specified level, with the assignment of grades based on achievement of objectives at specified levels.

mastery learning model   A five-step pattern of instruction that emphasizes the mastery of stated objectives by all students by allowing learning time to be flexible.

measurement   The assignment of numerical values to objects, events, performances, or products to indicate how much of a characteristic being measured they possess.

melting pot theory   The belief that other cultures should assimilate and blend into the dominant culture.

mental age   An age estimate of an individual's level of mental development, derived from a comparison of the individual's IQ score and chronological age.

mental retardation (MR)   Condition, usually present at birth, that results in below-average intellectual skills (below 70 IQ) and poor adaptive behavior.

mental set   A student's attitude toward beginning the lesson.

mentors   Experienced teachers who support, guide, and advise the development of younger or less experienced teachers.

metacognition   The process of thinking about and monitoring one's own thinking.

methodology   The patterned behaviors that form the definite steps by which the teacher influences learning.

middle school   School that has been planned for students ranging in age from 9 through 14 and generally has grades five through eight, with grades six through eight being the most popular organization.

mild mental retardation   The level of mental retardation that usually includes individuals with IQs between 50 and 75.

minority group   An ethnic or racial group that is a minority within a larger society.

mission statement   A broad statement of the unique purpose for which an organization exists and the specific function it performs.

mnemonic   A method to aid memory, such as keyword association and loci.

modality   See *sensory modality strength.*

modeling   The process of providing models to students by teacher or student demonstration or the provision of a finished or completed product or procedure.

moderate mental retardation   The level of mental retardation that usually includes individuals with IQs between 35 and 55.

motivation   The willingness or drive to accomplish something.

movement management behaviors   Those behaviors that the teacher uses to initiate, sustain, or terminate a classroom activity.

multicultural education   A structured process designed to foster understanding, acceptance, and constructive relations among people of various cultures.

multimedia   Software that combines text, sound, video, animation, and graphics into a single presentation.

multiple intelligences   A theory that proposes several different intelligences as opposed to just one general intelligence; other intelligences that have been described are linguistic, musical, logical-mathematical, spatial, kinesthetic, interpersonal, and intrapersonal.

NEA (National Education Association)   Largest professional educators organization in the United States; purpose includes working for improved education and enhancing the status of teachers.

negative reinforcement   Strengthening a behavior by release from a situation.

negligence Lack of ordinary care in one's action; failure to exercise due care.

no-lose tactic   A problem resolution tactic whereby a teacher and one or more students negotiate a solution such that no one comes out the loser.

nondiscriminatory testing   Assessment that properly takes into account a child's cultural and linguistic background.

noninstructional responsibility   Duties assumed by or assigned to teachers that are outside of their regular teaching responsibilities.

nonverbal cues   Eye contact, facial expressions, gestures, movement toward someone, placing a hand on someone's shoulder, or other physical act that communicates a message without the use of speech or writing.

nonverbal reinforcement   Using some form of physical action as a positive consequence to strengthen a behavior or event.

normal curve   Bell-shaped curve that describes the distribution of many natural phenomena; approximately 95 percent of the scores fall within two standard deviations of the mean.

norming group   A large sample of people who are similar to those for whom a particular standardized test is designed and who take the test to establish the group standards; serves as a comparison group for scoring the test.

norm-referenced test   A standardized test that focuses on a comparison of a student's score to the average of a norm group.

norms   Rules that apply to all members of a group.

novice   A person who is inexperienced in performing a particular activity.

objective   A clear and unambiguous description of instructional intent.

observable behavior   An overt act by an individual.

observation The process of looking and listening, noticing the important elements of a performance or a product.

on-task behavior   Student behavior that is appropriate to the task.

outcome-based education (OBE)   An effort designed to focus and organize all of the school's programs and instructional efforts around clearly defined outcomes that students are able to demonstrate.

overlapping   Attending to and supervising more than one thing at a time.

overlapping behaviors   Those behaviors by which the teacher indicates that he or she is attending to more than one thing when several things are going on at a particular time.

overlearning   Practicing beyond the point of mastery to improve retention.

pacing   Determining the speed of performance of a learning task.

paired-associate learning   A task involving the linkage of two items in a pair so that when one is presented, the other can be recalled.

paradigm   A pattern or model; sets of rules that establish boundaries.

paraprofessional   An adult who is not a credentialed teacher but works in the classroom with and under the supervision of a credentialed teacher (also called **teacher aide**).

parent   A person standing in parental relation to a child (TEC 26.002).

parenting styles   The different ways parents interact with their children, including (a) authoritarian—parents are restrictive, place limits and controls on the child, and offer very little give-and-take; (b) authoritative—parents are warm and nurturing and encourage the child to be independent, but still place limits, demands, and controls on the child's actions; (c) permissive indulgent—parents allow great freedom to the child and are undemanding, but are responsive and involved in the child's life; and (d) permissive indifferent—parents are neglectful, unresponsive, and highly uninvolved in the child's life.

PDAS (Professional Development and Appraisal System)   The state-adopted and -recommended appraisal process and performance criteria for (a) teachers, based on observable, job-related behavior, including teachers' implementation of discipline management procedures and the performance of teachers' students (TEC 21.351); (b) administrators (TEC 21.354); and (c) counselors (TEC.21.356).

pedagogy   The art and science of teaching.

PEIMS (Public Education Information Management System) A means of reporting attendance, personnel, management, special programs, and populations to the state (TEC 34.010).

percentile   A score at or below which a given percentage of the scores fall. *Example:* The 75th percentile is the score at or below which 75 percent of the scores fall.

peers   Individuals equal in age and/or status.

peer teaching   A procedure that provides teachers with an opportunity to practice new instructional techniques in a simplified setting, teaching lessons to small groups of their peers (other prospective or experienced teachers).

peer tutoring   An instruction practice in which students assist with the instruction of other students needing supplemental instruction; principal types are same-age tutoring, where the tutor is the same age as the tutee, and cross-age tutoring, where the tutor is older than the tutee.

performance assessment   See *authentic assessment.*

performance based instruction   Instruction designed around evaluating student achievement against specified and predetermined behavioral objectives.

phonics approach   An instructional strategy that emphasizes "sounding out" words based on letter-sound relationships.

planning   Decision-making process in which the teacher decides what, why, when, and how to teach; composed of three elements: task analysis, planning for student behaviors/outcomes, and planning for teacher behaviors/strategies.

portfolio   A collection of a student's work and achievements that is used to assess past accomplishments and future potential; can include finished work in a variety of media and can contain materials from several courses over time. In one method of portfolio assessment, the teacher or academic team confers and collaborates with the student on the portfolio, reviewing its contents, adding to it, selecting from it, and choosing a best work for review.

positive reinforcement   Strengthening a behavior by giving a desirable reward.

PQ4R   A study strategy where students preview the reading, create questions, read to answer questions, reflect, recite, and review the original material.

precision   Psychomotor ability to perform an act accurately, efficiently, and harmoniously.

primacy effect   The tendency to be able to recall the first things in a list.

primary motives   Forces and drives, such as hunger, thirst, and the need for security, that are basic and inborn.

primary reinforcers   Questions following a response that requires the respondent to provide more support, be clearer or more accurate, or offer greater specificity or originality.

principal   The instructional leader of the school (TEC 11.202).

principal autonomy   A system wherein the principal is authoritarian and makes all the decisions.

principle   A rule that explains the relationship between or among factors.

private speech   Children's self-talk.

probationary teacher   A teacher who is under a probationary contract that may not be for a term exceeding one school year, but may be renewed for two additional one-year periods, for a maximum permissible probationary contract period of three school years (TEC 21.102).

probing questions   Questions that follow a student response and require the student to think and respond more thoroughly than in the initial response.

problem solving   A strategy that involves the application of knowledge and skills to produce a result or solution.

procedure   A sequence of steps and activities that have been designed to lead to the acquisition of learning objectives.

productive questions   Broad, open-ended questions, with many correct responses, that require students to use their imagination, to think creatively, and to produce something unique.

professional autonomy   Freedom of professionals or groups of professionals to function independently.

professional development   The process of acquiring specialized knowledge and skills, as well as an awareness of the alternative actions that might be appropriate in particular situations.

profound mental retardation   The level of mental retardation that usually includes individuals with IQs below approximately 20 to 25.

progressivism   A learner-centered educational philosophy, popularized by John Dewey, based on the belief that the interaction of the student with the environment creates experience that encourages the student to learn by doing.

programmed instruction   A program in which students work through specially constructed print or electronic self-instructional materials at their own pace.

prompting questions   Questions that involve the use of hints and clues to aid students in answering questions or in correcting an initial response.

puberty   Developmental stage at which a person becomes capable of reproduction.

Public Law 94-142   Federal law requiring that all schools receiving federal funds must provide an education for every disabled child in the least restrictive environment.

pull-out programs   Programs in which students with special needs are taken out of regular classes for instructions.

punishment   Using unpleasant consequences to weaken or extinguish an undesirable behavior.

Pygmalion effect   The tendency of individuals who are treated as capable or incapable to act accordingly.

qualified reinforcement   Reinforcement of only the acceptable parts of an individual's response or action or of the attempt itself.

questionnaire   A list of written statements regarding attitudes, feelings, and opinions that are to be read and responded to.

rating scale   A scale of values arranged in order of quality, describing someone or something being evaluated.

ratio reinforcement schedule   A pattern in which reinforcement is dispensed after a desired observable behavior has occurred a certain number of times.

reality therapy   Therapy in which individuals are helped to become responsible and able to satisfy their needs in the real world.

receiving   Affective learning that involves being aware of and willing to freely attend to a stimulus.

recency effect   The tendency to be able to recall the last things in a list.

reciprocal teaching   An instructional approach in which the teacher helps the students learn to ask teacher-type questions; designed to help low achievers learn reading.

redirecting   The technique of asking several individuals to respond to a question in light of or to add new insight to the previous responses.

referent   That to which you compare the information you have about an individual to form a judgment.

reflection   Giving direct feedback to individuals about the way their verbal and nonverbal messages are being received; also, quiet thought or contemplation that includes analysis of past experience.

reflective listening   The act of listening with feeling as well as with cognition.

reflective practitioner   A teacher who systematically reflects on his or her own performance in the classroom and development as a teacher.

reflectivity   Examining and analyzing oneself and one's thoughts before taking action.

regular class   A typical classroom designed to serve students without disabilities.

reinforcement   Using consequences to strengthen the likelihood of a behavior or event.

reinforcement schedule   The frequency with which reinforcers are given; common schedules are fixed-ratio, which includes continuous reinforcement; variable-ratio; fixed-interval; and variable-interval.

relational concepts   Concepts that describe relationships between items.

reliability   The consistency of test scores obtained in repeated administrations to the same individuals on different occasions or with different sets of equivalent items.

remediation   Instruction given to students having difficulty learning that supplements whole-class instruction.

repertoire   A set of alternative routines or procedures, all of which serve some common purpose and each of which serves some additional, unique purpose.

reproduced data   Data that have been recorded in video, audio, or verbatim transcript form and can be reproduced when desired.

responding   Affective learning that involves freely attending to a stimulus as well as voluntarily reacting to it in some way.

restructuring   A radically altering reform of schools as organizations and the way schooling is delivered.

reteach   Instruction in the original objective that is substantially different from the initial instruction; differences may be reflected in an adjustment or modification of time allocation, practice depth/length, or instructional modality.

review closure   A type of closure technique whose main characteristic is an attempt to summarize the major points of a presentation or discussion.

reversibility   The ability to change direction in thinking and go back to a starting point.

ripple effect   The spreading of behaviors from one individual to others through imitation.

Ritalin   The most widely used drug to treat attention deficit disorder.

role playing   An activity in which students act out roles.

routine   An established pattern of behavior.

rote learning   Memorization of facts or associations.

salad-bowl theory   The belief that the various cultures should mix, but still retain their unique characteristics.

same-age tutoring   Peer tutoring in which one student teaches another student (usually a classmate) of the same age; runs the risk of being ineffective because resentment toward the same-age tutor (especially if he or she is a classmate) may develop.

SBEC (State Board for Educator Certification)   A 15-member appointed board created in 1995 by the 74th Texas Legislature to govern the standards of the education profession; oversees all aspects of public school educator certification, continuing education, and standards of conduct (TEC 21.031).

SBOC (State Board of Education)   A 15-member elected board that establishes rules and guidelines for public schools in Texas and, with the commissioner of education, oversees the public education system of Texas in accordance with the Texas Education Code (TEC 7.101).

scaffolding   Providing support for learning and problem solving, such as giving clues, reminders, encouragement, and examples; needed more during early stages of learning, but should be diminished later to allow the learner to become self-directed.

SCANS Report   A report issued in 1992 by the Secretary's (of Education) Commission on Achieving Necessary Skills that recommended changes in the school curricula and teaching methods in order to better prepare students for the work place.

schema   Mental diagrams that guide behavior.

schizophrenia   Abnormal behavior patterns and personality disorganization accompanied by less-than-adequate contact with reality.

school board   Governing board of trustees of a school who, as a body corporate, oversees the management of the district (TEC 11.051); trustees of an independent school district serve a term of three or four years (TEC 11.059).

secondary motives   Forces and drives, such as the desire for money or grades, that are learned through association with primary motives.

self-actualization   Reaching one's fullest potential.

self-concept   How a person thinks of himself or herself.

self-directed learning   Learning by designing and directing one's own learning activities.

self-efficacy   The confidence a person has that he or she has the power within himself or herself to be successful.

self-esteem   The value a person places on what he or she is; self-worth.

self-fulfilling prophecy   Phenomenon that occurs when one's biased beliefs about what should occur influences the results to conform to one's expectations.

semantic differential   A seven-point scale that links an adjective to its opposite; designed so that attitudes, feelings, and opinions can be measured by degree, from very favorable to highly unfavorable.

sensory modality strength   The predominant way an individual takes in information through the five senses (see, hear, smell, taste, touch).

set induction   Teacher actions and statements at the outset of a lesson to get student attention, to trigger interest, and to establish a conceptual framework.

severe mental retardation   The level of mental retardation that usually includes individuals with IQs between 20 and 40.

sexual harassment   unwelcome written or verbal comments or physical gestures or actions of a sexual nature.

short-term memory   Component of the memory system that can hold a limited amount of information for a short period.

silent time   The time the teacher waits following a student response before replying or continuing with the presentation.

simulation   An enactment of an artificial situation or event that represents real life as much as possible, but with most of the risk and complicating factors removed; works best when students are assigned roles and teacher acts as a facilitator, but does not become actively involved in the make-believe situation.

site-based decision making   State-mandated requirement that the campus-level committee be involved in decisions in the areas of planning, budgeting, curriculum, staffing patterns, staff development, and school organization (TEC 11.253).

site-based management (SBM)   School-level (campus) governance mandated by TEC 11.251; establishes district- and campus-level planning and decision-making committees that include representative professional staff, parents of students enrolled in the district, and community members.

small muscle activity   Physical movement involving the fine muscles of the hand.

social objective   A requirement of the cooperative learning model dealing with the social skills, roles and relationships, and group processes that students need to accomplish the learning task.

sociodrama   A form of role playing that focuses on a group solving a problem.

socioeconomic status (SES)   the relationship of an individual's economic status to social factors, including education, occupation, and place of residence.

special education   Programs designed to serve children with mental and/or physical disabilities.

standardized test   A commercially developed test that samples behavior under uniform procedures; used to provide accurate and meaningful information on students' levels of performance relative to others at their age or grade levels.

State Commissioner of Education   The educational leader of the state appointed by the governor; serves as executive officer of the Texas Education Agency and as executive secretary of the State Board of Education (TEC 7.055).

steering group   A group of pupils within the class who are carefully observed by the teacher to determine whether the class is understanding the content being discussed in the lesson.

stimulation approach   Emphasis on the viewpoint that factors outside the individual account for behaviors.

structuring the task   A step in the lesson, particularly in inductive-type lessons, that requires the teacher to specify the processes and procedures students are to follow to be successful with the learning experience.

success   Attainment, achievement, or accomplishment.

summative assessment   Assessment that follows instruction and evaluates at the end of a unit, semester, and so on; used to guide programs, curricula, and the like.

superintendent   The educational leader and the chief executive officer of the school district (TEC 11.201).

supervisor   Administrator responsible for specific programs in public schools, such as supervisor of special education, vocational education supervisor, or supervisor of elementary or secondary curriculum.

symbolic medium   A representational medium for acquiring concepts through symbols such as language.

synthesis Thinking that involves putting together ideas or elements to form a whole.

synthesis questions   Questions requiring the student to put together elements and parts to form a whole.

TAAS (Texas Assessment of Academic Skills)   A statewide assessment program created and implemented by the State Board of Education that is primarily performance-based to ensure school accountability for student achievement (TEC 39.022).

TAC (Texas Administrative Code)   State Board of Education rulings associated with the interpretation of the laws that affect Texas public schools.

target mistakes   The teacher stopping the wrong students or desisting a less serious misbehavior.

task analysis   Analyzing a task to determine its fundamental subskills.

taxonomy A classification system; used here in reference to a classification system of educational objectives or skills.

TEA (Texas Education Agency)   State agency composed of the Commission of Education and the TEA staff that oversees public education in Texas in accordance with the Texas Education Code (TEC 7.002).

teachable moment   A peak learning moment that usually occurs unexpectedly.

teacher certification   A process through which individuals are recognized by the state as having acquired the necessary skills and knowledge to teach in Texas; those certified must hold a bachelor's degree with coursework in three areas: (a) a broad general education, (b) academic specialization(s), and (c) teaching knowledge and abilities.

teacher empowerment   The concept of putting decision making in the hands of teachers, the school personnel closest to the student.

teacher expectations　A teacher's opinion of the likelihood that students will be successful.

teacher-made test　An assessment instrument developed and scored by a teacher to meet particular classroom needs.

teaching　The actions of someone who is trying to assist others to reach their fullest potential in all aspects of development.

teaching style　The way a teacher teaches; that teacher's distinctive mannerisms complemented by his or her choices of teaching behaviors and strategies.

Teams Games Tournaments (TGT)　A cooperative learning strategy in which teacher presentation is followed by team practice and individual mastery is tested in "tournaments," with two or three students of matched achievement, rather than tests.

TEC (Texas Education Code)　Statutes resulting from Senate Bill 1 of 1995 that govern public education in Texas.

TEKS (Texas Essential Knowledge and Skills)　The state foundation curriculum, developed by the State Board of Education, that requires all students to demonstrate the knowledge and skills necessary to read, write, compute, problem solve, think critically, apply technology, and communicate across all subject areas (TEC 39.021, TEC 28.001, TEC 28.002).

terminal behavior　That which has been learned as a direct result of instruction.

terminal goals　Goals one can expect to reach at the end of a given learning experience.

test　A device used to determine whether learning objectives have been met.

TFC (Texas Family Code)　Statutes governing family relationships in Texas.

thematic teaching　The organization of teaching and learning around a specific theme or topic. Although themes may be used in a single subject area, such as English, sociology, or literature, two or more subject areas may be integrated using a single thematic approach.

theoretical knowledge　Concepts, facts, and propositions that make up much of the content of the disciplines.

thinking　The act of withholding judgment in order to use past knowledge and experience to find new information, concepts, or conclusions.

time-out　A form of punishment in which the student is removed for a short while from the rest of the class (sit in the corner, stand out in the hall, and so on); used when the teacher believes the student misbehaves because he or she wants attention.

Title I　Shortened name for Title I of the Elementary and Secondary Act of 1965, a federal program that provides funding for remedial education programs to poor and disadvantaged children; formerly known as Chapter I.

Title VI　Shortened name for Title VI of the Civil Rights Act of 1964; bars discrimination in federally assisted programs and activities on the basis of race, color, or national origin.

Title VII　Shortened name for Title VII of the Elementary and Secondary Act, a federal program created in 1984 that provides funding to help make limited-English-proficient students proficient in the English language (also called the Bilingual Education Act).

Title IX   Shortened name for Title IX of the Education Amendments of 1972; bars gender discrimination in federally assisted programs and activities.

TOEFL (Test of English as a Foreign Language) A standardized test used to assess English language skills of nonnative individuals; frequently required of foreign students applying for admission to colleges and universities in the United States.

token reinforcement system   A system in which students perform actions or behaviors desired by the teacher in order to earn neutral tokens that can be exchanged periodically for rewards.

tracks Classes or curricula targeted for students of a specified achievement or ability level.

transfer The application of knowledge and skills in a new context.

trust   A value relationship between and among individuals; includes such subordinate terms as confidence, reliance, stability, and absence of deception.

unit plan   A plan for a sequence of several lessons dealing with the same general topic.

usability   In regard to a test, practical considerations, such as cost, time to administer, difficulty, and scoring procedure.

validity   The ability of a test to measure what it purports to.

value data   Data that involve a value judgment on the part of an observer.

values clarification   A teaching program that focuses on students' understanding and expressing their own values.

valuing   Affective learning that involves voluntarily giving worth to an object, a phenomenon, or a stimulus.

variable   A characteristic that varies from entity to entity.

variable-interval reinforcement schedule   A pattern for giving reinforcements in which the time at which reinforcement will occur is unpredictable; effective for maintaining a high rate of behavior and highly resistant to extinction. *Example:* Teachers' checking students' work at random intervals is variable-interval reinforcement.

variable-ratio reinforcement schedule   A pattern for giving reinforcements in which the number of desired responses before reinforcement is given is unpredictable; effective in motivating individuals to work a long time, even after reinforcement has stopped, and highly resistant to extinction. *Example:* Teachers' checking random samples of students' work is variable-ratio reinforcement.

verbal component   The actual words and meaning of a spoken message.

verbal reinforcement   Using positive comments as consequences to strengthen a behavior or event.

vocal component   The meaning attached to a spoken message, resulting from such variables as voice firmness, modulation, tone, tempo, pitch, and loudness.

wait time   The amount of time a teacher waits for a student to respond to a question before moving on to another student or giving the answer;

also, a term used to describe the time a teacher waits before calling on a student to answer after posing a question to the whole class.

whole-class discussion　A discussion among the whole class with the teacher as moderator; seating arrangements should be U-shaped or in a circle.

whole-language approach　An instructional strategy that emphasizes reading for meaning and in context.

within-class ability grouping　A system for accommodating differences between students by dividing a class into groups for instructional purposes (such as, reading groups, mathematics groups, science groups).

withitness　A teacher's awareness of what is going on in all parts of the classroom.

www (World Wide Web)　A segment of the global Internet computer network; also called the Web.

year-round school program　A school program whose calendar provides for instruction for the entire year, with short vacation periods throughout the year.

you-messages　Teacher messages that attack students.

zone of proximal development　Level of development one step above current level; learning in this zone requires assistance of peer or adult.

GUIDELINES FOR NEW TEACHERS

The Lesson Cycle

Guidelines for Writing Instructional Objectives

Guidelines for Working with Auditory, Visual, and Kinesthetic/Tactile Learners

Guidelines for Effective Classroom Management

Guidelines for Motivating Students

Guidelines for Effective Praise

Guidelines for Questioning

Guidelines for Using Cooperative Learning

Guidelines for Test Construction

Guidelines for Parent-Teacher Conferences

The Lesson Cycle

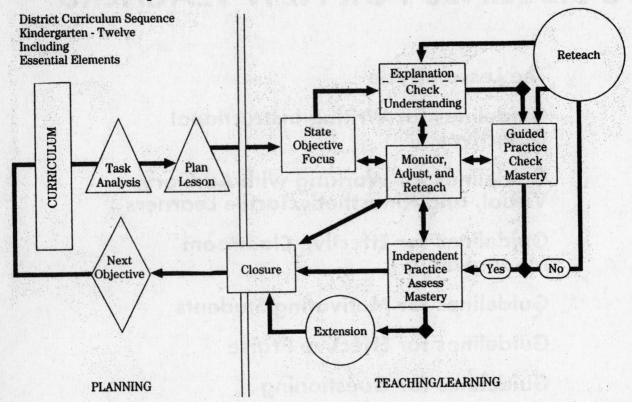

District Curriculum Sequence
Kindergarten - Twelve
Including
Essential Elements

Planning

The planning component focuses on the school district's curriculum scope and sequence of instructional objectives. The teacher reviews the unit plans, selects the appropriate lesson objective(s), and then prepares for the appropriate learning activities.

Task Analysis is a process used by the teacher to determine if the lesson objective is at an appropriate level of difficulty to enable the students to complete the lesson's learning activities with a high degree of success.

Teaching/Learning

Focus is a technique used at the beginning of the lesson to prepare students and focus their attention on the lesson's objective(s) and learning activities. Examples include novel or humorous stories, questions, objects, cartoons, and role play.

Objectives are statements that the teacher communicates to the students of what the student will be able to do as a result of the lesson's learning activities.

Explanation describes the techniques used by the teacher to present information or materials related to the lesson's objectives. Some techniques includes steps, processes, comparison, and contract.

Modeling refers to the kinds of techniques the teacher uses to demonstrate both verbally and visually the concepts presented during the explanation.

Check for Understanding enables the teacher to determine the degree to which students understand the concepts and essential information presented during the explaining and modeling.

Monitor and Adjust refers to the alternative strategies a teacher uses to increase effectiveness during instructional input while observing student behavior.

Guided Practice is the class time provided for students to practice learning activities that are directed and monitored by the teacher.

Check for Mastery is a method used by teachers to determine students' readiness to use the information presented during instructional input.

Independent Practice provides opportunities for students to learn by practicing the learning objective without assistance from the teacher.

Enrichment refers to the learning experiences that a teacher provides for students to extend learning and thinking after students have successfully completed guided practice and independent practice.

Reteach refers to the different methods and types of modeling a teacher uses to present content when learning has not occurred.

Closure refers to the activities a teacher uses to close the lesson.

Lesson Plan Formats and Two Sample Lesson Plans

Direct Teaching Model
Lesson Format

Class_____ Unit_____

Lesson Title _____

TAAS/TEKS_____

Objective(s): The student will...

Focus:

Explanation and Model:

Check for Understanding:

Guided Practice:

Check for Mastery:

Closure:

Reteach Strategies	Independent Practice	Resources

Cooperative Learning Model
Lesson Format

Class_____ Unit_____

Lesson Title _____

TAAS/TEKS_____

Objective(s): The student will...

Focus:

Structure Tasks:

Acquire Database:

Cooperative Practice/Application:

Closure:

Group Accountability	Individual Accountability	Resources

Constructivist Learning Model
Lesson Format

Class_____ Unit_____

Lesson Title _____

TAAS/TEKS_____

Objective(s): The student will...

Engage:

Explore:

Explain:

Elaborate:

Assess/Evaluate:

Inquiry/Discovery Model
Lesson Format

Class_____ Unit_____

Lesson Title _____

TAAS/TEKS_____

Objective(s): The student will...

Focus:

Inquiry or Discovery Experience:

Student Acquire Database:

Guided Application:

Closure:

Independent Practice	Extension	Resources

Laboratory Model
Lesson Format

Class_____ Unit_____

Lesson Title _____

TAAS/TEKS_____

Objective(s): The student will...

Focus:

Teacher Explanation:

Laboratory Experience(s):

Closure:

Group Accountability	Individual Accountability	Resources

Physical Education Classes
Lesson Format

Class_____ Unit_____

Lesson Title _____

TAAS/TEKS_____

Objective(s): The student will...

Skills to be Taught:

Class Size:_____   Equipment Needed:

Organizational Plan:

Introduction:

Explanation/Demonstration:

Closure:

Direct Teaching Model
Sample Lesson Plan*

Class: Second Grade   **Unit:** Division and Reading

Lesson Title: The Doorbell Rang—Introduction to Division

TAAS Objective: Objective 9—The student will use the operation of division to solve problems.

Objective: The learner will experiment with the process of dividing objects into equal groups through using literature and manipulatives.

Focus: The teacher will pass out a food sample to the class, giving each student one cookie and the last student one extra piece and see what happens.

Explanation and Model: After a discussion, distribute an extra cookie to the rest of the class. While reading the story *The Doorbell Rang*, the teacher will use magnetic cookies to show the division process along with the story.

Check for Understanding: The teacher will ask the students to explain what process was taking place in the story and why it is important to be able to divide things.

Guided Practice: Each student will be given his or her own paper children and cookies. The teacher will guide the student to divide the cookies among the children as he or she reads the story for a second time. First, they divide 12 cookies by 2 for Sam and Victoria, then they continue to divide as more and more children join the group.

Check for Mastery: The teacher will give each group a bag with a different number of objects and have them divide the objects among themselves.

Closure: The teacher will ask the students what has been discussed. The class will then discuss why it is important to learn how to divide things. The class will discuss different times that we use division every day. The class will also discuss that division is something we each use our entire life.

Reteach Strategies
Use mats to aid students in solving basic division problems. Make division mats for the numbers 2 to 10 by drawing patterns. Have students use the mats to complete basic division problems. Use a counter in each section until they have used all 12 counters.

Independent Practice
Describe a time when you had to share a number of items/treats with other people. How did you make sure everyone got a fair share? What did you do with any leftovers? Write your answer in your journal.

Resources
The Doorbell Rang, by Pat Hutchins
Hands-On Math, by Creative Teaching Press
Mathtivities, by Creative Publications

*Courtesy of Lori McGough Harkness, Department of Elementary Education, Stephen F. Austin State University.

Direct Teaching Model
Sample Lesson Plan*

Class: English IV   **Unit:** Anglo-Saxon Literature

Lesson Title: *Beowulf,* by Chaucer

TEKS Objective: English IV (1a)

Objective: Students will be able to recognize the characteristics of Anglo-Saxon literature in the epic poem *Beowulf.*

Focus: The students will be asked to list their ideas of what determines a hero. The teacher will list the characteristics of the Anglo-Saxon hero for comparison. Then the teacher will explain that our values are similar to the early Anglo-Saxons', and that our modern language developed from their language. At this point, the students will listen to a recording of Old English dialect while viewing a short section of a video about Anglo-Saxon life.

Explanation and Model: The students will be asked to scan quickly the questions in their study guide. The teacher will then read aloud section one of *Beowulf,* highlighting the different literary devices and different aspects of Anglo-Saxon culture. The teacher will give special consideration to the parts of the epic poem that illustrate religious overtones. The students will be asked to take notes.

Check for Understanding: The teacher will ask students to turn to a partner and explain the meaning gained from the section of *Beowulf* that the teacher had finished reading. The teacher will select students at random to share their responses with the total class.

Guided Practice: Students will be asked to complete the study guide provided by the teacher over section one in pairs.

Check for Mastery: The teacher will review with students the questions over section one of *Beowulf.* The groups will reach consensus on the best responses to each question.

Closure: The teacher will replay portions of the video on Anglo-Saxon life for clarity and summarize the main points in section one.

Reteach Strategies	**Independent Practice**	**Resources**
Ask students to complete vocabulary guide and remaining study questions over section one.	Provide students with an opportunity to complete additional research on the Internet on the life of Anglo-Saxons and write a feature story for the campus newspaper.	Audiocassette of Old English dialect Videocassette of Anglo-Saxon life Study guide over section one Lecture notes Transparencies Textbook

*Courtesy of Jerry Capps, student, Stephen F. Austin State University.

Guidelines for Writing Instructional Objectives*

Instructional objectives differ both in the types of learning involved and in the level of the learning involved. As a teacher you should know how to write and teach to an objective that results in the type and level of learning you desire for your students.

One of the most helpful guides in identifying and writing instructional objectives is the *Taxonomy of Educational Objectives* by Benjamin Bloom. It consists of a set of general and specific categories that encompass all possible learning outcomes that might be expected from instruction. The classification system was developed by psychologists, teachers, and test experts for use in curriculum development, teaching, and testing.

The taxonomy is divided into three main categories:

1. The cognitive domain
2. The affective domain
3. The psychomotor domain

The cognitive domain is the category for learning that involves the whole array of intellectual capabilities, from simple factual recall to the generation of new theories. Example: *By the end of class, the student will be able to write an essay comparing and contrasting at least three types of government.*

The affective domain is the category for learning that involves feelings and values. Objectives in the affective domain may range from stimulating interest in a school subject to encouraging healthy social attitudes to adopting a set of ethical standards. Example: *After the unit on ecology, the student will show an awareness of the importance of ecology by supplying pertinent newspaper clippings.*

The psychomotor domain is the category for learning that involves athletic, manual, and other such physical skill. Example: *The student will be able to demonstrate the ability to catch and pass the ball accurately while on the move during a basketball game.*

The subcategories in each of the domain areas are arranged in hierarchical order, from simplest outcomes to the most complex.

Cognitive Domain

Knowledge: Emphasizes remembering, memorizing, recognizing, recalling.

---

*Courtesy of Paulette Wright, Department of Secondary Education and Education Leadership, Stephen F. Austin State University.

Comprehension: Embraces interpreting, translating from one medium to another, describing in one's own words.

Application: Involves applying information to produce some results, problem solving.

Analysis: Involves the subdividing of something to show how it is put together, finding the underlying structure of a communication, identifying motives.

Synthesis: Entails the creation of a unique, original product that may be in verbal or physical form.

Evaluation: Involves making value decisions about issues, resolving controversies or differences of opinions.

One way to remember these six levels of the cognitive domain is "**K**ids **C**atch **A**pes **A**nd **S**illy **E**lephants."

Affective Domain

Receiving: Involves the willingness to be open to stimuli and messages in the environment; willingness to receive some message or to acknowledge that some phenomenon is taking place.

Responding: Involves the acceptance of a value and the willingness to be identified with it.

Valuing: Involves internalizing an idea, a phenomenon, or a stimulus.

Organizing: Involves the ordering and classifying of values; the determination of how values relate to each other; one's "philosophy of life."

Characterization by the Values or Value Complex: Involves the total commitment to certain attitudes, beliefs, or values as reflected in one's consistent behavior.

Remembering the mnemonic "**R**oy **R**eceived a **V**ery **O**ld **V**iolet **C**oat" might help you remember the five sublevels of the affective domain.

Psychomotor Domain

Generic movement: Includes the perception of body positions and motor acts and the arrangement of movement to achieve a skill.

Ordinate movement: Includes organizing, refining, and performing movement skillfully; the achievement of precision in motor performance.

Creative movement: Includes the invention or creation of movement personally unique to the performer; different ways of performing a specific movement without preinstruction.

The three levels of the psychomotor domain can be remembered by "**G**randma **M**oses' **O**ld **M**angy **C**at, **M**orris."

Guidelines for Working with Auditory, Visual, and Kinesthetic/Tactile Learners

Description of Learners

Auditory Learner	Visual Learner	Kinesthetic/Tactile Learner
Talks constantly	Notices small details	Needs to be mobile
Encourages people to laugh	Remembers where things are	Wants to feel, smell, taste everything
Good storyteller	Difficulty understanding oral	Always touching others
Hyperactive	directions	Has good motor skills
Poor fine-motor skills	Enjoys drawing pictures	Takes things apart
Can deliver messages	Enjoys looking at books	Enjoys doing things manually
Enjoys listening activities	Watches speaker's face	Appears immature and needs to
Memorizes easily	Avoids talking in class discussions	explore the environment
Enjoys being the "boss"	May have speech problems	Wants to use concrete objects as
Has an excuse for every occasion	Likes to work puzzles	learning aids
	Dislikes speaking before a group	Seems to be hyperactive

Ways of Learning

Auditory Learner	Visual Learner	Kinesthetic/Tactile Learner
Taped lessons	Videos	Outdoor activities
Language mastery activities	Memory games	Use tactile materials
Integrated computer-assisted	What's missing? games	Matching activities using all senses
instruction	Concentration games	Dramatic play, puppetry, and
Listening to stories	Repeating patterns	simulations
Verbalizing while learning	Using models	Musical instruments
Peer tutoring	Puzzles	Art (fingerpaint for writing words)
Recording own stories	Art activities	Playdough
Reading directions orally	Bulletin board games	Creative writing
Music activities	Demonstrations	Manipulatives
Group discussions		Freedom to move around classroom
Oral directions		

Guidelines for Effective Classroom Management

- Teach your students classroom rules and procedures at the beginning of the year.
- Involve your students in making classroom rules.
- Give reasons for consequences when going over the rules.
- Work with the whole class at first (even if you plan to group students later).
- Set clear standards and limits for classroom behavior.
- Plan well-organized lessons with objectives and activities to prevent discipline problems.
- Use simple, enjoyable tasks as activities for the first lessons of the school year.
- Begin lessons promptly and provide smooth transitions between activities.

- Make sure all students have access to instructional materials.
- Elicit your students' cooperation, and praise them when they give it.
- Maintain lesson momentum by using a brisk, but appropriate, pace.
- Keep your students busy.
- Limit the amount of time your students work alone at their desks.
- Hold your students accountable for completing their work.
- Monitor the classroom continuously.
- Reinforce and encourage appropriate behavior.
- Find out if any of your students have a physical impairment that might affect behavior.
- Anticipate problems and try to head them off.
- Use monitoring to prevent off-task behavior.
- Be quick to respond to and stop or redirect off-task or inappropriate behavior.
- Use the least intrusive intervention (such as a glance, rather than a verbal intervention) to stop or redirect inappropriate or disruptive behavior.
- Use a variety of verbal and nonverbal signals to stop inappropriate behavior.
- Use intervention techniques that ensure that the dignity of the student is preserved.
- Apply rules consistently and fairly, and follow through with consequences.
- Avoid using threats or giving your students long corrective lectures when they misbehave.
- Tell students who misbehave what they did wrong, why the behavior is unacceptable, and then explain what is acceptable behavior.
- If a student misbehaves, focus on the inappropriate behavior, not on the student.
- Use inappropriate behavior to teach your students what is appropriate.
- Model desired behavior.
- Tell your students whether your expectations have been met.
- Adapt instruction to meet your students' needs and special characteristics (learning style, modality strength, and so forth).
- Use a variety of teaching strategies and activities.
- Individualize lessons for students with special needs.
- Make sure the classroom is physically comfortable (temperature, light, and so forth).
- Learn about each student's needs, interests, and desires.
- Encourage your students to respect themselves and other people.
- Show your students that you have a sense of humor.
- Do not get into an argument or "shouting match" with a student.
- Be a good listener.
- Get ideas from your students on how to prevent and stop misbehavior.
- Consider placing misbehaving students in peer-tutoring arrangements, either as tutor or as tutee, as appropriate
- Encourage students to accept responsibility for their own behavior.
- Never mistreat a student or react to student misbehavior in anger.
- Be warm and friendly toward your students.
- Learn and use your students' names.

- Establish and maintain a positive rapport with students.
- Establish a climate of courtesy and respect.
- Maintain a warm, supportive environment where interactions serve to support dignity and promote learning.

Guidelines for Motivating Students

- Expect and demand the best from all your students.
- Relate the class content to your students' interests and experiences.
- Emphasize the value and importance of the activity or content.
- Reinforce and encourage your students' efforts and involvement.
- Model desired behavior (enthusiasm, interest, sense of humor, and so forth).
- Challenge your students.
- Use a variety of teaching strategies and activities.
- Maintain a warm, supportive atmosphere.
- Be warm and personable toward your students.
- Learn and use your students' names.
- Encourage slow and reluctant learners.
- Keep your students busy and actively involved.
- Be sure your students know what to do and how to do it.
- Use your students' ideas in planning instructional activities.
- Ask questions that provide high rates of correct responses, yet are challenging.
- Appeal to your students' natural curiosity, desire for fun, and need for social interaction.
- Appeal to your students' competitive spirits. (But don't overuse competition.)
- Appeal to your students' interests, ideals, attitudes, and goals.
- Be alert to an increase in student interest or curiosity and capitalize on it.
- Provide your students with opportunities for success.
- Establish and maintain a positive rapport with students.
- Try to build your students' trust in you.
- Make sure your students know you respect and value them and their contributions to the class.
- Create a risk-free environment.
- Establish a climate of courtesy and respect.

Guidelines for Effective Praise

Effective Praise	Ineffective Praise
• Is given for specific accomplishments.	• Is nonspecific and given in a random manner.
• Specifies why the behavior or accomplishment is worthy of praise.	• Is global in nature and the student is unable to determine the reason for the praise.
• Is spontaneous, deserving, and gets the attention of the students.	• Shows little emotion with regard to the value of students' accomplishments.
• Is given to students for demonstration of a specific behavior or effort.	• Rewards participation rather than the value of the accomplishment or behavior.
• Gives students specific information about their behavior or accomplishment and helps students understand its significance.	• Gives students little or no feedback regarding the quality of their accomplishments.
• Helps students develop more appreciation of their own task-related behavior and their problem-solving ability.	• Creates a competitive climate, and students compare themselves to other students in the classroom.
• Describes students' present accomplishments or achievements in the context of past performance.	• Describes students' accomplishments in the context of their peers.
• Is awarded because of the difficulty level of the task for particular students.	• Rewards students with little thought to meaning.
• Gives credit for success in terms of the effort and ability of students, implying that present success leads to high expectations for future successes.	• Attributes success to external forces rather than to the student's ability.
• Implies that students do well because they are intrinsically motivated to do well.	• Suggests that students are rewarded for pleasing the teacher or other external reasons.
• Focuses students' attention on their own task-specific behavior.	• Encourages a climate in which students feel manipulated by the teacher.
• Helps students to see the importance of their own behavior after the completion of the task.	• Inhibits the student's ability to focus on task-specific relevant behavior.

Guidelines for Questioning

Effective Questioning Techniques

- Evaluate your questions for clarity and level of difficulty.
- Relate questions to your lesson objectives.
- Praise students for correct or appropriate responses; however, strong praise should be used sparingly. Passive acceptance is more effective.
- Avoid sarcasm for incorrect responses.
- Provide many opportunities for student involvement during questioning.
- Ask questions appropriate to the ability levels in the class.
- Distribute questions in an equitable manner among the ability levels in the class.
- Ask the question and provide "wait time," approximately three to five seconds, for thought.
- Practice listening carefully to students' responses.
- Encourage students to ask questions and not to accept an incorrect response.
- Assist students in modifying their responses.
- Avoid asking, "Are there any questions?" or "Does everyone understand?"
- Use student responses to make a point.
- Use student responses to stimulate additional discussion.

- Be nonjudgmental in response to students' answers on higher-level questions.
- Avoid asking too many questions that give away answers, and avoid one-word-answer questions.
- Ask the question first, then identify the student by name.
- Extend answers to questions.
- Avoid answering your own questions.
- Avoid repeating student answers.
- Avoid give-away facial expressions as students respond.
- Replace lectures with a set of appropriate questions.
- Leave an occasional question unanswered at the end of the period.
- Keep the students actively involved in the learning process.

Socratic Questioning

Socratic questioning is a technique of using a questioning-and-interaction sequence designed to draw information out of the students. It provides opportunities for teachers to:

- Elicit from students a statement of belief or opinion.
- Examine the situation, belief, or opinion by the use of probing questions. In your questioning you should:

  - Try to bring out certain answers.

  - Challenge pupils to examine their own ideas and beliefs.

  - Ask your questions in a logical sequence.

  - Attempt to aid pupils to develop their own ideas.

  - Lead the pupils to your predetermined goal concept or belief.

Handling Pupil Questions

- Be courteous and kind.
- Use students' questions as springboards for further questions and discussion.
- Consider all questions that pupils ask to be relevant.
- Encourage pupils to ask questions that challenge the text or other students.
- Turn off trivial and irrelevant questions.

Question Types

Question Type	Student Activities	Examples
Knowledge	Remembering, memorizing, recognizing, recalling	• Who? • What? • Where? • When? • Why? • Define a word.
Comprehension	Interpreting, translating from one medium to another, describing	• What do the words "liberty and justice for all" mean? • What is the plot of the short story?
Application	Applying information to produce some results, problem solving	• Classify the activities as teacher-centered or student-centered. • How does California Proposition 187 affect legal immigrants?
Analysis	Identifying motives, making inferences, finding evidence to support, comparing	• Compare and contrast a liberal and a conservative on finance. • Examine the similarities and differences between butterflies and moths.
Synthesis	Creating something new, problem solving, making predictions, original communication	• Organize a plan to promote team spirit. • Think of some ways to encourage self-discipline.
Evaluation	Resolving differences of opinions, making value judgments	• Support the conclusion of your group with documented evidence. • Imagine yourself in the main character's position. What would you do?

Guidelines for Using Cooperative Learning

Cooperative learning is usually defined as students working together in small groups to achieve a common academic goal, such as the completion of a worksheet, assignment, quiz, or project. Responsibility for learning is placed on the learners, with the teacher assuming a facilitating role, providing guidance and support as needed.

To be most effective, cooperative learning groups should have all the following characteristics:

- A task for group discussion and resolution (if possible)
- Face-to-face interaction
- An atmosphere of cooperation and mutual helpfulness within each group
- Individual accountability
- Group processing of social skills

A cooperative learning group is created because:

- You want participants to model for each other.
- You want participants to reinforce each other.

- You want a variety of ideas for problem solving, decision making, and so forth.
- You want an ongoing support system for members.

Effective groups tend to be groups in which group members:

- Talk to each other and exchange many ideas and viewpoints.
- Show they like one another through reinforcing behavior.
- Are interested and active in helping one another.

Teachers who want to use cooperative learning groups should:

- Arrange the classroom to promote cooperative learning goals.
- Supply a variety of materials.
- Present the objectives as group objectives.
- Communicate expectations.
- Determine group sizes based on the task and goals for the group. For most activities, particularly problem-solving activities, groups of two to four work best.
- Assign students to groups to ensure heterogeneity (although students may be allowed to have input in the selection process).
- Assign each student a job or role.
- Make expectations of group behavior clear.
- Teach social skills (before and during activities) necessary for working with others.
- Devote time to monitoring group processes during activities.
- Follow up with informal evaluation after each session.
- Reward the group for successful completion of its task.

Assessment of student performance should include:

1. Individual assessment, which may be obtained from:

    - in-class tests or quizzes

    - take-home tests

    - homework assignments, and so forth

2. Group assessment, which may be determined in a number of ways:

    - One grade is given for a project or activity, and the group grade is equal to that grade.

    - One paper is selected at random from the group, and the group grade is the grade from the one paper.

    - The group grade is the average of the group members' grades.

    - The group grade is contingent on all members' individual grades reaching a certain level of performance.

    - The group grade is contingent on the average of all members' individual grades reaching a certain level of performance.

3. Social skills assessment, which may be obtained from:

    - Self-evaluation

    - Peer evaluation

    - Teacher evaluation of group participation and cooperation

Guidelines for Test Construction

In designing a test, a key decision you need to make is the form that test items should take. In selecting a test format, you will need to consider its *objectivity*. *Objective* questions tend to reduce the amount of teacher judgment used in the scoring, while *subjective* questions involve more teacher judgment when grading. As a general rule, true-false, matching, and multiple-choice questions are considered objective, and short answer and essay questions are considered subjective. As much as possible, you should try to design tests so that subjectivity in grading is reduced. The following guidelines should help you do that.

True-False Items

These require the student to mark a statement as true or false.

Advantages: Easy to construct, efficient way to test a lot of content, easy to grade

Disadvantages: Student guessing likely, too often directed at knowledge and comprehension cognitive levels, sometimes difficult to write nontrivial item, has little diagnostic value

Example. _____ George Washington was the first President of the United States.
(True)

Guidelines for construction:

- Design items based on significant facts, principles, and generalizations.
- Try to create items that test thinking beyond the knowledge level.
- Cite authorities when items contain controversial material or opinions.
- Design items so that the main idea in the statement is apparent to the student.
- Create items that deal with a single idea, not a combination of several ideas.
- Express items simply and clearly; avoid ambiguous language; include no more than one qualifying phrase.
- Avoid copying statements directly from the book.
- Create items that are entirely true or entirely false, not partially true and partially false.
- Avoid tricky items or items whose responses rest on a trivial detail.
- Avoid statements that could read more than one way.
- Make true and false items about the same length.
- Use positive statements; avoid negative statements, which tend to be confusing.
- Avoid "giveaway" words like *sometimes, never, always, often,* or *usually.* These frequently provide clues to the correctness of the statement.
- Include about equal numbers of true and false items on the test and make sure correct responses do not fall in a pattern.
- Provide a simple method for indicating the answer ("Write T for True or F for False.").

Matching Items

These require the student to match two sets of terms to show some indicated relationship (words with definitions, dates with events, and so forth).

Advantages: Checks student recognition of relationships, easy to construct, efficient way to test a lot of information, easy to grade

Disadvantages: Too often directed at knowledge and comprehension cognitive levels, sometimes difficult to construct plausible incorrect items.

Example: _____ Indicate the capital of the state by marking the letter of the correct answer in the blank provided.

_____ 1. Arkansas   A. Albuquerque
_____ 2. California   B. Austin
_____ 3. Lousiana   C. Baton Rouge
_____ 4. New Mexico   D. Houston
_____ 5. Texas   E. Little Rock
                 F. Sacramento
                 G. Santa Fe

(Correct answers are 1-E; 2-F; 3-C; 4-G; 5-B)

Guidelines for construction:

- Design questions based on significant facts, principles, and generalizations.
- Make the response options short.
- Use no more than 10 to 12 response options.
- Make lists that are similar in content.
- Include 1 or 2 response options that do not match up, or allow a response option to be used more than once.
- Arrange terms in a sequential order when feasible (for example, alphabetically).
- Put both sets of terms on the same page.
- Write clear and specific directions. Explain how the matching is to be done ("Write the letter of the correct answer . . .") and if terms may be used more than once.

Multiple-Choice Items

These require the student to select the correct or best response from a number of possible responses.

Advantages: Can be used to test at higher cognitive levels, substantially reduce guessing; easy to grade, have high diagnostic value

Disadvantages: time-consuming to prepare, difficult to present situations briefly, subjectivity may creep in

Example: _____ What is the area of a square that measures 5 meters on a side?

    A. 10 square meters
    B. 20 square meters
    C. 25 square meters
    D. 50 square meters

(Correct answer is C.)

Guidelines for construction:

- Design items based on significant facts, principles, and generalizations.
- Try to create items that test thinking beyond the knowledge level.
- Cite authorities when items contain controversial material or opinions.
- Design items that test one, and only one, central idea.
- Write simply, clearly, and briefly; avoid ambiguous language.
- Avoid copying statements directly from the book.
- Make sure items are independent of each other. One item should not aid in answering another item.
- Avoid negatively stated items.
- Avoid "giveaway" words like *sometimes*, *never*, *always*, *often*, or *usually*, which frequently provide clues to the correct response.
- Write item stems that contain sufficient information to indicate clearly one correct response.
- Provide four or five response choices.
- Arrange the response choices in a logical order when feasible (alphabetically, by magnitude, and so forth).
- Be sure all response choices are grammatically consistent with the stem.
- Be sure all response choices are parallel in construction.
- Design items for which there is one, and only one, correct response. The distractors (incorrect response options) should be clearly incorrect or inadequate.
- Be sure all distractors are plausible to students who do not know the correct answer.
- Use distractors that represent common mistakes or misconceptions.
- Avoid using "all of the above" or "none of the above" to complete the list of response options.
- Make sure the position of the correct response does not fall in a pattern.
- Write clear and specific directions. Provide a simple method for indicating the answer ("Circle the letter. . .").

Short Answer and Completion Items

These require the student to write a brief answer or to fill in a blank with a brief answer.

Advantages: Easy to construct, reduce student guessing

Disadvantages: Focus on rote memory and lower cognitive levels; grading may be subjective

Example: The author of *The Adventures of Tom Sawyer* is _____ .

(Mark Twain)

Guidelines for construction:

- Design items based on significant facts, principles, and generalizations.
- Cite authorities when items contain controversial material or opinions.
- Try to create items that test thinking beyond the knowledge level.
- Write items that contain sufficient information to indicate clearly one correct response.
- Avoid copying statements directly from the book.
- Try to create items that have a single word or short phrase as the correct response.
- Avoid statements that could read more than one way.
- Leave out key words or phrases, not trivial material.
- For completion items, put blanks at or near the end and use a maximum of two blanks.
- Leave plenty of space for writing the response.
- Write clear and specific directions.

Essay Questions

These require the student to write an extended response.

Advantages: Allow assessment at higher cognitive and affective levels, allow greater latitude in content, form, and length of answers

Disadvantages: hard to construct, may result in answers produced through rote memorization or bluffing, difficult to grade reliably, time-consuming to grade, number per test is limited

Example: Compare and contrast the Norse gods with the Roman gods.

Guidelines for construction are

- Design questions based on significant content.
- State questions clearly, specifically, and unambiguously.
- Begin questions with phrases such as *compare and contrast, present the arguments for and against, give the reasons for, explain how (or why), give an example of,* and similar phrases.
- Create questions that are interesting and challenging.
- Design questions that can be reasonably answered in the given time frame. If more than one essay question is used, indicate a reasonable time limit and give a point value for each on the test.
- Write clear and specific directions. Make sure students understand if mechanical skills (spelling, punctuation, grammar) will be given weight in the grading.

Guidelines for Parent-Teacher Conferences

Preparing for the Conference

- Schedule the conference at a definite day and time.
- Inform the principal.
- Invite the student to attend the conference, if appropriate and parents agree.
- Provide parents with topics to be discussed prior to the conference.
- Have a written conference agenda to keep you on task.
- Anticipate questions you think parents might have.
- Study the student's cumulative records.
- Review current daily grades, test results, and anecdotal records.
- Observe the student in different situations (for example, class, group work, playground).
- Collect samples of the student's work and obtain information from other teachers who work with the student, if needed.
- Determine whether the information gathered is pertinent to the conference objective.
- If there is reason to believe the child may have special needs, have a handout for the parents regarding the services offered by the school.
- Explain to the student the reason for the conference (age will determine how much detail).
- Make sure the setting for the conference is warm and inviting.
- Make sure the seating is comfortable and arranged so there are no physical barriers between you and the parents.
- Ask another teacher or the principal to attend as a witness, if possible—particularly if you anticipate difficulties.

During the Conference

- Think of the conference as a partnering with parents to help the student.
- Greet the parents warmly.
- Introduce yourself using first and last name.
- Offer refreshments.
- Be professional at all times.
- Stay poised and focused.
- Be respectful of and sensitive to the parents' cultural and social background.
- Address the parents often by their names.
- Establish and maintain eye contact (unless you sense it is making the parents uncomfortable, defensive, or hostile).
- Be sensitive to the parents' feelings throughout the conference.
- Accentuate the positive; always begin and end on a positive note.
- Be tactful, but honest and truthful.
- Respect confidentiality.
- Avoid comparing the student to other siblings.
- Stay away from psychological references as to why a student is not doing well. Avoid "diagnosing" or "labeling" students.

- Avoid candycoating problems when explaining difficulties to parents.
- Avoid bringing up past issues that have already been dealt with.
- Avoid discussing other students.
- Talk "with" parents instead of "at" them.
- Be a good listener and encourage parental input.
- Avoid becoming defensive when parents question your judgment.
- Make constructive suggestions and offer solutions, but always have a back-up plan.
- Use language and terminology that parents can easily understand.
- Avoid using jargon and overwhelming parents with irrelevant material.
- Share any notes taken and review them with parents, summarizing key points.
- Collaboratively develop a teacher-parent-student plan.
- Suggest what parents can do to help at home.
- Set a timetable for contacting parents with a progress report.
- Explain to parents the procedures and practices that will be followed.
- Provide the parents and student with a written copy of the plan.
- Schedule another conference if warranted.
- Invite parents to visit and participate.

Following the Conference

- Engage in self-reflection and evaluation (What went well? What didn't?)
- Review notes and comments, and file for further reference.
- Document, date, and file what was proposed.
- Provide the principal with a brief, written report.
- Write a personal note to the parents, thanking them for their time and informing them when you will contact them with an update.
- Make positive comments to the student as soon as possible.

Effective Interpersonal Skills During the Conference

- *Good Listener*—hearing what is implied as well as what is said; reading body language
- *Genuine*—being real; showing consistency between verbal and nonverbal language
- *Concrete*—being specific, but tactful when communicating
- *Warm*—being caring; giving concerned looks; using warm tone of voice
- *Respect*—being accepting, objective, nonjudgmental
- *Empathy*—showing feeling; understanding from another's perspective
- *Open*—being accepting of different views, inviting
- *Trustworthy*—being faithful, reliable

Hostile Conference

- If threatened, ask for an end to the conference.
- If the principal is not present, ask that the meeting be moved to his or her office.
- If you need one, ask for a break.
- Remember to stay calm; speak slowly, keep it short, and do not become defensive or angry.
- If parents make complaints, ask that they write them down.
- State that you will respond in writing.
- Avoid walking out of the conference unless you have been given permission by the principal to do so.
- Be aware that the student's right to privacy prohibits the involvement of legal representation for the teacher in a noninvestigatory setting such as a parent-teacher conference.

A LEGISLATIVE SUMMARY FOR NEW TEACHERS

Senate Bill 1

The revised Texas Education Code (TEC) adopted in 1995 (address: www.capitol.state.tx.us/statutes/edtoc.html).

TEC 21.041: Unprofessional Practices

A violation of any rule or provision of the Code of Ethics and Standards Practices for Texas Educators [TAC 19.247] shall be deemed to be unprofessional practice that shall constitute grounds for "suspension or revocation of an educator certificate."

TEC 21.102: Probationary Contract

"(a) Any person who is employed as a teacher by any school district for the first time, or who has not been employed by the district for two consecutive school years . . . shall be employed under a probationary contract.

"(b) A probationary contract may not be for a term exceeding one school year. The probationary contract may be renewed for two additional one-year periods, for a maximum permissible probationary contract period of three school years."

TEC 21.203: Employment Policies

"(a) The employment policies adopted by a board of trustees must require a written evaluation of each teacher at annual or more frequent intervals."

TEC 21.351: Recommended Appraisal Process and Performance Criteria

"(a) The commissioner shall adopt a recommended appraisal process and criteria on which to appraise the performance of teachers. The criteria must be based on observable, job-related behavior, including: (1) teachers' implementation of discipline management procedures; and (2) the performance of teachers' students."

TEC 21.352: Appraisals

"(c) Appraisal must be done at least once during each school year. The district shall maintain a written copy of the evaluation of each teacher's performance in the teacher's personnel file. Each teacher is entitled to receive a written copy of the evaluation on its completion. After receiving a written copy of the evaluation, a teacher is entitled to a second appraisal by a different appraiser or to submit a written rebuttal to the evaluation to be attached to the evaluation in the teacher's personnel file. The evaluation and any rebuttal may be given to another school district at which the teacher has applied for employment at the request of that district.

"(d) A teacher may be given advance notice of the date or time of an appraisal, but advance notice is not required."

TEC 21.355: Confidentiality

"A document evaluating the performance of a teacher . . . is confidential."

TEC 21.401: Minimum Service Required

"(a) A contract between a school district and an educator must be for a minimum of 10 months' service.

"(b) An educator employed under a 10-month contract must provide a minimum number of days of service as determined by the [formula in this section]."

TEC 21.402: Minimum Salary

"(a) [A] school district must pay each classroom teacher or full-time librarian not less than the minimum monthly salary, based on the employee's level of experience, determined by the [formula in this section]."

TEC 21.404: Planning and Preparation Time

"Each classroom teacher is entitled to at least 450 minutes within each two-week period for instructional preparation, including parent-teacher conferences, evaluating students' work, and planning. A planning and preparation period under this section may not be less than 45 minutes within the instructional day. During a planning and preparation period, a classroom teacher may not be required to participate in any other activity."

TEC 21.405: Duty-Free Lunch

"(a) . . . [E]ach classroom teacher or full-time librarian is entitled to at least a 30-minute lunch period free from all duties and responsibilities connected with the instruction and supervision of students. Each school district may set flexible or rotating schedules for each classroom teacher or full-time librarian in the district for the implementation of the duty-free lunch period."

TEC 21.406: Denial of Compensation Based on Absence for Religious Observance Prohibited

"A school district may not deny an educator a salary bonus or similar compensation given in whole or in part on the basis of educator attendance because of the educator's absence from school for observance of a holy day observed by a religion whose places of worship are exempt from property taxation under Section 11.20, Tax Code."

TEC 21.407: Political Affairs

"(b) A school district board of trustees or school district employee may not directly or indirectly coerce any teacher to refrain from participating in political affairs in the teacher's community, state, or nation."

TEC 21.408: Professional Associations

"This chapter does not abridge the right of an educator to join any professional association or organization or refuse to join any professional association or organization."

TEC 21.409: Leave of Absence

"(a) Each full-time educator employed by a school district shall be given a leave of absence for temporary disability at any time the educator's condition interferes with the performance of regular duties. The contract or employment of the educator may not be terminated by the school district while the educator is on a leave of absence for temporary disability. 'Temporary disability' in this section includes the condition of pregnancy."

TEC 22.001: Salary Deductions for Professional Dues

"(a) A school district employee is entitled to have an amount deducted from the employee's salary for membership fees or dues to a professional organization."

TEC 22.003: Minimum Personal Leave Program

"(a) A state minimum personal leave program consisting of five days per year personal leave with no limit on accumulation and transferable among districts shall be provided for school district employees. School districts may provide additional personal leave beyond this minimum. The board of trustees of a school district may adopt a policy governing an employee's use of personal leave granted under this subsection, except that the policy may not restrict the purposes for which the leave may be used.

"(b) In addition to all other days of leave provided by this section or by the school district, an employee of a school district who is physically assaulted during the performance of the employee's regular duties is entitled to the number of days of leave necessary to recuperate from all physical injuries sustained as a result of the assault."

TEC 22.004: Group Health Benefits

"(a) Each district shall make available to its employees group health coverage."

TEC 22.051: Immunity from Liability

"(a) A professional employee [superintendent, principal, teacher, supervisor, social worker, counselor, nurse, or teacher's aide] of a school district is not personally liable for any act that is incident to or within the scope of the duties of the employee's position of employment and that involves the exercise of judgment or discretion on the part of the employee, except in circumstances in which a professional employee uses excessive force in the discipline of students or negligence resulting in bodily injury to students.

"(b) This section does not apply to the operation, use, or maintenance of any motor vehicle."

TEC 22.052: Administration of Medication

"(a) [S]chool district . . . employees are immune from civil liability from damages or injuries resulting from the administration of medication to a student if:

"(1) the school district has received a written request to administer the medication from the parent, legal guardian, or other person having legal control of the student; and (2) when administering prescription medication, the medication appears to be in the original container and to be properly labeled."

TEC 22.082: Access to Criminal History Records by State Board for Educator Certification

"The State Board for Educator Certification shall obtain from any law enforcement or criminal justice agency all criminal history record information that relates to an applicant for or holder of a[n educator] certificate."

TEC 22.083: Access to Criminal History Records by Local and Regional Education Authorities

"(a) A school district . . . may obtain from any law enforcement or criminal justice agency all criminal history record information that relates to a person:

"(1) whom the district . . . intends to employ in any capacity. . . .

"(b) A school district . . . may obtain from any law enforcement or criminal justice agency all criminal history record information that relates to:

"(1) . . . [an] employee of the district."

TEC 22.085: Discharge of Employees Convicted of Offenses

"A school district . . . may discharge an employee if the district or school obtains information of the employee's conviction of a felony or of a misdemeanor involving moral turpitude that the employee did not disclose to the State Board for Educator Certification or the district."

TEC 22.901: Unlawful Inquiry into Religious Affiliation

"(a) A person employed or maintained to obtain or aid in obtaining positions for public school employees may not directly or indirectly ask about, orally or in writing, the religion or religious affiliation of anyone applying for employment in the public schools of this state."

TEC 25.082: School Day

"(a) A school day shall be at least seven hours each day, including intermissions and recesses.

"(b) A school district may provide for a period of silence at the beginning of the first class of each school day during which a student may reflect or meditate."

TEC 25.083: School Day Interruptions

"The board of trustees of each school district shall adopt and strictly enforce a policy limiting interruptions of classes during the school day for nonacademic activities such as announcements and sales promotions. At a minimum, the policy must limit announcements other than emergency announcements to once during the school day."

TEC 25.085: Compulsory School Attendance

"(b) Unless specifically exempted . . . a child who is at least six years of age . . . and who has not yet reached the child's 18th [19th] birthday shall attend school."

TEC 25.087: Excused Absences

"(a) A child required to attend school may be excused for temporary absence resulting from any cause acceptable to the teacher, principal, or superintendent of the school in which the child is enrolled.

"(b) A school district shall excuse a student from attending school for the purpose of observing religious holy days . . . if before the absence the parent, guardian, or person having custody or control of the student submits a written request for the excused absence. A school district shall excuse a student for temporary absence resulting from health care professionals if that student commences classes or returns to school on the same day of the appointment. . . . A student whose absence is excused under this subsection shall be allowed a reasonable time to make up school work missed on those days."

TEC 25.111: Student/Teacher Ratios

"[E]ach school district must employ a sufficient number of teachers . . . to maintain an average ratio of not less than one teacher for each 20 students in average daily attendance."

TEC 25.112: Class Size

"(a) [A] school district may not enroll more than 22 students in a kindergarten, first, second, third, or fourth grade class.

"(d) On application of a school district, the commissioner may except the district from the limit in Subsection (a) if the commissioner finds the limit works an undue hardship on the district. An exception expires at the end of the semester for which it is granted, and the commissioner may not grant an exception for more than one semester at a time."

TEC 25.901: Exercise of [Students'] Constitutional Right to Pray

"A public school student has an absolute right to individually, voluntarily, and silently pray or meditate in school in a manner that does not disrupt the instructional or other activities of the school. A person may not require, encourage, or coerce a student to engage in or refrain from such prayer or meditation during any school activity."

TEC 26.004: [Parents'] Access to Student Records

"A parent is entitled to access to all written records of a school district concerning the parent's child, including: (1) attendance records; (2) test scores; (3) grades; (4) disciplinary records; (5) counseling records; (6) psychological records; (7) applications for admission; (8) health and immunization information; (9) teacher and counselor evaluations; and (10) reports of behavioral patterns."

TEC 26.008: [Parents'] Right to Full Information

"(a) A parent is entitled to full information regarding the school activities of a parent's child.

"(b) An attempt by any school district employee to encourage or coerce a child to withhold information from the child's parent is grounds for discipline."

TEC 26.010: Exemption from Instruction

"(a) A parent is entitled to remove the parent's child temporarily from a class or other school activity that conflicts with the parent's religious or moral beliefs if the parent presents or delivers to the teacher of the parent's child a written statement authorizing the removal of the child from the class or other school activity."

TEC 28.001: [Essential Knowledge and Skills] Purpose

"[T]he essential knowledge and skills developed by the State Board of Education . . . shall require all students to demonstrate the knowledge and skills necessary to read, write, compute, problem solve, think critically, apply technology, and communicate across all subject areas. The essential knowledge and skills shall also prepare and enable all students to continue to learn in postsecondary educational, training, or employment settings."

TEC 28.002: Required Curriculum

"(a) Each school district that offers kindergarten through grade 12 shall offer . . .

(1) a foundation curriculum that includes: (A) English language arts; (B) mathematics; (C) science; and (D) social studies, consisting of Texas, United States, and world history, government, and geography; and

"(2) an enrichment curriculum that includes: (A) to the extent possible, languages other than English; (B) health; (C) physical education; (D) fine arts; (E) economics, with emphasis on the free enterprise system and its benefits; (F) career and technology education; and (G) technology applications.

"(h) . . . A primary purpose of the public school curriculum is to prepare thoughtful, active citizens who understand the importance of patriotism and can function productively in a free enterprise society with appreciation for the basic democratic values of our state and national heritage.

"(i) . . . [The State Board of Education] may not adopt rules that designate the methodology used by a teacher or the time spent by a teacher or a student on a particular task or subject."

TEC 28.004: Human Sexuality Instruction

"(a) Any course materials and instruction relating to human sexuality, sexually transmitted diseases, or human immunodeficiency virus or acquired immune deficiency syndrome . . . must: (1) present abstinence from sexual activity as the preferred choice of behavior in relationship to all sexual activity for unmarried persons of school age. . . .

"(b) A school district may not distribute condoms in connection with instruction relating to human sexuality.

"(h) A school district shall notify a parent of each student enrolled in the district of: (1) the basic content of the district's human sexuality instruction to be provided to the student; and (2) the parent's right to remove the student from any part of the district's human sexuality instruction."

TEC 28.005: Language of Instruction

"(a) English shall be the basic language of instruction in public schools.

　"(b) It is the policy of this state to ensure the mastery of English by all students, except that bilingual instruction may be offered or permitted in situations in which bilingual instruction is necessary to ensure students' reasonable proficiency in the English language and ability to achieve academic success."

TEC 28.021: Student Advancement

"(a) A student may be promoted only on the basis of academic achievement or demonstrated proficiency of the subject matter of the course or grade level."

TEC 29.303: Unique Communication

"Students who are deaf or hard of hearing must have an education in which their unique communication mode is respected, used, and developed to an appropriate level of proficiency."

TEC 29.307: Role Models

"A student who is deaf or hard of hearing shall be given the opportunity to be exposed to deaf or hard-of-hearing role models."

TEC 29.051: [Bilingual Education] State Policy

"English is the basic language of this state. Public schools are responsible for providing a full opportunity for all students to become competent in speaking, reading, writing, and comprehending the English language. Large numbers of students in the state come from environments in which the primary language is other than English. . . . Bilingual education and special language programs can meet the needs of those students and facilitate their integration into the regular school curriculum. Therefore, in accordance with the policy of the state to ensure equal educational opportunity to every student, and in recognition of the educational needs of students of limited English proficiency, this subchapter provides for the establishment of bilingual education and special language programs in the public schools."

TEC 29.055: [Bilingual] Program Content; Method of Instruction

"(a) A bilingual education program established by a school district shall be a full-time program of dual-language instruction that provides for learning basic skills in the primary language of the students enrolled in the program and for carefully structured and sequenced mastery of English language skills. A program of instruction in English as a second language established by a school district shall be a program of intensive instruction in English from teachers trained in recognizing and dealing with language differences.

　"(b) A program of bilingual education or of instruction in English as a second language shall be designed to consider the students' learning experiences and shall incorporate the cultural aspects of the students' backgrounds.

"(c) In subjects such as art, music, and physical education, students of limited English proficiency shall participate fully with English-speaking students in regular classes provided in the subjects."

TEC 31.104: Distribution and Handling [of Textbooks]

"(c) . . . Each teacher shall keep a record of the number or other identifying mark of each textbook issued to each student. Each textbook . . . must be covered by the student under the direction of the teacher. Subject to availability, each school district . . . shall, at the request of a parent or guardian of a student enrolled in the district . . . allow the student to take home any textbook . . . used by the student. The student must return the textbook to school at the beginning of the next school day. A student must return all textbooks to the teacher at the end of the school year or when the student withdraws from school.

"(d) Each student, or the student's parent or guardian, is responsible for each textbook not returned by the student."

TEC 33.081: Extracurricular Activities

"(c) A student . . . shall be suspended from participation in any extracurricular activity . . . after a grade evaluation period in which the student received a grade lower than the equivalent of 70 on a scale of 100 in any academic class other than an identified honors or advanced class. A suspension continues for at least three weeks and is not removed during the school year until the conditions of Subsection (d) are met.

"(d) Until the suspension is removed . . . a school district shall review the grades . . . at the end of each three-week period following the date on which the suspension began. At the time of a review, the suspension is removed if the student's grade in each class, other than an identified honors or advanced class, is equal to or greater than the equivalent of 70 on a scale of 100. The principal and each of the student's teachers shall make the determination concerning the student's grades.

"(f) A student suspended under this section may practice or rehearse with other students for an extracurricular activity but may not participate in a competition or other public performance."

TEC 37.001: Student Code of Conduct

"(a) The board of trustees of an independent school district shall . . . adopt a student code of conduct for the district.

"(b) A teacher with knowledge that a student has violated the student code of conduct shall file with the school principal or the other appropriate administrator a written report, not to exceed one page, documenting the violation. The principal or the other appropriate administrator shall, not later than 24 hours after receipt of a report from a teacher, send a copy of the report to the student's parents or guardians."

TEC 37.002: Removal by Teacher

"(a) A teacher may send a student to the principal's office to maintain effective discipline in the classroom.

"(b) A teacher may remove from class a student: (1) who has been documented by the teacher to repeatedly interfere with the teacher's ability to communicate effectively with the students in the class or with the ability of the student's classmates to learn; or (2) whose behavior the teacher determines is so unruly, disruptive, or abusive that it seriously interferes with the teacher's ability to communicate effectively with the students in the class or with the ability of the student's classmates to learn.

"(c) If a teacher removes a student from class . . . the principal may not return the student to that teacher's class without the teacher's consent unless the [Placement Review] committee [composed of two teachers and one member of the professional staff] . . . determines that such placement is the best or only alternative available."

TEC 37.004: Placement of Students with Disabilities

"The placement of a student with a disability who receives special education services may be made only by a duly constituted admission, review, and dismissal committee. A student with a disability who receives special education services may not be placed in alternative education programs [AEP]. . . ."

[Except: (1) when appropriate, special education students may be suspended or removed to an AEP for up to 10 days (to the extent such alternatives would be applied to children without disabilities) without approval of the ARD committee, but districts must continue to provide services defined in each student's IEP; (2) for certain drug and weapons offenses, special education students may be removed to an AEP for up to 45 days without approval of the ARD committee; (3) school personnel have the option of asking a hearing officer to move children with disabilities to an interim alternative educational setting for up to 45 days without approval of the ARD committee, if they are substantially likely to injure themselves or others in their current placement. IDEA 97: Section 615(k)]

TEC 37.007: Expulsion for Serious Offenses

"(g) A school district shall inform each teacher of the conduct of a student who has engaged in any violation [that could result in expulsion]. . . . A teacher shall keep the information received . . . confidential. The State Board for Educator Certification may revoke or suspend the certification of a teacher who intentionally violates this subsection."

TEC 37.008: Alternative Education Programs

"(a) Each school district shall provide an alternative education program that . . . is provided in a setting other than a student's regular classroom."

TEC 37.009: Conference; Hearing; Review

"(a) Not later than the third class day after the day on which a student is removed from class by the teacher . . . the principal . . . shall schedule a conference among the principal . . . , a parent or guardian of the student, the teacher, . . . and the student. At the conference, the student is entitled to written or oral notice of the reasons for the removal, an explanation of the basis for the removal, and an opportunity to respond to the reasons for the removal. The student may not be returned to the regular classroom pending the conference. Following the conference . . . the principal shall order the placement of the student . . . for a period consistent with the student code of conduct.

"(e) A student placed in an alternative education program . . . shall be provided a review of the student's status . . . at intervals not to exceed 120 days. At the review, the student or the student's parent or guardian must be given the opportunity to present arguments for the student's return to the regular classroom or campus. The student may not be returned to the classroom of the teacher who removed the student without that teacher's consent. The teacher may not be coerced to consent.

"(f) Before a student may be expelled . . . the board or the board's designee must provide the student a hearing at which the student is afforded appropriate due process as required by the federal constitution."

TEC 37.016: Report of Drug Offenses; Liability

"A teacher . . . is not liable in civil damages for reporting to a school administrator or governmental authority, in the exercise of professional judgment within the scope of the teacher's . . . duties, a student whom the teacher suspects of using, passing, or selling, on school property: (1) marihuana or a controlled substance, . . . (2) a dangerous drug, (3) an abusable glue or aerosol paint, . . . or a volatile chemical, . . . or (4) an alcoholic beverage."

TEC 37.018: Information for Educators

"Each school district shall provide each teacher . . . with a copy of [Subchapter A. Alternative Settings for Behavior Management] and with a copy of the local policy relating to [it]."

TEC 37.082: Possession of Paging Devices

"(a) The board of trustees of a school district may adopt a policy prohibiting a student from possessing a paging device while on school property or while attending a school-sponsored, school-related activity on or off school property."

TEC 37.083: Discipline Management Programs; Sexual Harassment Policies

"(a) Each school district shall adopt and implement a discipline management program. . . .
"(b) Each school district may develop and implement a sexual harassment policy."

TEC 37.121: Fraternities, Sororities, Secret Societies, and Gangs

"(a) A person commits an offense if the person: (1) is a member of, pledges to become a member of, joins, or solicits another person to join or pledge to become a member of a public school fraternity, sorority, secret society, or gang; or (2) is not enrolled in a public school and solicits another person to attend a meeting of a public school fraternity, sorority, secret society, or gang or a meeting at which membership in one of those groups is encouraged.

"(b) A school district board of trustees or an educator shall recommend placing in an alternative education program any student under the person's control who violates Subsection (a).

"(c) An offense under this section is a Class C misdemeanor.

"(d) In this section, 'public school fraternity, sorority, secret society, or gang' means an organization composed wholly or in part of students of public primary or secondary schools that seeks to perpetuate itself by taking in additional members from the students enrolled in school on the basis of the decision of its membership rather than on the free choice of a student in the school who is qualified by the rules of the school to fill the special aims of the organization. The term does not include an agency for public welfare, including Boy Scouts, Hi-Y, Girl Reserves, DeMolay, Rainbow Girls, Pan-American Clubs, scholarship societies, or other similar educational organizations sponsored by state or national education authorities."

TEC 38.005: Protective Eye Devices in Public Schools

"Each teacher and student must wear industrial-quality eye-protective devices in appropriate situations as determined by school district policy."

TEC 38.006: Tobacco on School Property

"The board of trustees of a school district shall: (1) prohibit smoking or using tobacco products at a school-related or school-sanctioned activity on or off school property."

TEC 38.007: Alcohol-Free School Zones

"(a) The board of trustees of a school district shall prohibit the use of alcoholic beverages at a school-related or school-sanctioned activity on or off school property."

TEC 39.021: Essential Skills and Knowledge

"The State Board of Education . . . shall establish the essential skills and knowledge that all students should learn."

TEC 39.022: Assessment Program

"The State Board of Education by rule shall create and implement a statewide assessment program that is primarily performance-based to ensure school accountability for student achievement."

TEC 39.023: Adoption and Administration of Instruments

"(a) The agency shall adopt appropriate criterion-referenced assessment instruments designed to assess competencies in . . . (1) reading and mathematics, annually in grades three through eight; (2) writing, in grades four and eight; and (3) social studies and science, at an appropriate grade level determined by the State Board of Education.

"(c) The agency shall also adopt secondary exit-level assessment instruments designed to assess competencies in mathematics and English language arts. The English language arts section must include the assessment of writing competencies.

"(d) The agency shall adopt end-of-course assessment instruments for students in secondary grades who have completed Algebra I, Biology I, English II, and United States history.

"(e) [T]he agency shall release the questions and answer keys to each assessment instrument . . . after the last time the instrument is administered for a school year."

TEC 39.030: Confidentiality; Performance Reports

"(b) The results of individual student performance on academic skills assessment instruments administered under this subchapter are confidential. . . . However, overall student performance data shall be [dis]aggregated by ethnicity, sex, grade level, subject area, campus, and district and made available to the public. . . . The information may not contain the names of individual students or teachers."

TEC 39.051: Academic Excellence Indicators

"(a) The State Board of Education shall adopt a set of indicators of the quality of learning on a campus.

"(b) Performance on the indicators adopted under this section shall be compared to state-established standards. . . . The indicators must be based on information that is disaggregated with respect to race, ethnicity, sex, and socioeconomic status and must include: (1) the results of [state-required] assessment instruments . . . ; (2) dropout rates; (3) student attendance rates; (4) the percentage of graduating students who attain [passing] scores on the secondary [state-required] exit-level assessment instruments . . . ; (5) the percentage of graduating students who meet the course requirements established for the recommended high school program . . . ; (6) the results of the Scholastic Assessment Test (SAT) and the American College Test; (7) the percentage of students taking end-of-course assessment instruments . . . ; (8) the percentage of students exempted . . . from the assessment program . . . ; and (9) any other indicator the State Board of Education adopts."

TEC 39.072: Accreditation Standards

"(a) The State Board of Education shall adopt rules to evaluate the performance of school districts and to assign to each district a performance rating as follows: (1) exemplary (meets or exceeds state exemplary standards); (2) recognized (meets or exceeds required improvement and within 10 percent of state exemplary standards); (3) academically acceptable (below the exemplary and recognized standards but exceeds the academically unacceptable standards); or (4) academically unacceptable (below the state clearly unacceptable performance standard and does not meet required improvement).

"(b) The academic excellence indicators . . . shall be the main consideration of the agency in the rating of the district."

Texas Family Code (TFC) 261.101: Report of Child Abuse or Neglect

"(b) If a [teacher] has cause to believe that a child has been or may be abused or neglected, the [teacher] shall make a report not later than the 48th hour after the hour the [teacher] first suspects that the child has been or may be abused or neglected. A [teacher] may not delegate to or rely on another person to make the report.

"(d) The identity of an individual making a report under this chapter is confidential."

TFC 261.103: Report [of Child Abuse or Neglect] Made to Appropriate Agency

"A report shall be made to: (1) any local or state law enforcement agency; (2) the [Department of Protective and Regulatory Services] if the alleged or suspected abuse involves a person responsible for the care, custody, or welfare of the child; (3) the state agency that operates, licenses, certifies, or registers the facility in which the alleged abuse or neglect occurred; or (4) the agency designated by the court to be responsible for the protection of children."

TFC 261.104: Contents of Report [of Child Abuse or Neglect]

"The person making a report shall identify, if known: (1) the name and address of the child; (2) the name and address of the person responsible for the care, custody, or welfare of the child; and (3) any other pertinent information concerning the alleged or suspected abuse or neglect."

TFC 261.106: Immunities [for Reporting Child Abuse or Neglect]

"(a) A person acting in good faith who reports . . . alleged child abuse or neglect . . . is immune from civil or criminal liability."

TFC 261.107: False Report [of Child Abuse or Neglect]; Penalty

"(a) A person commits an offense if the person knowingly or intentionally makes a report [of alleged child abuse or neglect] that the person knows is false or lacks factual foundation. The first offense under this section is a Class A misdemeanor; a subsequent offense under this section is a state jail felony."

TFC 261.109: Failure to Report [Child Abuse or Neglect]; Penalty

"(a) A person commits an offense if the person has cause to believe that a child's physical or mental health or welfare has been or may be adversely affected by abuse or neglect and knowingly fails to report. . . .

"(b) An offense under this section is a Class B misdemeanor."

19 Texas Administrative Code §§ 74, 110-128: Texas Essential Knowledge and Skills

The essential knowledge and skills developed by the State Board of Education. (address: www.sos.state.tx.us/tac/19/II/) Authority: TEC 28.002, TEC 28.005, and TEC 29.051.

Chapter I (formerly Title I) of the Elementary and Secondary Education Act of 1965 (ESEA)

Provided a comprehensive plan for addressing the inequality of educational opportunity for economically underprivileged children. Highlights of current Title I legislation include:

- Coordinates the state, local education agency, and schools' programs to ensure high standards for all children.
- Provides students with an accelerated curriculum and instruction that will allow them to meet the high standards.

- Emphasizes extended learning time and/or schoolwide programs that will allow Title I students to receive instruction at least equivalent to that received by other children.
- Promotes schoolwide reform, effective instructional methods, and challenging academic content.
- Enhances the quality of instruction by expanding professional development opportunities.
- Aligns services under all sections of Title I with each other, with other educational programs, and with health and social services, when feasible.
- Strengthens parent involvement in their children's education.
- Allocates resources to areas where the need is greatest.
- Uses state assessment systems to improve accountability and to demonstrate how well children are achieving the state's performance standards.
- Allows schools and teachers more authority in making decisions in return for greater responsibility for student performance (1994). [Source: The National Clearinghouse for Bilingual Education at www.ncbe.gwu.edu]

Title VII of the Elementary and Secondary Education Act Amendments of 1968 (The Bilingual Education Act)

Made federal funds available for bilingual education programs.

Public Law 91-230: The Elementary and Secondary Education Act Amendments of 1970

Included Title VI, the Education of the Handicapped Act. Established a core grant program for local education agencies, now known as part B, and it authorized a number of discretionary programs. [Source: www.nichcy.org]

Section 504 of the Rehabilitation Act of 1973

Prohibits schools (and other institutions receiving federal funds) from discriminating against students who have disabilities.

Public Law 93-280: The Education Amendments of 1974

Established two laws. One was the Education of the Handicapped Act Amendments of 1974, which was the first to mention an appropriate education for all children with disabilities. It also reauthorized the discretionary programs. The second law, the Family Education Rights and Privacy Act, gave parents and students over the age of 18 the right to examine records kept in the student's personal file. [Source: www.nichcy.org]

Public Law 94-142: The Education for All Handicapped Children Act of 1975

Mandated a free appropriate public education (FAPE) for all children with disabilities, ensured due process rights, and mandated IEPs and LRE. As such, it is the core of federal funding for special education. This law was passed in 1975 and went into effect in October 1977, when the regulations were finalized. [Source: www.nichcy.org]

Public Law 101-476: The Education of the Handicapped Act Amendments of 1990

Renamed the law the Individuals with Disabilities Education Act. It reauthorized and expanded the discretionary programs, mandated transition services, defined assistive technology devices and services, and added autism and traumatic brain injury to the list of categories of children and youth eligible for special education and related services. [Source: www.nichcy.org]

Public Law 105-17: The Individuals with Disabilities Education Act Amendments of 1997

The current law. Strengthens the role of parents; ensures access to the general curriculum and reforms; focuses on teaching and learning while reducing unnecessary paperwork requirements; assists educational agencies in addressing the costs of improving special education and related services to children with disabilities; gives increased attention to racial, ethnic, and linguistic diversity to prevent inappropriate identification and mislabeling; ensures schools are safe and conducive to learning; and encourages parents and educators to work out their differences by using nonadversarial means. [Source: www.nichcy.org]

Lau v. Nichols

A 1974 case in which the Supreme Court decided that all students, regardless of their English ability, must not be denied "a meaningful opportunity to participate in the public educational program."

Plyler v. Doe

A 1982 case in which the Supreme Court decided that a state's statute denying school enrollment to children of illegal immigrants "violates the Equal Protection Clause of the Fourteenth Amendment."

14th Amendment

The 14th Amendment to the Constitution ensures due process; legal procedures and safeguards; rights of parents to examine school records; requirement that parents have prior notification of changes; parental consent for evaluation and/or placement.

Buckley Amendment/Family Educational Rights and Privacy Act

A 1974 law regarding the privacy of student records; parents have the right to view their children's educational records; students over 18 years of age also have this right. Allows all parents, even those not having custody of their children, access to records. Only parents who have restraining orders against them are barred from seeing records. Seek parental permission in writing before disclosing any personally identifiable record on a child to anyone other than professional personnel employed in the district. Parents in Texas have a right to know if the teacher is certified in the area of assignment.

Title VI of the Civil Rights Act of 1964

Protects people from discrimination based on race, color, or national origin in programs or activities that receive federal funds.

Title VII, Civil Rights Act of 1964

Prohibits discriminatory practices, including sexual harassment in the workplace.

Title IX Education Amendment

Prohibits discrimination on the basis of sex in education programs receiving federal financial assistance. Title IX also protects students from unlawful sexual harassment in all of a school's programs or activities, whether they take place in the facilities of the school, on a school bus, at a class or training program sponsored by the school at another location, or elsewhere. Title IX protects both male and female students from sexual harassment, regardless of who the harasser is.

Rodriguez v. San Antonio ISD

A 1973 court case that urged states to devise new school tax plans to provide equality in education. Texas school funding not in violation of federal Constitution.

Edgewood ISD v. Kirby

A 1984 school finance case; suit to end discrepancies between rich and poor districts.

Honig v. Doe ("Stay-put Provision")

A 1988 case in which the Supreme Court reaffirmed that an educational placement of a student with disabilities cannot be changed without exhausting due process proceedings outlined in P.L. 94-142. The court found that school officials may temporarily suspend a student with disabilities up to 10 days. Under this ruling, disciplinary exclusion for more than 10 days constitutes a change of placement under P.L. 94-142. After the initial 10-day period, the student must return to his or her placement and remain there ("stay-put") during any due process hearing or court appeal. However, school officials may seek court action if "maintaining the child in his/her current placement is substantially likely to result in injury to himself or others."

Greer v. Rome City School District

A 1992 case in which the court decided in favor of parents who objected to the placement of their daughter in a self-contained special education classroom. Specifically, the court said: "Before the school district may conclude that a handicapped child should be educated outside of the regular classroom it must consider whether supplemental aids and services would permit satisfactory education in the regular classroom." The district argued that the costs of providing services in the classroom would be too high. However, the court said that the district cannot refuse to serve a child because of added cost. On the other hand, the court also said that a district cannot be required to provide a child with his or her own full-time teacher.

Public Law 94-553: Copyright Law

Allows teachers to copy for scholarly use certain amounts of printed materials. Copying is only for one course and must include the copyright notice. Other guidelines must be adhered to, including no pirating of computer software.

CODE OF ETHICS AND STANDARD PRACTICES FOR TEXAS EDUCATORS*

(A) PROFESSIONAL RESPONSIBILITY

The Texas educator should strive to create an atmosphere that will nurture to fulfillment the potential of each student.

The educator should comply with standard practices and ethical conduct toward students, professional colleagues, school officials, parents, and members of the community.

In conscientiously conducting his or her affairs, the educator shall exemplify the highest standards of professional commitment.

(B) PRINCIPLE I: PROFESSIONAL ETHICAL CONDUCT

The Texas educator should endeavor to maintain the dignity of the profession by respecting and obeying the law, demonstrating personal integrity, and exemplifying honesty.

Standards

1. The educator shall not intentionally misrepresent official policies of the school district or educational organization and shall clearly distinguish those views from his personal attitudes and opinions.

2. The educator shall honestly account for all funds committed to his charge and shall conduct his financial business with integrity.

3. The educator shall not use institutional or professional privileges for personal or partisan advantage.

4. The educator shall accept no gratuities, gifts, or favors that impair professional judgment.

5. The educator shall not offer any favor, service, or thing of value to obtain special advantage.

6. The educator shall not falsify records, or direct or coerce others to do so.

*Adopted by the State Board for Educator Certification
(Effective March 1, 1998) Available at http://www.sos.state.tx.us/tac/19/VII/247/247.2.html.

(C) PRINCIPLE II: PROFESSIONAL PRACTICES AND PERFORMANCE

The Texas educator, after qualifying in a manner established by law or regulation, shall assume responsibilities for professional administrative or teaching practices and professional performance and shall demonstrate competence.

Standards

1. The educator shall apply for, accept, offer, or assign a position or a responsibility on the basis of professional qualifications and shall adhere to the terms of a contract or appointment.

2. The educator shall not deliberately or recklessly impair his or her mental or physical health or ignore social prudence, thereby affecting his or her ability to perform the duties of his or her professional assignment.

3. The educator shall organize instruction that seeks to accomplish objectives related to learning.

4. The educator shall continue professional growth.

5. The educator shall comply with written local school board policies, state regulations, and other applicable state and federal laws.

(D) PRINCIPLE III: ETHICAL CONDUCT TOWARD PROFESSIONAL COLLEAGUES

The Texas educator, in exemplifying ethical relations with colleagues, shall accord just and equitable treatment to all members of the profession.

Standards

1. The educator shall not reveal confidential information concerning colleagues unless disclosure serves professional purposes or is required by law.

2. The educator shall not willfully make false statements about a colleague or the school system.

3. The educator shall adhere to written local school board policies and state and federal laws regarding dismissal, evaluation, and employment processes.

4. The educator shall not interfere with a colleague's exercise of political and citizenship rights and responsibilities.

5. The educator shall not discriminate against, coerce, or harass a colleague on the basis of race, color, religion, national origin, age, sex, disability, or family status.

6. The educator shall not intentionally deny or impede a colleague in the exercise or enjoyment of any professional right or privilege.

7. The educator shall not use coercive means or promise special treatment in order to influence professional decisions or colleagues.

8. The educator shall have the academic freedom to teach as a professional privilege, and no educator shall interfere with such privilege except as required by state and/or federal laws.

(E) PRINCIPLE IV: ETHICAL CONDUCT TOWARD STUDENTS

The Texas educator, in accepting a position of public trust, should measure success by the progress of each student toward realization of his or her potential as an effective citizen.

Standards

1. The educator shall deal considerately and justly with each student and shall seek to resolve problems including discipline according to law and school board policy.

2. The educator shall not intentionally expose the student to disparagement.

3. The educator shall not reveal confidential information concerning students unless disclosure serves professional purposes or is required by law.

4. The educator shall make reasonable effort to protect the student from conditions detrimental to learning, physical health, mental health, or safety.

5. The educator shall not deliberately distort facts.

6. The educator shall not unfairly exclude a student from participation in a program, deny benefits to a student, or grant advantage to a student on the basis of race, color, sex, disability, national origin, religion, or family status.

7. The educator shall not unreasonably restrain the student from independent action in the pursuit of learning or deny the student access to varying points of view.

(F) PRINCIPLE V: ETHICAL CONDUCT TOWARD PARENTS AND COMMUNITY

The Texas educator, in fulfilling citizenship responsibilities in the community, should cooperate with parents and others to improve the public schools of the community.

Standards

1. The educator shall make reasonable effort to communicate to parents information which should be revealed in the interest of the student.

2. The educator shall endeavor to understand community cultures and relate the home environment of students to the school.

3. The educator shall manifest a positive role in school public relations.

LEARNER-CENTERED PROFICIENCIES FOR TEXAS TEACHERS*

The State Board for Educator Certification standards for the preparation of teachers in Texas are listed below and are correlated with the present ExCET professional development competencies.

LEARNER-CENTERED KNOWLEDGE

The teacher possesses and draws on a rich knowledge of content, pedagogy, and technology to provide relevant and meaningful learning experiences for students.

The teacher exhibits a strong working knowledge of subject matter and enables students to better understand patterns of thinking specific to a discipline. The teacher stays abreast of current knowledge and practice within the content area, related disciplines, and technology; participates in professional development activities; and collaborates with other professionals. Moreover, the teacher contributes to the knowledge base and understands the pedagogy of the discipline.

As the teacher guides learners to construct knowledge through experiences, they learn about relationships among and within the central themes of various disciplines while also learning how to learn. Recognizing the dynamic nature of knowledge, the teacher selects and organizes topics so students make clear connections between what is taught in the classroom and what they experience outside the classroom. As students probe these relationships, the teacher encourages discussion in which both the teacher's and the students' opinions are valued. To further develop multiple perspectives, the teacher integrates other disciplines, learners' interests, and technological resources so that learners consider the central themes of the subject matter from as many different cultural and intellectual viewpoints as possible.

This standard correlates with the following competencies:

Competency 002: The teacher considers environmental factors that may affect learning in designing a supportive and responsive classroom community that promotes all students' learning and self-esteem.

Competency 004: The teacher understands how learning occurs and can apply this understanding to design and implement effective instruction.

Competency 007: The teacher uses effective verbal, nonverbal, and media communication techniques to shape the classroom into a community of learners engaged in active inquiry, collaboration, exploration, and supportive interactions.

Competency 008: The teacher uses a variety of instructional strategies and roles to facilitate learning and to help students become independent

*Available at http://www.sbec.state.tx.us/sbec/publ/learncen.htm#teacher

thinkers and problem solvers who use higher-order thinking in the classroom and the real world.

Competency 009: The teacher uses a variety of instructional materials and resources (including human and technological resources) to support individual and group learning.

Competency 012: The teacher is a reflective practitioner who knows how to promote his or her own professional growth and can work cooperatively with other professionals in the system to create a school culture that enhances learning and encourages positive change.

LEARNER-CENTERED INSTRUCTION

To create a learner-centered community, the teacher collaboratively identifies needs; and plans, implements, and assesses instruction using technology and other resources.

The teacher is a leader of a learner-centered community, in which an atmosphere of trust and openness produces a stimulating exchange of ideas and mutual respect. The teacher is a critical thinker and problem solver who plays a variety of roles when teaching. As a coach, the teacher observes, evaluates, and changes directions and strategies whenever necessary. As a facilitator, the teacher helps students link ideas in the content area to familiar ideas, to prior experiences, and to relevant problems. As a manager, the teacher effectively acquires, allocates, and conserves resources. By encouraging self-directed learning and by modeling respectful behavior, the teacher effectively manages the learning environment so that optimal learning occurs.

Assessment is used to guide the learner community. By using assessment as an integral part of instruction, the teacher responds to the needs of all learners. In addition, the teacher guides learners to develop personally meaningful forms of self-assessment.

The teacher selects materials, technology, activities, and space that are developmentally appropriate and designed to engage interest in learning. As a result, learners work independently and cooperatively in a positive and stimulating learning climate fueled by self-discipline and motivation.

Although the teacher has a vision for the destination of learning, students set individual goals and plan how to reach the destination. As a result, they take responsibility for their own learning, develop a sense of the importance of learning for understanding, and begin to understand themselves as learners. The teacher's plans integrate learning experiences and various forms of assessment that take into consideration the unique characteristics of the learner community. The teacher shares responsibility for the results of this process with all members of the learning community.

Together, learners and teachers take risks in trying out innovative ideas for learning. To facilitate learning, the teacher encourages various types of learners to shape their own learning through active engagement, manipulation, and examination of ideas and materials. Critical thinking, creativity, and problem solving spark further learning. Consequently, there is an appreciation of learning as a lifelong process that builds a greater understanding of the world and a feeling of responsibility toward it.

This standard correlates with the following competencies:

Competency 001: The teacher uses an understanding of human developmental processes to nurture student growth through developmentally appropriate instruction.

Competency 002: The teacher considers environmental factors that may affect learning in designing a supportive and responsive classroom community that promotes all students' learning and self-esteem.

Competency 004: The teacher understands how learning occurs and can apply this understanding to design and implement effective instruction.

Competency 005: The teacher understands how motivation affects group and individual behavior and learning and can apply this understanding to promote student learning.

Competency 006: The teacher uses planning processes to design outcome-oriented learning experiences that foster understanding and encourage self-directed thinking and learning in both individual and collaborative settings.

Competency 008: The teacher uses a variety of instructional strategies and roles to facilitate learning and to help students become independent thinkers and problem solvers who use higher-order thinking in the classroom and the real world.

Competency 009: The teacher uses a variety of instructional materials and resources (including human and technological resources) to support individual and group learning.

Competency 010: The teacher uses processes of informal and formal assessment to understand individual learners, monitor instructional effectiveness, and shape instruction.

EQUITY IN EXCELLENCE FOR ALL LEARNERS

The teacher responds appropriately to diverse groups of learners.
The teacher not only respects and is sensitive to all learners but also encourages the use of all their skills and talents. As the facilitator of learning, the teacher models and encourages appreciation for students' cultural heritage, unique endowments, learning styles, interests, and needs. The teacher also designs learning experiences that show consideration for these student characteristics.

Because the teacher views differences as opportunities for learning, cross-cultural experiences are an integral part of the learner-centered community. In addition, the teacher establishes a relationship between the curriculum and community cultures. While making this connection, the teacher and students explore attitudes that foster unity. As a result, the teacher creates an environment in which learners work cooperatively and purposefully, using a variety of resources to understand themselves, their immediate community, and the global society in which they live.

This standard correlates with the following competencies:

Competency 003: The teacher appreciates human diversity, recognizing how diversity in the classroom and the community may affect learning and creating a classroom environment in which both the diversity of groups and the uniqueness of individuals are recognized and celebrated.

Competency 004: The teacher understands how learning occurs and can apply this understanding to design and implement effective instruction.

Competency 006: The teacher uses planning processes to design outcome-oriented learning experiences that foster understanding and encourage self-directed thinking and learning in both individual and collaborative settings.

Competency 011: The teacher structures and manages the learning environment to maintain a classroom climate that promotes the lifelong pursuit of learning and encourages cooperation, leadership, and mutual respect.

Competency 014: The teacher understands how the school relates to the larger community and knows strategies for making interactions between school and community mutually supportive and beneficial.

LEARNER-CENTERED COMMUNICATION

While acting as an advocate for the student and the school, the teacher demonstrates effective professional and interpersonal communication skills.

As a leader, the teacher communicates the mission of the school with learners, professionals, families, and community members. With colleagues, the teacher works to create an environment in which taking risks, sharing new ideas, and innovative problem solving are supported and encouraged. With citizens, the teacher works to establish strong and positive ties between the school and the community.

Because the teacher is a compelling communicator, students begin to appreciate the importance of expressing their views clearly. The teacher uses verbal, nonverbal, and media techniques so that students explore ideas collaboratively, pose questions, and support one another in their learning. The teacher and students listen, speak, read, and write in a variety of contexts; give multimedia and artistic presentations; and use technology as a resource for building communication skills. The teacher incorporates techniques of inquiry that enable students to use different levels of thinking.

The teacher also communicates effectively as an advocate for each learner. The teacher is sensitive to concerns that affect learners and takes advantage of community strengths and resources for the learners' welfare.

This standard correlates with the following competencies:

Competency 002: The teacher considers environmental factors that may affect learning in designing a supportive and responsive classroom community that promotes all students' learning and self-esteem.

Competency 007: The teacher uses effective verbal, nonverbal, and media communication techniques to shape the classroom into a community of learners engaged in active inquiry, collaboration, exploration, and supportive interactions.

Competency 008: The teacher uses a variety of instructional strategies and roles to facilitate learning and to help students become independent thinkers and problem solvers who use higher-order thinking in the classroom and the real world.

Competency 009: The teacher uses a variety of instructional materials and resources (including human and technological resources) to support individual and group learning.

Competency 014: The teacher understands how the school relates to the larger community and knows strategies for making interactions between school and community mutually supportive and beneficial.

LEARNER-CENTERED PROFESSIONAL DEVELOPMENT

The teacher, as a reflective practitioner dedicated to student success, demonstrates a commitment to learn, to improve the profession, and to maintain professional ethics and personal integrity.

As a learner, the teacher works within a framework of clearly defined professional goals to plan for and profit from a wide variety of relevant learning opportunities. The teacher develops an identity as a professional, interacts effectively with colleagues, and takes a role in setting standards for teacher accountability. In addition, the teacher uses technological and other resources to facilitate continual professional growth.

To strengthen the effectiveness and quality of teaching, the teacher actively engages in an exchange of ideas with colleagues, observes peers, and encourages feedback from learners to establish a successful learning community. As a member of a collaborative team, the teacher identifies and uses group processes to make decisions and solve problems.

The teacher exhibits the highest standard of professionalism and bases daily decisions on ethical principles. To support the needs of learners, the teacher knows and uses community resources, school services, and laws relating to teacher responsibilities and student rights. Through these activities, the teacher contributes to the improvement of comprehensive educational programs as well as programs within specific disciplines.

This standard correlates with the following competencies:

Competency 012: The teacher is a reflective practitioner who knows how to promote his or her own professional growth and can work cooperatively with other professionals in the system to create a school culture that enhances learning and encourages positive change.

Competency 014: The teacher understands how the school relates to the larger community and knows strategies for making interactions between school and community mutually supportive and beneficial.

Competency 015: The teacher understands requirements, expectations, and constraints associated with teaching in Texas, and can apply this understanding in a variety of contexts.

REFERENCES AND RELATED SUPPLEMENTAL RESOURCE MATERIALS

The following list of references and resources should assist you in preparing to take the Professional Development ExCET. You should be able to locate the materials listed without difficulty; nevertheless, do not limit yourself to what is listed here. There may be other good materials, including your classnotes, that would be helpful to you as you prepare for the test.

TEACHER EDUCATION TEXTBOOKS

Bennett, C. I. (1998). *Comprehensive multicultural education: Theory and practice* (2nd ed.). Boston: Allyn and Bacon.

Biehler, R. F., & Snowman, J. (1996). *Psychology applied to teaching* (7th ed.). Boston: Houghton Mifflin.

Borich, G. D. (1995). *Effective teaching methods.* New York: Macmillan.

Callahan, J. F., & Clark, L. C. (1990). *Teaching in the Secondary School: Planning for Competence.* New York: Macmillan.

Callahan, J. F., Clark, L. C., & Kellough, R. (1997). *Teaching in the middle and secondary schools* (4th ed.). New York: Macmillan.

Clark, L. H., & Starr, I. S. (1995). *Secondary and middle school teaching methods* (6th ed.). New York: Macmillan.

Cooper, J. M., ed. (1999). *Classroom teaching skills* (4th ed.). Lexington, MA: Heath.

Eggen, P., & Kauchak, D. (1999). *Educational psychology* (2nd ed.). New York: Macmillan.

Emmer, E. T. (1997). *Classroom management for secondary teachers: Windows on the classroom* (2nd ed.). Boston: Allyn and Bacon.

Funkhouser, C. W. (1996). *Education in Texas: Policies, practices, and perspectives* (6th ed.). Scottsdale, AR: Gorsuch Scarisbrick.

Henson, K. T. (1996). *Methods and strategies for teaching in secondary and middle schools.* White Plains, NY: Longman.

Johnson, J. A. (1999). *Introduction to the foundations of American education* (8th ed.). Boston: Allyn and Bacon.

Logan, J. W., & Moss, R. K. (1983). *Secondary education: An introduction— instructor's manual.* New York: Macmillan.

Moore, K. D. (1997). *Classroom teaching skills* (3rd ed.). New York: McGraw-Hill.

Mosston, M., & Ashworth, S. (1990). *The spectrum of teaching styles: From command to discovery.* New York: Longman Press.

Ornstein, A. C., & Levine, D. U. (1992). *Foundations of education* (4th ed.). Boston: Houghton Mifflin.

Ross, S. M. (1994). *Educational psychology theory and practice* (4th ed.). Boston: Allyn and Bacon.

Savage, M. K., & Savage, T. V. (1990). *Secondary education: An introduction* (2nd ed.). New York: Macmillan.

Slavin, R. E. (1996). *Educational psychology: Theory and practice* (4th ed.). Boston: Allyn and Bacon.

Sprinthall, N. A., & Sprinthall, R. C. (1994). *Educational psychology: A developmental approach* (6th ed.). New York: McGraw Hill.

Vaughan, J. L., & Estes, T. H. (1986). *Reading and reasoning beyond the primary grades.* Boston: Allyn and Bacon.

Wilson, J. D. (1994). *Methods for effective teaching.* Needham Heights, MA: Allyn and Bacon.

Winitzsy, N., & Arends, R. I. (1988). *Learning to teach: Instructor's manual.* New York: Random House.

Wolfgang, C. H. (1998). *Solving discipline problems: Methods and models for today's teachers* (2nd ed.). Boston: Allyn and Bacon.

JOURNALS

ASCD Update, Newsletter of the Association for Supervision and Curriculum Development.

Creative Classroom, Children's Television Workshop.

Educational Leadership, Association for Supervision and Curriculum Development.

Exceptional Children, Council for Exceptional Children.

Instructor, Scholastic, Inc.

Phi Delta Kappan, Phi Delta Kappa.

Teaching Pre-K–8, Early Years, Inc.

Teaching Tolerance, 400 Washington Ave., Montgomery, Alabama 36104.

OTHER REFERENCES AND SOURCES

Arizona Department of Education (1991). *Impact: A handbook of creative teaching methods.* Phoenix, AZ: Author.

Association for Supervision and Curriculum Development (1989). *Toward the thinking curriculum: Current cognitive research* (1989 Yearbook). Alexandria, VA: Author.

Association of Texas Professional Educators (1994). *A new teacher handbook* 1993–94. Austin: Author.

Banks, James (1993). *Multiethnic education: Theory and practice* (2nd ed.). Boston: Allyn and Bacon.

Banks, J. A., & McGee, C. A., eds. (1996). *Multicultural education: Issues and perspectives.* Boston: Allyn and Bacon.

Berliner, David C. (1988). *The development of expertise in pedagogy.* Alexandria, VA: American Association of Colleges for Teacher Education.

Bertcher, H. J., & Maple, F. F. (1996). *Creating groups.* Beverly Hills, CA: Sage.

Blake, S., & Sugrue, B. (1991). *Applying educational psychology in the classroom* (4th ed.). New York: Longman.

Bloom, B. S. (1984). *Taxonomy of educational objectives handbook.* New York: Longman.

Bogue, E. G. (1991). *Journey of the heart: The call to teaching.* Bloomington, IN: Phi Delta Kappa Education Foundation.

Brandt, Ronald S., ed. (1989). *Conversations with leading educators: From educational leadership.* Alexandria, VA: Association for Supervision and Curriculum Development.

Brookfield, S. D. (1992). *The skillful teacher: On techniques, trust, and representativeness in the classroom.* San Francisco: Jossey-Bass.

Brooks, J. G., & Brooks, M.G. (1993). *In search of understanding: The case for constructivist classrooms.* Alexandria, VA: Association for Supervision and Curriculum Development.

Burden, P. R., & Byrd, D. M. (1994). *Methods for effective teaching.* Boston: Allyn and Bacon.

California Department of Education (1987). *Caught in the middle: Education reform for young adolescents in California public schools*. Sacramento, CA: California State Department of Education.

Carnegie Council on Adolescent Development (1989). *Turning points: Preparing American youth for the 21st century*. New York: Carnegie Corporation of New York.

Casey, M. B., & Tucker, E. C. (October 1994). Problem-centered classrooms: Creating lifelong learners. *Phi Delta Kappan*, 139–143.

Cohen, E. F. (1986). *Designing groupwork*. New York: Teachers College Press.

Cohen, E. G. (1994). Restructuring the classroom: Conditions for productive small groups. *Review of Educational Research, 64*, 1–35.

Commission on Reading (1990). *Becoming a nation of readers*. Washington, DC: The National Institute of Education, the National Academy of Education, and the Center for the Study of Reading.

Costa, A.L., & Kallick, B., eds. (1995). *Assessment in the learning organization: Shifting the paradigm*. Alexandria, VA: Association for Supervision and Curriculum Development.

Darling-Hammond, L., et al. (June, 1990). *The teaching internship: Practical preparation for a licensed profession*. The RAND Corporation.

Davidman, L., & Davidman, P. T. (1997). *Teaching with a multicultural perspective* (2nd ed.). New York: Longman.

Davidson, N. (1990). *Cooperative learning in mathematics*. Menlo Park, CA: Addison-Wesley.

Davis, M., Hawley, P., McMullan, B., & Spilka, G. (1997). *Design as a catalyst for learning*. Alexandria, VA: Association for Supervision and Curriculum Development.

Davis, R., & Davis, K. (1978). *Teaching students through their independent language styles*. Englewood Cliffs, NJ: Prentice Hall.

Dede, C., ed. (1998). *1998 ASCD Yearbook: Learning with technology*. Alexandria, VA: Association for Supervision and Curriculum Development.

Delpit, L. D. (August, 1988). The silenced dialogue: Power and pedagogy in educating other people's children. *Harvard Educational Review*, 280–298.

Diez, M. (1988). A thrust from within: Reconceptualizing teacher education at Alverno College. *Peabody Journal of Education*, Winter, 280–298.

Duckett, W. D., ed. (1988). *Observation and evaluation of teaching*. Bloomington, IN: Phi Delta Kappa.

Eby, J. W. (1998). *Reflective planning, teaching, and evaluation K–12* (2nd ed.). Upper Saddle River, NJ: Prentice Hall.

Eggen, P. D., & Kauchak, D. P. (1996). *Strategies for teachers: Teaching content and thinking skills*. Boston, MA: Allyn and Bacon.

Elliot, J., & Kratochwill, T., eds. (1994). *Reader in psychology and education*. Dubuque, IA: Brown and Benchmark.

Epanchin, B. C., Townsend, B., & Stoddard, K. (1994). *Constructive classroom management*. Belmont, CA: Brooks/Cole.

Esler, W. K., & Sciortino, P. (1991). *Methods for teaching: An overview of current practices*. Raleigh, NC: Contemporary Publishing Co.

Fredericks, A. D. (1990). Conferencing with parents: Successful approaches. *Reading Teacher, 44*, 174–176.

Froyen, L. A., & Iverson, A. M. (1998). *Schoolwide and classroom management: The reflective educator-leader* (3rd ed.). Upper Saddle River, NJ: Merrill.

Frymier, J. (November, 1992). Children who hurt, children who fail. *Phi Delta Kappan*, 257–259.

Gajar, A., Goodman, L., & McAfee, J. (1993). *Secondary schools and beyond: Transition of individuals with mild disabilities*. New York: Macmillan.

Garrod, A., Smulyan, L., Powers, S. I., & Kilkenny, R. (1995). *Adolescent portraits: Identity, relationships, and challenges* (2nd ed.). Boston: Allyn and Bacon.

Gallagher, J. J. (1994). *Teaching the gifted child*. Boston: Allyn and Bacon.

Glasser, W. (1986). *Control theory in the classroom*. New York: HarperCollins.

Glasser, W. (1998). *The quality school*. New York: HarperCollins.

Glatthorn, A. A., ed. (1995). *Content of the curriculum* (2nd ed.). Alexandria, VA: Association for Supervision and Curriculum Development.

Good, T. L., & Brophy, J. E. (1980). *Educational psychology: A realistic approach* (2nd ed.). New York: Holt, Rinehart, & Winston.

Good, T. L., & Brophy, J. E. (1996). *Looking in classrooms* (3rd ed.). New York: Harper & Row.

Goodlad, J. I. (November, 1990). Better teachers for our nation's schools. *Phi Delta Kappan, 72*, 185–194.

Goodman, G., Blake, S., & Sugrue, B. (1991). *Instructor's manual with test items for Myron H. Dembo's Applying educational psychology in the classroom* (4th ed.). New York: Longman.

Grabe, M., & Grabe, C. (1998). *Integrating technology for meaningful learning* (2nd ed.). Boston, MA: Houghton Mifflin.

Grant, C. A., & Gomez, M. L. (1996). *Making schooling multicultural: Campus and classroom*. Englewood Cliffs, NJ: Merrill.

Hargreaves, A. (Ed.). (1997). *Rethinking educational change with heart and mind: ASCD Yearbook*. Alexandria, VA: Association for Supervision and Curriculum Development.

Harmin, M. (1994). *Inspiring active learning: A handbook for teachers*. Alexandria, VA: Association for Supervision and Curriculum Development.

Hewitt, J. S., & Whittier, K. S. (1997). *Teaching methods for today's schools: Collaboration and inclusion*. Boston: Allyn and Bacon.

Hunter, Madeline. (1984). *Mastery teaching: Increasing instructional effectiveness in secondary schools, colleges, and universities*. El Segundo, CA: TIP Publications.

Jensen, E. (1998). *Teaching with the brain in mind*. Alexandria, VA: Association for Supervision and Curriculum Development.

Johnson, D. (1982). *Every minute counts*. Palo Alto, CA: Dale Seymour.

Johnson, R. T., Johnson, D. W., & Holebec, E. J. (1987). *Structuring cooperative learning lesson plans for teachers*. Edina, MN: Interaction Book Co.

Jones, V. F., & Jones, L. S. (1995). *Comprehensive classroom management* (4th ed.). Boston: Allyn and Bacon.

Kauchak, D. P., & Eggen, P. D. (1998). *Learning and teaching: Research-based methods* (3rd ed.). Boston: Allyn and Bacon.

Kindsvatter, R., Wilen, W., & Isher, M. (1996). *The dynamics of effective teaching* (3rd ed.). White Plains, NY: Youngman.

Knox, L., & Candelaria, C. (1987). Tips for more productive parent-teacher conferences. *Learning, 16*, 60–61.

Kohn, A. (1996). *Beyond discipline: From compliance to community*. Alexandria, VA: Association for Supervision and Curriculum Development.

Kohut, Jr., S., & Range, D. G. (1986). *Classroom discipline: Case studies and viewpoints*. Washington, DC: National Education Association.

Knowles, J. G., Cole, A. L., & Presswood, C. S. (1994). *Through preservice teachers' eyes*. New York: Macmillan.

Kulik, J. A., & Kulik, C. L. (1987). Effects of ability grouping on student achievement. *Equity and Excellence, 23*, 22–30.

Lemlech, J. K. (1988). *Classroom management* (2nd ed.). Prospects Heights, IL: Waveland Press.

LeTendre, M. J. (1991). The continuing evolution of a federal role in compensatory education. *Educational Evaluation and Policy Analysis, 13* (4), 328–334.

Lewin, L., & Shoemaker, B. J. (1998). *Great performances: Creating classroom-based assessment tasks*. Alexandria, VA: Association for Supervision and Curriculum Development.

Lezotte, L., & Jacoby, B. (1990). *A Guide to the school improvement process based on effective schools research*. Okemos, MI: Effective Schools Products, Ltd.

Long, J. D., Frye, V. H., & Long, E. W. (1989). *Making it until Friday: A guide to successful classroom management*. Princeton, NJ: Princeton Book Co.

Lyman, L., & Foyle, H. C. (1990). *Cooperative grouping for interactive learning: Students, teachers, and administrators.* Washington, DC: National Education Association.

Marlowe, B. A., & Page, M. L. (1998). *Creating and sustaining the constructivist classroom.* Thousand Oaks, CA: Corwin Press, Inc.

Marsh, D. D., ed. (1999). *ASCD Yearbook: Preparing our schools for the 21st century.* Alexandria, VA: Association for Supervision and Curriculum Development.

Meyers, K., & Pawlas, G. (1989). Simple steps assure parent-teacher conference success. *Instructor, 99,* 64–68.

Mills, C. J., & Durden, W. G. (1992). Cooperative learning and ability grouping: An issue of choice. *Gifted Child Quarterly, 36* (1), 1–16.

Oakes, J., & Lipton, M. (1999). *Teaching to change the world.* Boston: McGraw-Hill College.

Price, H. B. (November, 1992). Multiculturalism: Myths and realities. *Phi Delta Kappa, 74,* 208–213.

Reynolds, A. (1992). What is competent beginning teaching? A review of the literature. *Review of Educational Research, 62,* 1–35.

Rich, S. J. (1985). Restoring power to teachers: The impact of "whole language." *Academic Therapy, 23,* 405–415.

Richardson, V., ed. (1997). *Constructivist teacher education: Building a world of new understandings.* Washington, DC: Falmer Press.

Riepe, L. (1989). Make parent conferences more productive. *Learning, 18,* 46–47.

Santrock, J. W. (1998). *Adolescence* (7th ed.). Boston: McGraw-Hill.

Savage, T. V. (1991). *Discipline for self-control.* Englewood Cliffs, NJ: Prentice Hall.

Slavin, R. E. (1994). *Using student team learning.* Baltimore: Johns Hopkins University Press.

Slavin, R. E. (1995). *Cooperative learning: Theory, research, and practice.* Englewood Cliffs, NJ: Prentice Hall.

Texas Education Agency. (1993). *ExCET: Examination for the Certification of Educators in Texas preparation manual: Professional development.* Austin: Author.

Texas Education Agency. (1994). *Texas school law bulletin.* Austin: Author.

Texas Education Agency. (1997). *Learner-centered schools for Texas: A vision of Texas educators.* Austin: Author.

Texas Education Agency. (1998). *Preparation manual for the ExCET Test: Professional development.* Austin: Author.

Texas Education Agency. (1998). *State Board of Education rules for curriculum.* Austin: Author.

U.S. Department of Education. (1991). *America 2000: An education strategy.* Washington, DC: Author.

U.S. Department of Labor. (1992). *A Blueprint for high performance: A SCANS report for America 2000.* Washington, DC: Author.

Vallin, R. (1988). Making parent-teacher conferences pay off. *Instructor, 97,* 96–98.

VanHorn, R. (1991). *Advanced technology in education.* Pacific Grove, CA: Brooks/Cole.

Weinstein, C. S., & Mignano, Jr., A. J. (1993). *Elementary classroom management.* New York: McGraw-Hill.

Wiggins, G., & McTighe, J. (1998). *Understanding by design.* Alexandria, VA: Association for Supervision and Curriculum Development.

Wilson, J. D. (1994). *Instructor's manual with test bank for Burden and Byrd's Methods for Effective Teaching.* Boston: Allyn and Bacon.

Witrock, M. C., ed. (1986). *Handbook of research on teaching* (3rd ed.). New York: Macmillan.

Zahorik, J. (1995). *Constructivist Teaching.* Bloomington, IN: Phi Delta Kappa.

ANSWER SHEET—DIAGNOSTIC TESTS

Elementary

1. Ⓐ Ⓑ Ⓒ Ⓓ
2. Ⓐ Ⓑ Ⓒ Ⓓ
3. Ⓐ Ⓑ Ⓒ Ⓓ
4. Ⓐ Ⓑ Ⓒ Ⓓ
5. Ⓐ Ⓑ Ⓒ Ⓓ
6. Ⓐ Ⓑ Ⓒ Ⓓ
7. Ⓐ Ⓑ Ⓒ Ⓓ
8. Ⓐ Ⓑ Ⓒ Ⓓ
9. Ⓐ Ⓑ Ⓒ Ⓓ
10. Ⓐ Ⓑ Ⓒ Ⓓ
11. Ⓐ Ⓑ Ⓒ Ⓓ
12. Ⓐ Ⓑ Ⓒ Ⓓ
13. Ⓐ Ⓑ Ⓒ Ⓓ
14. Ⓐ Ⓑ Ⓒ Ⓓ
15. Ⓐ Ⓑ Ⓒ Ⓓ
16. Ⓐ Ⓑ Ⓒ Ⓓ
17. Ⓐ Ⓑ Ⓒ Ⓓ
18. Ⓐ Ⓑ Ⓒ Ⓓ
19. Ⓐ Ⓑ Ⓒ Ⓓ
20. Ⓐ Ⓑ Ⓒ Ⓓ
21. Ⓐ Ⓑ Ⓒ Ⓓ
22. Ⓐ Ⓑ Ⓒ Ⓓ
23. Ⓐ Ⓑ Ⓒ Ⓓ

24. Ⓐ Ⓑ Ⓒ Ⓓ
25. Ⓐ Ⓑ Ⓒ Ⓓ
26. Ⓐ Ⓑ Ⓒ Ⓓ
27. Ⓐ Ⓑ Ⓒ Ⓓ
28. Ⓐ Ⓑ Ⓒ Ⓓ
29. Ⓐ Ⓑ Ⓒ Ⓓ
30. Ⓐ Ⓑ Ⓒ Ⓓ
31. Ⓐ Ⓑ Ⓒ Ⓓ
32. Ⓐ Ⓑ Ⓒ Ⓓ
33. Ⓐ Ⓑ Ⓒ Ⓓ
34. Ⓐ Ⓑ Ⓒ Ⓓ
35. Ⓐ Ⓑ Ⓒ Ⓓ
36. Ⓐ Ⓑ Ⓒ Ⓓ
37. Ⓐ Ⓑ Ⓒ Ⓓ
38. Ⓐ Ⓑ Ⓒ Ⓓ
39. Ⓐ Ⓑ Ⓒ Ⓓ
40. Ⓐ Ⓑ Ⓒ Ⓓ
41. Ⓐ Ⓑ Ⓒ Ⓓ
42. Ⓐ Ⓑ Ⓒ Ⓓ
43. Ⓐ Ⓑ Ⓒ Ⓓ
44. Ⓐ Ⓑ Ⓒ Ⓓ
45. Ⓐ Ⓑ Ⓒ Ⓓ
46. Ⓐ Ⓑ Ⓒ Ⓓ

47. Ⓐ Ⓑ Ⓒ Ⓓ
48. Ⓐ Ⓑ Ⓒ Ⓓ
49. Ⓐ Ⓑ Ⓒ Ⓓ
50. Ⓐ Ⓑ Ⓒ Ⓓ
51. Ⓐ Ⓑ Ⓒ Ⓓ
52. Ⓐ Ⓑ Ⓒ Ⓓ
53. Ⓐ Ⓑ Ⓒ Ⓓ
54. Ⓐ Ⓑ Ⓒ Ⓓ
55. Ⓐ Ⓑ Ⓒ Ⓓ
56. Ⓐ Ⓑ Ⓒ Ⓓ
57. Ⓐ Ⓑ Ⓒ Ⓓ
58. Ⓐ Ⓑ Ⓒ Ⓓ
59. Ⓐ Ⓑ Ⓒ Ⓓ
60. Ⓐ Ⓑ Ⓒ Ⓓ
61. Ⓐ Ⓑ Ⓒ Ⓓ
62. Ⓐ Ⓑ Ⓒ Ⓓ
63. Ⓐ Ⓑ Ⓒ Ⓓ
64. Ⓐ Ⓑ Ⓒ Ⓓ
65. Ⓐ Ⓑ Ⓒ Ⓓ
66. Ⓐ Ⓑ Ⓒ Ⓓ
67. Ⓐ Ⓑ Ⓒ Ⓓ
68. Ⓐ Ⓑ Ⓒ Ⓓ
69. Ⓐ Ⓑ Ⓒ Ⓓ

70. Ⓐ Ⓑ Ⓒ Ⓓ
71. Ⓐ Ⓑ Ⓒ Ⓓ
72. Ⓐ Ⓑ Ⓒ Ⓓ
73. Ⓐ Ⓑ Ⓒ Ⓓ
74. Ⓐ Ⓑ Ⓒ Ⓓ
75. Ⓐ Ⓑ Ⓒ Ⓓ
76. Ⓐ Ⓑ Ⓒ Ⓓ
77. Ⓐ Ⓑ Ⓒ Ⓓ
78. Ⓐ Ⓑ Ⓒ Ⓓ
79. Ⓐ Ⓑ Ⓒ Ⓓ
80. Ⓐ Ⓑ Ⓒ Ⓓ
81. Ⓐ Ⓑ Ⓒ Ⓓ
82. Ⓐ Ⓑ Ⓒ Ⓓ
83. Ⓐ Ⓑ Ⓒ Ⓓ
84. Ⓐ Ⓑ Ⓒ Ⓓ
85. Ⓐ Ⓑ Ⓒ Ⓓ
86. Ⓐ Ⓑ Ⓒ Ⓓ
87. Ⓐ Ⓑ Ⓒ Ⓓ
88. Ⓐ Ⓑ Ⓒ Ⓓ
89. Ⓐ Ⓑ Ⓒ Ⓓ
90. Ⓐ Ⓑ Ⓒ Ⓓ

ANSWER SHEET—DIAGNOSTIC TESTS

Secondary

1. Ⓐ Ⓑ Ⓒ Ⓓ 24. Ⓐ Ⓑ Ⓒ Ⓓ 47. Ⓐ Ⓑ Ⓒ Ⓓ 70. Ⓐ Ⓑ Ⓒ Ⓓ
2. Ⓐ Ⓑ Ⓒ Ⓓ 25. Ⓐ Ⓑ Ⓒ Ⓓ 48. Ⓐ Ⓑ Ⓒ Ⓓ 71. Ⓐ Ⓑ Ⓒ Ⓓ
3. Ⓐ Ⓑ Ⓒ Ⓓ 26. Ⓐ Ⓑ Ⓒ Ⓓ 49. Ⓐ Ⓑ Ⓒ Ⓓ 72. Ⓐ Ⓑ Ⓒ Ⓓ
4. Ⓐ Ⓑ Ⓒ Ⓓ 27. Ⓐ Ⓑ Ⓒ Ⓓ 50. Ⓐ Ⓑ Ⓒ Ⓓ 73. Ⓐ Ⓑ Ⓒ Ⓓ
5. Ⓐ Ⓑ Ⓒ Ⓓ 28. Ⓐ Ⓑ Ⓒ Ⓓ 51. Ⓐ Ⓑ Ⓒ Ⓓ 74. Ⓐ Ⓑ Ⓒ Ⓓ
6. Ⓐ Ⓑ Ⓒ Ⓓ 29. Ⓐ Ⓑ Ⓒ Ⓓ 52. Ⓐ Ⓑ Ⓒ Ⓓ 75. Ⓐ Ⓑ Ⓒ Ⓓ
7. Ⓐ Ⓑ Ⓒ Ⓓ 30. Ⓐ Ⓑ Ⓒ Ⓓ 53. Ⓐ Ⓑ Ⓒ Ⓓ 76. Ⓐ Ⓑ Ⓒ Ⓓ
8. Ⓐ Ⓑ Ⓒ Ⓓ 31. Ⓐ Ⓑ Ⓒ Ⓓ 54. Ⓐ Ⓑ Ⓒ Ⓓ 77. Ⓐ Ⓑ Ⓒ Ⓓ
9. Ⓐ Ⓑ Ⓒ Ⓓ 32. Ⓐ Ⓑ Ⓒ Ⓓ 55. Ⓐ Ⓑ Ⓒ Ⓓ 78. Ⓐ Ⓑ Ⓒ Ⓓ
10. Ⓐ Ⓑ Ⓒ Ⓓ 33. Ⓐ Ⓑ Ⓒ Ⓓ 56. Ⓐ Ⓑ Ⓒ Ⓓ 79. Ⓐ Ⓑ Ⓒ Ⓓ
11. Ⓐ Ⓑ Ⓒ Ⓓ 34. Ⓐ Ⓑ Ⓒ Ⓓ 57. Ⓐ Ⓑ Ⓒ Ⓓ 80. Ⓐ Ⓑ Ⓒ Ⓓ
12. Ⓐ Ⓑ Ⓒ Ⓓ 35. Ⓐ Ⓑ Ⓒ Ⓓ 58. Ⓐ Ⓑ Ⓒ Ⓓ 81. Ⓐ Ⓑ Ⓒ Ⓓ
13. Ⓐ Ⓑ Ⓒ Ⓓ 36. Ⓐ Ⓑ Ⓒ Ⓓ 59. Ⓐ Ⓑ Ⓒ Ⓓ 82. Ⓐ Ⓑ Ⓒ Ⓓ
14. Ⓐ Ⓑ Ⓒ Ⓓ 37. Ⓐ Ⓑ Ⓒ Ⓓ 60. Ⓐ Ⓑ Ⓒ Ⓓ 83. Ⓐ Ⓑ Ⓒ Ⓓ
15. Ⓐ Ⓑ Ⓒ Ⓓ 38. Ⓐ Ⓑ Ⓒ Ⓓ 61. Ⓐ Ⓑ Ⓒ Ⓓ 84. Ⓐ Ⓑ Ⓒ Ⓓ
16. Ⓐ Ⓑ Ⓒ Ⓓ 39. Ⓐ Ⓑ Ⓒ Ⓓ 62. Ⓐ Ⓑ Ⓒ Ⓓ 85. Ⓐ Ⓑ Ⓒ Ⓓ
17. Ⓐ Ⓑ Ⓒ Ⓓ 40. Ⓐ Ⓑ Ⓒ Ⓓ 63. Ⓐ Ⓑ Ⓒ Ⓓ 86. Ⓐ Ⓑ Ⓒ Ⓓ
18. Ⓐ Ⓑ Ⓒ Ⓓ 41. Ⓐ Ⓑ Ⓒ Ⓓ 64. Ⓐ Ⓑ Ⓒ Ⓓ 87. Ⓐ Ⓑ Ⓒ Ⓓ
19. Ⓐ Ⓑ Ⓒ Ⓓ 42. Ⓐ Ⓑ Ⓒ Ⓓ 65. Ⓐ Ⓑ Ⓒ Ⓓ 88. Ⓐ Ⓑ Ⓒ Ⓓ
20. Ⓐ Ⓑ Ⓒ Ⓓ 43. Ⓐ Ⓑ Ⓒ Ⓓ 66. Ⓐ Ⓑ Ⓒ Ⓓ 89. Ⓐ Ⓑ Ⓒ Ⓓ
21. Ⓐ Ⓑ Ⓒ Ⓓ 44. Ⓐ Ⓑ Ⓒ Ⓓ 67. Ⓐ Ⓑ Ⓒ Ⓓ 90. Ⓐ Ⓑ Ⓒ Ⓓ
22. Ⓐ Ⓑ Ⓒ Ⓓ 45. Ⓐ Ⓑ Ⓒ Ⓓ 68. Ⓐ Ⓑ Ⓒ Ⓓ
23. Ⓐ Ⓑ Ⓒ Ⓓ 46. Ⓐ Ⓑ Ⓒ Ⓓ 69. Ⓐ Ⓑ Ⓒ Ⓓ

ANSWER SHEET—PRACTICE TESTS

Elementary

1. Ⓐ Ⓑ Ⓒ Ⓓ	24. Ⓐ Ⓑ Ⓒ Ⓓ	47. Ⓐ Ⓑ Ⓒ Ⓓ	70. Ⓐ Ⓑ Ⓒ Ⓓ
2. Ⓐ Ⓑ Ⓒ Ⓓ	25. Ⓐ Ⓑ Ⓒ Ⓓ	48. Ⓐ Ⓑ Ⓒ Ⓓ	71. Ⓐ Ⓑ Ⓒ Ⓓ
3. Ⓐ Ⓑ Ⓒ Ⓓ	26. Ⓐ Ⓑ Ⓒ Ⓓ	49. Ⓐ Ⓑ Ⓒ Ⓓ	72. Ⓐ Ⓑ Ⓒ Ⓓ
4. Ⓐ Ⓑ Ⓒ Ⓓ	27. Ⓐ Ⓑ Ⓒ Ⓓ	50. Ⓐ Ⓑ Ⓒ Ⓓ	73. Ⓐ Ⓑ Ⓒ Ⓓ
5. Ⓐ Ⓑ Ⓒ Ⓓ	28. Ⓐ Ⓑ Ⓒ Ⓓ	51. Ⓐ Ⓑ Ⓒ Ⓓ	74. Ⓐ Ⓑ Ⓒ Ⓓ
6. Ⓐ Ⓑ Ⓒ Ⓓ	29. Ⓐ Ⓑ Ⓒ Ⓓ	52. Ⓐ Ⓑ Ⓒ Ⓓ	75. Ⓐ Ⓑ Ⓒ Ⓓ
7. Ⓐ Ⓑ Ⓒ Ⓓ	30. Ⓐ Ⓑ Ⓒ Ⓓ	53. Ⓐ Ⓑ Ⓒ Ⓓ	76. Ⓐ Ⓑ Ⓒ Ⓓ
8. Ⓐ Ⓑ Ⓒ Ⓓ	31. Ⓐ Ⓑ Ⓒ Ⓓ	54. Ⓐ Ⓑ Ⓒ Ⓓ	77. Ⓐ Ⓑ Ⓒ Ⓓ
9. Ⓐ Ⓑ Ⓒ Ⓓ	32. Ⓐ Ⓑ Ⓒ Ⓓ	55. Ⓐ Ⓑ Ⓒ Ⓓ	78. Ⓐ Ⓑ Ⓒ Ⓓ
10. Ⓐ Ⓑ Ⓒ Ⓓ	33. Ⓐ Ⓑ Ⓒ Ⓓ	56. Ⓐ Ⓑ Ⓒ Ⓓ	79. Ⓐ Ⓑ Ⓒ Ⓓ
11. Ⓐ Ⓑ Ⓒ Ⓓ	34. Ⓐ Ⓑ Ⓒ Ⓓ	57. Ⓐ Ⓑ Ⓒ Ⓓ	80. Ⓐ Ⓑ Ⓒ Ⓓ
12. Ⓐ Ⓑ Ⓒ Ⓓ	35. Ⓐ Ⓑ Ⓒ Ⓓ	58. Ⓐ Ⓑ Ⓒ Ⓓ	81. Ⓐ Ⓑ Ⓒ Ⓓ
13. Ⓐ Ⓑ Ⓒ Ⓓ	36. Ⓐ Ⓑ Ⓒ Ⓓ	59. Ⓐ Ⓑ Ⓒ Ⓓ	82. Ⓐ Ⓑ Ⓒ Ⓓ
14. Ⓐ Ⓑ Ⓒ Ⓓ	37. Ⓐ Ⓑ Ⓒ Ⓓ	60. Ⓐ Ⓑ Ⓒ Ⓓ	83. Ⓐ Ⓑ Ⓒ Ⓓ
15. Ⓐ Ⓑ Ⓒ Ⓓ	38. Ⓐ Ⓑ Ⓒ Ⓓ	61. Ⓐ Ⓑ Ⓒ Ⓓ	84. Ⓐ Ⓑ Ⓒ Ⓓ
16. Ⓐ Ⓑ Ⓒ Ⓓ	39. Ⓐ Ⓑ Ⓒ Ⓓ	62. Ⓐ Ⓑ Ⓒ Ⓓ	85. Ⓐ Ⓑ Ⓒ Ⓓ
17. Ⓐ Ⓑ Ⓒ Ⓓ	40. Ⓐ Ⓑ Ⓒ Ⓓ	63. Ⓐ Ⓑ Ⓒ Ⓓ	86. Ⓐ Ⓑ Ⓒ Ⓓ
18. Ⓐ Ⓑ Ⓒ Ⓓ	41. Ⓐ Ⓑ Ⓒ Ⓓ	64. Ⓐ Ⓑ Ⓒ Ⓓ	87. Ⓐ Ⓑ Ⓒ Ⓓ
19. Ⓐ Ⓑ Ⓒ Ⓓ	42. Ⓐ Ⓑ Ⓒ Ⓓ	65. Ⓐ Ⓑ Ⓒ Ⓓ	88. Ⓐ Ⓑ Ⓒ Ⓓ
20. Ⓐ Ⓑ Ⓒ Ⓓ	43. Ⓐ Ⓑ Ⓒ Ⓓ	66. Ⓐ Ⓑ Ⓒ Ⓓ	89. Ⓐ Ⓑ Ⓒ Ⓓ
21. Ⓐ Ⓑ Ⓒ Ⓓ	44. Ⓐ Ⓑ Ⓒ Ⓓ	67. Ⓐ Ⓑ Ⓒ Ⓓ	90. Ⓐ Ⓑ Ⓒ Ⓓ
22. Ⓐ Ⓑ Ⓒ Ⓓ	45. Ⓐ Ⓑ Ⓒ Ⓓ	68. Ⓐ Ⓑ Ⓒ Ⓓ	
23. Ⓐ Ⓑ Ⓒ Ⓓ	46. Ⓐ Ⓑ Ⓒ Ⓓ	69. Ⓐ Ⓑ Ⓒ Ⓓ	

ANSWER SHEET—PRACTICE TESTS

Secondary

1. Ⓐ Ⓑ Ⓒ Ⓓ
2. Ⓐ Ⓑ Ⓒ Ⓓ
3. Ⓐ Ⓑ Ⓒ Ⓓ
4. Ⓐ Ⓑ Ⓒ Ⓓ
5. Ⓐ Ⓑ Ⓒ Ⓓ
6. Ⓐ Ⓑ Ⓒ Ⓓ
7. Ⓐ Ⓑ Ⓒ Ⓓ
8. Ⓐ Ⓑ Ⓒ Ⓓ
9. Ⓐ Ⓑ Ⓒ Ⓓ
10. Ⓐ Ⓑ Ⓒ Ⓓ
11. Ⓐ Ⓑ Ⓒ Ⓓ
12. Ⓐ Ⓑ Ⓒ Ⓓ
13. Ⓐ Ⓑ Ⓒ Ⓓ
14. Ⓐ Ⓑ Ⓒ Ⓓ
15. Ⓐ Ⓑ Ⓒ Ⓓ
16. Ⓐ Ⓑ Ⓒ Ⓓ
17. Ⓐ Ⓑ Ⓒ Ⓓ
18. Ⓐ Ⓑ Ⓒ Ⓓ
19. Ⓐ Ⓑ Ⓒ Ⓓ
20. Ⓐ Ⓑ Ⓒ Ⓓ
21. Ⓐ Ⓑ Ⓒ Ⓓ
22. Ⓐ Ⓑ Ⓒ Ⓓ
23. Ⓐ Ⓑ Ⓒ Ⓓ

24. Ⓐ Ⓑ Ⓒ Ⓓ
25. Ⓐ Ⓑ Ⓒ Ⓓ
26. Ⓐ Ⓑ Ⓒ Ⓓ
27. Ⓐ Ⓑ Ⓒ Ⓓ
28. Ⓐ Ⓑ Ⓒ Ⓓ
29. Ⓐ Ⓑ Ⓒ Ⓓ
30. Ⓐ Ⓑ Ⓒ Ⓓ
31. Ⓐ Ⓑ Ⓒ Ⓓ
32. Ⓐ Ⓑ Ⓒ Ⓓ
33. Ⓐ Ⓑ Ⓒ Ⓓ
34. Ⓐ Ⓑ Ⓒ Ⓓ
35. Ⓐ Ⓑ Ⓒ Ⓓ
36. Ⓐ Ⓑ Ⓒ Ⓓ
37. Ⓐ Ⓑ Ⓒ Ⓓ
38. Ⓐ Ⓑ Ⓒ Ⓓ
39. Ⓐ Ⓑ Ⓒ Ⓓ
40. Ⓐ Ⓑ Ⓒ Ⓓ
41. Ⓐ Ⓑ Ⓒ Ⓓ
42. Ⓐ Ⓑ Ⓒ Ⓓ
43. Ⓐ Ⓑ Ⓒ Ⓓ
44. Ⓐ Ⓑ Ⓒ Ⓓ
45. Ⓐ Ⓑ Ⓒ Ⓓ
46. Ⓐ Ⓑ Ⓒ Ⓓ

47. Ⓐ Ⓑ Ⓒ Ⓓ
48. Ⓐ Ⓑ Ⓒ Ⓓ
49. Ⓐ Ⓑ Ⓒ Ⓓ
50. Ⓐ Ⓑ Ⓒ Ⓓ
51. Ⓐ Ⓑ Ⓒ Ⓓ
52. Ⓐ Ⓑ Ⓒ Ⓓ
53. Ⓐ Ⓑ Ⓒ Ⓓ
54. Ⓐ Ⓑ Ⓒ Ⓓ
55. Ⓐ Ⓑ Ⓒ Ⓓ
56. Ⓐ Ⓑ Ⓒ Ⓓ
57. Ⓐ Ⓑ Ⓒ Ⓓ
58. Ⓐ Ⓑ Ⓒ Ⓓ
59. Ⓐ Ⓑ Ⓒ Ⓓ
60. Ⓐ Ⓑ Ⓒ Ⓓ
61. Ⓐ Ⓑ Ⓒ Ⓓ
62. Ⓐ Ⓑ Ⓒ Ⓓ
63. Ⓐ Ⓑ Ⓒ Ⓓ
64. Ⓐ Ⓑ Ⓒ Ⓓ
65. Ⓐ Ⓑ Ⓒ Ⓓ
66. Ⓐ Ⓑ Ⓒ Ⓓ
67. Ⓐ Ⓑ Ⓒ Ⓓ
68. Ⓐ Ⓑ Ⓒ Ⓓ
69. Ⓐ Ⓑ Ⓒ Ⓓ

70. Ⓐ Ⓑ Ⓒ Ⓓ
71. Ⓐ Ⓑ Ⓒ Ⓓ
72. Ⓐ Ⓑ Ⓒ Ⓓ
73. Ⓐ Ⓑ Ⓒ Ⓓ
74. Ⓐ Ⓑ Ⓒ Ⓓ
75. Ⓐ Ⓑ Ⓒ Ⓓ
76. Ⓐ Ⓑ Ⓒ Ⓓ
77. Ⓐ Ⓑ Ⓒ Ⓓ
78. Ⓐ Ⓑ Ⓒ Ⓓ
79. Ⓐ Ⓑ Ⓒ Ⓓ
80. Ⓐ Ⓑ Ⓒ Ⓓ
81. Ⓐ Ⓑ Ⓒ Ⓓ
82. Ⓐ Ⓑ Ⓒ Ⓓ
83. Ⓐ Ⓑ Ⓒ Ⓓ
84. Ⓐ Ⓑ Ⓒ Ⓓ
85. Ⓐ Ⓑ Ⓒ Ⓓ
86. Ⓐ Ⓑ Ⓒ Ⓓ
87. Ⓐ Ⓑ Ⓒ Ⓓ
88. Ⓐ Ⓑ Ⓒ Ⓓ
89. Ⓐ Ⓑ Ⓒ Ⓓ
90. Ⓐ Ⓑ Ⓒ Ⓓ

3:30

790 → 610 — Exit San Felipe

H# 713-626-1544 W→

C# 713-553-9001   Santoche right ↓

sage
~~cross post oak~~
Corner of sage
→ Nations Bank
   Bank of America
Randalls.
↓
Cross sage
|
come 50 yards corner of
School at Sage
little ± St
York Town
_____
|
Big building

Marathon oil

Four way stop sign
Big high rise condo
at St James
very next apt
complex
"Creole"

at Creole come to
   leasing office
get to parking
walk up gate.

Fee $25 hour